ENCORE TRICOLORE 1

nouvelle édition

TEACHER'S BOOK

Sylvia Honnor and Heather Mascie-Taylor

ICT Consultant: Terry Atkinson

OXFORD
UNIVERSITY PRESS

Great Clarendon Street, Oxford, OX2 6DP, United Kingdom

Oxford University Press is a department of the University of Oxford. It furthers the University's objective of excellence in research, scholarship, and education by publishing worldwide. Oxford is a registered trade mark of Oxford University Press in the UK and in certain other countries

First published by Nelson Thornes Ltd in 2000

British Library Cataloguing in Publication Data
Data available

978-0-17-440272-5

20 19

Printed in the United Kingdom by Ashford Colour Press Ltd.

Acknowledgements

Cover: G&E 2000
Page make-up and editorial: Michael Spencer

The authors and publishers would like to thank the following for their help in producing this book: Alan Wesson, The Collège Chante Cigale in Gujan-Mestras, Sheila Blackband, Andrew Colley, Arnold Klein, Jackie Coe, all schools who took part in the formal and informal research on *Encore Tricolore* and provided valuable feedback.

CONTENTS

Encore Tricolore 1
nouvelle édition

Section 1
Introduction to the course

Section 2
Activities for language learning

Section 3
Teacher's notes

Introduction

Encore Tricolore nouvelle édition builds on the proven strengths and approach of ***Tricolore*** and ***Encore Tricolore*** and incorporates new features to bring it into line with current teaching requirements.

The course features:

- a systematic and comprehensive approach to grammar progression, with clear explanations and extensive practice
- interesting topics, set in authentic contexts, from France and other French-speaking countries
- user-friendly vocabulary and grammar reference sections to encourage independent learning
- differentiation which is integral to the course and fully referenced and explained in the Teacher's Book
- the development of study skills, with systematic training in strategies for listening and reading

Key features of the new edition are:

- *Écoute et parle* – systematic teaching of the interrelationship of sounds and writing
- assessment materials, both informal and formal, as an integral part of the course
- *Presse-Jeunesse* – magazine-style reading sections in the Students' Book
- two Student CDs for independent listening and speaking practice
- an English–French glossary in addition to the French–English glossary

Components

Encore Tricolore 1 nouvelle édition is planned to give a wealth of teaching material in as compact and easily usable form as possible. The components are:

Students' Book
Teacher's Book
Copymasters
6 CDs
100 Flashcards

These five components are planned to cover one complete year's work. They are fully integrated and cross-referenced and designed to be motivating, thorough, practical and easy to use.

1 Students' Book

The Students' Book is the main teaching tool of the course and contains the essential core material, reference sections and a full range of items for consolidation, extension and revision. There are also sections for reading for pleasure and systematic practice in linking sounds and writing. It comprises:

- **10 units**

These contain all the core material, with a full range of practice tasks and with regular grammar explanations in the *Dossier-langue* boxes.

At the beginning of each unit students can see what they will learn and the end of unit summaries (*Sommaires*) provide comprehensive reference lists.Together these provide a complete learning framework for the unit. These summaries are also provided on copymasters for retention by the students.

- **Au choix**

This section contains further practice material and extension tasks for each unit. There are often parallel tasks for support provided on copymasters.

- **Presse-Jeunesse**

Starting after *Unité 4* and at regular intervals throughout the book, these four magazine-style sections provide material for reading for pleasure. They can be used when they appear in the Students' Book or at any time later and are intended for students to work on alone. Although they use mainly the vocabulary and structures introduced by that time in the core units, they also contain a small amount of additional language.

No exercises are included in the *Presse-Jeunesse* sections in the Students' Book, but they are accompanied by optional copymasters which give comprehension and practice tasks and systematic training in reading strategies, including help with working out the meaning of unfamiliar words.

- **Rappel**

These double-page sections are placed after *Unités 3, 5, 7* and *9*, alternating with the *Presse-Jeunesse* sections. They can be used at any point after the unit which they follow, for revision and consolidation. Each *Rappel* section provides reading and writing activities which are self-instructional and can be used by students working individually, for homework or during cover lessons. They contain a variety of tasks including practice of vocabulary, genders, grammar and topic revision.

- **À l'ordinateur**

For easy reference, these three pages list vocabulary and expressions linked with computers, the Internet, sending e-mails etc.

- **Écoute et parle**

This section provides material for the teaching and practice of the interrelationship between sounds and writing, which is a major requirement of the new curriculum. It introduces all the main sounds of French and provides practice of pronunciation and speaking.

- **Grammaire**

A reference section covering the main grammar points and irregular verbs taught in ***Encore Tricolore 1 nouvelle édition***.

- **Glossaires**

Two glossaries are provided at the end of the Students' Book, French–English and English–French.

- **Vocabulaire de classe**

Useful classroom phrases and rubrics are summarised with their meaning, for easy reference.

2 Teacher's Book

This book has three sections:

Section 1: general information

Section 2: games, songs, ICT activities, background information

Section 3: detailed teaching notes and solutions for all items in the Students' Book and in the Copymasters and a full transcript of all recorded items; notes on informal assessment (*Épreuves*) and formal assessment (*Contrôles*)

Section 1

- a detailed teaching plan of ***Encore Tricolore 1 nouvelle édition*** which can form the basis for a Scheme of Work
- suggestions for:
  - developing language skills
  - developing language-learning skills
  - linking sounds and writing
  - grammar
  - assessing progress
  - using ICT
  - differentiation
  - developing cultural awareness
- complete lists of:
  - flashcards
  - copymasters
  - recordings
- notes about:
  - the National Curriculum (with details of levels and coverage of the 'Knowledge, skills and understanding' section)
  - the QCA Scheme of Work for Key Stage 3
  - the National Literacy Strategy
  - the Scottish Guidelines
  - the Curriculum in Northern Ireland

Section 2

This gives details of a wide range of games and practice activities for use in pairs, groups or as a class. It also includes notes on songs, background information and ongoing ICT activities.

Section 3

This section gives unit by unit suggestions for teaching with the materials.

Each unit begins with a clear plan, setting out the language and functions of the unit and the links with the National Curriculum. It lists exactly which materials will be needed.

The teaching suggestions which follow are divided into a logical sequence of Areas. These include solutions for each task, transcripts of recorded items and suggestions for follow-up work.

The unit notes also include solutions for copymasters and other items which can be used with that unit but are not in the Students' Book itself, e.g. *Tu comprends?* (listening comprehension practice) and *Épreuves* (informal assessment), both on copymasters.

Also in this section of the Teacher's Book are notes and solutions for the *Rappel* pages and for copymasters which are not attached to any one unit, e.g. *Presse-Jeunesse* and *Contrôles* (formal assessment).

Activity labels (such as reading, speaking, extension, support) are supplied for every task, indicating which skills etc. are involved.

The following symbols are also used:

SB 56	Students' Book page number
1	Task number
1 (grey)	*Au choix* task number
[1]	*Écoute et parle* task number
CM 2/4	Copymaster number (unit/number)
CM 115	Copymaster page number
FC 18–26	Flashcard number(s)
TB 30	Teacher's Book page number
(headphones) **1/14**	Recorded item (CD number/track)
(headphones) **SCD 1/2**	(Student CD number/track)
(headphones, dotted line)	Transcript
(pairwork icon)	Pairwork activity
(computer icon)	ICT activity

3 CDs

There are six CDs, all containing a wide variety of lively material, recorded by French native speakers and at a speed and level which the students can understand.

List of CDs

Class CD 1

Tracks 1–11: *Unité 1*

Tracks 12–21: *Unité 2*

Tracks 22–34: *Unité 3*

Tracks 35–49: *Unité 4*

Class CD 2

Tracks 1–11: *Unité 5*

Tracks 12–27: *Unité 6*

Tracks 28–40: *Unité 7*

Class CD 3

Tracks 1–13: *Unité 8*

Tracks 14–25: *Unité 9*

Tracks 26–40: *Unité 10*

Class CD 4

Contrôle

Student CD 1

(Student CD for independent study)

Tracks 1–52: *Écoute et parle, Unités 1–7*

Student CD 2

(Student CD for independent study)

Tracks 1–21: *Écoute et parle, Unités 8–10*

Tracks 22–45: *Tu comprends?*

List of recorded items

Class CD 1

Unité 1

SB 6 (1)	*Bonjour!*
SB 6 (2)	*Comment t'appelles-tu?*
SB 7 (4)	*Ça va?*
TB (Area 5)	*Quel âge as-tu?*
SB 7 (5)	*Qui parle?*
SB 126 (1)	*Une conversation*
SB 8 (1)	*Des affaires scolaires*
SB 126 (3)	*C'est quel nombre?*
CM 1/2	*Écoutez bien!*

Unité 2

SB 10 (1)	*J'habite ici*
CM 2/2	*Trois conversations*
SB 11 (4)	*Qui habite où?*
SB 11	*Chantez! Un, deux, trois*
SB 12 (1)	*Télé-jeu: 30 secondes*
SB 12 (2)	*Je pense à quelque chose (Section A et Section B)*
SB 12 (2)	*Je pense à quelque chose (Section C)*
SB 127 (3)	*Qu'est-ce que c'est?*
SB 127 (4)	*Jean-Pierre a des problèmes*

Unité 3

SB 14 (1)	*Ma famille*
SB 15 (5)	*Trois familles*
SB 17 (4)	*La semaine*
SB 17 (5)	*Quel jour sommes-nous?*
SB 18 (1)	*La maison de la famille Laurent*
SB 18 (2)	*C'est quelle pièce?*
SB 19 (4)	*Notre chambre*
SB 128 (2)	*La maison de la famille Lambert*
SB 19 (6)	*Samedi*
CM 3/7	*Épreuve (Unités 1–3): Écouter*

Unité 4

TB (Area 1)	*Sondage*
SB 24 (2)	*Vote, vote, vote!*
SB 129 (2)	*Chat perdu*
SB 26 (1)	*Trois interviews*
TB (Area 3)	*On parle à Grégory et à Roseline*
SB 27 (5)	*C'est quelle phrase?*
SB 28 (1)	*Des animaux extraordinaires*
SB 28 (2)	*Des opinions*
SB 29	*Chantez! L'alphabet*
CM 4/8	*Épreuve: Écouter*
SB 33	*Presse-Jeunesse 1: Deux comptines*

Class CD 2

Unité 5

SB 34 (1)	*C'est quelle date?*
SB 36 (1)	*Le Mardi gras*
SB 38 (1)	*L'année en France*
SB 41 (2a)	*On parle des vêtements*
SB 131 (4)	*Des vêtements pour le week-end*
SB 42 (1)	*Vous cherchez un cadeau?*
SB 43 (4)	*L'anniversaire de Marc*
SB 46 (4)	*Des cadeaux pour Suzanne*
CM 5/10	*Épreuve: Écouter*

Unité 6

SB 50 (2)	*On téléphone à Suzanne*
SB 51 (5)	*Voici la météo*
SB 52	*Chantez! Le premier mois*
SB 133 (3)	*La météo*
SB 53 (7)	*Comment ça s'écrit?*
SB 54 (1)	*Au club de sports*
SB 56 (1)	*À la maison*
SB 56 (2)	*Un film de Tom et Jojo*
SB 57 (5)	*Pendant les vacances*
SB 59 (5)	*Deux interviews*
SB 60 (3)	*Au téléphone*
CM 6/11	*Épreuve: Écouter*
SB 65	*Presse-Jeunesse 2: Encore une comptine*

Unité 7

SB 67 (1)	*Voici La Rochelle*
SB 69 (4)	*À l'office de tourisme*
SB 69 (6)	*Les touristes à La Rochelle*
SB 70 (2)	*C'est loin?*
TB (Area 4)	*C'est où?*
SB 71 (5)	*Pardon, Monsieur*
SB 135 (3)	*Deux conversations*
SB 136 (5)	*Où sont-ils?*
SB 71 (7)	*C'est à ...?*
SB 74 (1)	*Coralie est au lit*
CM 7/10	*Épreuve: Écouter*

Class CD 3

Unité 8

SB 80 (1)	*C'est à quelle heure?*
SB 81 (3)	*Rendez-vous à quelle heure?*
SB 82 (1)	*Une journée typique*
SB 85 (4)	*C'est quel jour?*
SB 86 (1)	*Six élèves*
SB 87 (5)	*Un nouvel élève*
SB 139 (7)	*Deux amies très différentes*
SB 89 (4)	*Au collège*
CM 8/11	*Épreuve: Écouter*
SB 93	*Presse-Jeunesse 3: Chantez! Attention, c'est l'heure!*

Unité 9

SB 97 (1)	*Trois familles*
SB 100 (1)	*Le petit déjeuner*
SB 141 (3)	*Qu'est-ce qu'ils mangent?*
SB 142 (5)	*On gagne des prix*
SB 102 (4)	*Mon repas préféré*
SB 103 (6)	*À table*
SB 104	*Chantez! Pique-nique à la plage*
TB (Area 7)	*C'est bon, ça?*
CM 9/10	*Épreuve: Écouter*

Unité 10

SB 110 (2)	*Faites-vous du sport?*
SB 112 (1b)	*On aime la musique*
SB 113 (4)	*Le jeu des interviews*
SB 144 (4)	*Spécial-loisirs*
TB (Area 4)	*Quiz sonore*
SB 115 (4)	*Tu aides à la maison?*
TB (Area 5)	*Vingt-quatre heures*
SB 117 (5)	*C'est quand?*
SB 118 (1b)	*Lucie part en vacances*
SB 120	*Chantez! Samedi, on part en vacances*
CM 10/10	*Épreuve: Écouter*

Class CD 4

CM 109–110	*Premier contrôle (Écouter)*
CM 115–116	*Deuxième contrôle (Écouter)*
CM 121–122	*Troisième contrôle (Écouter)*
CM 127	*Troisième contrôle (Écouter)* (alternative)

Student CD1

SB 150	*Écoute et parle 1*
SB 151	*Écoute et parle 2*
SB 152	*Écoute et parle 3*
SB 153	*Écoute et parle 4*
SB 154	*Écoute et parle 5*
SB 155	*Écoute et parle 6*
SB 156	*Écoute et parle 7*

Student CD 2

SB 157	*Écoute et parle 8*
SB 158	*Écoute et parle 9*
SB 159	*Écoute et parle 10*
CM 4/6	*Tu comprends?*
CM 5/8	*Tu comprends?*
CM 6/9	*Tu comprends?*
CM 7/8	*Tu comprends?*
CM 8/9	*Tu comprends?*
CM 9/8	*Tu comprends?*
CM 10/8	*Tu comprends?*

4 Flashcards

There are 100 single-sided colour flashcards, including many photographs. In this edition the flashcards are also available on CD-ROM. This allows the teacher to view and print images individually and in groups, as needed. Full details accompany the CD-ROM.

They provide:

- the main visual aid for presenting vocabulary
- a stimulus for oral work
- the key element in many oral games and activities.

See below for a full list of flashcards and TB 27 for ideas for flashcard games.

List of flashcards

1 happy face
2 sad face

Places
3 town
4 village
5 house and garden
6 flat
7 farm
8 street
9 grocer's shop
10 supermarket
11 café
12 cinema

Rooms
13 bedroom
14 kitchen
15 bathroom
16 lounge
17 dining room

Animals
18 hamster
19 dog
20 cat
21 rabbit
22 fish
23 horse
24 mouse
25 budgerigar
26 guinea pig

Weather
27 hot weather
28 cold weather
29 raining
30 fine sunny weather
31 windy weather
32 snow
33 fog

Activities
34 watching TV
35 listening to radio/cassettes/CDs
36 doing homework
37 using computer
38 playing table tennis
39 playing basketball
40 playing volleyball
41 playing with games console
42 playing cards

Places in town
43 market
44 restaurant
45 station
46 swimming pool
47 post office
48 campsite
49 hospital
50 church
51 museum
52 town hall
53 school
54 tourist office
55 youth hostel

Food and drink
56 ham
57 roast chicken
58 roast red meat
59 fish
60 omelette
61 potatoes
62 chips
63 carrots
64 peas
65 cauliflower
66 cabbage
67 French/green beans
68 lettuce
69 apple
70 orange
71 pear
72 peach
73 banana
74 grapes
75 strawberries
76 baguette
77 croissants
78 cheese
79 yoghurts
80 cake
81 wine
82 mineral water
83 lemonade
84 coke
85 fruit juice
86 coffee
87 tea
88 hot chocolate
89 milk

Leisure activities
90 playing chess
91 skate-boarding
92 roller skates/blades
93 mountain bike
94 drumkit
95 drawing

Household tasks
96 washing up
97 shopping
98 cooking/baking
99 hoovering
100 washing car

5 Copymasters

There are 125 copymasters, containing a wide variety of material and giving practice in all four skills and training in language-learning strategies.

- **Support sheets**

Some copymasters are designed to give easy practice of vocabulary and structures to support the teaching in the Students' Book. These could be used by some students while others are doing extension tasks in *Au choix*.

- **Expendable material**

Some of the copymaster worksheets are intended to be expendable, e.g. those containing crosswords, word searches or grids for completion by the student. Others can be cut up and used for pair or group activities. The *Sommaire* and grammar practice sheets can be stuck into the student's exercise book or file for future reference.

- **ICT**

Besides regular links with ICT in the core units, there are also three copymasters which give specific practice linked with ICT.

- **Reading strategies**

The copymasters linked to each *Presse-Jeunesse* section give systematic training in reading skills and strategies.

- **Assessment**

The students' sheets for assessment tests, *Épreuves* (informal) and *Contrôles* (formal) are also provided on copymasters.

- **Tu comprends?**

Self-instructional listening tasks, with accompanying CD, provide useful material for homework or for students working independently in class.

List of copymasters

Unité 1
1/1 *La France* [support]
1/2 *Écoutez bien!* [listening]

Unité 2
2/1 *J'habite en France* [support]
2/2 *Trois conversations* [listening]
2/3 *Mots et images* [consolidation]
2/4 *Sommaire*

Unité 3
3/1 *Lire, c'est intéressant* [extension]
3/2 *La famille Techno* [speaking: information gap]
3/3 *À la maison* [consolidation]
3/4 *Masculin, féminin* [grammar: gender]
3/5 *Jeux de vocabulaire* [consolidation]
3/6 *Sommaire*
3/7 *Épreuve: Écouter*
3/8 *Épreuve: Lire*
3/9 *Épreuve: Écrire et grammaire*

Unité 4
4/1 *Les animaux* [mini-flashcards/support]
4/2 *Les animaux de mes amis* [extension]
4/3 *Questions et réponses* [speaking/writing]
4/4 *À l'ordinateur* [ICT]
4/5 *C'est moi!* [support]
4/6 *Tu comprends?* [independent listening]
4/7 *Sommaire*
4/8 *Épreuve: Écouter*
4/9 *Épreuve: Lire*
4/10 *Épreuve: Écrire et grammaire*

Unité 5
5/1 *Des dates* [speaking: pairwork]
5/2 *être* [grammar]
5/3 *Des vêtements* [mini-flashcards/support]
5/4 *Jeux de vocabulaire* [support]
5/5 *Des cadeaux et des vêtements* [reading/speaking/writing]
5/6 *Une lettre pour dire «merci»* [grammar: adjectival agreement]
5/7 *avoir* [grammar]
5/8 *Tu comprends?* [independent listening]
5/9 *Sommaire*
5/10 *Épreuve: Écouter*
5/11 *Épreuve: Lire*
5/12 *Épreuve: Écrire et grammaire*

Unité 6
6/1 *Le temps et les saisons* [mini-flashcards/support]
6/2 *La France en été et en hiver* [consolidation]
6/3 *La météo* [speaking: information gap]
6/4 *Les chiffres* [support]
6/5 *Taper les accents français* [ICT]
6/6 *Tom et Jojo* [grammar: verbs]
6/7 *Les verbes* [grammar]
6/8 *Des cartes postales* [extension]
6/9 *Tu comprends?* [independent listening]
6/10 *Sommaire*
6/11 *Épreuve: Écouter*
6/12 *Épreuve: Lire*
6/13 *Épreuve: Écrire et grammaire*

Unité 7
7/1 *Une ville de France* [mini-flashcards/support]
7/2 *En ville* [support]
7/3 *C'est quelle direction?* [consolidation]
7/4 *Où va-t-on?* [grammar: *à, au* etc.]
7/5 *aller* [grammar]
7/6 *C'est où?* [grammar: prepositions]
7/7 *Un plan à compléter* [speaking: information gap]
7/8 *Tu comprends?* [independent listening]
7/9 *Sommaire*
7/10 *Épreuve: Écouter*
7/11 *Épreuve: Lire*
7/12 *Épreuve: Écrire et grammaire*

Unité 8
8/1 *Quelle heure est-il?* [mini-flashcards/support]
8/2 *Quelle journée!* [support]
8/3 *Qui est-ce?* [speaking: information gap]
8/4 *La page des jeux* [support]
8/5 *La vie scolaire* [extension]
8/6 *Conversations au choix* [speaking]
8/7 *Mon, ton, son* [grammar]
8/8 *Jeux de vocabulaire – informatique* [ICT]
8/9 *Tu comprends?* [independent listening]
8/10 *Sommaire*
8/11 *Épreuve: Écouter*
8/12 *Épreuve: Lire*
8/13 *Épreuve: Écrire et grammaire*

Unité 9
9/1 *On mange et on boit* [mini-flashcards/support]
9/2 *C'est quel mot?* [grammar]
9/3 *Des jeux de vocabulaire* [support]
9/4 *La page des jeux* [extension]
9/5 *À table* [speaking]
9/6 *Ça ne va pas!* [grammar: negative; support]
9/7 *La forme négative* [extension]
9/8 *Tu comprends?* [independent listening]
9/9 *Sommaire*
9/10 *Épreuve: Écouter*
9/11 *Épreuve: Lire*
9/12 *Épreuve: Écrire et grammaire*

Unité 10
10/1 *Les loisirs* [extension]
10/2 *faire* [grammar]
10/3 *À la maison* [support]
10/4 *Sébastien et Vivienne* [speaking: information gap]
10/5 *24 heures* [grammar]
10/6 *C'est à qui?* [grammar]
10/7 *La page des lettres* [extension]
10/8 *Tu comprends?* [independent listening]
10/9 *Sommaire*
10/10 *Épreuve: Écouter*
10/11 *Épreuve: Lire*
10/12 *Épreuve: Écrire et grammaire*

CM 103 *Presse-Jeunesse 1* (for SB 32–33)
CM 104 *Presse-Jeunesse 2* (for SB 63–65)
CM 105–106 *Presse-Jeunesse 3* (for SB 93–95)
CM 107–108 *Presse-Jeunesse 4* (for SB 122–125)

CM 109–110 *Premier contrôle: Écouter*
CM 111 *Premier contrôle: Parler*
CM 112–113 *Premier contrôle: Lire*
CM 114 *Premier contrôle: Écrire*

CM 115–116 *Deuxième contrôle: Écouter*
CM 117 *Deuxième contrôle: Parler*
CM 118–119 *Deuxième contrôle: Lire*
CM 120 *Deuxième contrôle: Écrire*

CM 121–122 *Troisième contrôle: Écouter*
CM 123 *Troisième contrôle: Parler*
CM 124–125 *Troisième contrôle: Lire*
CM 126 *Troisième contrôle: Écrire*

CM 127–128 *Troisième contrôle:* alternative tasks

CM 128 *Contrôles:* Record sheet

Planning the course

1 Covering the National Curriculum

Encore Tricolore 1 nouvelle édition covers attainment levels 1–4 of the National Curriculum.

Developing knowledge, skills and understanding

1 Acquiring knowledge and understanding of the target language *Pupils should be taught:*	***Encore Tricolore 1 nouvelle édition***
a *the principles and interrelationship of sounds and writing in the target language*	*Écoute et parle*
b *the grammar of the target language and how to apply it*	A major feature of the course. Grammar is explained in *Dossier-langue* sections of the Students' Book and presented and practised extensively.
c *how to express themselves using a range of vocabulary and structures.*	A major feature of the course.
2 Developing language skills *Pupils should be taught:*	
a *how to listen carefully for gist and detail*	A major feature of the course with regular practice tasks for class and individual work. Strategies for listening set out in teacher's notes in *Unité 2*.
b *correct pronunciation and intonation*	*Écoute et parle*
c *how to ask and answer questions*	Taught and practised throughout the course, with numerous pairwork activities. Questions with *Est-ce que* introduced in *Unité 4*; other question words and forms used throughout. *Questions et réponses* is a series of tasks which practises matching correct answers to questions.
d *how to initiate and develop conversations*	Many activities practise this, e.g. *Inventez des conversations* and information gap tasks on copymaster.
e *how to vary the target language to suit context, audience and purpose*	Practised through substitution tables, but mainly covered in later stages of ***Encore Tricolore***.
f *how to adapt language they already know for different contexts*	Covered mainly in later stages of ***Encore Tricolore***.
g *strategies for dealing with the unpredictable [for example, unfamiliar language, unexpected responses]*	Reading strategies set out in several units of the teacher's notes, beginning in *Unité 3*. Also in: CM 3/1 *Lire, c'est intéressant!* *Presse-Jeunesse* sections in the Students' Book and related copymasters with five cut-out sections: *Lire, c'est facile*.
h *techniques for skimming and for scanning written texts for information, including those from ICT-based sources*	*Presse-Jeunesse* sections in the Students' Book and related copymasters (as above).
i *how to summarise and report the main points of spoken or written texts, using notes where appropriate*	*Complète le résumé* tasks in Students' Book. Tasks on copymaster, linked with *Presse-Jeunesse* pages.
j *how to redraft their writing to improve its accuracy and presentation, including the use of ICT.*	Suggestions in the Teacher's Book for using ICT for preparing letters, messages, brochures etc.
3 Developing language-learning skills *Pupils should be taught:*	
a *techniques for memorising words, phrases and short extracts*	Grouping words into topics (*Sommaires*), colour-coding genders, identifying word endings of nouns to indicate gender, memory games, routine practice of useful phrases and expressions with flashcards.
b *how to use context and other clues to interpret meaning [for example, by identifying the grammatical function of unfamiliar words or similarities with words they know]*	*Presse-Jeunesse* sections in the Students' Book and related copymasters.
c *to use their knowledge of English or another language when learning the target language*	Question boxes in the Students' Book focus on comparisons with English.
d *how to use dictionaries and other reference materials appropriately and effectively*	Tasks such as *C'est utile, le dictionnaire* provide practice in using the glossary or dictionaries. Reference material for grammar and vocabulary provided in the Students' Book.
e *how to develop their independence in learning and using the target language.*	Many tasks are self-instructional, e.g. in *Rappel*, *Écoute et parle* and *Presse-Jeunesse* sections. *Tu comprends?* is a series of listening tasks with a student CD for independent use. *Vocabulaire de classe* sections provide support for using target language in class.

4 Developing cultural awareness *Pupils should be taught about different countries and cultures by:*	***Encore Tricolore 1 nouvelle édition***
a *working with authentic materials in the target language, including some from ICT-based sources [for example, handwritten texts, newspapers, magazines, books, video, satellite television, texts from the Internet]*	Authentic printed materials used in the Students' Book, where appropriate. Suggestions for Internet sites given in the Teacher's Book. *Presse-Jeunesse* sections include slightly adapted articles from French magazines for young people.
b *communicating with native speakers [for example, in person, by correspondence]*	Suggestions in Teacher's Book for forming class links and video-conferencing.
c *considering their own culture and comparing it with the cultures of the countries and communities where the target language is spoken*	Festivals (*Unité* 5), mealtimes (*Unités 8, 9*), school life and everyday routine (*Unité* 8)
d *considering the experiences and perspectives of people in these countries and communities.*	Recordings, letters, articles etc. from people from different French-speaking countries and communities.
5 Breadth of study *During Key Stages 3 and 4, pupils should be taught the knowledge, skills and understanding through:*	
a *communicating in the target language in pairs and groups, and with their teacher*	A major feature of the course, with detailed suggestions in the Teacher's Book and Students' Book.
b *using everyday classroom events as an opportunity for spontaneous speech*	Suggestions in the Teacher's Book. *Vocabulaire de classe* sections in the Students' Book provide support for this.
c *expressing and discussing personal feelings and opinions*	Likes, dislikes (*Unités 4, 6, 8, 10*), opinions (*Unités 8, 10*)
d *producing and responding to different types of spoken and written language, including texts produced using ICT*	A major feature of the course, with detailed suggestions in the Teacher's Book and Students' Book.
e *using a range of resources, including ICT, for accessing and communicating information*	Suggestions in the Teacher's Book and Students' Book for useful resources, including Internet sites.
f *using the target language creatively and imaginatively*	*À toi!* sections in the Students' Book encourage students to personalise and vary language learnt.
g *listening, reading or viewing for personal interest and enjoyment, as well as for information*	Recorded stories, songs, *Presse-Jeunesse* sections etc.
h *using the target language for real purposes [for example, by sending and receiving messages by telephone, letter, fax or e-mail]*	Tasks in the Students' Book for writing letters, messages and e-mails (e.g. *Unité* 8).
i *working in a variety of contexts, including everyday activities, personal and social life, the world around us, the world of work and the international world.*	***Encore Tricolore 1 nouvelle édition*** covers the following contexts: • everyday activities • personal and social life • the world around us. Other contexts are covered in later stages.

2 Covering the QCA Scheme of Work

Encore Tricolore nouvelle édition has taken into account the QCA Scheme of Work for Key Stage 3, with its emphasis on clear progression in language learning. ***Encore Tricolore 1–3*** covers all the language content and contexts for learning, although sometimes the order is slightly different. Classroom instructions are covered in the Teacher's Book and in the *Vocabulaire de classe* sections in the Students' Book. Pronunciation and spelling rules are taught mainly in the *Écoute et parle* section. As recommended by QCA, students are introduced to grammatical rules and terminology at an early stage so that they are equipped with the knowledge to construct their own sentences and become independent language learners.

3 Building on the National Literacy Strategy

Encore Tricolore nouvelle édition builds on the knowledge about language that students will bring with them from their primary school, based on their work using the National Literacy Strategy, in the following ways:

- identifying points of grammar to understand how the French language works
- using appropriate grammatical terminology in the *Dossier-langue* and *Grammaire* sections
- familiarising students with spelling and pronunciation patterns to encourage greater accuracy
- making comparisons between English and French to increase general awareness of language.

4 Covering the Scottish Guidelines

The table below is based on the Modern Languages Guidelines (5–14) consultation draft, published by the Scottish Consultative Council on the Curriculum, 1999. It indicates how ***Encore Tricolore 1 nouvelle édition*** covers the strands for each skill.

A key feature of these guidelines is knowing about language, and this is also a central aim of ***Encore Tricolore nouvelle édition***. The course emphasises learning how to use grammar and structures in a flexible way and how to recognise the spelling patterns and unique features of the language. Grammar is first presented in use, then explained in a *Dossier-langue* section, then practised through a variety of different activities and games. Students are also encouraged to identify similarities and differences between English and French.

Modern Language Guidelines (draft)	***Encore Tricolore 1 nouvelle édition***
Listening *Knowing about language*	Identifying sounds, intonation, recognising linguistic patterns (subject + verb etc.).
Listening for information and instructions	Use of the target language for class activities, general listening activities for gist and detail. Listening strategies suggested throughout Teacher's Book from *Unité* 2 onwards.
Listening and reacting to others	Pairwork, group and class activities.
Listening for enjoyment	Songs, *Comptines, Des phrases ridicules.*
Speaking *Knowing about language*	Structured practice through *Inventez des conversations* and other speaking activities. Appropriate pronunciation and intonation.
Speaking to convey information	Personal conversations, role-play activities, information gap tasks, colour-coded conversations – expanding and adapting basic dialogues.
Speaking and interacting with others	Pair, group and class activities, games etc.
Speaking about experiences, feelings and opinions	Say how they feel (*Unité 1*), express likes/dislikes, e.g. *j'aime/je n'aime pas/j'adore/je déteste* + noun (*Unité 5*), *aimer/détester* + infinitive (*Unité 10*), opinions, e.g. *c'est (ce n'est pas) intéressant/utile/ennuyeux* etc. (*Unité 8*).
Reading *Knowing about language*	Use reading strategies to help access unfamiliar language, use grammatical and contextual clues, skim and scan texts, practice in using a dictionary.
Reading for information and instructions	Read rubrics, signs, labels, captions, simple postcards, e-mail messages, letters, route directions etc.
Reading aloud	Practice in pronunciation. Sound out new words on basis of pronunciation patterns (*Écoute et parle* sections). Read parts in scripted conversations.
Reading for enjoyment	Stories, poems, short articles (*Presse-Jeunesse* sections).
Writing *Knowing about language*	Noticing similarities and differences between English and French. Awareness of language patterns, e.g. regular *-er* verbs, adjectival agreement etc. Using a dictionary to check genders, irregular plurals etc.
Writing to exchange information and ideas	Copy words, complete questionnaires, adapt model letters etc. Use a word processor to amend and present written information.
Writing to establish and maintain personal contact	Write short messages, e-mails and letters.
Writing imaginatively	Prepare poster of useful classroom phrases. *À toi!* sections – expressing personal opinions and production of language. Invent simple word puzzles. Write entries for a diary.

5 Covering the Curriculum in Northern Ireland

At the time of writing, the Northern Ireland Curriculum was under review. The following table indicates how ***Encore Tricolore nouvelle édition*** covers the Contexts for Learning and Associated Topics for Key Stage 3 in current use (April 2000).

Context 1: Everyday Activities	***Encore Tricolore 1 nouvelle édition***
Topics	
a Home and school life	*Unité 2, Unité 3, Unité 4, Unité 8*
b Food and drink	*Unité 9*
c Shopping	*(**Encore Tricolore 2**)*
d Eating out	*(**Encore Tricolore 2**)*
Context 2: Personal Life and Social Relationships	
Topics	
a Self, family and friends	*Unité 1, Unité 3, Unité 10*
b Health	*(**Encore Tricolore 2**)*
c Holidays and Leisure	*Unité 6, Unit10*
d Celebrations and special occasions	*Unité 5*
Context 3: The World Around Us	
Topics	
a House and home	*Unité 2, Unité 10*
b Town and countryside	*Unité 7*
c Getting around	*(**Encore Tricolore 2**)*
d Weather	*Unité 6*

6 Encore Tricolore 1 nouvelle édition: Teaching Plan

Unité 1	**Bonjour!**
When	Autumn Term
Topics	• meeting, greeting and saying goodbye to a French person • exchanging of names in French • talking about how people are • asking and giving ages
Grammar	• introduction to masculine and feminine • numbers up to 20
Classroom language	• understanding basic task rubrics • naming classroom objects
ICT	• using word processing and clip art for an illustrated word list • using a CD-ROM for vocabulary practice
Écoute et parle: Interrelationship between sounds and writing	• pronunciation of *i* (*six, dix*) • intonation: even stress on syllables in French • spotting regular spelling patterns in French (this is practised in all units from this point onwards)
National Curriculum Levels	All students = Level 1

Unité 2	**J'habite ici**
When	Autumn Term
Topics	• saying where you live • asking others where they live • introduction to La Rochelle
Grammar	• *à* + town, *en/au/dans* + country etc. • numbers up to 30 • introduction to the negative • *combien? il y a …*
Classroom language	• understanding instructions from the teacher • naming more classroom items
ICT	• setting up an electronic phrase book
Écoute et parle: Interrelationship between sounds and writing	• acute accent on e (*écouter, déjeuner*) • discriminating between -e and -ez • differentiating between *un* and *une*
National Curriculum Levels	Most students = Levels 1–2 All students = Level 1

Unité 3	**Chez moi**
When	Autumn Term
Topics	• talking about families and homes • saying who things belong to • talking about the days of the week
Grammar	• definite and indefinite articles (singular) • prepositions (*sur, sous, dans*) • singular paradigm (present tense) of *être* • possessive adjectives (1st and 2nd person singular) • numbers up to 70 • introduction to the plural of nouns
Classroom language	• understanding homework instructions • saying where classroom objects are
ICT	• making labels and vocabulary lists for classroom display • using text reconstruction activities
Écoute et parle: Interrelationship between sounds and writing	• pronunciation of *qu* (*quel? qu'est-ce que?*) • grave accent on *e* (*père, frère, mère*)
National Curriculum Levels	Some students = Level 2 Most students = Levels 1–2 All students = Level 1
Rappel (after *Unité 3*)	Revision of vocabulary and structures learnt in *Unités 1–3*

Unité 4	**Les animaux**
When	Autumn Term
Topics	• talking about animals/pets • describing animals and objects (colour, size) • expressing likes, dislikes and preferences
Grammar	• adjectival agreement (singular) • concept of *tu* and *vous* • singular paradigm (present tense) of *avoir* • questions with *est-ce que...?* • French alphabet and spelling (this is practised in every unit from this point onwards)
Classroom language	• differentiating between instructions to individuals and to whole class
ICT	• naming the main parts of a computer • setting up a file of personal information
Écoute et parle: Interrelationship between sounds and writing	• pronunciation of *h* (*cahier, huit*) • pronunciation of *r* (*revoir, livre, trois*)
Reading strategies	• using clues to interpret meaning: illustrations, cognates, known vocabulary, prefixes and suffixes (introduced in CM 103 which accompanies *Presse-Jeunesse* at end of *Unité 4*)
National Curriculum Levels	Some students = Levels 2–3 Most students = Level 2 All students = Levels 1–2
Formal assessment	• *Premier contrôle*: assessment of language and vocabulary introduced in the first four units. The marking scheme gives guidelines for determining National Curriculum levels attained in all four Attainment Targets.

Unité 5	**Des fêtes et des festivals**
When	Autumn/Spring Term
Topics	• asking for and giving the date • discussing important events of the year • understanding and giving greetings • talking about birthdays and presents (e.g. stationery, items of clothing)
Grammar	• complete paradigm (present tense) of *être* • plural forms (nouns and adjectives) • adjectival agreement (singular and plural) • complete paradigm (present tense) of *avoir*
Classroom language	• understanding more complicated task rubrics
ICT	• looking up information on French Internet sites • sending a virtual greetings card
Écoute et parle: Interrelationship between sounds and writing	• differentiating between *ou* and *u* (*sous, sur*) • introduction to liaison (*nous avons*)
Reading strategies	• use of a dictionary or glossary to interpret meaning (introduced and practised from this point onwards, on a regular basis, in a section in the SB entitled *C'est utile, le dictionnaire*)
National Curriculum Levels	Some students = Level 3 Most students = Levels 2–3 All students = Level 1–2
Rappel (after *Unité 5*)	• revision of vocabulary and structures learnt in *Unités 4–5*

Unité 6	**Qu'est-ce que tu fais?**
When	Spring Term
Topics	• talking about the weather, temperature and seasons • understanding simple weather information • talking about sport and other leisure activities
Grammar	• complete paradigm (present tense) regular *-er* verbs • use of *on* • numbers up to 100 and some minus numbers
Classroom language	• useful phrases for students to use
ICT	• typing French accents on the computer • looking at weather details on the Internet • using the table facility to build a personal verb table
Écoute et parle: Interrelationship between sounds and writing	• nasal vowels (*janvier, trente* and *bonjour, on*) • circumflex on e (*fenêtre, être*) • further work on endings of words
Reading strategies	• reading for detail and reading for gist (skimming) – two different comprehension techniques (introduced in CM 104 that accompanies *Presse-Jeunesse* section at end of *Unité 6*)
National Curriculum Levels	Some students = Level 3 Most students = Levels 2–3 All students = Levels 1–2

Unité 7	**Une ville de France**
When	Spring Term
Topics	• talking about places in a town • asking for, understanding and giving directions • obtaining information and maps from the tourist office • discussing how far away places are
Grammar	• at/to (*à, à la, à l', au, aux, en*) • present tense of *aller* • prepositions (*devant, derrière* and *entre*)
Classroom language	• useful phrases for students to use
ICT	• further work with obtaining information from French Internet sites • making a brochure using DTP or word processing • sending a virtual postcard
Écoute et parle: Interrelationship between sounds and writing	• nasal vowels (*cinq, lundi*) • intonation: raising voice towards end of sentence
National Curriculum Levels	Some students = Level 3 Most students = Levels 2–3 All students = Levels 1–2
Rappel (after *Unité 7*)	• revision of vocabulary and structures learnt in *Unités 6–7*
Formal assessment	• *Deuxième contrôle*: assessment of language and vocabulary introduced in *Unités 5–7*. The marking scheme gives guidelines for determining National Curriculum levels attained in all four Attainment Targets.

Unité 8	**Une journée scolaire**
When	Spring/Summer Term
Topics	• understanding and giving the time • asking what the time is or when something is happening • talking about a typical day (at home or at school) • saying which subjects you like or dislike and giving opinions about them
Grammar	• present tense of *manger* and *commencer* • possessive adjectives (all forms, singular and plural) • some examples of reflexive verbs
Classroom language	• further work on task rubrics
ICT	• contact with French schools via e-mail and the Internet • creating a database based on the results of a questionnaire • producing school timetable in French on computer • using graphics software to produce a graph of favourite subjects
Écoute et parle: Interrelationship between sounds and writing	• use of cedilla to soften c (*commençons*) • use of e to soften g before o (*mangeons*) • pronunciation of *ph* (*pharmacie*) • pronunciation of *th* (*thé, théâtre*) • pronunciation of *ch* (*chambre, chaise*)
Reading strategies	• techniques to use before consulting a dictionary (introduced in CM 106 that accompanies *Presse-Jeunesse 3* at end of *Unité 8*)
National Curriculum Levels	Some students = Level 3+ Most students = Levels 2–3 All students = Levels 1–2

Unité 9	**Mmm – c'est bon, ça!**
When	Summer Term
Topics	• talking about food and drink (including giving opinions) • talking about meals • accepting or declining food and drink
Grammar	• partitive article (*du, de la, de l', des*) • present tense of *prendre* • use of the negative
Classroom language	• useful negative sentences
ICT	• mentioning problems with ICT equipment • creating an electronic verb table
Écoute et parle: Interrelationship between sounds and writing	• pronunciation of *oi* (*soixante, histoire*) • pronunciation of *ai* (*vrai, saison*) • further work on liaison
National Curriculum Levels	Some students = Levels 3–4 Most students = Levels 2–3 All students = Levels 1–2
Rappel (after *Unité 9*)	• revision of vocabulary and structures learnt in *Unités 8–9*
Formal assessment	• Alternative tasks make it possible to adapt the *Troisième contrôle* for use at the end of *Unité 9* instead of *Unité 10* – some schools may prefer to do this, for reporting purposes.

Unité 10	**Amuse-toi bien!**
When	Summer Term
Topics	• talking about leisure activities including sport and music (including opinions) • using and understanding the 24-hour clock • saying what you do to help at home, giving reasons and opinions
Grammar	• present tense of *faire* • use of *jouer à* with sports and games • use of *jouer de* with music • use of verb followed by infinitive
Classroom language	• useful questions and answers
ICT	• discussing ICT as a hobby (games, web-browsing) • making an electronic phrase book • setting up whole class e-mail exchanges • using the Internet to find French-speaking penfriends
Écoute et parle: Interrelationship between sounds and writing	• pronunciation of *-tion* (*natation, solution*) • pronunciation of *-ui-* (*huit, pluie*) • pronunciation of 'ye' sound (*cahier, viande*)
Reading strategies	• reading to obtain specific information – scanning the text rather than reading every word • using grammatical clues – identifying verbs, adjectives and nouns by their context as an aid to understanding (introduced in CM 107–108 that accompany *Presse-Jeunesse* at the end of *Unité 10*)
National Curriculum Levels	Some students = Levels 3–4 Most students = Levels 2–3+ All students = Level 2
Formal assessment	• *Troisième contrôle*: assessment of language and vocabulary introduced in *Unités 8–10*. The marking scheme gives guidelines for determining National Curriculum levels attained in all four Attainment Targets.

Developing skills

1 Developing listening skills

Training in careful listening for detail and for gist is a key feature of the course. The strategies for using recorded texts, on which much of the teaching is based, are set out in the teacher's notes for *Unité 2* (see TB 54).

There are no 'paused' recordings as it is left to the teacher's discretion to decide the number of times the CD is played, when there should be pauses, and the speed of building up from simple to more demanding tasks. The only exception to this is in the *Contrôles*, which simulate examination-type conditions.

The full text of all recorded items appears in Section 3 of the Teacher's Book.

Recorded listening material can be broadly grouped as follows:

- **Intensive listening**
Students know what to listen for and have to select specific information from the recorded text and listen in sufficient detail to respond, e.g. by matching a description to a picture or answering simple *Vrai ou faux?* questions.

Sometimes there is an additional task, at a higher level, in which students listen for an opinion or for additional details.

Most of the listening practice in ***Encore Tricolore 1*** is intensive.

- **Listening for gist**
In this type of listening, students listen to find out what happened at the end of a story or to discover the mood of the speakers. In items of this kind the teacher should make it clear that students should not worry if they can't understand every word but should just listen for the main points as they probably will do when they hear real French people talking.

- **Interrelationship between sounds and writing**
Student CD 1 and Student CD 2 (Tracks 1–21) are devoted to intensive practice linked with different sounds, French and English pronunciation, linking sounds with spelling patterns etc. These sections appear on SB 150–159 entitled *Écoute et parle*.

- **Independent listening**
From *Unité 4* onwards, there are recorded listening items, with linked tasks on the copymaster, for students to use on their own, either at home or at school. These *Tu comprends?* sections, to be found on Student CD 2 (Tracks 22–45), are based on the language content of the unit and are graded in difficulty.

2 Developing speaking skills

The National Curriculum states that students should learn how to express themselves using a range of vocabulary and structures.

Particular emphasis is placed on the following:

- correct pronunciation and intonation
- how to ask and answer questions
- how to initiate and develop conversations
- how to vary the target language to suit context, audience and purpose.

These are addressed fully in the course, both by on-going training in listening and speaking, in every unit, and also with more targeted training linked with the above points. Examples of this are:

a individual pronunciation practice, using the *Écoute et parle* items in the Students' Book and the Student CDs

b questions – using *Est-ce que* (*Unité 4*), asking for personal details (*Unités 1–4*), more general questions (*Unités 5–10*)

c pairwork and role-play practice based in the Students' Book and 'information gap' activities, using copymasters

d 'colour-coded conversations', called *Inventez des conversations*, which appear regularly throughout the Students' Book. Students practise a basic conversation, then vary and adapt it by substituting other words and expressions from the colour-coded sections.

Consolidation
At the end of each *Écoute et parle* section there is a recorded conversation to provide extra practice of the language in the unit.

3 Developing reading skills

There is a wide range of reading material in ***Encore Tricolore 1***, including practice in intensive reading to discover specific information and reading for gist, e.g. to find out a story line.

Reading is formally introduced in *Unité 3* and reading strategies are outlined in this unit, through the list of ways of using recorded text to teach reading (TB 64) and through copymasters, e.g. 3/1 *Lire, c'est intéressant*.

- **Presse-Jeunesse**
These Students' Book magazine sections can just be used alone as reading for pleasure. However, for specific training in reading skills, they should be used with the accompanying copymasters. These systematically introduce and practise reading strategies, as listed in the National Curriculum requirements, e.g.
    - techniques for skimming and for scanning written texts for information, including those from ICT-based sources
    - how to use context and other clues to interpret meaning, for example, by identifying the grammatical function of unfamiliar words or similarities with words
    - using ICT.

- **ICT and reading skills**
In many units of the Students' Book, there are suggestions for using ICT programmes such as *Fun with Texts* to allow students to work on a reading passage at their own pace, involving such activities as unjumbling text, sequencing and cloze procedure activities.

- **Using dictionaries and other reference material**

Practice in using dictionaries and the Students' Book French–English and English–French glossaries 'appropriately and effectively' is given regularly through Students' Book items such as *C'est utile, le dictionnaire* and through activities on copymaster.

4 Developing writing skills

Training in writing is in line with National Curriculum requirements and plenty of practice activities are provided, e.g.

- **Copywriting**

In the early units, the main emphasis is inevitably on copywriting, of words and phrases, but simple creative activity is introduced quite quickly, especially through the copymasters, e.g. through word games, sorting words and making lists according to gender.

Students also use computers to make labels or posters for the classroom.

- **Learning new words**

Students soon begin to practise writing familiar words, then phrases from memory, mainly through a wide range of games and word activities.

The *Sommaire* sections, at the end of each unit and on copymasters, encourage students to learn lists of vocabulary on a regular basis.

ICT activities such as *Fun with Texts* also train students to learn spelling patterns.

- **Adapting a model by substituting text/ adapting known language to new contexts**

There are a lot of Students' Book activities based on writing sentences using substitution tables. They begin with simple sentence work, but more creative and open-ended writing is gradually introduced, especially through the *À toi!* items in which students adapt the language they have learnt to make personal statements, state likes and dislikes and express opinions.

Sometimes option boxes in the Students' Book can be used in cut and paste activities on a computer.

- **Developing independence in learning and using the target language**

Students are encouraged to use dictionaries and other reference materials appropriately and are trained through such activities as *C'est utile, le dictionnaire* to use dictionaries and the *Glossaires* at the back of the book.

The vocabulary in the *Sommaires* is listed alphabetically within topics to make it easy for students to refer to.

Students are also trained to refer to the *Dossier-langue* explanations and to the grammar section at the back of the book. In addition, they are encouraged to make their own ICT verb tables and 'electronic phrase book' (see TB 40).

- **Using the Target Language creatively and imaginatively/Producing different types of written language**

These skills are built up gradually through many easy tasks on copymasters or through Students' Book items such as writing simple e-mails to individuals or a class in France. For more able students, this builds up to more open-ended tasks such as *À toi!* In these items, students adapt the language they have learnt to make personal statements, state likes and dislikes and express opinions.

- **Re-drafting writing to improve its accuracy**

Although this is quite advanced work for students using ***Encore Tricolore 1***, early training is given by the following types of task:

  - *Vrai ou faux?* tasks, followed by correcting false statements
  - *Chasse à l'intrus* activities in which students add explanations for their answers
  - sentence completion tasks, based on information from short articles or letters
  - working on the computer with text re-sequencing activities
  - unjumbling and completing sentences
  - using substitution tables.

5 Developing understanding and application of grammar

Grammar is a central feature of ***Encore Tricolore***. Throughout the course, new grammatical structures are introduced through oral/aural and sometimes reading activities. Students are encouraged to work out rules for themselves before referring to the English explanation, in the *Dossier-langue* sections. This is immediately followed by practice activities and games, to help students to absorb the grammatical patterns and use them.

There is a grammar reference section, including verb tables, at the back of the Students' Book and students are encouraged to make up their own computer-generated verb tables.

- **Grammar in Action**

Grammar in Action is a series of workbooks designed to accompany each stage of ***Encore Tricolore***. The books provide extensive practice in French grammar and reinforce and extend students' grammar skills. The existing edition of *Grammar in Action 1* is designed to accompany ***Encore Tricolore 1*** (original edition) and includes page references to the Students' Book.

Grammar in Action 1 can continue to be used both independently and with ***Encore Tricolore 1 nouvelle édition***.

6 Developing language-learning skills

The National Curriculum emphasises training in language-learning skills stating that pupils should be taught:

- **techniques for memorising words, phrases and short extracts**

In ***Encore Tricolore 1 nouvelle édition***, students are given regular hints for memorising, e.g. learning nouns with their gender.

Useful tips are given where relevant and are indicated in the Students' Book by the following symbol: [!]

Genders are also often shown by red and blue colour-coding of nouns, and students are encouraged to use similar reminders when compiling their own vocabulary lists.

The *Masculin, féminin* tasks in the *Rappel* sections are supported by a *Pour t'aider* note which indicates common word endings linked to masculine or feminine words.

The *Sommaire* and *Vocabulaire de classe* sections at the end of each unit bring vocabulary together for easy reference. This gives a sense of progress and emphasises the importance of regular learning as an essential language-learning skill.

- **to use their knowledge of English or another language when learning the target language**

Grammar is explained in English, and the *Dossier-langue* sections and a range of notes in the Teacher's Book all use knowledge of English to help in learning the target language.

Comparisons between English and French are highlighted by question boxes. These boxes appear whenever a point of this nature occurs in context on the pages of the Students' Book.
They are indicated by the following symbol: [?]

- **to look out for clues**

Through training in reading strategies (CM 103–108), students are taught to use clues to discover meaning, such as similarities to English (cognates), as well as context and grammatical function.

Differentiation

1 Early units

Encore Tricolore 1 nouvelle édition contains material for most of the ability range. In the first few units it is assumed that the class will work at much the same pace, although suggestions for varying the level of difficulty are included in the teacher's notes, even at this early stage, e.g. answering in full sentences or with single words, saying or writing down answers.

2 Support and extension material

At a later stage some separate items are provided for practical differentiation using both the *Au choix* section of the Students' Book and the Copymasters.

- **Au choix**

This section of the Students' Book provides teachers and students with extension (harder items) and consolidation (more practice at the same level). This should prove useful for students who work quickly as no extra materials need to be given out and students can work on most of the tasks independently.

- **Copymasters**

Some of these are for support and some for consolidation. There are also a few copymasters for extension, usually where the task itself involves writing on the sheet. Copymasters involving word puzzles, testing material etc. are expendable, but many other sheets are re-usable.

In addition, many copymasters have an incline of difficulty, to allow even the less able students to try harder items if they wish.

3 Differentiation by task

This can be done using *Au choix* and copymasters as suggested above. Some students can work on an extension task, others on a support task, possibly even a third group on a consolidation task. Usually this range of options is indicated in the teacher's notes and this choice of task could also form part of a Carousel lesson (see below).

4 Differentiation by outcome

Some tasks, especially the open-ended ones such as *À toi!* can be carried out at various levels according to the level of ability of the student. For example, to offer more support for the less able, the item could be treated as a class activity and a description built up on the board to be copied down. In other cases, gap-filling tasks can be made easier by giving students options to choose from, which can be written on the board and copied.

5 Selective use of items

The teaching of each new area of language follows a sequence of steps: presentation, discovery and explanation of new language, practice of new vocabulary and structures, leading to full communicative use.

The initial presentation, through oral/aural work, the explanation of new structures and some practice is appropriate for all.

After this, there is room for selection, for example, by using some of the materials for differentiation, listed above, or choosing from the suggestions for practice tasks, games and ICT activities, listed in Section 2 and in the notes for the individual units. This selection will be influenced by the time available and the abilities and needs of students.

One useful way to practise a range of items is to use the Carousel technique, as explained below.

Carousel group work

It can be useful sometimes to organise a lesson on a 'Carousel' system. This involves groups doing a series of activities in sequence. Some of these can be harder than others and, depending on the plan for moving round, some activities can be made more demanding than others for differentiation purposes. Also, fairly straightforward tasks (even exercises) can alternate with something more light-hearted. It is best to have at least one more activity in progress than there are groups, so that no-one is waiting around until the next activity is available.

For this type of group work, group leaders will be needed. They can be chosen by their group or the teacher. Some time will need to be spent training the group leaders and helping them to prepare materials, but people who have done this have found it very rewarding in terms of progress and enjoyment, and the activities set up can often be re-used or adapted for other groups or occasions.

Developing cultural awareness

In ***Encore Tricolore nouvelle édition*** students are introduced to a variety of countries in which French is spoken and throughout the course, the emphasis is on authenticity of language and of background information. In ***Encore Tricolore 1 nouvelle édition***, the focus is mainly on France and French family life, but some items relate to the wider francophone community such as Sénégal (*Unité* 8) and various religious festivals (*Unité* 9). The illustrations include a varied selection of recent photos of life in France, mainly featuring young people.

Students are encouraged to look up background information on the Internet and also gradually build up direct contacts with French-speaking individuals or school classes.

Assessment

Assessment is an integral part of ***Encore Tricolore 1 nouvelle édition*** and is of two types:

1 Épreuves (informal assessment)

These informal tests are on copymasters and appear after *Unité 3* and all subsequent units. The teacher's notes, solutions and mark allocations appear at the end of each unit of Section 3 of this book.

The skills tested are listening, reading and writing combined with grammar, with between two and four tasks per skill, at different levels (starting with easy tasks at Level 1 in each skill, but with a built-in incline of difficulty on each copymaster).

Students will find the *Épreuves* useful to check their own progress and pinpoint areas that need further revision before they carry out the more formal assessment (*Contrôles*).

The *Épreuves* relate specifically to the unit just completed and each involve no more than two periods, probably one period for listening and another for reading and writing.

The listening material relating to these informal tests is at the end of each unit.

These tests can be used for continuous assessment or more informally in class, for homework or for a cover lesson as extra practice and consolidation.

2 Contrôles (formal assessment)

Encore Tricolore 1 nouvelle édition includes three blocks of formal assessment which form an integral part of the course. The students' sheets can be found in one section at the end of the Copymasters, the mark scheme is in the Teacher's Book and the recordings for the listening assessment are on Class CD 4.

These assessments, or *Contrôles*, take place, in all four language skills, at the following points in the course:

Premier contrôle – after *Unité 4*
Deuxième contrôle – after *Unité 7*
Troisième contrôle – after *Unité 10*

Alternative tasks are also provided to make it possible to carry out the *Troisième contrôle* after *Unité 9*, if schools find this fits in better with their examination and reporting arrangements.

The *Contrôles* have been designed to provide:

- a means of checking how much of the language and structures taught in preceding units has been assimilated by students
- evidence to help determine the National Curriculum Levels attained by students in each of the four language skills (Attainment Targets)
- a way of recording progress made by students – a Record sheet for students (CM 128) is provided for this purpose
- a pointer towards lack of progress in any language skill (enabling the teacher to take the necessary steps for support)
- an introduction, at a basic level, to the type of target-language testing used at GCSE level, giving students a head start in developing the examination techniques they are going to need at a later date.

The three *Contrôles* each provide a series of tasks at various levels, with an incline of difficulty within each paper, so that all students can start together at the beginning and work through the tasks as far as they are able.

Premier contrôle: Levels 1–2
Deuxième contrôle: Levels 1–3
Troisième contrôle: Levels 2–4

The mark schemes for the *Contrôles* (TB 200–206) provide the teacher with:

- instructions for administering the tasks, where necessary
- solutions for all tasks that are not open-ended
- a points system, adding up to 100 points for each *Contrôle*, for easy conversion to percentages
- information for converting the points scored to National Curriculum levels
- transcripts for the recorded material.

The mark scheme, and the tasks themselves, are closely linked to the approach set out by the QCA Exemplification Materials and Optional Tests and Tasks for Key Stage 3.

The following points should be borne in mind in relation to the various sets of papers:

Listening

- The papers for listening are, except for the alternative tasks, designed to be expendable.
- Each item is recorded twice, without any sound effects or interruptions and is clearly spoken by a native French speaker. It must be remembered that playing the material a third time, except where specified, could affect a student's performance and cause an artificially high score to be obtained.

Speaking

- These sheets are designed to be re-used and there is no need for students to write on them.
- The teacher is best placed to decide when to give out the tasks prior to the assessment and whether to allow students to record their own work (see individual mark schemes for more detailed information).

Reading

- As with the listening, these papers are, except for the alternative tasks, designed to be expendable.
- The use of dictionaries should not be permitted, in line with the latest GCSE directive.

Writing

- These sheets are designed to be re-used.
- The use of dictionaries should not be permitted, in line with the latest GCSE directive.
- Because these tasks are open-ended, the marking is quite complicated, but full details are provided in the individual mark schemes.

Finally, it is important to remember that the assessment tasks of the three *Contrôles* should not be used in isolation to determine the National Curriculum levels attained by students. They are designed to supplement rather than replace knowledge accumulated by the teacher from everyday assessment of student performance as they work through the various activities.

Using Information and Communication Technology (ICT)

1 Introduction

ICT has been fully integrated into the various components of ***Encore Tricolore 1 nouvelle édition***. There is a planned approach to teaching French ICT vocabulary and phrases for classroom use so that these can be introduced, practised, revised and integrated consistently into every aspect of the course. As a result, ICT is seen as a routine part of learning French and of life in French-speaking countries.

In the Teacher's Book, the guidelines for each unit contain specific suggestions for incorporating ICT into the learning process. Some ICT activities, however, are ongoing and are suitable for use with many different units – these are listed in Section 2 (TB 40). The final two pages of the Teacher's Book (TB 207–208) list useful websites for teachers and students.

There is a three-page section entitled *À l'ordinateur* at the back of the Students' Book (SB 147–149).

Three ICT worksheets to reinforce this technical language are included in the Copymasters (CM 4/4, CM 6/5, CM 8/8).

ICT symbols on the pages of the Students' Book indicate clearly which tasks are most suitable for adapting or extending to become ICT activities.

Some of the activities suggested are ones in which ICT is used as a tool to support the learning of French. Examples include:

- text manipulation activities such as gap-filling
- use of CD-ROMs to practise vocabulary
- use of word processing in phrase and vocabulary building.

There are genuinely communicative activities based on the use of ICT as a communications medium, for example:

- World Wide Web activities in which students can learn about aspects of life and culture in French-speaking countries from authentic materials
- communicating with other learners and native speakers via e-mail
- live interaction with a correspondent via a video conference link.

Thus, ***Encore Tricolore 1 nouvelle édition*** will enable ICT to add value to the process of learning French. Whenever ICT is advocated, care has been taken to design activities which genuinely add something to the learning process that could not be achieved without the technology – it's not just ICT for the sake of it!

2 ICT and the National Curriculum

The integrated approach to ICT is fully in line with the National Curriculum for Modern Foreign Languages in England and Wales and with similar requirements elsewhere. Through this integrated approach students will benefit to the full from frequent opportunities to use technology, as prescribed by the National Curriculum. The table below sets out some of the key skills, as listed in the section entitled **Developing knowledge, skills and understanding** (TB 9–10) that can be developed through using ICT:

1 *Acquiring knowledge and understanding of the target language* • *the grammar of the target language and how to apply it*	1 • using CD-ROMs to study language patterns • using text manipulation to encourage thinking about language patterns
2 *Developing language skills* • *how to listen carefully for gist and detail* • *how to adapt language they already know for different contexts* • *techniques for skimming and for scanning written texts for information, including those from ICT-based sources*	2 • using multi-media software for listening practice • using word processing to present language in revised format • reading web pages on the Internet
3 *Developing language learning skills* • *how to use dictionaries and other reference materials appropriately and effectively*	3 • using electronic dictionaries and glossaries and electronic encyclopaedia
4 *Developing cultural awareness* • *working with authentic materials in the target language, including some from ICT-based sources* • *communicating with native speakers [in person or by correspondence]*	4 • reading web pages on the Internet • sending and receiving e-mail
5 *Breadth of study* • *producing and responding to different types of spoken and written language, including texts produced using ICT* • *using a range of resources, including ICT, for accessing and communicating information* • *using the target language creatively and imaginatively* • *using the target language for real purposes [for example e-mail messages]*	5 • reading web pages on the Internet • producing own writing, posters, brochures etc. using word processing and desktop publishing packages • sending and receiving e-mail

3 Key ICT uses

E-mail

E-mail provides the opportunity to communicate with native speakers. There are a host of tasks that can be used with e-mail. For beginners, the basic tasks that could be covered include:

- reading an e-mail in French from a correspondent in the link school
- replying to an e-mail
- writing an e-mail message and sending it to a correspondent
- sending an e-mail greetings card (advice on this is given on TB 207).

Databases and spreadsheets

These programs can be used for simple activities like:

- collating information about pets, members of the class or other topics which can then be displayed in graphs, updated and edited, and later used as a basis for oral work
- working with figures to add up prices or convert currencies.

Word processing

There are many uses for word processing in languages lessons including:

- developing electronic phrase books (see TB 40)
- building up a file in which students write a self-description (see TB 40)
- creative writing – framework poems (poems made out of a list of words supplied by the teacher), captions for interesting images, simple narratives, unusual menus
- descriptive writing – postcards, letters, shopping lists, menus.

Text manipulation

Good language practice can be provided with text manipulation software, e.g. *Fun with Texts*. Students can work on ready-made texts which are commercially available or teachers can develop texts themselves, thereby ensuring that the level and the language are relevant to the class. Text manipulation can help develop grammatical awareness, comprehension and spelling. If the text used is a model text, e.g. a letter, work on it gives excellent practice prior to proceeding to writing an original or personalised version of the model.

Desktop publishing
Many schools have publishing software that allows the user to lay out text and images. If your students have been taught how to use this software in their ICT lessons they will be able to make things in French such as:

- a one-sentence poster of a useful classroom request in French to display on the wall
- a wanted poster
- an invitation to a party
- a greetings card.

CD-ROMs and multi-media
CD-ROMs can be very useful at the practice stage to enable students to work intensively at their own pace and level. Suitable practice is provided by a variety of language learning programs. These programs offer a variety of exercises such as matching, multiple choice, true or false and games which provide simple vocabulary practice of the basic topics.

The CD-ROM is really just a mass storage device. It is particularly useful for multi-media software which involves vast amounts of data. This type of software is very useful in modern languages because it makes it possible to include sound in the program as well as images, animation and video.

Working with graphics and images
Images can be used in many different ways, both by students and teachers. Images may be ready made in the form of clip-art or symbol fonts or can be drawn on the computer using a paint package or the built in drawing facilities of word processing or desktop publishing. The Internet is an excellent source of images – for famous people, for objects and for places in France and other French-speaking countries.

Presentation
The computer makes a very powerful presentation tool that can be used to present new vocabulary, grammar points, dialogues and simple picture stories. It can also be used by students to support simple oral presentations.

The basic equipment needed for this includes a computer (laptop or desktop machine) and a projection device: the computer can be linked to a data projector if the school has one. It is also possible to connect a computer to an overhead projector, but this requires additional hardware.

Alternatively, computers can be connected up to television sets – this requires a large screen television and a television adaptor.

Finally, some classrooms are being equipped with electronic whiteboards that produce a large screen display and are also interactive.

Internet/World Wide Web
If students have access to the World Wide Web via the Internet they may like to consult relevant web pages to support their learning about aspects of French life and culture. They will not understand all of the information given but will be able to work out the gist of sections particularly where they are interested in the topic and where lively presentation and good use of graphics aid comprehension and boost motivation.

There are many possible ways to use the Internet:

- to look for information
- to read for pleasure
- to do practice activities available via the Internet
- to produce a web page for the class.

Video conferencing
If video conferencing facilities are available in schools it is possible for students to watch and listen to a video correspondent via a video conferencing link and to speak themselves to the correspondent. This can be a demanding activity as it calls for maturity. For beginners, it may be best if they speak in their mother tongue. The main learning benefit will come from listening to their correspondents speaking French to them. This can be highly motivating but calls for extensive preparation by the teachers in each country.

4 Points to note

Guidance on hardware
If you are able to specify hardware for use by students learning French, here are some points to consider:

- Is there a fast CD-ROM drive to allow rapid access to sound and pictures?
- Is there a DVD-ROM drive to allow access to new software sold in that medium?
- What monitor size is available? (A large 17" screen is good for pair work.)
- Computer sound: is there a playback and record facility?
- Are there headphones with a splitter to allow two sets of headphones to be used with one computer?
- Is there an easy-to-use microphone?
- Video conferencing: is there a record facility so that pupils can see a replay of the exchange? (Note that this facility is often claimed but can be very hard to get to work!)
- Network: can the network run a CD-ROM?
- Data projector: does the school have a portable data projector that you can use in your own classroom for wide screen display of a computer screen? (It could be useful for presentations and demonstrations by teacher and students.)
- Electronic whiteboard: this also provides a large screen for class viewing, but with the added advantage that you can operate the computer from the screen with a pointer that works like a mouse.

Copyright issues
The issue of copyright in dealing with electronic materials should be regarded in the same way as for any other published materials. However, there are some particular points that should be kept in mind:

- legally obtained clip-art images can be used for making teaching and learning materials
- web pages are often copyright free but it is important to consider the source of the web page – does the web page developer own the copyright for the material on the page? Some images on the Web may be copyrighted but many are not.

However, the images may have been placed on the Web without the copyright holder's permission. In the circumstances, it is hard to give clear advice. For those who wish to make absolutely certain of this issue, there is usually a contact e-mail address on web pages which could be used to seek permission. Having said all of this, much on the Web is freely copiable and this is often stated. It will sometimes be a question of judgement. If the image is to be used solely in your own school for educational purposes then it is unlikely to infringe copyright. This area is a difficult one and teachers must follow their own judgement or be advised by head teachers or ICT managers.

5 Classroom organisation

There are three main ways in which ICT can be an integral part of your French lessons:

1 Access to a computer room, with about 15 computers, i.e. roughly one computer between two pupils

The computers will probably be linked to the school network and possibly also to the Internet. It is often useful to ask students to work together in pairs and some of the best learning occurs as a result of collaboration and discussion. Sometimes you will want your students to work individually, e.g. when writing a self-description. In that case, it may be possible for half the class to work on computer and the other half to do related work.

2 A small number of computers available in the modern languages area which may or may not be linked to the school network/Internet

This facility is useful to provide:

- differentiated work for individuals and small groups, e.g. vocabulary building using a CD-ROM for students who have missed work or fallen behind
- an ICT activity as part of a carousel of other activities that students work through in groups
- part of a jigsaw of activities in which students collect information from different sources (print, listening, ICT) and then collate this in groups

It is very useful to have someone to provide support for students if they are using the computers outside the teaching room. This could be provided by a sixth former, a Foreign Language Assistant (FLA) or a student teacher. It is important that students have had an introduction to the program that they are to use and some hands-on experience. Alternatively, distribute computer literate students across the groups so that there is always at least one person in each group who can provide help if anyone gets stuck.

3 A single computer in the ML classroom, usually not linked to network or Internet

This can be very useful if there is some facility for projection or large screen display. The teacher can use the computer for presentations or demonstrations. Students can use the computer to support them in giving a simple oral presentation. Even with one computer, it is possible for students to work in pairs on an activity at the computer and for each pair to have completed the activity over the course of two or three lessons.

6 How to enter accents

Students will need to know how to enter accents in the various programs that they use – word processing, e-mail, text manipulation, desktop publishing, presentation, web pages etc. Some of these programs have a simple method for entering accents, e.g. Microsoft Word. This is fine if that is the only program used but the method will not work for other programs. The way around this is to make sure that students understand the ALT code method because it works on most programs (CM 6/5). The Toolbar method is also effective if your school computers are equipped with it and is explained in the help section of your word processing package. Ultimately, students will need to know a range of methods since they are likely to use different computers at school, at home and in libraries.

7 Summary

For further information on using ICT, please refer to:

- the list of ongoing ICT activities in Section 2 (TB 40)
- the specific suggestions incorporated into the guidelines given for each unit
- the suggestions for which aspects of ICT would fit best with each unit in the Teaching Plan (TB 12–16)
- the list of ICT vocabulary in the Students' Book (SB 147–149)
- the three ICT worksheets in the Copymasters (CM 4/4, CM 6/5 and CM 8/8)
- the list of useful websites (TB 207–208)

Games

Many of the games described here are applicable for a wide range of language practice. A game which is particularly appropriate for a specific area is mentioned in the relevant unit notes.

In many games the teacher is the caller at the beginning, but students can soon be encouraged to take over this role.

1 Number games

- **Continue!**

The caller counts aloud, stopping at intervals and pointing at someone, who must say the next number or s/he is out.

- **Chef d'orchestre**

This is a more complicated version of *Continue!* For this the class is divided into two teams (*en avant* and *en arrière*). The 'conductor' says any number and points to one of the teams who must call out the next or the previous number depending on which team is indicated.

- **Avancez et reculez**

In this game, the class stands up and counts aloud in sequence until the teacher (or a student) gives the command *Avancez* or *Reculez*, at which point they change to counting backwards or forwards again. Anyone who makes a mistake has to sit down. This can also be played as a team game, with the counting passed to the other team as soon as a mistake is made. The team left with the most people standing at an agreed finishing time has won.

- **Comptez comme ça!**

The caller starts by saying *Comptez comme ça!* and begins to count in a particular way, either forwards or backwards or alternate numbers or later in multiples of 2, 3 etc. Students join in as soon as they can with the right sequence and are out if they count a wrong number. The caller changes the sequence at intervals by saying *Maintenant, comptez comme ça!* and beginning again.

A group version of this can be played in which only the group the caller points at counts in the sequence which s/he begins.

- **Dice games**

Ordinary dice can be used for number games or special ones made using higher numbers or with words on, such as the six persons of the verb paradigm etc.

The simplest form of dice games is for a player to throw the dice, marked with a selection of numbers, and then say aloud the number or word that they throw. One group can throw for another and students unable to say the right words are out.

Alternatively, players in pairs or groups can simply throw the dice in turns, say the numbers or words aloud and jot them down, keep their own scores and eventually add them up aloud in French and see who has the most after, say, six throws.

- **Loto (Bingo)**

Students can make a class set of Bingo cards, as illustrated below, and play with buttons as counters.

Similarly, they can play a simpler version by just writing any four numbers on a scrap of paper and crossing them off as they are said by the caller. This game is useful when the numbers are learnt as words, as the winner must show her/his paper to the teacher and will be eliminated if the words are incorrectly spelt.

1	9	1	12	3	10	8	15	7	12	5	11	5	12	7	10	14	19
11	16	10	17	12	19	16	17	18	19	14	16	14	17	19	20	16	17
16	14	6	15	3	11	6	12	2	11	4	12	4	10	4	13	8	11
6	17	17	18	13	20	17	18	13	16	14	19	15	17	15	20	18	19
8	10	2	10	5	14	2	8	9	11	3	12	3	9	2	9	9	12
14	15	12	15	16	19	17	19	19	20	14	15	6	18	11	20	17	18
7	16	9	14	5	13	9	13	7	9	1	7	6	12	4	11	1	8
17	18	15	16	15	18	18	19	13	16	18	20	13	15	13	18	10	15

The above is a series of 36 cards, all bearing a different group of numbers, which is included for teachers' convenience, so that each child can be given a different group to make. Further cards including numbers 20–40 and 40–60 could be prepared.

This type of Bingo is also an excellent standby for practice of almost any set of vocabulary, days of the week, months, colours, parts of a verb etc. For example, when learning the date, students write four days or months in words on a piece of paper and cross them off as the caller says them, saying *Loto!* when all four have been said.

- **Le dix magique**

This is a pontoon-type game. The French for pontoon is *vingt et un*, but this version uses a total of ten so is called *Le dix magique*.

Students make a simple set of cards with numbers 1–10. They place the cards upside down and turn them over one at a time, saying the number, until they get exactly 10. If they get 11 or more they are 'bust' (*fichu!*) and they must start again. The best of five turns is the winner.

2 The time and the date

- **Quelle heure est-il?**

This is a 'signalling' game in which the teacher (or caller) holds her/his arms upright to symbolise the hour, to the right to symbolise quarter past, to the left to symbolise quarter to and downwards to symbolise half past and the class or individuals say the time.

The game could be played in the manner of *Jacques a dit* (see TB 29), with the teacher saying the time and the students doing the hand signals. Alternatively, students could write down a sequence of times signalled and check them back orally.

- **Devine la date**

Write twelve dates on the board (one from each month). Students work in pairs, and each write down one of the dates without showing their partner. The partners then take it in turn to guess the dates (using the ones on the board as a guide). The first person to guess the date gains a point, and the first person to get, say, four points wins.

Sets of A5 sized cards, one set numbered 1–31 and

the other numbered 1–12, can be made and used as cue cards, with someone holding the cards up in pairs to represent the date. These cards can be used for pairwork or for team games with each team holding up a pair of cards in turn and guessing each other's against the clock.

The cards can also be used for other flashcard games (see TB 27).

- **Loto des mois/jours**

Students write down any four months (or days) on a scrap of paper and cross them off as they are said by the caller.

3 General vocabulary games

These can be used for practising numbers and areas of vocabulary, e.g. food, pets etc.

- **Attention!**

Everyone in the class is given a word or number at the beginning of a week and a list of these is written on a notice or at the side of the board. At any odd time during the French lessons for that week, the teacher will call out one of the words or numbers listed and the correct student should stand up. If not, s/he is out and crossed off the list. The winners are those still in at the end of the week.

This game can be used to practise any vocabulary, each member of the class being allocated a colour, fruit, part of a verb etc.

- **Effacez!**

Numbers, pictures or words are written on the board in random order. When the caller names an item on the board, a student must rush out and rub the item off.

This can be played by the teacher just pointing at the next student, who has five seconds only to locate and erase the right item. It can also be played in groups or in teams. In the latter case it is advisable to write two sets of items, one set on each half of the board, and to provide two board rubbers. If the teacher wants the items left on for further practice they could be ringed in coloured chalk or pen instead of being rubbed off.

This is an excellent game for matching the written word to vocabulary previously met only aurally.

- **Les deux échelles (a dice game)**

Two or more six-rung ladders can be drawn on the board with a number (or word, part of verb etc.) on each rung. Each team or group throws the dice and reads out the number or word and, if it is the next on the ladder, it is crossed off and the team moves up to the next rung. No number or word must be crossed off until that rung is reached and the first team to reach the top of the ladder wins.

See also **Dice games** and **Loto** (TB 25).

- **Qu'est-ce qu'il y a dans la boîte?**

This game can be played with any selection of objects linked with a recent vocabulary topic, e.g. classroom objects, pictures of animals, clothes etc.

First show the class the things to be used and practise the vocabulary. The objects are then taken out of sight and placed one at a time in a box for the class to guess which one is there each time.

- **Vrai ou faux? (True and false chairs)**

This is a useful game for mixed or lower ability classes as it does not involve all the class in speaking or writing. Each team has two chairs labelled *vrai* and *faux*.The teacher (or a student) makes any statement and a member of each team comes out and sits on the true chair if s/he thinks the statement is true and on the false one if not. Sitting on the right chair wins a point for that team. (If the teams are too level, points can be given for the first child to sit on the right chair each time.)

- **Je touche**

This is a cumulative game (chain game), in which the first person gets up and touches something, saying what he/she is doing, e.g. *Je touche le livre de Jean*, and then chooses someone to continue. The next person repeats what has been said and adds on something else, and so on.

For writing practice the class could try to write the whole list down from memory at the end.

Another alternative is to make, from memory, a numbered list of drawings. This list can be used again for pairwork, e.g. *Numéro 4, qu'est-ce que c'est?*

- **Il y a une erreur (Deliberate mistake game)**

Students work in groups on text from a book (or on tape). When they are reasonably familiar with it, they each make up a 'deliberate mistake' (which must be factual, not a spelling or grammar error). Then each reads out the whole or a section of the passage and the others try to spot the mistake.

- **Touché-coulé (Battleships)**

This well-known game (best played in pairs) can be adapted to practise various bits of language. In its simplest form students are given the area of vocabulary to be practised, e.g. a verb paradigm, numbers, days of the week etc. or a set of flashcards is put up as a reminder. Each person writes down on paper any three of the alternatives. Each player in turn guesses one item that the other person has written and if guessed correctly, the player must cross it out. The first one to eliminate their partner's items has won.

More complicated versions, nearer to the original, involve writing the items in a particular place on squared paper or a plan so that one player says to their opponent, e.g. *A3, tu as …!*)

- **Using Battleships to practise the verb être**

(as for *Unités 3* or *5*)

Each partner marks where s/he is on a simple plan of a house or flat. Then each asks the other, in turn, e.g. *Es-tu dans la cuisine?* answering, e.g. *Oui, je suis dans la cuisine* or *Non* if incorrect. The first one to discover where the other is has won.

When the whole paradigm has been learnt, the game can be extended to include the third person and the plural persons of the verb, e.g. *Les enfants sont dans le salon* etc.

- **Je pense à quelque chose**

The basic guessing game, in which someone thinks of a word (within a given range) and the others have to guess it by asking *C'est un/une …?* (See *Unité 2* – SB 12.)

- **Le jeu des Scarabées (Beetle)**

Again, various areas of vocabulary which can have visual interpretation can be adapted to this, e.g. Beetle house. Students draw a square divided into four for a house. They throw the dice and fill in the correct parts as follows:

1 *la cuisine*
2 *la salle à manager*
3 *la salle de bains*
4 *la chambre*
5 *la porte*
6 *le jardin*

The first to complete her/his house has won. Other possible subjects are pets (*Unité 4*), clothes (*Unités 5* and *10*), lessons on a timetable (*Unité 8*) and courses of a meal (*Unité 9*).

- **Jeu de mémoire (Kim's game)**

Everyone looks at a set of objects, words or information for a set time (say, 2 minutes). Then one or more of these is removed or the whole lot are covered up, and the class has to remember as many objects, facts or words as possible.

4 Flashcard games

For guessing games involving flashcards the class should always be shown all the cards to be used first and the French for these should be practised or checked before the game begins.

- **Qu'est-ce que c'est? (Guess the back of the flashcard)**

It is better to limit the cards to a single topic, so that there are not too many to choose from.

The pile of flashcards is shuffled and the caller holds up a card with the picture facing her/him and says *Qu'est-ce que c'est?* Other students ask *C'est un/une* (+ noun)? and the person who guesses correctly comes out and acts as caller.

- **Qu'est-ce qu'il/elle fait?**

This game is similar to the one above but is played with flashcards depicting actions (e.g. flashcards 34–42 and 90–100).

- **Quel temps fait-il?**

This is played in the same way as above, but with cards 27–33.

- **Ce n'est pas ... (Guess what the card <u>isn't</u>)**

This is played with the whole class, as a group game or in pairs. One player holds up a card, face away, and the other person(s) guess what it is not, e.g.

– *Ce n'est pas un chien.*

– *Vrai.*

– *Ce n'est pas une souris.*

– *Vrai.*

– *Ce n'est pas un lapin.*

– *Faux – c'est un lapin.*

This is a good morale booster as the answer is more often right than wrong!

- **Des questions**

The teacher picks up one of a group of flashcards and asks a question about it. S/he gives the card to the student who answers correctly. When all the cards are given out, the students with them come to the front and ask a question about their card to someone else in the class who then receives the card if s/he answers correctly. This goes on until all the class have had a turn.

- **Où vas-tu?**

To practise the verb *aller*, all the flashcards referring to places should be put up around the room. The teacher or a student tells someone, e.g. *Va à la gare!* The student gets up and goes to the relevant place and on the way is asked *Où vas-tu?* If s/he answers correctly s/he continues and the teacher asks someone else *Où va-t-il/elle?* If s/he replies incorrectly s/he sits down and someone else is told to go somewhere. If s/he replies correctly and arrives at the destination s/he has a point.

- **Morpion (Flashcards noughts and crosses)**

This game can be played with a variety of vocabulary. The example given practises places in a town.

Stick nine 'places in a town' flashcards to the board, face outwards if you want the activity to be easy and face inwards if you want it to be difficult (in which case you will have to memorize the positions of the cards yourself!). Students play this in two teams, with each team asking the way to a place (*pour aller au ...*) in turn. The card representing the place they asked the way to is then removed and replaced with X or 0. The object of the game is to get three in a row.

- **Trois questions (Mind reading)**

This is good for practising verbs + nouns.

Tell students that you are going to read their minds. Put up a number of flashcards and tell a student to think hard about one of them (get the thinker to tell her/his neighbour or write down which s/he has chosen, as a safeguard). Then ask three questions and if you have read her/his mind by then you get a point, if not the class gets a point.

Examples:

1 *être* (+ room)
Teacher: *Tu es dans la salle à manger?*
Student: *Non, je ne suis pas dans la salle à manger.*
Teacher: *Tu es dans le salon?*
Student: *Non, je ne suis pas dans le salon.*
Teacher: *Tu es dans la cuisine?*
Student: *Oui, je suis dans la cuisine.*
or *Non, je ne suis pas dans la cuisine.*
or *Non, je suis* (+ correct place)

2 *avoir* (+ pets)
Teacher: *Tu as un lapin.*
Student: *Oui, j'ai un lapin.*
or *Non, je n'ai pas de lapin* etc.

3 *aller* (+ place)
Teacher: *Tu vas à l'église.*
Student: *Oui, je vais à l'église.*
or *Non, je ne vais pas à l'église* etc.

This game can be adapted for use with a wide range of structures and can be played teacher v class, group v group, team v team, girls v boys etc.

5 Mini-flashcard games

The flashcard games which follow can be played in pairs or small groups, with the sets of mini-flashcards made from the worksheets.

- **Pelmanism (group or pair game)**

Use double sets of word cards, mini-flashcards or picture cards + matching word cards. In turn, students turn over a pair of cards to see if they match. They say the word on or represented by the cards, then turn them face downwards again in the same place – unless they form a pair, in which case they pick them up and keep them.

- **Le jeu des sept familles (Happy Families or Fish!)**

Using four sets of mini flashcards for each group, or a set of home-made cards, this game can be played as normal, using *As-tu...?/Oui, j'ai/Non, je n'ai pas ...*

- **Loto de vocabulaire (Flashcard Bingo)**

Students could make their own sets of *Loto* cards with four divisions and either draw or cut out and stick on pictures of four of the things depicted on the flashcards. Each group of students could make sets of cards dealing with a different vocabulary area and then change them round for vocabulary revision games. The example below uses vegetables and fruit.

potato	carrot	carrot	cabbage	cabbage	cauliflower
cabbage	cauliflower	cauliflower	chips	chips	peas
cauliflower	chips	chips	peas	peas	beans
peas	beans	beans	lettuce	lettuce	apple
beans	lettuce	lettuce	apple	apple	pear
apple	pear	pear	orange	orange	peach
pear	orange	orange	peach	peach	banana
peach	banana	banana	strawberry	strawberry	grapes

Players need four counters or buttons each.

The caller should shuffle the pile of relevant flashcards and turn them up one at a time saying *Voilà des pommes de terre* etc.

The winner (who must shout *Loto!*) is the player whose card is first full and who can also say the four things shown on it in French. If the first to finish cannot say the words in French s/he is out and the caller continues until the next card is full.

Suitable vocabulary areas for this are *En ville, À la maison, Les animaux* and weather.

The statements to be made by the caller can be extended to practise relevant structures, e.g. *J'aime les pommes de terre. Il y a des carottes.*

- **Oui ou non?**

The leader has a pile of flashcards in front of her/him. S/he picks one up at a time and shows it to the group, making a statement about it in French followed by *Oui ou non?*

If the statement is true, everyone says *Oui* and repeats it; if it is not, they say *Non*. Anyone speaking in the wrong place or failing to repeat a true statement is out. The winner becomes the new leader.

This type of game can be adapted to almost any topic, with or without flashcards. Students can make statements about classroom objects, pictures etc. and follow the statement with *(Répondez) oui ou non(?)*

The game could also be played with individuals. The group leader shows a card to one person at a time and makes a statement about it. The student replies *Oui* and repeats the statement, or *Non*.

- **'Carousel' version**

Each group could have sets of flashcards, each on a different subject. Then groups could rotate after five minutes or so to practise different sets of vocabulary.

- **Games with 2 sets of cards**

Bataille! (Snap)
Flashcard snap in which they say the name of each card as they put it down. The first player to call *Bataille* wins the pile of cards.

Contre la montre
This is a race against time in which each student sorts their cards into fruit and vegetables, masculine and feminine, good and bad weather, inside or outside, as appropriate.

Mots et images
One player says the name of an object from their hand. The other player selects the appropriate card from their own hand and puts it on the table. Then this player says a name and the first player puts the appropriate card on the table, and so on.

6 Games for practising verbs

These are in addition to those already mentioned.

- **Verb dice**

Make a big cardboard dice, but instead of numbers write on it *je, tu, il/elle/on, nous, vous, ils/elles*. Students throw the dice in turn and must say (or write on the board) the correct part of whatever verb they are practising. Each group could make its own cube dice or use a six-sided pencil. The verbs could also be used in sentences, e.g. *Je suis à l'épicerie*.

- **Loto des verbes**

Students write down three or four persons of a verb on their paper and play as before. Alternatively, about ten infinitives (of regular verbs) should be put on the board and everyone writes down the same person of four of them (this enables one person + relevant ending to be practised at a time).

- **Le jeu des mimes (Miming)**

Students take turns to mime an action. The teacher or group leader says *Qu'est-ce qu'il/elle fait?* Students guess the action by asking *Tu regardes la télévision? Tu écoutes la radio?* etc. The actor answers *Oui, je regarde la télévision* or *Non, je ne regarde pas la télévision*, as appropriate.

- **Le jeu des mimes (Group version)**

Students could work in groups of four or five, a representative of each group doing a mime in turn, and the members of the other groups writing down a guess for each mime. When enough mimes have been done (say, two or three per group), the groups can then be asked to guess in turn and to score a point for each correct guess. The points are totalled to find the winning group.

• **Chef d'orchestre**
(See **Number games**, TB 25.) The teams must give the next person before or after the one quoted, in the standard paradigm or any agreed order. (Some classes will need the pronouns in order on the board as a visible prompt.)

• **Les verbes en cercle (Circle paradigm practice)**
A number of subjects (nouns and pronouns) are written on the board, in random order, in the form of a circle, e.g.

Christophe

Je *Magali et Olivier*

Nous *Tu*

On *Ils*

Vous

The teacher calls out a sentence, e.g. *Je joue au tennis*, and then points to any of the subjects in the circle and asks someone to modify the sentence accordingly. The person chosen then continues clockwise round the circle until stopped by the teacher. This practice drill should move quickly, with frequent changes of speaker, sentence and points on the circle. Different nouns and pronouns should be used whenever this is played.

• **Jacques a dit (or Simon dit)**
An old favourite in which students carry out actions preceded by *Jacques a dit* (or *Simon dit*) but not otherwise, e.g. *Jacques a dit (Simon dit): jouez au football! Asseyez-vous!* etc.

• **Les verbes en désordre (Scrambled verbs)**
Write the pronouns and the six (or nine) parts of the verb in random order on each side of the board. One from each team comes out and rings *je* and the part which goes with it. Then, when this is done correctly, the next marker comes out and rings *tu* and the verb in a different colour, and so on until one team has correctly unscrambled the verb.

7 Spelling games

• **Dix secondes**
Words linked with a particular topic are written on the board. A member of each team in turn has to see how many of the words s/he can spell correctly in, say, ten seconds. (The speller stands facing away from the board.) The words are crossed out or ticked when spelt so the choice gets smaller.

• **Je vois (I spy)**
Play as in English: *Je vois quelque chose qui commence par …*

This game is particularly useful from *Unité 4* onwards, when the French alphabet has been introduced.

Spelling consequences
Students in groups spell words one letter at a time, in turn. Each group has to say a new letter and must be 'on the way' to making a French word that makes sense, preferably from a given vocabulary area, e.g. *En ville* or *Les fruits et les légumes*.

If anyone thinks they know the word, they put their hand up, the spelling stops and they guess. If correct, their group gets a point and takes over, starting a new word. If wrong, the speller says which word they were spelling and the speller's group start a new word, gaining one point. If anyone suspects that a group has added a letter when they had not got a word in mind, they can challenge. If they were right, they gain a point and take over with a new word. If wrong, the speller's group gets a point and starts a new word.

8 Extra practice activities (vocabulary and verbs)

• **Numbered lists for pair work**
There are several versions of this activity:

a Each student writes a numbered list of the words to be learnt, with the French words on one side of the paper and the English on the back. They then test each other, one looking at the French side of the sheet and the other at the English. If one doesn't know the answer, the other tells her/him the number.

b Students try to catch each other out by saying a number the other one doesn't know. This can also be played by two pairs competing against each other.

c **Les mots contre la montre**
The game is played as above, but against the clock – use a stopwatch if possible. Each partner in turn has to identify ten items from numbers given by the other partner, in as short a time as possible.

One of the advantages of these games is that the very fact of making the cards or lists themselves is helping students to learn the vocabulary.

• **Making wordsearches to set to each other**
Limit each one to, say, ten words to be chosen from a given topic. Clues to be given in the opposite language to the words in the square.

• **Group brainstorming**
After revision of topic or homework learning of vocabulary, give groups 5/10 minutes to write down as many words as they can connected with the topic, e.g. *Les vacances, Dans la maison, La famille*.

Then check by letting each group in turn read out an answer. Groups score 1 point for any expression which others also have but 5 points for any correct answer which no-one else has. (Teacher can check winning group's answers for correct spelling etc.)

• **Memory masters**
Some students find it useful to make their own 'memory masters' on which they write important new grammatical rules, lists of topic vocabulary or verb paradigms. These are pieces of card small enough to go in the pocket and the idea is that they should be brought out and learnt and referred to at odd moments. Teachers could have a regular Friday check to see if the week's 'memory master' has been learnt or pupils could quiz each other on them at regular intervals.

If the cards are made with the English on one side and the French on the other, the language can be practised with the following pair game:

Partner A holds up a card so that s/he can see one side and Partner B can see the other. Points are awarded for the first one to say correctly what is on the other side of the card. The sides are changed round periodically and double points are awarded for the answers from the French side.

A similar sort of personal record of vocabulary etc. can be made on a computer – see **Electronic phrase book** in the ICT section, TB 40.

9 The Universal Board Game

This game is very useful for practising almost any vocabulary item, structure, phrase or model question/answer combination. It is very undemanding in terms of teacher time, easy to organize and play and very adaptable.

The game basically comprises an A4 sheet on which is drawn a path of approximately 100 squares, numbered in sequence from 1–100. This can take whatever form you like, from very artistic 'snake patterns' to simply dividing the sheet into squares to make a grid pattern, numbered in sequence like this:

100	99	98	97	96	95	94	93	92	91
81	82	83	84	85	86	87	88	89	90
80	79	78	77	76	75	74	73	72	71
61	62	63	64	65	66	67	68	69	70
60	59	58	57	56	55	54	53	52	51
41	42	43	44	45	46	47	48	49	50
40	39	38	37	36	35	34	33	32	31
21	22	23	24	25	26	27	28	29	30
20	19	18	17	16	15	14	13	12	11
1	2	3	4	5	6	7	8	9	10

Make two sets of cards with questions on. These can vary widely, but some suggestions are below. These sets of cards can also be used for other games, e.g. Happy Families, Snap! or Pelmanism. Also they can be built up into a store of revision packs – different groups work with different topic packs and then exchange topics with another group, e.g. clothes, sport, food, school, leisure activities etc.

Students then throw a dice and move:

- if they land on an even-numbered square, they turn over a card from one pile;
- if they land on an odd-numbered square they pick up a card from the other pile.

One pile can contain words in French to be said in English. The other can contain either words in English or picture stimuli which have to be said in French.

The cards are in the piles face downwards. When students have used a card, it goes on the bottom of its pile.

If they answer the questions correctly, students get another throw (up to a maximum of three!), and if they answer them wrongly or not at all they go back two squares.

The winner is the first to 100 or the one who has got furthest in the time available.

- **Variations**

a Some subjects are suitable for using in a 'split format' – i.e. either pile can form the question and the other automatically gives the answer (e.g. English/French: chips/*les frites* – if you pick up the English you give the French and vice-versa – **but** make sure the piles are kept level and 'synchronised'!

b Other question/answer combinations are not reversible, e.g.

Question: *Il y a combien de jours dans une semaine?*
Answer: *Il y en a sept.*

In this case the answer must appear on the reverse of the card and will be visible to the other contestants (when it is held up) but not to the person answering the question.

If the cards do not contain the answers either on the reverse or on the other pile, it will be necessary somehow to make the answers available to the players, e.g. by providing a sheet with the answers on for each group of players.

- **Easy ideas for cards**

1 Numbers
Figures and words, e.g.
2/deux, 85/quatre-vingt-cinq

Simple sums in figures, to be read out in French, e.g. 5 + 17 = 22,
or in words: *cinq et dix-sept font vingt-deux*

2 Vocabulary
French/English (as above)

French/picture

Missing word, e.g.
La souris … petite./est

3 Simple grammar
Adjectives, e.g. *une fleur/(blanc/blanche)*
or *une fleur* (white)/*blanche*

Verbs, e.g.
nous (manger)/mangeons
or *nous* (eat)/*mangeons*
or *À midi nous … le déjeuner./mangeons*

Masculine/feminine, e.g.
homme/femme, beau/belle.

- **A bit harder**

4 Questions and answers
Things students sometimes muddle, e.g.
Qui?/Who?
Qui est-ce qui?/Who?
Qu'est-ce qui?/What?
Qu'est-ce que?/What?

or in sentences, e.g.
*Qu'est-ce que tu aimes comme fruit?/
J'aime les pommes* etc.

*Est-ce que tu aimes les pommes?/
Oui, j'aime les pommes.*

5 Negatives
J'aime les pommes/Je n'aime pas les pommes.

There are endless possibilities!

Resource material

1 French names and saints' days (Unité 5)

In the past, French children had to be given a Christian name from the official list of saints. This is no longer necessary and some English or American names such as Linda and Morgan(e) are now popular, though Kévin, one of the commonest names in recent years, does have a saint's day (*le 3 juin*). However, many children do still have at least one saint's name and celebrate their *fête*, often receiving one or two small gifts and cards from close family and friends.

Most French calendars and diaries have the saints' names listed.

For information about finding saints' days on the Internet, see TB 207.

- **List of French names and saints' days**

Name	Saint's day
A	
André(e)	30 novembre
Annick	26 juillet
Antoine	13 juin
Arnaud	10 février
B	
Bernadette	18 février
Bernard	20 août
Brigitte	23 juillet
Bruno	6 octobre
C	
Catherine	25 novembre
Chantal	12 décembre
Charles	4 novembre
Charlotte	17 juillet
Christian	12 novembre
Christine	24 juillet
Christophe	21 août
Claire	11 août
Claude	6 juin
Claudine	15 février
Colette	6 mars
D	
Damien	26 septembre
Daniel	11 décembre
David	29 décembre
Delphine	26 novembre
Dominique	8 août
E	
Emma	19 avril
Éric	18 mai
F	
Fabien(ne)	20 janvier
Ferdinand	30 mai
Florent	4 juillet
François	24 janvier
Françoise	9 mars
Frédéric	18 juillet
G	
Georges	23 avril
Gérard	3 octobre
Grégoire/Grégory	3 septembre
Guillaume	10 janvier
Guy	12 juin
H	
Hélène	18 août
I	
Isabelle	22 février
J	
Jacqueline	8 février
Jacques	3 mai
Jean	27 décembre
Julien	2 août
K	
Kévin	3 juin
L	
Laurence	10 août
Laurent	10 août
Léon	10 novembre
Louis	25 août
Louise	15 mars
Luc	18 octobre
Lucien	8 janvier
M	
Marc	25 avril
Marcel	16 janvier
Marie	15 août
Martine	30 janvier
Mathieu	21 septembre
Michel	29 septembre
Monique	27 août
N	
Nathalie	28 juillet
Nicolas	6 décembre
Nicole	6 décembre
Norbert	6 juin
O	
Odette	20 avril
Olivier	12 juillet
P	
Pascal(e)	17 mai
Paul	29 janvier
Philippe	3 mai
Pierre	29 juin
R	
Richard	3 avril
Robert	30 avril
Roland	15 septembre
Rosalie	4 septembre
Roseline	17 janvier
S	
Sandrine	2 avril
Sébastien	20 janvier
Sophie	25 mai
Suzanne	11 août
Sylvain	4 mai
Sylvie	5 novembre
T	
Thérèse	1 octobre
Thierry	1 juillet
Thomas	28 janvier
V	
Vincent	22 janvier
Y	
Yves	19 mai
Yvette	13 janvier

2 The calendar (Unité 5)

In English the words 'month' and 'moon' have the same root. Originally, the period of a month was linked to the time taken for the moon to go round the earth, about 29·5 days.

In the Islamic calendar, the months are still linked to each new moon. However, in the western calendar, the months are fixed and do not now correspond to each new moon.

The names of the months often have interesting meanings.

janvier – named after the Roman god, Janus, who had two faces and could look backwards and forwards.

février – named after the Roman festival of purification held on 15th February.

mars – named after the Roman god, Mars, god of war. Also known as a rough and windy month.

avril – from the Latin word *aperire* meaning to open.

mai – takes its name from Maia, the goddess of growth and increase.

juin – named after the Roman goddess, Juno, the wife of Jupiter.

juillet – named in honour of Julius Caesar.

août – named in honour of the Roman emperor Augustus.

septembre – from the Latin word *septem* – this used to be the seventh month when the Roman year had only ten months and started in March.

octobre – from the Latin word *octo*, meaning eight.

novembre – from the Latin word *novem*, nine.

décembre – from the Latin word *decem*, ten.

The names of the last four months show that there used to be ten months in the Roman year.

- **The Gregorian calendar**

Throughout history, there have been attempts to change the calendar, for instance during the French Revolution, but the calendar we use today is the one fixed by Pope Gregory XIII in 1582 and is known as the Gregorian calendar.

If students are interested in learning about other calendars, perhaps this could be linked with work in other subjects. Different groups could find out about different calendars as suggested below and report back to the class.

- **The Islamic calendar**

The Islamic calendar is based on lunar months (when the new moon is visible at Mecca) and is shorter than our calendar year, which results in the festivals taking place at different seasons of the year.

- **The Chinese calendar**

The Chinese calendar has a New Year festival in February and each year is represented by an animal. According to legend, the Buddha summoned all the animals to him one year and only twelve obeyed. These twelve were given a year each, as a reward. The twelve years are used in rotation and always follow the same order: Rat, Buffalo, Tiger, Cat, Dragon, Snake, Horse, Goat, Monkey, Cockerel, Dog and Pig.

3 Notes on La Rochelle (mainly Unités 2 and 7)

- **History**

La Rochelle is an old seaport on the west coast of France. It began as a fishing village in the 10th century on a rocky platform in the middle of surrounding marshland.

The town has several interesting links with England and was, in fact, the property of the English crown from 1152 to 1224 and from 1360 to 1372.

The town became a free port and a Protestant stronghold. Protected by the city walls and an efficient fleet, it thrived on the salt and wine trade and resisted attack until the Wars of Religion, when it was besieged twice by the Catholics in 1573 and 1627. The second time, the attack was led by Cardinal Richelieu who was trying to unite a Catholic France. His army succeeded in building a huge dam across the bay, with an opening in the middle for the tide, which was heavily guarded. This effectively sealed off the city and reduced it to famine. Fifteen months later, in 1628, the city under its mayor, Jean Guiton, was finally starved into submission and La Rochelle became part of France. The city walls (with the exception of the three towers) were flattened. After the siege, the population had been reduced from 28,000 to 5,000.

The city flourished again in the 18th century as a result of trading links with Canada (furs) and the West Indies (sugar). The founders of Montreal and some of the first French-Canadian settlers left from La Rochelle.

The town later declined in importance until a large deep new harbour at La Pallice was built in 1891.

- **La Rochelle today**

Today, besides being a popular place for holidays, La Rochelle is a thriving administrative and commercial centre. It is still an important commercial port (eighth in France) and fishing port (fifth in France).

It has become an important yachting centre with several international races taking place from there, notably the Plymouth–La Rochelle race held every two years.

A number of local festivals are organised in La Rochelle throughout the year, and, of special appeal to the young, there is now an annual festival of French song, in July, called *Les Francofolies*. An interesting feature of the town are the famous yellow bikes, which are available free of charge from the *esplanade du Parc* for use by residents and visitors.

- **Main points of interest**

Le vieux port

The old port, with its small fishing boats and pleasure craft, and the quay with restaurants and cafés, is a very picturesque sight. It is bounded by two towers (the *tour Saint-Nicolas* and the *tour de la Chaîne*).

During the holiday season, many entertainers keep passers-by amused with a wide range of 'free' shows on the quayside and create a very lively atmosphere.

La tour Saint-Nicolas

The three towers, built to guard the harbour, date from the 14th and 15th centuries and survived the destruction of the surrounding walls after the siege of

1628. The *tour Saint-Nicolas* is the highest of the three and is connected by a wall to the *tour de la Lanterne*.

La tour de la Chaîne
This tower owes its name to the enormous chain which used to be stretched across the entrance to the harbour to the *tour Saint-Nicolas*, to prevent ships from entering the harbour. Inside the tower, there is a model of La Rochelle in medieval times, and a *Son et Lumière* presentation.

La tour de la Lanterne
This circular tower, with a spire and a turret, was once a lighthouse. There is an external balcony, half-way up the spire, which offers good views of the town, port and off-shore islands. This tower also features slide shows, models and *Son et Lumière*.

L'hôtel de ville
This old and interesting building dates mainly from the 15th and 16th centuries. The surrounding wall has battlements and a bell-tower.

La Grosse Horloge
This gothic tower was one of the medieval gateways to the town in the old city wall, which separated the walled town from the port.

La cathédrale Saint-Louis
This has been built on the site of the church of Saint-Barthélemy, which was destroyed during the Wars of Religion. Most of the building dates from the 18th century, but the square bell-tower was preserved from an earlier church.

L'église Saint-Sauveur
The church has a 15th century tower, but the rest of the building was rebuilt in the 17th and 18th centuries.

Les rues à arcades
La Rochelle has the greatest number of *rues à arcades* in France and there are many old buildings in the streets of the old town; some timbered houses date from the 15th century. Streets to look out for are the *rue des Merciers*, the *rue des Gentilshommes*, the *rue du Palais* and the *rue du Minage*.

La Pallice and l'Île de Ré
The port of La Rochelle is situated about five kilometres north-west of the centre. From La Pallice there are car ferries and a variety of excursions by boat to the Île de Ré. By ferry the journey takes about 15 minutes, but there is now also a road bridge linking the island to the mainland.

This flat, sandy island, with beautiful beaches, is largely given over to vineyards and market gardening. It is about 30 kilometres long and five kilometres wide and there are several picturesque fishing villages. It can get very crowded in August.

For information about the La Rochelle website and useful addresses see TB 208.

Songs

1 Using the songs

There are six songs on the CDs, especially written and performed for ***Encore Tricolore 1***. The words of the songs can be found in the Students' Book. The musical scores, comprising melodies, guitar chords and words, are on photocopiable pages of this Teacher's Book, TB 34–39 (except for *Attention, c'est l'heure!* which is a rap).

Un, deux, trois (Unité 2)	CD 1 Track 15	SB 11	TB 36
L'alphabet (Unité 4)	CD 1 Track 43	SB 29	TB 34–5
Le premier mois (Unité 6)	CD 2 Track 14	SB 52	TB 37
Attention, c'est l'heure! (after Unité 8)	CD 3 Track 9	SB 93	
Pique-nique à la plage (Unité 9)	CD 3 Track 20	SB 104	TB 38
Samedi, on part en vacances (Unité 10)	CD 3 Track 35	SB 120	TB 39

There are two recorded versions of each song, one version including the words and the other an instrument-only version.

The version of each song which includes the words can be:

- listened to by the students simply for enjoyment
- used as the stimulus material for various types of listening comprehension tasks or games
- used as a device to teach the song to students – they may be able to sing along with this version on CD, or sing along with the teacher (who may choose to play the accompaniment or not) independently of the CD.

The instrument-only version of each song may be used in class as a means of encouraging students to perform the song unaided by vocal support from the CD or the teacher, and thus this version lends itself to independent preparation and performance by small groups.

Students preparing the songs in this way may be encouraged to perform them in extra- or cross-curricular contexts, for example departmental parents' evenings, school assemblies or as projects in conjunction with performing arts departments within the school.

The instrumental backing of the songs has been designed to be accessible and relatively simple in terms of musical structure and progression; thus, students with some musical training (in conjunction with music teachers or musically-able language teachers) might be expected to be able to produce full instrumental and vocal interpretations of these songs, by study of the CD and melody/guitar chords score, in any of the extra- or cross-curricular contexts described above. Have fun!

2 Words and music for the songs in *Encore Tricolore 1 nouvelle édition*

L'alphabet

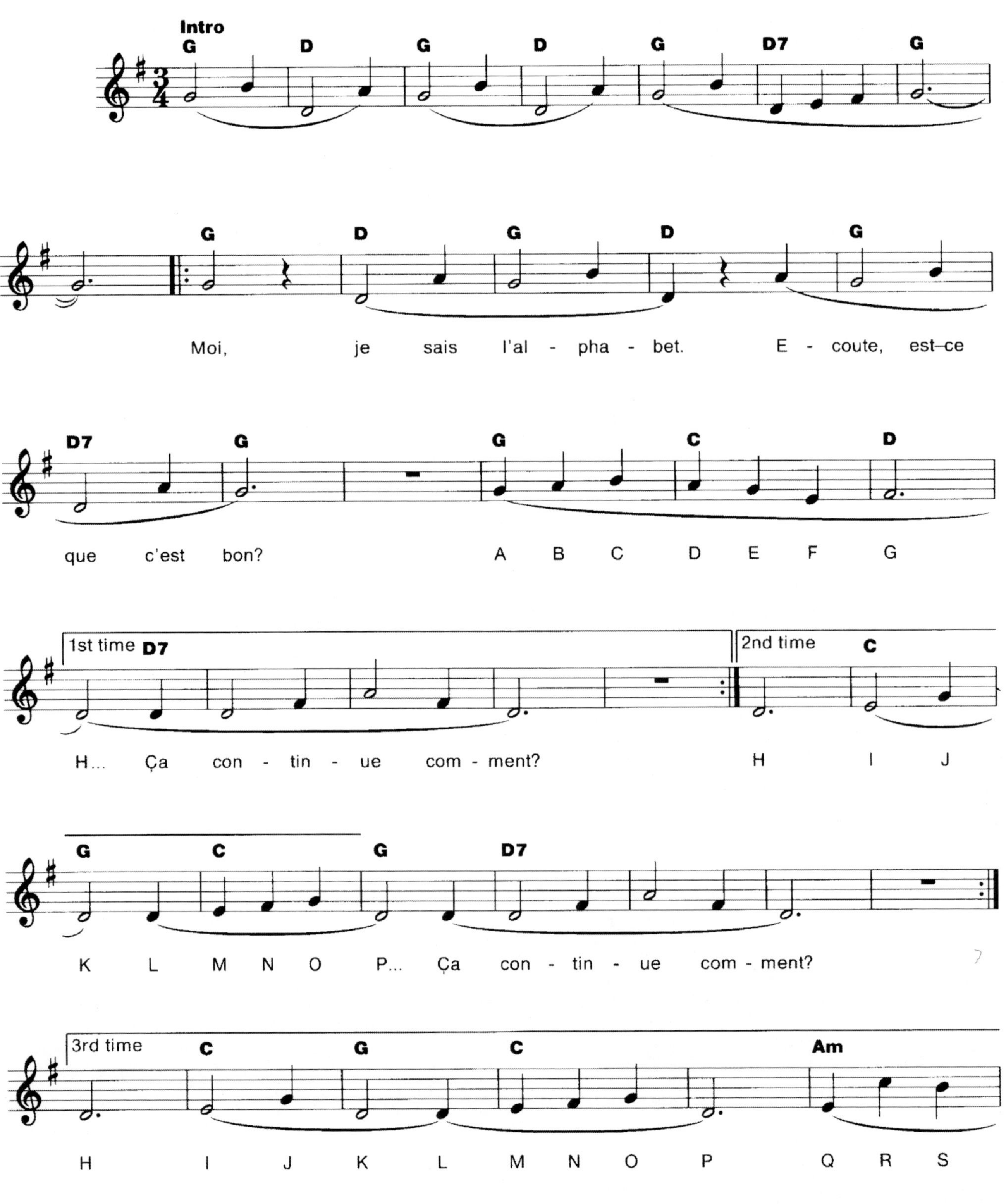

 Encore Tricolore 1 nouvelle édition © Oxford University Press 2014 ISBN 0-17-440272-4

D
D7
T U V W... Ça con - tin - ue com - ment?
4th and final time
C G C Am
H I J K L M N O P Q R S T U V
D Am D7 G D7
W... X Y Z... Ça con - tin - ue com -
Am D7 G G
- ment? I - di - ote, c'est tout, c'est bon!! A B C
C D C G C G
D E F G H I J K L M N O P
Am D7 Am D7 G
Q R S T U V W X Y Z.

Un, deux, trois

– 1, 2, 3,
Salut! C'est moi!

4, 5, 6,
J'habite à Nice.

7, 8, 9,
Dans la rue Elbeuf.

10, 11, 12,
Et toi?

– Toulouse.
13, 14, 15,
Dans l'avenue de Reims.

16, 17,
Je m'appelle Colette.

18, 19, 20,
C'est la fin!

Recommence au numéro un …

  ISBN 0-17-440272-4

Le premier mois

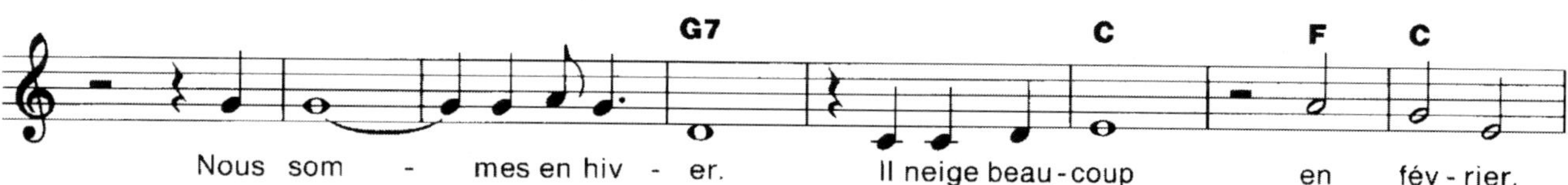

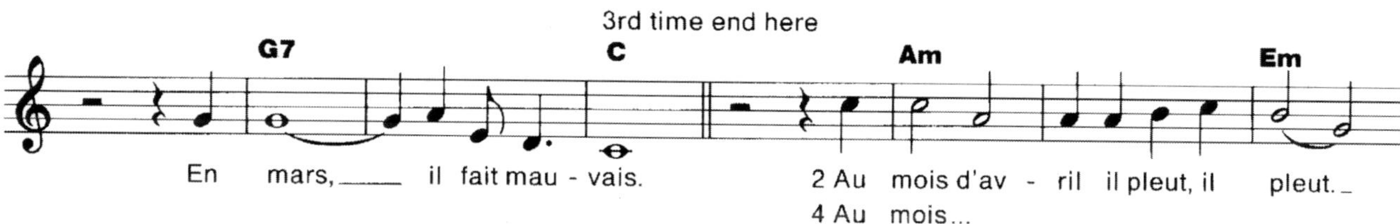

1 Le premier mois, c'est janvier.
Nous sommes en hiver.
Il neige beaucoup en février,
En mars, il fait mauvais.

2 Au mois d'avril, il pleut, il pleut.
Nous sommes au printemps.
Il fait très beau au mois de mai,
La météo dit: beau temps!

3 Et puis c'est juin, et juillet, août.
Nous sommes en été.
Il fait très chaud pour les vacances,
Ma saison préférée.

4 Au mois de septembre la rentrée.
Octobre, c'est l'automne.
Du brouillard pendant novembre.
Oh! qu'est-ce qu'il fait du vent!

5 Le dernier mois, on fête Noël.
Nous sommes en décembre.
Il fait très froid, mais moi, j'ai chaud –
Je reste dans ma chambre!

Pique-nique à la plage

1 Bonne journée! Bonne journée!
Tout le monde va pique-niquer.
Va chercher le panier!
Pique-nique, pique-nique à la plage.

2 Bonne journée! Bonne journée!
Qu'est-ce que nous allons manger?
Des sandwichs, une grande quiche.
Pique-nique, pique-nique à la plage.

3 Bonne journée! Bonne journée!
Regarde dans le panier.
Oh, chouette, une galette!
Pique-nique, pique-nique à la plage.

4 Bonne journée! Bonne journée!
Il ne faut pas oublier
Les chips, le vin, les petits pains.
Pique-nique, pique-nique à la plage.

5 Quelle journée! Quelle journée!
Tout le monde va pique-niquer.
Allons trouver le soleil!
Pique-nique, pique-nique à la plage.

Encore Tricolore 1 nouvelle édition © Oxford University Press 2014 ISBN 0-17-440272-4

Samedi, on part en vacances

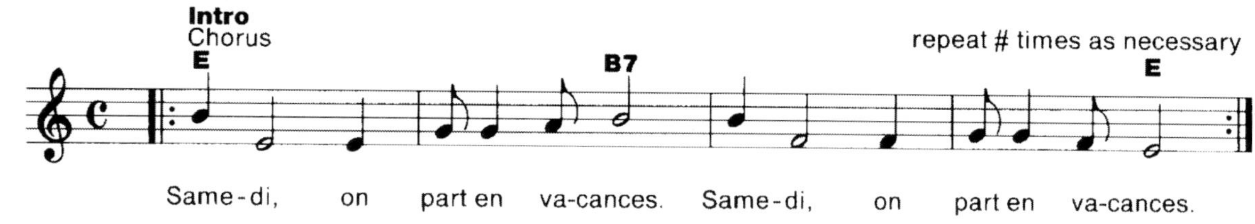

Samedi, on part en vacances.
Samedi, on part en vacances.

1 Nice et Cannes, Toulouse et Sète,
Ma valise est presque faite.
Samedi, on part en vacances.
Samedi, on part en vacances.

2 Oui, c'est vrai on part demain.
Où est mon maillot de bain?
Nice et Cannes, Toulouse et Sète,
Ma valise est presque faite.
Samedi, on part en vacances.
Samedi, on part en vacances.

3 Pour le soleil, mes lunettes,
Pour le volley, mes baskets.
Oui, c'est vrai on part demain.
Où est mon maillot de bain?
Nice et Cannes, Toulouse et Sète,
Ma valise est presque faite.
Samedi, on part en vacances.
Samedi, on part en vacances.

4 Faire du vélo, faire du ski,
Faire du camping, allons-y!
Pour le soleil, mes lunettes,
Pour le volley, mes baskets.
Oui, c'est vrai on part demain.
Où est mon maillot de bain?
Nice et Cannes, Toulouse et Sète,
Ma valise est presque faite.
Samedi, on part en vacances.
Samedi, on part en vacances.

5 Sète, Toulouse et Nice et Cannes,
Nous allons en caravane.
Faire du vélo, faire du ski,
Faire du camping, allons-y!
Pour le soleil, mes lunettes,
Pour le volley, mes baskets.
Oui, c'est vrai on part demain.
Où est mon maillot de bain?
Nice et Cannes, Toulouse et Sète,
Ma valise est presque faite.
Samedi, on part en vacances.
Samedi, on part en vacances.

6 Que nous avons de la chance,
C'est bientôt les vacances.
Sète, Toulouse et Nice et Cannes,
Nous allons en caravane.
Faire du vélo, faire du ski,
Faire du camping, allons-y!
Pour le soleil, mes lunettes,
Pour le volley, mes baskets.
Oui, c'est vrai on part demain.
Où est mon maillot de bain?
Nice et Cannes, Toulouse et Sète,
Ma valise est presque faite.
Samedi, on part en vacances.
Samedi, on part en vacances.

ICT activities

1 Word processing idea – self-description file

The self-description file is introduced for the first time in *Unité 4* but is really a thread that can run through the whole of ***Encore Tricolore 1 nouvelle édition*** and on into further stages. The idea is simply that pupils write a self-description based on the language and phrases learnt in each unit. This is done using word processing so it can then be added to, amended and redrafted in subsequent units and stages. Teachers might wish to make this a regular activity after each or every two or three units.

2 Using the table facility of a word processor

Using tables is an easy option with most word processing programs and provides a wealth of possibilities in language learning. Below are three examples.

- **Verb tables**

Students can use a template to lay out verb paradigms and keep a record of all the verbs they meet on disk and print this out from time to time for ease of reference.

Here is the basic template:

Tense	**Present**		
Infinitive			
je		I	
tu		you (sing.)	
il/elle/on		he/she/one	
nous		we	
vous		you (pl./polite)	
ils/elles		they	

Here is a completed example for *regarder* in the present tense:

Tense	**Present**		
Infinitive	**regarder**	to look at, to watch	
je	regarde	I	look at, watch
tu	regardes	you (sing.)	look at, watch
il/elle/on	regarde	he/she/one	looks at, watches
nous	regardons	we	look at, watch
vous	regardez	you (pl./polite)	look at, watch
ils/elles	regardent	they	look at, watch

For regular verbs, it is a simple matter to use FIND and REPLACE (found in the EDIT menu) to substitute the stem of the verb with that of another, e.g. *regarder* » *travailler*.

- **Electronic phrase book**

Students can create an electronic vocabulary/phrase book using tables to lay out the columns. This is best done using a word processing package such as Microsoft® Word or Word Perfect – choose whichever program is the school's preferred option.

Set up the file by using a table with two columns of equal width. The phrase book can be organised according to the following principles:

- sections on each topic or unit (i.e. cumulatively rather than alphabetically), French to English only
- other non-topic specific vocabulary, e.g. conjunctions, prepositions etc.
- classroom vocabulary, including that for use in ICT lessons, also listed in the order that the new phrases and words are met
- combined section made up of all the words from the first three sections. This section can be sorted into alphabetical order using the SORT function (in Word this is found in the Table menu). Include both French–English and English–French sections.

The electronic phrase book can be saved on the school network, depending on disk space available, but students should also take copies on their own floppy disks.

A printed copy is also very useful.

A starter phrase book could be produced by the teacher based on the first few units.

This phrase book can then be used by students when working on the computer. For example, when writing self-descriptions or e-mails, students can copy and paste phrases from the phrase book to their sentences. The phrase book can be added to when undertaking reading exercises with *Fun with Texts* or websites by copying and pasting words. Phrase book use and maintenance should be encouraged whenever students use the computers.

Periodically, teachers could check the phrase books. Later, students can use spell-checking software in French to check their own phrase books.

- **Phrase generator**

Any word processor can be used in phrase generation work. It is best to use the standard school program as the students should be familiar with this. A table is very helpful in setting up the phrase generator. On most programs there will be a simple menu command to INSERT A TABLE through which you specify the number of rows and the number and width of columns – this should be planned on paper in advance. The final table may then look like this (example from *Unité 5*)

En France, on	mange un gâteau spécial	à Pâques
	mange des œufs en chocolat	
	danse dans les rues	le 6 janvier
	regarde un feu d'artifice	
	offre des cadeaux	à Noël
	chante des chants de Noël	
	mange un grand repas	le 14 juillet

The students can use copy and paste to create the phrases. Some may have good ICT skills and can use the mouse to drag and drop.

3 Types of text manipulation activities

Most programs allow the teacher (or well-chosen student!) to set up a text by typing it in. There are then a number of activities that students can do with that text such as:

- cloze exercises where students have to fill in missing letters
- cloze exercises where students have to fill in missing words
- cloze exercises where students have to fill in missing lines
- re-ordering of jumbled lines of the text
- re-ordering of jumbled words on a line
- re-ordering of jumbled letters in words.

All of these tasks are variations of pencil and paper exercises but they do have certain added elements such as instant feedback on whether something is right or wrong, a scoring facility and a help facility. Small scale research studies have shown various benefits for learning and accuracy. The software is easy to use and can be adapted to almost any content, so you could develop text manipulation exercises for all units.

Some ready-made texts have been devised and can be purchased from software suppliers or downloaded from the Internet. Some websites offer on-line learning materials developed by language teachers (see TB 207–208 for website addresses).

Word processing software can also be used to develop text-manipulation activities, but it will not correct the students' work automatically. It may be preferable, however, if you want to create open-ended or creative activities, such as the phrase generation activity (TB 40).

4 The CD-ROM as a language-practising tool

CD-ROMs can be very useful to enable students to work intensively at their own pace and level. Suitable practice is provided by a variety of language-learning programs. These programs offer a variety of exercises such as matching, multiple choice, true or false and games which provide simple vocabulary practice of the basic topics.

5 Suggestions for working with graphics and images

Ideas for students to use images include:

- adding images to students' written work
- making a poster for classroom display
- making an electronic poster for a simple oral presentation using data projector or electronic whiteboard.

6 Ideas for teaching with images

These include:

- flashcards, e.g. Simpsons, Mr Men, tourist attractions
- overhead transparencies – symbol fonts such as Wingdings give useful images which can help to emphasise meaning in role-plays, e.g.

- worksheets with images to provide guidance and hints on what students are expected to write or say
- activities where students add labels to pictures and vice-versa
- writing a simple phrase or sentence to describe an image
- making sets of cards for word games.

7 Further information

Please see the section at the end (TB 207–208) for further information about:

- publications giving information about ICT in the Modern Languages Classroom
- more information about CDs listed above
- a list of useful website addresses.

unité 1 Bonjour!

Areas	Topics	Grammar
Introduction	Map of France	
1	Greetings and some classroom commands	
2	Introducing yourself	
3	Identifying people	
4	Asking 'How are you?'	
5	Numbers and ages	Using numbers 1–20
6	Identifying classroom objects	Introduction to gender
7	Discussing quantity	
8	Further activities and consolidation	

National Curriculum information

All students Level 1

Refer also to the information about coverage of 'Knowledge, skills and understanding' (TB 9).

Revision

The vocabulary and structures introduced in this unit are revised in the *Rappel* section following *Unité 3* (SB 22–23, TB 75).

Sounds and writing

- pronunciation of *i*
- intonation and stress
- see *Écoute et parle* (SB 150, TB 50)

ICT opportunities

- using word processing and clip art to make up an illustrated word list (TB 49)
- using a CD-ROM to practise vocabulary for classroom items (TB 49)

Assessment

- Informal assessment is provided by the *Épreuves* after *Unité 3* (TB 74).
- Formal assessment is in the *Premier contrôle* following *Unité 4* (TB 200).

Students' Book

Map of France SB 3 (TB 44)

Unité 1 SB 6–8

Au choix SB 126 1 (TB 47), 2, 3, 4 (TB 49)

Écoute et parle SB 150 (TB 50)

Flashcards

1 smiley face

2 sad face

CDs

1/1–11

Student CD 1/1–7

Copymasters

1/1 *La France* [support] (TB 44)

1/2 *Écoutez bien!* [listening] (TB 50)

Language content

Greetings (Area 1)

Bonjour (+ name)
Au revoir
Salut!

People (Areas 2, 3)

enfant (m)
fille (f) (girl)
garçon (m)
madame
mademoiselle
monsieur

General

oui, non
merci
s'il vous plaît
Qui a gagné?
J'ai gagné
(Name) *a gagné*

Asking 'How are you?' (Area 4)

Ça va?
Oui, ça va bien. Et toi?
Non, pas très bien.

Numbers (Area 5)

1–20

Classroom objects etc. (Area 6)

boîte (f)
cahier (m)
calculette (f)
cartable (m)
cassette (f)
chaise (f)
classeur (m)
crayon (m)
gomme (f)
livre (m)
magnétophone (m)
ordinateur (m)
règle (f)
sac à dos (m)
stylo (m)
table (f)
taille-crayon (m)
trousse (f)

Classroom language and rubrics

Assieds-toi/Asseyez-vous
Commence/Commencez
Complète/Complétez
Compte/Comptez
Continue/Continuez
Écoute/Écoutez
Écris/Écrivez
Ferme/Fermez
Lève-toi/Levez-vous
Ouvre/Ouvrez (le livre à la page ...)
Rangez vos affaires
Regarde/Regardez
Répète/Répétez
Réponds/Répondez
Retourne à ta place/Retournez à vos places
Travaillez à deux/en groupes/avec un(e) partenaire
Trouve/Trouvez
Viens ici/Venez ici

Note

Unité 1 is intended to be fairly short, so that students will quickly feel a sense of achievement. The work is almost all oral/aural, although there is a small amount of written French (see *Au choix* SB 126).

Introduction

SB 3
CM 1/1

Voici + place

Ça, c'est ... (for comprehension only)

SB 3 **PRESENTATION**

La France

Some teachers might like to precede the beginning of learning French with a look at France itself, using this map and Copymaster 1/1. However, these items could equally well be used later for interest or consolidation.

Begin by showing the class the map and speaking about it very simply in French, e.g.

Voici la France. Ça, c'est Paris – voici la Tour Eiffel et Disneyland Paris. Voici les montagnes, les Alpes, les Pyrénées etc.

Ask a few questions to find out how many of the class have visited France, how to get there, if they know any French people or can speak any French etc. Talk about France from your own point of view, perhaps showing some photos, and tell the class about other countries where French is spoken and how useful it is as an international language.

CM 1/1 **SUPPORT**

La France

This multi-choice quiz could be used with the map as a basis for class discussion or as a written task, for homework or in class, for example in pairs or as a group quiz against the clock.

Solution:

1 **Voici la France**
1a, 2b, 3a, 4b, 5a, 6c

2 **Mots mêlés**

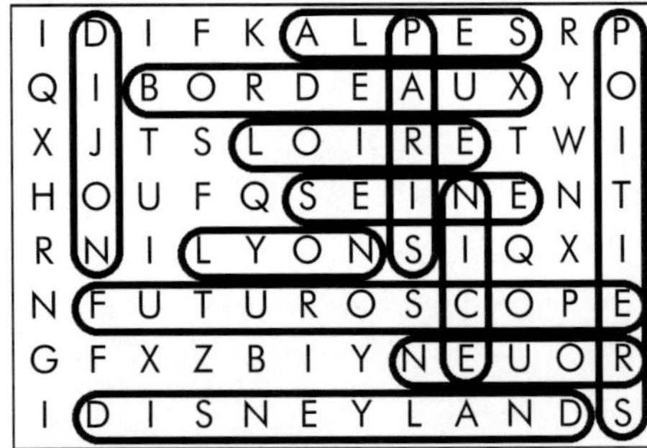

3 **Chasse à l'intrus**
1 *la Seine,* **2** *le Rhône,* **3** *Le Massif Central,* **4** *Dieppe* (others are capital cities), **5** *la Manche,* **6** *Le Mans,* **7** *La Corse,* **8** *Poitiers* (others are on coast)

4 **La France et l'Angleterre**
1 *Paris,* **2** *France,* **3** *Paris,* **4** *30km,* **5** *Londres* (or London)

Students could be encouraged to find out more about France themselves, such as obtaining leaflets from a travel agent for a classroom display round a centrally placed map.

Area 1
Greetings and some classroom commands

SB 6, 1
CD 1/1

Bonjour Monsieur/Madame/Mademoiselle.
Salut (+ name). *Au revoir.*

Greetings **PRESENTATION**

Introduce the class to French greetings and appropriate replies, both when addressed as a class and individually, e.g.

1 – *Bonjour les enfants/les élèves/la classe!*
– *Bonjour Monsieur/Madame/Mademoiselle.*

2 – *Bonjour Katie/Christopher etc.*
– *Bonjour M./Mme/Mlle.*

Greet individuals by name, perhaps shaking hands with them.

Explain the use of *Salut* as a more informal greeting (Hi!) and bring this into the conversation as well.

Salut Lauren, Salut Harry etc.

Introduce the other titles one at a time by using cards with names on, e.g. *M. Duval, Mme Cresson, Mlle Leclerc.*

Give out one or two cards and introduce those holding them to the class.

– *Voici Monsieur Duval. Répétez.*
– *Bonjour Monsieur* etc.

To make things more amusing, you could attach the name labels to hats which can then be put on a variety of children, who, in turn, exchange greetings with the class or individuals.

When the class is confident with this, introduce *Au revoir* and practise in a similar way.

SB 6, 1/1 **LISTENING SPEAKING**

1 Bonjour!

The class listens to the greetings while looking at the photos.

Then play the recordings again, this time with the students repeating after the speakers and then gradually trying out the conversations without the support of the recording.

As you do this, begin to introduce some classroom commands, e.g.

Écoute! Écoutez! Ouvrez le livre à la page ... Regardez le livre.

Comment, if you wish, on the fact that shaking hands and sometimes kissing each other on the cheek, as shown in the photos, is quite usual in France for both boys, girls and adults.

Bonjour!

– Bonjour Coralie.
– Bonjour Sébastien.
– Bonjour M. Garnier.

- Bonjour Jean-Marc.
- Salut Olivier!
- Salut Magali!
- Au revoir Isabelle.
- Au revoir Loïc.

As a follow-up, after a short demonstration, ask students to get up and each say hello, then goodbye to four other people in French.

Integrate with this the teaching and practice of the commands:

Lève-toi/Levez-vous, Assieds-toi/Asseyez-vous, Viens/Venez ici and *Retourne à ta place.*

The game *Jacques a dit* (TB 29) could also be used.

Sometime during the first lesson, students will probably like to learn to say *Bonjour maman!* and *Bonjour papa!* so that they can demonstrate at home that they have actually 'started French'.

Area 2 Introducing yourself

SB 6, 2
CD 1/2

Comment t'appelles-tu? Je m'appelle ...

1/2 — PRESENTATION LISTENING

Comment t'appelles-tu?

Explain that the class will now hear some of the people shown in the photographs being asked what their names are. Ask the class to listen carefully to see how they reply.

Comment t'appelles-tu?

- Comment t'appelles-tu?
- Je m'appelle Coralie.
- Comment t'appelles-tu?
- Je m'appelle Sébastien.
- Comment t'appelles-tu?
- Je m'appelle Olivier.
- Comment t'appelles-tu?
- Je m'appelle Magali.
- Comment t'appelles-tu?
- Je m'appelle Loïc.
- Comment t'appelles-tu?
- Je m'appelle Isabelle.

After playing the recording, introduce yourself: *Je m'appelle* (+ name) and then point to several students and get them to say *Je m'appelle* (+ name).

Gradually start to ask the question *Comment t'appelles-tu?* and practise this question and answer work until most students can answer correctly.

Note – French names: whilst it is quite reasonable for a teacher, unfamiliar with a new class's names, to ask them *Comment t'appelles-tu?* it seems less sensible for students to practise asking each other's names, if they know them already. One solution is to give the students French names (see TB 31), but an alternative is to write a selection of common French *prénoms* on cards, and ask the class to repeat them. Then spread the cards out, upside down and ask students to take turns to pick up and look at one of the cards. At first, choose a different student to ask *Comment t'appelles-tu?* and receive the correct answer. Next, several students could pick up cards and ask each other's names as a chain game.

Devinez le prénom — SPEAKING

This simple group or class game would provide useful consolidation. One student picks up a card and the others have three chances to guess her/his correct name, asking *Tu t'appelles Jean?* etc. Anyone who guesses correctly becomes the caller and turns over a name card. If no one guesses correctly, the teacher chooses another student to ask the caller *Comment t'appelles-tu?* and this person then becomes the caller.

SB 6 — SPEAKING

2 Une conversation

This illustrated dialogue shows the printed form and could prove a useful prompt for practice of this short conversation in pairs. Make sure that everyone understands the rubric *Travaillez à deux.*

Area 3 Identifying people

SB 6, 3

Qui est-ce? C'est (+ name)*? Oui, c'est* (+ name).

C'est ...? — PRESENTATION

Point to a student and ask *Comment t'appelles-tu?* The student replies. Then point to the student and say to the class. *C'est ...*

Gradually expand this as follows:

1 **Teacher:** *C'est ...? Oui/Oui, c'est ...*
2 **Teacher:** *Qui est-ce? C'est ...? Oui? Oui, c'est ...*
3 **Teacher:** *Qui est-ce?*
Student: *C'est ...*
Teacher: *Oui, c'est ...*
4 **Teacher:** *Qui est-ce? C'est* (+ wrong name)*?*
Non, c'est (+ correct name).
5 **Teacher:** *Qui est-ce? C'est* (+ wrong name)*?*
Student: *Non, c'est* (+ correct name).

SB 6 — SPEAKING

3 Qui est-ce?

These are the same people featured in *Bonjour!* (Task 1 above), with one missing. Students jot down the numbers and match them up with the people, just writing down their initials, to find out who is missing.

This short item could be corrected orally, with the teacher asking *Qui est-ce?* and students answering *C'est M. Garnier* etc.

Solution: **1** *Coralie,* **2** *M. Garnier,* **3** *Olivier,* **4** *Isabelle,* **5** *Magali,* **6** *Loïc,* **7** *Sébastien (Jean-Marc est absent.)*

Un jeu: Qui est-ce?

PRACTICE

This game would give useful practice of *Qui est-ce?* and *C'est* (+ name).

Send someone out of the classroom and everybody except one person has to do something, e.g. cross their legs, close or open their text book. Invite the person back in and see how long it takes them to discover who is the odd one out. (A volunteer can time them.) Prompt them by asking *C'est Richard? C'est Sarah? Alors, qui est-ce?*

Area 4
Asking 'How are you?'

SB 7, 4
FC 1–2
CD 1/3

Ça va? Oui, ça va bien. Et toi?
Non, pas très bien.

FC 1–2 **PRESENTATION**

Ça va?

Tell the class they are going to learn how to ask people how they are or if they're OK. The class should first repeat *Ça va?* several times. Then get some students to ask you the question and, showing flashcard 1 (happy face), say *Oui, ça va bien, merci.* After a while, add to this *Et toi?* Hand the card to the questioner and get her/him to reply.

When everyone has practised this question and answer routine, introduce the possibility of not feeling too good, miming pain or sadness and using flashcard 2 (sad face) to teach *Non, pas très bien.*

SB 7, 1/3 **LISTENING**

4 Ça va?

Students copy down the names of the six people illustrated or just write the numbers, then listen to the conversations between Nicole and her friends and put a tick or a cross to show if each person is OK or not.

Pause the recording after the first conversation, refer to the example to make sure everyone knows what to do before playing the rest of the recording. Eventually correct the item orally with the class, perhaps playing the recording again and stopping after each conversation to say *Ça va? Oui ou non?*

Solution: **1** *Lucie* ✔, **2** *Daniel* ✔, **3** *Sanjay* ✔, **4** *Sarah* ✘, **5** *Sophie* ✔, **6** *Marc* ✘

Ça va?

1 – Bonjour Lucie.
– Ah, bonjour Nicole. Ça va?
– Oui, ça va bien, merci, et toi?
– Oui, oui. Ça va très bien.

2 – Bonjour Daniel, c'est Nicole.
– Ah, bonjour Nicole. Ça va?
– Oui, ça va bien, merci, et toi?
– Oui. Ça va très bien, merci.

3 – Bonjour Sanjay.
– Ah, salut Nicole.
– Ça va, Sanjay?
– Oui, oui, ça va bien.

4 – Bonjour Sarah.
– Qui est-ce?
– C'est Nicole. Ça va, Sarah?
– Non, Nicole. Pas très bien.

5 – Bonjour Sophie.
– Qui est-ce? C'est Nicole?
– Oui, oui, c'est moi. Ça va, Sophie?
– Ah, salut, Nicole! Oui, oui, ça va bien, merci.

6 – Bonjour Marc, c'est Nicole.
– Ah, bonjour Nicole. Ça va?
– Oui, ça va bien, merci, et toi?
– Non, non. Ça ne va pas très bien.

For further practice, choose pairs of students to come out and ask each other *Ça va?* and cue their replies with the flashcards. This practice could continue as pair or group work, using mini-flashcards made quickly by the students.

Area 5
Numbers and ages

SB 7, 5–6
Au choix SB 126, 1
CD 1/4–6
Écoute et parle SB 150, 4, 6
Student CD 1/5, 7

Numbers 1–20
Quel âge as-tu? Tu as quel âge?
J'ai (+ number) ans.
Comptez!

Numbers 1–20

PRESENTATION

Many students will have at least a hazy idea of the French numbers, but it is important to get pronunciation right at this point. It is a good idea to teach the numbers three at a time with students repeating them after you, and only move on to the next three when the previous group is properly learnt.

Number games

There is a wide selection of these (see TB 25). The simplest form of bingo is good at this stage to get students to identify numbers, and students can take turns at being the caller. For games which have a winner, teach *J'ai gagné* and (Name) *a gagné*.

Some other suitable number games are: *Continue!*, *Comptez comme ça!* and *Le dix magique* (see TB 25)

The numbers need plenty of practice, so one or two number games could be played in each lesson during the first few weeks of French, with higher numbers being added unit by unit as they are introduced. *Zéro* could also be taught, perhaps as part of a 'countdown'.

SB 150, TB 51, SCD 1/5 **LISTENING**

4 C'est quel nombre?

In *Écoute et parle* there is a task on numbers for individual practice at home. For details see SB 150 and TB 51.

SB 6, 🎧 1/4 **PRESENTATION LISTENING**

Quel âge as-tu?

This task uses the photos for *Bonjour!* (SB 6). Tell the children to look at the photos as they are going to hear some of the children shown there being asked their age and replying. Then play the following recording – they should listen and try to find out how to say their age in French.

🎧 Quel âge as-tu?

– Sébastien, quel âge as-tu?
– J'ai douze ans.

– Coralie, quel âge as-tu?
– J'ai treize ans.

– Olivier, quel âge as-tu?
– J'ai quatorze ans.

– Magali, quel âge as-tu?
– J'ai quinze ans.

– Isabelle, quel âge as-tu?
– J'ai seize ans.

Play the recording several times, pausing after each speaker and getting students to answer the same questions as if they were the children on the recording. Extend this question and answer practice until most students can say their own ages.

SB 7, 🎧 1/5 **LISTENING**

5 Qui parle?

The five speakers from the previous recording are listed with their ages, but this time they speak in a different order and anonymously. Students look at page 7, listen to the recording and identify the speakers by their ages writing down the names (or initials) in order.

Solution: **1** *Olivier,* **2** *Isabelle,* **3** *Sébastien,* **4** *Magali,* **5** *Coralie*

🎧 Qui parle?

1 – Tu as quel âge?
– J'ai quatorze ans.

2 – Quel âge as-tu?
– J'ai seize ans.

3 – Tu as quel âge?
– J'ai douze ans.

4 – Quel âge as-tu?
– J'ai quinze ans.

5 – Tu as quel âge?
– J'ai treize ans.

SB 7 **SPEAKING**

6 Quel âge as-tu?

Students can be helped to work out how to slot different ages into the same answer structure. They can then go on to practise this with the puzzle.

1 Students follow the lines and work out each person's age, perhaps noting them down – N(icole) 11.

2 They work in pairs, in turns asking the age of their partner who replies for the person named, as in the example.

Dialogue **SPEAKING**

Students could now add age into the dialogue they used previously to ask each other's name (see SB 6, Task 2)

First revise greetings and asking names, demonstrating with a student.

Teacher: (shaking hands) *Bonjour.*
Student: *Bonjour M./Mme/Mlle.*
Teacher: *Comment t'appelles-tu?*
Student: *Je m'appelle ...*
Teacher: (shaking hands) *Au revoir* (name).
Student: *Au revoir M./Mme/Mlle.*

Get students to practise this in pairs, choosing a few to demonstrate this to the class.

Then add in the new question and answer and get pairs of students to practise the complete dialogue, perhaps recording some of them.

The recording of a complete conversation used in *Au choix* Task 1 (SB 126) could be used as a model for this activity. (See text below.)

AU CHOIX SB 126, 🎧 1/6 **LISTENING**

1 Une conversation

Students who are ready for the printed version of the new structures can do this task, listening to the recording and just writing down the correct letter for the missing words.

They could then use the completed conversation as a script for further practice in pairs.

Solution: **1b, 2a, 3d, 4c, 5e**

🎧 Une conversation

– Bonjour. Comment t'appelles-tu?
– Bonjour. Je m'appelle (Sophie). Et toi?
– Je m'appelle (Robert). Quel âge as-tu?
– J'ai (douze) ans. Et toi?
– J'ai (onze) ans. Au revoir Sophie.
– Au revoir Robert.

SB 150, TB 51, 🎧 SCD 1/7 **LISTENING**

6 Une conversation

There is a similar conversation in *Écoute et parle*, paused for individual practice at home.

Area 6
Identifying classroom objects
An introduction to gender

SB 8, 1
Au choix SB 126, 2
CD 1/7

C'est un garçon/une fille.
Qu'est-ce que c'est?
C'est un stylo/livre/cahier/crayon/cartable/taille-crayon/ordinateur
C'est une règle/chaise/trousse/table/gomme/boîte/calculette

Gender

PRESENTATION

Grammatical gender is still a difficult concept and it seems best to introduce it gradually, stressing its importance but not making it sound too difficult. The words *garçon* and *fille* have occurred in the number games, but in any case they are good ones to start with.

Revise the questions and answers learnt already and move on from *Qui est-ce? C'est Jean* to *Qui est-ce? C'est un garçon. C'est un garçon? Oui, c'est un garçon.*

Then introduce the French for five masculine classroom objects (*un livre, un stylo, un cahier, un crayon, un cartable*) with the question *Qu'est-ce que c'est?*

These five nouns can be practised until most students can answer correctly the question *Qu'est-ce que c'est?*

Then help students to deduce that the word for 'a' used with the other words is *un* (like *un* before *garçon*).

Next point to a girl and say *C'est un garçon?* When you get the answer *Non*, say *Non, c'est une fille. Répétez. C'est une fille.*

Now teach five feminine objects (*une chaise, une règle, une table, une gomme, une boîte*) with *Qu'est-ce que c'est?*

Draw attention to the word *une* and link it with *une fille*.

Explain briefly that, in French, all objects are either *un* or *une* words, and mention the terms masculine and feminine. Tell the students to make sure that they always learn whether a word is masculine or feminine.

Next, teach a few more classroom objects (*un ordinateur, un classeur, un sac à dos, un magnétophone, un taille-crayon, une calculette, une trousse*) and practise these as before.

SB 8, 1/7

LISTENING

1 Des affaires scolaires

Ask the class to look at the pictures of classroom objects, noticing that they are divided into masculine (*un*) and feminine (*une*) words (surrounded with red or blue frames as an added reminder).

Explain *affaires* if they have not already met the phrase *Rangez vos affaires!*

Then ask questions about the things illustrated, widening the conversation, if wished, to include actual objects again, e.g.

Ça, (b), qu'est-ce que c'est? C'est un crayon? Non, c'est un stylo.

Voici une trousse. C'est ta trousse, Claire. Et ça, (h), qu'est-ce que c'est? C'est une règle? Oui, c'est une règle. Et regardez ça. C'est une calculette, non? Et ça, c'est un ordinateur – c'est important, n'est-ce pas?

Some of the students could ask similar questions or they could practise in pairs.

Next, everyone should write down the numbers from 1–13 and then listen to the recording and write down the letter for each object as it is mentioned in the recording. This task could be corrected by playing the recording again and stopping to check each answer in turn.

The written form of the names for classroom objects has not been supplied in this unit, but you might wish to introduce this if students are confident enough in their pronounciation. If so, they could refer to the list in the *Sommaire* at the end of *Unité* 2 (SB 13).

Solution: 1c, 2h, 3i, 4a, 5e, 6m, 7b, 8d, 9f, 10l, 11k, 12j, 13g

Des affaires scolaires

1 – Qu'est-ce que c'est?
– C'est un cahier.

2 – Et ça? C'est une règle?
– Ah oui, c'est une règle.

3 – Qu'est-ce que c'est?
– C'est une gomme.

4 – C'est un livre?
– Oui, c'est un livre.

5 – Qu'est-ce que c'est?
– C'est un cartable.

6 – Et voici une chaise.
– Oui, oui, c'est une chaise.

7 – Et ça, qu'est-ce que c'est?
– C'est un stylo.

8 – Voici un crayon.
– C'est vrai. C'est un crayon.

9 – Et ça, qu'est-ce que c'est?
– C'est un taille-crayon – c'est mon taille-crayon.

10 – Et une calculette, regarde!
– Ah bon, c'est ma calculette, ça!

11 – Oui? Dans la trousse? C'est ça?
– Oui, oui. Dans la trousse.

12 – Et ça, c'est une boîte?
– Oui, c'est une boîte.

13 – Et voici un ordinateur.
–Oui, un ordinateur. Ça, c'est très important!

Use some games to practise the new vocabulary and the article, e.g. *Jeu de mémoire, Effacez!* (TB 26–27). Put some classroom objects into a 'feely box'. Students put their hand through a hole in a cardboard box and say what they are touching.

Au choix SB 126 **WRITING**

2 Deux listes

A short task suitable for students thought ready to write. The lists contain some of the new vocabulary with the article and the meaning.

Solution:

un (masculine)	*une* (feminine)
un livre = a book	*une calculette* = a calculator
un cartable = school bag	*une boîte* = a box
un crayon = a pencil	*une chaise* = a chair
un stylo = a pen	*une règle* = a ruler

If students have access to a computer with a CD-ROM drive, there will probably be a task practising the words for classroom objects, e.g. matching labels to pictures, since many basic French CD-ROMs have this vocabulary.

As an alternative, using word processing and clip art, students could make up an illustrated list of the vocabulary.

Area 7
Discussing quantity
SB 8, 2
Au choix 126, 3
CD 1/8
Combien? Il y a combien de (+ noun)?
Il y a (number) (+ noun).

Combien? PRESENTATION

Teach *Combien?* and *C'est combien?* orally using groups of classroom objects, holding up fingers, writing figures on the board etc., first asking and answering the questions yourself then getting students to do so.

Gradually use numbers plus nouns, saying: *Il y a combien de* (+ noun)? *Il y a* (+ noun).

SB 8  **SPEAKING**

2 Combien?

First ask a few questions based on the pictures to show what is required, then get the class to work in pairs asking each other *Il y a combien de* (+ noun)? They could answer using the structure suggested (*Il y a trois crayons*) or just give the number.

Solution: **1** *Il y a 3 crayons,* **2** *Il y a 7 taille-crayons,* **3** *Il y a 8 règles,* **4** *Il y a 5 livres,* **5** *Il y a 4 calculettes,* **6** *Il y a 9 gommes,* **7** *Il y a 2 stylos,* **8** *Il y a une trousse.*

Note: The written form of the numbers has not been given in this unit, but teachers might wish to introduce this if students are confident in their pronuncation. If so, they could refer to the lists on SB 21, SB 162 (and also to the numbers at the bottom of each page).

Au choix SB 126, 1/8 **LISTENING**

3 C'est quel nombre?

Practice in understanding numbers, alone and when followed by nouns.

Solution: 1f, 2c, 3a, 4h, 5j, 6g, 7b, 8d, 9e, 10i

C'est quel nombre?

1 six
2 dix-huit
3 deux
4 douze
5 seize
6 trois livres
7 trois cahiers
8 sept crayons
9 deux gommes
10 quatre stylos

Area 8
Further activities and consolidation
SB 8
Au choix SB 126, 4
CM 1/2
CD 1/9–11
Écoute et parle SB 150, 5, 1–6
Student CD 1/2–7

SB 8 **PRACTICE**

Vocabulaire de classe

In each unit, a selection of classroom commands or similar useful phrases are included in the Students' Book just before the *Sommaire* with an accompanying task. Students could copy and complete the list and gradually build up a useful vocabulary list for reference in this way.

Solution: 1c, 2f, 3d 4g, 5b, 6e, 7h, 8a

SB 8, SB 150, TB 51, SCD 1/6 **LISTENING**

5 Vocabulaire de classe

This listening task in the *Écoute et parle* section is linked with the above task and could be done now or at the end of the unit. In this case, the instructions are recorded in random order (see TB 51).

Au choix SB 126 **READING**

4 C'est quelle image?

Students ready for reading can do this task in which they match the conversations to the pictures.

Solution: 1b, 2a, 3g, 4c, 5d, 6e, 7f, 8h

CM 1/2, 🎧 1/9–11

Écoutez bien!

This is a listening quiz on the language taught in the unit. Students write down Section 1 and number from 1–5. They look at the pictures and write the letter of the correct one as they hear each name on the recording.

Solution: 1d, 2b, 3e, 4a, 5c

🎧 **Écoutez bien!**

Section 1

1 Bonjour! Je m'appelle Pierre.
2 Bonjour! Je m'appelle Françoise.
3 Bonjour! Je m'appelle Catherine.
4 Bonjour! Je m'appelle Jean-Pierre.
5 Bonjour! Je m'appelle Michèle.

In Section 2, the class number again from 1–5, then listen for the age of each speaker.

Solution: 1e, 2a, 3b, 4d, 5c

🎧 **Écoutez bien!**

Section 2

1 – Quel âge as-tu?
– J'ai six ans.

2 – Quel âge as-tu?
– J'ai quatre ans.

3 – Quel âge as-tu?
– J'ai douze ans.

4 – Quel âge as-tu?
– J'ai cinq ans.

5 – Quel âge as-tu?
– J'ai dix ans.

In Section 3, students number from 1–10, then listen for classroom objects.

Solution: 1j, 2c, 3b, 4d, 5g, 6a, 7i, 8f, 9h, 10e

🎧 **Écoutez bien!**

Section 3

1 C'est une gomme.
2 C'est un livre.
3 C'est un cartable.
4 C'est une règle.
5 C'est une boîte.
6 Qu'est-ce que c'est?
C'est un crayon.
7 Qu'est-ce que c'est?
C'est un cahier.
8 Qu'est-ce que c'est?
C'est une table.
9 Qu'est-ce que c'est?
C'est un stylo.
10 Qu'est-ce que c'est?
C'est une chaise.

Copymasters such as this one can also be used for a variety of games, e.g.

Loto
Section 3 can be mounted on card and cut up to make ten smaller cards which could be supplemented by four more made by students (perhaps for homework) to represent, say, pencil sharpener, calculator, pencil case and rucksack. These can be used for *Loto* (Bingo). The winner becomes the next caller.

Un jeu de mémoire
Students place cards face downwards without looking at them. Each student in turn puts a finger on a card and guesses what it is. The card is then turned over. If guessed correctly, the person takes the card. If not, the card is turned back and the next person has a go. The winner is the student with most cards at the end.

SB 150, 🎧 SCD 1/2–7 INDEPENDENT LISTENING READING

Écoute et parle – Unité 1

These recordings are intended primarily for individual work, but, as this is the first unit, it will probably be worth spending a little time explaining and demonstrating their use and going through a few items with the class.

Any of the items could serve as useful consolidation.

The text for all the items in *Unités 1–10* is given together from SB 150–159, and each unit follows a similar pattern. The transcripts for all the tasks for a particular unit are given near the end of the Teacher's Notes for the relevant unit. There is a recorded introduction at the beginning of this first unit.

🎧 **Écoute et parle**

Introduction

In this section, you will learn about the main sounds of French and have a chance to practise pronunciation and speaking in French, using the CD.

Here are some points to bear in mind:

- In French, each syllable of a word is normally stressed equally, whereas in English, there is often a stronger emphasis on one syllable.

  Listen to the difference in pronunciation of these words which are spelt in the same way in both languages. First you will hear the English pronunciation, then the French.

  table, table
  parent, parent
  article, article
  nature, nature
  solution, solution
  impossible, impossible

- If *t*, *d* or *p* (and most other consonants) come at the end of a French word, they are not normally pronounced. Compare the English and French pronunciation of these words.

  content, content
  art, art
  concert, concert
  sport, sport
  camp, camp

- However, if there is an e after the consonant, then the consonant is sounded, but not the e. Listen to these examples, first in English, then in French.

  post, poste
  salad, salade
  tent, tente
  list, liste
  artist, artiste
  visit, visite

- The same sounds can be spelt in different ways in French. Listen to these groups of words – the endings all rhyme, but they are spelt differently.

  trois, moi, droit
  nous, joue, où
  et, parlez, cahier, café
  gros, beau, mot, faux

  Now you are ready to start work on the practice items.

  You will soon build up your pronunciation skills with regular practice on these units.

1 Les sons français

Solution: (a) 1d, 2e, 3b, 4a, 5c, 6f

Les sons français. La lettre i

a **1** riche
2 il
3 lis
4 dix
5 merci
6 famille

b six, écris, livre, dis, oui, fille

2 Une phrase ridicule

Une phrase ridicule

La souris lit dix livres à Paris et dit «merci».

3 C'est anglais ou français?

Solution: (a) 1c, 2a, 3d, 4e, 5b

C'est anglais ou français?

a **1** bouquet
2 café
3 ballet
4 papier maché
5 pâté

b **1** serviette
2 croissant
3 route

c **1** chef
2 Champagne
3 chauffeur
4 chic

4 C'est quel nombre?

C'est quel nombre?

douze, onze, vingt, huit, trois
quinze, dix, neuf, cinq, seize

5 Vocabulaire de classe

Solution: 2, 5, 7, 4, 1, 8, 6, 3

Vocabulaire de classe

Regarde la page 8. Écoute le CD et écris le nombre de chaque instruction dans l'ordre du CD.
Exemple: 2

Regarde
Écris
Trouve
Réponds
Écoute
Complète
Répète
Travaillez à deux.

6 Une conversation

Une conversation

a Écoute les questions et réponds pour Alex.

– Bonjour! Comment t'appelles-tu? (pause)
– Je m'appelle Alex.
– Quel âge as-tu? (pause)
– J'ai onze ans.
– Ça va? (pause)
– Oui, ça va bien.

b Écoute les questions et réponds pour toi.

– Bonjour! Comment t'appelles-tu?
– (pause)
– Quel âge as-tu?
– (pause)
– Ça va?
– (pause)

SPEAKING

À toi!

For extra practice students could be asked to test themselves by trying the following pairwork activity.

Without looking at your books, see how much of this you can do from memory:

- Say hello to each other in French.
- Ask each other's name and age.
- Ask how you both are.
- See if you can count from 1–20 in French.
- Try to do it backwards, ending with *zéro*.

A French website for children

As a follow-up to work on names and ages, students could visit a French website for children (see TB 208) and look up *Correspondants*. Although they will not be able to understand a lot of the text, they could find out a few French names and ages and perhaps where in France some of the children live. Teachers could previously look up the site themselves first and perhaps direct students' research by getting them to answer some questions about one or two chosen correspondents.

Encore Tricolore 1
nouvelle édition
unité 2 J'habite ici

Areas	Topics	Grammar
1	Introduction to La Rochelle	
2	Saying where you live Asking other people where they live	
3	Using different ways of saying 'in'	*en/au/dans* (+ country etc.) *à* (+ town)
4	Using numbers up to 30	*Combien? Il y a ...*
5	More about things in the classroom	Introduction to the negative Singular and plural *ce sont des* (+ plural noun)
6	Further activities and consolidation	

National Curriculum information

Most students	Levels 1–2
All students	Level 1

Refer also to the information about coverage of 'Knowledge, skills and understanding' (TB 9).

Revision

The vocabulary and structures introduced in this unit are revised in the *Rappel* section following *Unité 3* (SB 22–23, TB 75).

ICT opportunities

- looking up La Rochelle and other French towns on websites (TB 208 and 54)
- text reconstruction activity – basic self-description (TB 56)
- setting up an electronic phrase book (TB 40 and 59)
- using word processing and clip art to make up an illustrated word list (TB 59)
- using a CD-ROM to practise vocabulary for classroom items (TB 59)

Sounds and writing

- *é* and *ez*
- see *Écoute et parle* (SB 151, TB 61)

Assessment

- Informal assessment is provided by the *Épreuves* after *Unité 3* (TB 74).
- Formal assessment is in the *Premier contrôle* following *Unité 4* (TB 200).

Students' Book

Unité 2 SB 9–13

Au choix SB 127 1, 2 (TB 56), 3 (TB 59), 4 (TB 60)

Écoute et parle SB 151 (TB 61)

CDs

1/12–21

Student CD 1/8–15

Flashcards

3–4	town, village
5–7	house, flat, farm
8–12	places in a town

Copymasters

2/1	*J'habite en France* [support] (TB 55)
2/2	*Trois conversations* [listening] (TB 56)
2/3	*Mots et images* [consolidation] (TB 60)
2/4	*Sommaire* (TB 60)

Language content

Talking about where you live (Areas 2 and 3)

Où habites-tu?
J'habite ...
dans une maison/un appartement/une ferme
dans une ville/un village
à Londres / près de Paris
en France
en Angleterre
en Écosse
en Irlande (du Nord)
au Pays de Galles

People and places (Areas 2 and 3)

un/une enfant
une femme
une fille
un homme
un café
un cinéma
une rue

Basic questions and answers

Qui est-ce?
Qu'est-ce que c'est?
C'est
Ce n'est pas
Ce sont
Oui, c'est ça
Non, ce n'est pas ça
Voici
Voilà
Il y a

Classroom items (Area 5)

masculine words	feminine words
un baladeur	*une boîte*
un cahier	*une calculette*
un cartable	*une chaise*
un classeur	*une fenêtre*
un crayon	*une gomme*
un lecteur de CDs	*une porte*
un livre	*une règle*
un magnétophone	*une table*
un ordinateur (de poche)	*une trousse*
un sac (à dos)	
un stylo (à bille)	
un taille-crayon	

Classroom language and rubrics

Asseyez-vous.
Ouvrez le livre.
Regardez les images.
Écoutez le CD.
Comptez.
Fermez le livre.
Rangez vos affaires.
Levez-vous.
Jouez à deux.
Vrai ou faux?
Donne-moi un/une ..., s'il te plaît.
Je voudrais un/une ...
Merci bien.
Je ne sais pas.

Introductory note

Links with France

It is a good idea to establish a link with a French class and this can be arranged through the Central Bureau for International Education and Training (see TB 208).

The first term's work is mainly on the theme of talking about oneself and one's family. This lends itself well to the creation of a composite class website or a regular exchange of e-mails, or recording a cassette in which students speak about their own families etc. Preparing material for this exchange link could be part of normal classwork right through ***Encore Tricolore 1 nouvelle édition***. (See website addresses TB 208)

Area 1
An introduction to La Rochelle
SB 9, 1
FC 3, 4, 8, 11

SB 9, FC 3, 4, 8, 11, — PRESENTATION

Venez à La Rochelle

This montage of photos serves as an introduction to La Rochelle.

Tell the class a little about La Rochelle, using the photos and as much French as is likely to be understood, e.g.

Voici la France.
Voici La Rochelle – c'est une ville. (Use flashcard 3.)
Et voici des photos de La Rochelle.
Voici le port – La Rochelle est un port etc.

Use flashcards to teach key words such as *ville, rue* and *café*.

Ask questions, pointing to a photo and saying *C'est un port/une rue/un café etc. Oui ou non?*

Some students could read the captions aloud.

Follow-up

Check whether anyone has visited La Rochelle. Ask students to look it up on the map (SB 3) or to find out information from an atlas or a CD-ROM such as *Encarta*, or if possible, from a website (see TB 208).

There is some background information on La Rochelle on TB 32–33. However, not too much time needs to be spent on this at this stage as more work will be done in *Unité 7*.

SB 9 — READING

1 La Rochelle

Teach *Vrai ou faux?* by making statements about members of the class or classroom objects, e.g. *Voici Charles. Il est le professeur – c'est vrai ou faux?*

Use the example to check that everyone knows how to do the task.

The task could be done as a class activity or individually with the answers checked orally. Some students might be ready to read out some of the statements being checked or they could just be repeated by the class.

Solution: 1F, 2V, 3V, 4F, 5F, 6F, 7V, 8F

Area 2
Say where you live
Ask other people where they live
Learning to listen
SB 10, 1–2
Au choix SB 127, 1
CM 2/1
FC 3–7
CD 1/12
J'habite à (+ town) près de
dans une maison etc.
Où habites-tu?

FC 3–7 — PRESENTATION, SPEAKING

J'habite ...

Teach how to say where you live using flashcards and repetition of *J'habite à* (+ place). Then students say the phrase in answer to the question *Où habites-tu?* Eventually some students could question others.

Using flashcards 3 and 4, gradually teach *C'est une ville/un village* and ask:
(Name of place), *c'est une ville? C'est un village?*

C'est une ville/un village?

Write the names of some well-known towns or villages in Britain and France on the board and use them for oral practice, e.g.

– (Student A), *Paris, c'est une ville?*
– *Oui, c'est une ville.*

Une maison, un appartement, une ferme

Using the flashcards, teach *une maison* and *un appartement*. Then ask *Tu habites dans une maison ou dans un appartement?* Teach *une ferme* and practise these nouns using a flashcard game (TB 27).

Strategies for listening

(See also TB 17, **Developing listening skills**.)
Some simple training in strategies for listening should be built into the use of the materials from the outset.

These strategies fall into two main categories:

1 Building up confidence so that students believe they can understand, and constantly proving this to be so.

2 Developing the skills of guessing what it is reasonable to guess, and 'ignoring positively' and carrying on without knowing things that don't really matter anyway!

The first strategy is linked with attitude: the teacher must believe that the students will be able to understand what they hear, so long as the items are introduced gradually with a build-up of what is to be listened for.

The second strategy can be helped along more directly by the content of the materials themselves. For example, in the following item, *J'habite ici*, several new, but easily guessable, words are 'slipped in': *moderne, fantastique, importante*.

The key language is reinforced by many repetitions of such phrases as *J'habite ici. Je m'appelle ... C'est une ville/un village* etc., but the different speakers in the recording recombine these statements, and some give more and some less information than is presented in the Students' Book text. So only part of what they say is supported directly by the written word. This should encourage careful listening and begin to train students to make an informed guess.

SB 10, 1/12 — **LISTENING SPEAKING**

1 J'habite ici

Before you start, use the photos to teach or revise *garçon, fille, homme, femme*, e.g.
Voici une femme (repeat several times).
Elle s'appelle Mme Meyer. Elle habite ici.
Et voici une fille. Elle habite dans une maison.

Next look at all the pictures in turn, speaking briefly about them, e.g.
Voici Paris. C'est une ville? Oui, c'est une ville.

Et voici Strasbourg. C'est une ville aussi.
Répétez – Strasbourg.
Mme Meyer habite à Strasbourg.

Et voici un village. C'est une ville? Non, c'est un village, près de Trouville.
Et voici une fille. La fille habite ici, dans la maison.

Et voici un homme. Répétez. Il s'appelle M. Lafitte etc.

Students could look up the places mentioned on the map on SB 3.

Now use the recording with the Students' Book text. Play the whole of the recording once while students follow in their books. Play it a second time, using the pause button to give them time to identify each speaker and write down the appropriate letter.

Note: in this case, the recording and the Students' Book text are similar but not exactly the same.

Solution: 1b, 2c, 3a, 4d, 5h, 6f, 7g, 8e

J'habite ici

1. Moi, je m'appelle Vivienne. J'habite ici, dans un village près de Trouville. Voici ma maison.
2. Bonjour. Je m'appelle Hassan. J'habite ici, à Paris. C'est fantastique! J'habite dans un appartement moderne.
3. Moi, je m'appelle M. Jean Lafitte. J'habite ici, dans une ferme. La ferme est dans un village, près de Cherbourg.
4. Moi, je m'appelle Philippe et j'habite ici, à La Rochelle. J'habite dans un appartement.
5. Je m'appelle Séverine. Salut! Moi, j'habite dans un village près de Grenoble. Ma maison est près des Alpes et j'adore le ski.
6. Je m'appelle Madame Meyer. J'habite à Strasbourg, dans une maison.
7. Moi, je m'appelle Sika. J'habite dans une maison, à Toulouse. Toulouse, c'est une ville importante.
8. Salut! Je m'appelle Luc. J'habite à Poitiers, dans un appartement. Poitiers est près du Futuroscope. Ça, c'est fantastique!

SPEAKING

Oui ou non?

The photographs in Task 1 above could be used for oral work. First revise numbers 1–8, then play the game *Répondez oui ou non* – a student chooses a person from the photos, whom s/he will represent, then writes down the letter of the photo and gives it to the teacher as a check. The other students have to guess the identity of the person chosen by asking questions which may only be answered by *Oui* or *Non*, e.g. *Tu habites à Toulouse?*
Tu t'appelles Vivienne? etc.

CM 2/1 — **LISTENING SUPPORT**

J'habite en France

1 J'habite ici

As a support activity to the above item, students listen again to the recording, first identifying the speakers and noting down the names, then filling in the grid on the sheet This activity is ideal for use with individual listening facilities.

Solution:

	ville	village	maison	appartement	ferme
1		✔	✔		
2	✔			✔	
3		✔			✔
4	✔			✔	
5		✔	✔		
6	✔		✔		
7	✔		✔		
8	✔			✔	

2 Où sont les voyelles?

This could be done for further consolidation in class or for homework.

Solution: **1** *village*, **2** *Paris*, **3** *village*, **4** *appartement*, **5** *Grenoble*, **6** *maison*, **7** *ville*, **8** *habite*

Solution: 3 Mots mêlés

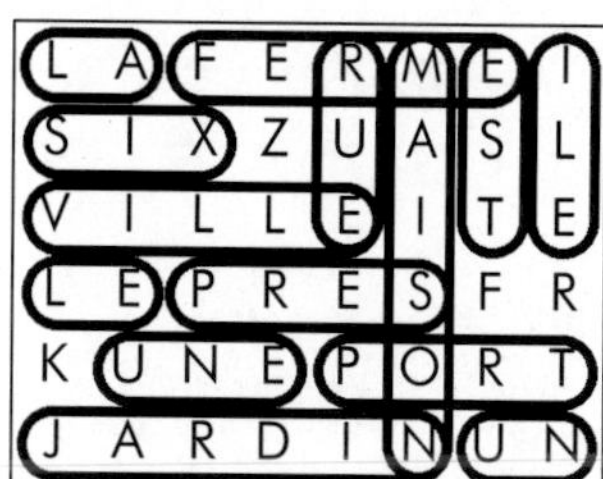

SB 10 — **READING WRITING**

2 Où habites-tu?

Students find the correct words from the box to complete these core sentences.

They could just note down the numbers and matching letters and the answers could be checked orally, with students supplying the full sentence. Any students ready to start writing could copy down the complete sentences.

Solution: 1b, 2f, 3c, 4a, 5e, 6d, 7h, 8g

Au choix SB 127 **READING EXTENSION**

1 C'est moi!

This task is suitable for students ready for independent reading. In part **a**, students match up the two halves of sentences Part **b** is a *Vrai ou faux?* task, based on part **a**.

Solution: (a) 1b, 2a, 3e, 4f, 5d, 6c
(b) 1V, 2V, 3F, 4F, 5F

Language awareness **EXTENSION**

As optional follow-up, students might be interested to see how a lot of town names in French end in *-ville*, e.g. Trouville, Deauville, Contrexéville etc., just as a lot of English town names end in -town or -ton, e.g. Newtown, Bolton, Taunton, Darlington.

They could perhaps add to these lists themselves, looking up some more French ones in an atlas or on the Internet.

They might be surprised to see how names often reflect local features or industries, e.g. Montceaux-les-Mines, Villedieu-les-Poêles (where copper pots are made), Colombey-les-Deux-Églises. They could also look at British place names which contain French words, e.g. Bellevue.

Area 3
Using different ways of saying 'in'
SB 11, 3
CM 2/2
Au choix SB 127, 2
CD 1/13
Écoute et parle, SB 151, 8
Student CD 1/15

Presentation

Ask several students again where they live, then add the name of the town or village and a country, e.g. (Name), *c'est une ville/un village en Angleterre/en Écosse/au Pays de Galles/en Irlande (du Nord)* etc.

With the names of villages, *c'est près de* can be re-introduced, e.g.

- *Bardsey, c'est une ville (en Angleterre)?*
- *Non, c'est un village (en Angleterre).*
- *Oui, c'est un village (en Angleterre). C'est près de Leeds.*

SB 11 **SPEAKING**

3 À toi!

Go through the conversation in speech bubbles to teach students to make up their own answer to the question about where they live. Draw attention to the substitution table *Pour t'aider* and help them to spot the two different ways of saying in + country and to work out the reason for this. They can now prepare their own answer.

They could practise the short conversation in pairs first, then go round the class asking other people where they live.

CM 2/2, 1/13 **SUPPORT LISTENING**

Trois conversations

This copymaster brings together some of the main structures of *Unités 1–2* (name, age, where you live).

Students first look through the illustrations for the conversations and the multiple-choice items, before working on the recorded version and ticking the correct options.

This item could be used with individual listening equipment or in a multi-media facility, in which case, the recorded conversations could also be used for 'listen and repeat' practice.

Solution: 1 Ab, Bc, Cb, Dc
2 Aa, Bc, Ca, Da
3 Aa, Bb, Ca, Db

Trois conversations

Conversation 1

– Bonjour. Je m'appelle Monique. Comment t'appelles-tu?
– Je m'appelle Marcel.
– Quel âge as-tu, Monique?
– J'ai quatorze ans. Et toi?
– J'ai dix ans.

Conversation 2

– Bonjour. Je m'appelle Marc. Comment t'appelles-tu?
– Je m'appelle Françoise. Tu habites où?
– J'habite dans un village, près de La Rochelle. Et toi?
– J'habite dans un village, près de Marseille.

Conversation 3

– Bonjour. Je m'appelle Philippe. Et toi? Tu t'appelles comment?
– Je m'appelle Martine. Tu habites où?
– J'habite à Sainte-Marie. C'est un village. Et toi?
– J'habite à Bordeaux. C'est une ville en France.

The completed text of part **a** of this item would be suitable for a text reconstruction activity on self-description, e.g. using *Fun with Texts – Textsalad* or *Copywrite*.

Au choix SB 127,  **GRAMMAR**

2 C'est où?

Students use the appropriate prepositions with the names of towns and countries. This could be an oral or written activity.

A similar activity could involve the use of a text reconstruction package such as *Fun with Texts*.

Solution:

1 *Glasgow, c'est une ville en France.*
2 *Manchester, c'est une ville en Angleterre.*
3 *Paris, c'est une ville en France.*
4 *La Rochelle, c'est une ville en France.*
5 *Bordeaux, c'est une ville en France.*

6 *Dublin, c'est une ville en Irlande.*
7 *Leeds, c'est une ville en Angleterre.*
8 *Belfast, c'est une ville en Irlande du Nord.*
9 *Aberdeen, c'est une ville en Écosse.*
10 *Swansea, c'est une ville au Pays de Galles.*

SB 151, TB 61, SCD 1/15 — **LISTENING SPEAKING**

8 Une conversation

This is the final task in the *Écoute et parle* section for this unit. It is on the student CD for independent study and could be used now or at the end of the unit.

SB 11 — **LANGUAGE AWARENESS**

This is one of several points about specific language which appear throughout the book. Students might have worked out the answer to this question, while using *j'habite*.

Explain that *h* is often not sounded in French and acts as if it's not there. With *habite*, this has the effect of making it seem as if the word begins with a vowel.

Area 4
Using numbers up to 30

SB 11, 4
Chantez!
CD 1/14–16
Écoute et parle, SB 151, 4
Student CD 1/11

Numbers 1–30 — PRESENTATION

Revise the numbers from 1–15 and teach the new numbers from 16–30, using repetition, *Comptez de 3 à 8* etc. and some of the number games (TB 25).

SB 151, TB 61, SCD 1/11 — **LISTENING**

4 C'est quel nombre?

This *Écoute et parle* task gives further practice of numbers and could be used now or later for consolidation.

SB 11, 1/14 — **LISTENING**

4 Qui habite où?

Revise the pronunciation of the names and ask the class to read aloud the numbers of the houses. Then play the recording, pausing after the first speaker to look at the example, and again after each speaker for students to write down the correct answers. Check the results orally, perhaps with further questions, e.g. *Qui habite au numéro sept? Où habite Magali?* etc.

Solution: **1** 7, **2** 21, **3** 25, **4** 30, **5** 14, **6** 28, **7** 5, **8** 15

Qui habite où?

1 – Où habites-tu, Olivier?
– J'habite à Paris, dans la Villa Violette.
– C'est quel numéro?
– Numéro sept.

2 – Et toi, Coralie? Où habites-tu?
– J'habite à La Rochelle, dans la rue Gambetta.
– Quel numéro?
– Vingt et un.

3 – Salut, Magali. Est-ce que tu habites au numéro vingt-cinq?
– Oui, c'est ça. Au vingt-cinq.

4 – Et toi, Loïc Tu habites dans cette rue, non?
– Oui, j'habite au numéro trente.

5 – Salut Sébastien.
– Salut!
– Où habites-tu, Sébastien?
– À La Rochelle, au numéro quatorze, rue du Pont.

6 – Et vous habitez aussi dans la rue du Pont, M. Garnier. C'est vrai?
– Oui, mais moi, j'habite au numéro vingt-huit.

7 – Et Jean-Marc, aussi. Il habite au numéro cinq.
– Oui, c'est ça. Moi, j'habite au cinq.

8 – Et toi, Isabelle. Où habites-tu?
– Moi, j'habite à Rennes, dans la rue de Paris.
– Quel numéro?
– Quinze, j'habite au numéro quinze.

SB 11, TB 33, TB 36, 1/15–16 — **LISTENING**

Chantez! Un, deux, trois

A song revising numbers which could be used now and repeated at the end of the unit for consolidation. See the notes on the use of songs (TB 33).

Chantez! Un, deux, trois

– 1, 2, 3,
Salut! C'est moi!
4, 5, 6,
J'habite à Nice.
7, 8, 9,
Dans la rue Elbeuf.
10, 11, 12,
Et toi?
– Toulouse.
13, 14, 15,
Dans l'avenue de Reims.
16, 17,
Je m'appelle Colette.
18, 19, 20,
C'est la fin!
Recommence au numéro un …

Area 5
More about classroom vocabulary
Masculine and feminine
Singular and plural

SB 12, 1–2
CD 1/17–20
CM 2/3
Au choix SB 127, 3

Ce n'est pas un/une (+ noun)
Ce sont des (+ plural noun)

Revision of nouns PRESENTATION

Revise classroom objects already taught (*cahier, cartable, crayon, livre, stylo*) using the structure *Qu'est-ce que c'est? C'est un …*
Voici/Voilà un … Oui/Non.

Then teach *tableau, ordinateur, lecteur de CDs, baladeur, magnétophone à cassettes* and *télévision*.

Introduction of classroom instructions

Gradually introduce *s'il te plaît* and *merci bien* and, if wished, *Je ne sais pas/Je voudrais un …*

Begin to use as often as possible such commands as *regardez, ouvrez, fermez, écrivez*, so that the class gets used to the lesson being conducted in French.

SB 12, 1/17 LISTENING SPEAKING

1 Télé-jeu: 30 secondes

This item is designed to reinforce the new vocabulary items and to give listening and speaking practice.

Ask students to look at the picture on SB 12, then explain it to them briefly:
Voilà, c'est un jeu à la télévision. Regardez. Voici une fille, Hélène, et un garçon, Marc, et voici les prix. Helène gagne quatre choses et Marc gagne six choses. Regardez les prix.

Explain *gagne*, if not guessed. Then go through all the prizes to check vocabulary:
Numéro 1, qu'est-ce que c'est?

Explain that the two contestants must watch the prizes go by, then identify them from memory to win them.

First play the recording right through with the class looking at the picture. Then play the recording again and ask them to jot down the number of the prizes each person wins, reporting back using the actual words for the prizes.

Some teachers may wish to give their class the written words here, and if so, they could be written on the board in random order and later listed with their meanings, in vocabulary books (or in an electronic vocabulary list – see TB 40).

Finally, students can play the game themselves. One student sees how many prizes s/he can win in thirty seconds, without looking at the book and with suitable applause from the class.

Soon, a student can play the quizmaster, or the game can be played in groups. More prizes could be added.

Solution: Hélène 1, 2, 4, 6; Marc 1, 3, 5, 7, 8, 9

Télé-jeu: 30 secondes

– Voilà, Hélène et Marc, regardez les prix – ce sont des prix fantastiques, non?
– Oui, oui, fantastiques!
– Bon, c'est à toi Hélène – ça va?
– Ça va.
– Bon, tu as trente secondes: 3 … 2 … 1 … zéro!
– Eh bien, numéro un, c'est un lecteur de CDs et deux, euh, c'est un magnétophone.
– Très bien, splendide! Continue!
– Alors trois, numéro trois, c'est … c'est une télévision?
– Ah, non. Mais …
– Ah non, euh, la télé, c'est numéro quatre. Et numéro six, euh, c'est un baladeur …
– Trente secondes! Très bien, Hélène. Tu as gagné un lecteur de CDs, un magnétophone, une télé et un baladeur.
– Oh, merci, merci, Monsieur.
– Et maintenant, Marc. Ça va?
– Euh … oui, oui, ça va.
– Tu as trente secondes: 3 … 2 … 1 … zéro! Commence!
– Numéro un est un lecteur de CDs, euh … oui, numéro trois, c'est une calculette, numéro cinq, des crayons, numéro sept, un sac à dos, numéro huit, un ordinateur de poche, numéro neuf, un cartable et …
– Trente secondes! Fantastique, Marc! Tu as gagné six prix, six. Voilà – un lecteur de CDs, une calculette, des crayons, un sac à dos, un ordinateur de poche et un cartable. Félicitations – et au revoir!

SB 12, 1/18, PRESENTATION SPEAKING LISTENING

2 Je pense à quelque chose (Section A et Section B)

First teach the class how to play the game *Je pense à quelque chose*, saying *Oui, c'est ça* or *Non, ce n'est pas ça* depending on whether their guess is right or not.

Play this a few times, using first the objects in the masculine box (A), then in the feminine box (B) and then playing a few more rounds with students taking the teacher's role.

Students then listen to the recording of French children playing *Je pense à quelque chose*, using a mixture of masculine and feminine nouns (from Section A and Section B only). They should write down the numbers of any objects mentioned.

Solution: 5, 3, 8, 1; 12, 2, 6, 4

Je pense à quelque chose (Section A et Section B)

– Je pense à quelque chose. Qu'est-ce que c'est?
– C'est un livre?
– Non, ce n'est pas ça.
– C'est un magnétophone?
– Non, ce n'est pas ça.
– C'est une fenêtre?

- Non, ce n'est pas ça.
- C'est un ordinateur?
- Oui, c'est un ordinateur. Très bien!

- Je pense à quelque chose. Qu'est-ce que c'est?
- C'est une règle?
- Non, ce n'est pas ça.
- C'est un cartable?
- Non, ce n'est pas ça.
- C'est un sac à dos?
- Non, ce n'est pas ça.
- C'est un baladeur?
- Oui, c'est ça. C'est un baladeur.

Students can now play this game in pairs or groups, using both masculine and feminine singular nouns.

At this point, many teachers will wish to supply students with the written words for the classroom vocabulary. They could do this by playing a matching game in which the words for the pictures in Sections A and B on SB 12 are written on the board, with numbers from 1–12, but in random order. Students come out and ring a number and matching word, saying them as they do it. Alternatively, students could pick a number from a box, read it out and point to and say the matching word.

The words and their meanings could eventually be added to students' vocabulary book lists or students could work on the computer to make their own bilingual electronic phrase book (see TB 40) or perhaps some illustrated vocabulary posters for the classroom (see TB 41). The words are listed on SB 13.

For further practice of classroom vocabulary, students could play one of the following games: *Vrai ou faux?/* True and false chairs, *Loto* or *Qu'est-ce que c'est?* (see TB 25–27).

Several French CD-ROMs practise classroom vocabulary and could be useful here.

The plural of nouns

PRESENTATION
SPEAKING

It is important for students to be familiar with plural forms orally before seeing the written form, as they will be tempted to pronounce the final *-s*.

Plurals can be practised as follows:
Donne-moi un …! Merci bien.
Qu'est-ce que c'est? C'est un …
(Student A)*, donne-moi un autre … Merci bien.*
Qu'est-ce que c'est? C'est un …
Regardez! Ce sont des …

When this is readily understood, students, in turn, can collect two or three similar objects and ask *Qu'est-ce que c'est?* to produce the answer *Ce sont des …*

SB 12, 1/19, **LISTENING** **SPEAKING**

2 Je pense à quelque chose (Section C)

Now ask the class to look at Section C and note that here all the pictures show groups of things (i.e. they are plural).

Use the pictures for some more oral work, e.g. *Regardez, ce sont des règles. Ce sont des crayons? Non, ce sont des règles. Répétez* etc.

Point out that these words sound the same in the plural as in the singular, although they are preceded by *des* instead of *un* or *une*. Help the class to work out what this word means and also tell them that the plural nouns end with an *s*, but this is usually silent.

Students listen to the recording and write down the number of each thing mentioned, as for Sections A and B.

Solution: 16, 18, 14, 15

Je pense à quelque chose (Section C)

- Je pense à quelque chose. Qu'est-ce que c'est?
- Ce sont des règles?
- Non, ce n'est pas ça.
- Ce sont des crayons?
- Non, ce n'est pas ça.
- Alors, des cahiers, ce sont des cahiers.
- Non, non, ce n'est pas ça. Ce ne sont pas des cahiers.
- Je sais, ce sont des calculettes.
- Oui, c'est ça. Ce sont des calculettes. Très bien! À toi, maintenant!

Students in pairs can now play *Je pense à quelque chose* again, first with just the plural objects, and then (or perhaps later on) using all 16 pictures or extending the choices to other vocabulary they know.

Oui ou non?

For further practice play *Oui ou non?* (perhaps as a team game or in groups). This will also be good for revising numbers and practising plurals. Make a statement about one of the pictures and the next person has to agree or disagree with it, e.g.
– Numéro 3 – c' est un magnétophone. Oui ou non?
– Oui, c'est un magnétophone.

– Numéro 17 – ce sont des calculettes. Oui ou non?
– Non, ce sont des gommes.

AU CHOIX SB 127, 1/20 **LISTENING** **WRITING**

3 Qu'est-ce que c'est?

This activity gives further practice of singular and plural and of *c'est* and *ce sont*. In part **a**, students listen and match the captions with the pictures.

Solution: 1c, 2a, 3d, 4e, 5b, 6g, 7f, 8h

In part **b**, students write sentences about the eight pictures, using the substitution table to help them.

Qu'est-ce que c'est?

1 C'est une boîte.
2 Ce sont des baladeurs.
3 Ce sont des boîtes.
4 Ce sont des enfants.
5 C'est un baladeur.
6 C'est une calculette.
7 C'est un enfant.
8 Ce sont des calculettes.

Area 6
Further activities and consolidation

CM 2/3–2/4
Au choix SB 127, 4
CD 1/21
Écoute et parle, SB 151, 7, 1–8
Student CD 1/8–15

CM 2/3 **SUPPORT**

Mots et images

Some students could do this copymaster while others do the extension task in *Au choix*.

1 C'est quelle image?

Students match captions to pictures. These pictures could be mounted on card and used with those from CM 1/2 – for suggestions for use see TB 50.

Solution: 1C, 2E, 3G, 4F, 5B, 6H, 7D, 8A, 9J, 10I

2 Oui ou non?

Students look at the pictures and answer *Oui* or *Non* to the questions.

Solution: 1 *Oui,* **2** *Non,* **3** *Non,* **4** *Non,* **5** *Oui*

AU CHOIX SB 127, 1/21 **LISTENING EXTENSION**

4 Jean-Pierre a des problèmes

Students first listen straight through to get the gist of the story. They then look at the things which the teacher asks for and listen to the recording, writing down the order in which the objects are asked for (numbering from 1–6).

Finally see if the class can explain why Jean-Pierre has apparently come without a lot of his equipment.

Solution: 1c, 2d, 3f, 4e, 5a, 6b

Jean-Pierre a des problèmes

– Jean-Pierre, donne-moi ton cahier, s'il te plaît.
– Oui, monsieur ... euh ... mon cahier ... mais Monsieur, mon cahier est dans mon cartable.
– Bien. Voici ton cartable. Donne-moi ton cahier de mathématiques.
– Mais monsieur, mon cahier n'est pas ici.
– Ah ... ton cahier n'est pas là. Montre-moi ta calculette alors.
– Ma calculette ... mais monsieur, ma calculette n'est pas dans le cartable.
– Jean-Pierre, c'est la leçon de mathématiques et dans ton cartable, il n'y a pas ton cahier et il n'y a pas ta calculette! Eh bien, regarde bien dans le cartable. Il y a des crayons?
– Oui, monsieur, il y en a deux. Mais monsieur, ...
– Et il y a une gomme?
– Oui, monsieur, il y a une gomme, mais monsieur, ...
– Tais-toi, Jean-Pierre! Il y a une règle?
– Oui, monsieur, il y en a une, mais monsieur, ...
– Et un livre? Il y a un livre de mathématiques?
– Oui, monsieur, ...
– Ah bon – c'est bien, alors!
– Mais non, monsieur, ce n'est pas bien!
– Jean-Pierre, qu'est-ce qu'il y a, alors?
– Monsieur, ça, ce n'est pas mon cartable. Ça, c'est le cartable de Sébastien. Voilà mon cartable et voici mon cahier et ma calculette!!

Qu'est-ce qu'il y a dans la boîte?

SPEAKING

This is a useful game for oral practice of the vocabulary of this unit. See TB 26.

SB 13 **LISTENING**

Vocabulaire de classe

Students could do this task at any time, perhaps for homework or to break up the sessions of *Je pense à quelque chose*.

Begin by saying the commands in order, for repetition, and then in random order for them to spot which number you are saying. Make sure they are able to understand and pronounce these expressions orally before they do the matching task.

Use these commands at odd times to play the game *Jacques a dit* (TB 29) and also as often as possible in everyday classroom routine.

Solution: 1c, 2i, 3e, 4g, 5h, 6f, 7b, 8d, 9a, 10j

SB 13, SB 151, TB 61, SCD 1/14 **LISTENING**

7 Vocabulaire de classe

This listening task in the *Écoute et parle* section is linked with the above task and could be done now or at the end of the unit. In this case, the instructions are recorded in random order.

SB 13, CM 2/4

Sommaire

A summary of the main structures and vocabulary of *Unités 1–2* appears on SB 13 and on CM 2/4 for filing or sticking in to the students' books.

In their first few weeks of French the students have met a lot of new language and at least one lesson towards the end of their first month should be spent just consolidating all this, going over the questions and answers orally and playing games to reinforce both structures and vocabulary (see TB 25–30).

Several ways to add interest to this are:

a a competition, in groups, pairs or individually, to see who can make the most correct statements in French

b getting students to have a first attempt at talking about themselves on tape.

To help with **b**, students can look at the *Sommaire* as a reminder of what they can now say about themselves. Record about four students first and let the class hear them, then record a few more saying the same sort of thing.

The class could play some vocabulary games on the computer, using *Fun with Texts*, update their own vocabulary lists or electronic phrase book (see TB 40) or make further picture-vocabulary posters for the classroom or to put up at home.

SB 151, SCD 1/8–15 INDEPENDENT LISTENING READING

Écoute et parle – Unité 2

1 Les sons français

Solution: é: (a) 1c, 2e, 3a, 4f, 5b, 6d
-ez: (a) 3a, 1b, 5c, 2d, 4e

Les sons français

La lettre é

a 1 détail
2 école
3 écoute
4 éléphant
5 cinéma
6 énorme

b Écosse
écris
télévision
réponds
téléphone

La terminaison -ez

a 1 Parlez
2 Chantez
3 Travaillez
4 Rangez
5 Écrivez

b Répétez
Commencez
Devinez
Tournez

2 Une phrase ridicule

Une phrase ridicule

Un éléphant énorme écrit une encyclopédie en Écosse.

3 C'est anglais ou français?

Solution: (b) 1F, 2A, 3F, 4F, 5A, 6F, 7A, 8F

C'est anglais ou français?

a 1 *concert*, concert
2 *accident*, accident
3 *sport*, sport
4 *biscuit*, biscuit
5 *Jonathan*, Jonathan
6 *Julie*, Julie
7 *jaguar*, jaguar
8 *judo*, judo

b 1 concert
2 *accident*
3 sport
4 biscuit
5 *Jonathan*
6 Julie
7 *jaguar*
8 judo

4 C'est quel nombre?

Solution: 1d 28, **2e** 15, **3a** 20, **4b** 22, **5f** 25, **6c** 14

C'est quel nombre?

1 vingt-huit
2 quinze
3 vingt
4 vingt-deux
5 vingt-cinq
6 quatorze

5 C'est un ou une?

C'est un ou une?

1 un appartement
2 un ordinateur
3 une porte
4 une ville
5 un classeur
6 une maison

6 C'est au pluriel?

Solution: 1b, 2b, 3a, 4b, 5a, 6b

C'est au pluriel?

1 des calculettes
2 des gommes
3 un cahier
4 des livres
5 un sac
6 neuf règles

7 Vocabulaire de classe

Solution: 4, 2, 7, 3, 5, 1, 6, 8

Vocabulaire de classe

Regarde la page 13. Écoute le CD et écris le nombre de chaque instruction dans l'ordre du CD.

Écoutez la cassette.
Ouvrez le livre.
Rangez vos affaires.
Regardez les images.
Comptez.
Asseyez-vous.
Fermez le livre.
Levez-vous.

8 Une conversation

Une conversation

a Écoute les questions et réponds pour Chris.

– Bonjour! Comment t'appelles-tu? (pause)
– Je m'appelle Chris.
– Quel âge as-tu? (pause)
– J'ai douze ans.
– Ça va? (pause)
– Non, pas très bien.
– Où habites-tu? (pause)
– J'habite à Bristol, en Angleterre.
– Tu habites dans une maison ou un appartement? (pause)
– J'habite dans une maison.

b Écoute les questions et réponds pour toi.

– Bonjour! Comment t'appelles-tu?
– (pause)
– Quel âge as-tu?
– (pause)
– Ça va?
– (pause)
– Où habites-tu?
– (pause)
– Tu habites dans une maison ou un appartement?
– (pause)

Encore Tricolore 1
nouvelle édition

unité 3 Chez moi

Areas	Topics	Grammar
1	Talking about the family	Using* 3rd person singular Masculine and feminine articles (D-L SB 15)
2	More about family relationships	Using* *tu as (as-tu), j'ai, je suis*
3	Talking about your family and your possessions	Possessive adjectives (D-L SB 16) *mon, ma, mes, ton, ta, tes*
4	Days of the week	
5	Saying who things belong to	*C'est le/la* (+ noun) *de* (+ name)
6	Describing rooms in the house	
7	Saying where things are	Prepositions – *dans, sur, sous* (SB 19)
8		Singular paradigm of verb *être* (D-L SB 19)
9		Masculine and feminine (D-L SB 20)
10	Further activities and consolidation	

*As a deliberate policy, new grammar is introduced gradually in a unit, sometimes over several areas, before it is explained in a *Dossier-langue*. In the table above, the word 'using' means that the item is introduced. When it is actually explained the *Dossier-langue* page reference is given, e.g. (D-L SB 19).

National Curriculum information

Some students	Level 2
Most students	Levels 1–2
All students	Level 1

Refer also to the information about coverage of 'Knowledge, skills and understanding' (TB 9).

Revision

The vocabulary and structures introduced in *Unités 1–3* are revised in the *Rappel* section following this unit (SB 22–23, TB 75).

Sounds and writing

- e + grave accent (*père* etc.)
- *qu* (*quatre, question* etc.)
- see *Écoute et parle* (SB 152, TB 73)

ICT opportunities

- making labels and vocabulary lists for classroom displays (TB 72)
- using text reconstruction activities (e.g. *Fun with Texts*) (TB 72)

Assessment

- Informal assessment is in the *Épreuves* at the end of this unit (TB 74).
- Formal assessment is in the *Premier contrôle* following *Unité 4* (TB 200).

Students' Book

Unité 3 SB 14–21

Au choix SB 128 1 (TB 66), 2, 3, 4 (TB 70)

Écoute et parle SB 152 (TB 73)

Rappel 1 SB 22–23 (TB 75)

Flashcards

1–2 smiley/sad faces

5–6 house etc.

13–17 rooms

CDs

1/22–34

Student CD 1/16–23

Copymasters

3/1 *Lire, c'est intéressant* [extension: reading strategies] (TB 64)

3/2 *La famille Techno* [speaking: information gap] (TB 66)

3/3 *À la maison* [consolidation: household/family vocab.] (TB 70)

3/4 *Masculin, féminin* [grammar: gender] (TB 72)

3/5 *Jeux de vocabulaire* [consolidation] (TB 73)

3/6 *Sommaire*

3/7 *Épreuve: Écouter* (TB 74)

3/8 *Épreuve: Lire* (TB 75)

3/9 *Épreuve: Écrire et grammaire* (TB 73), (TB 75)

Additional

Grammar in Action 1, page 3

Language content

Talking about the family (Areas 1–3)

Tu as des frères ou des sœurs?

Tu as des grands-parents?

ma famille

J'ai *un père*
une mère
une sœur
deux sœurs
un frère
trois frères
un demi-frère
une demi-sœur
un(e) cousin(e)
un grand-père
une grand-mère
des parents
des grands-parents

Je suis *fils unique*
fille unique
enfant unique
l'ami(e) de …

Il/Elle s'appelle comment?

I/Ellel s'appelle …

Il/Elle a quel âge?

Il/Elle a … ans

Il/Elle habite où?

Il/Elle habite à …

Qui est-ce?

C'est …

Days of the week (Area 4)

Quel jour sommes-nous?

les jours de la semaine

lundi, mardi, mercredi, jeudi, vendredi, samedi, dimanche

Saying who things belong to (Area 5)

C'est l'ordinateur de Guy.

C'est le frère de Dani.

Talking about your home (Area 6)

Dans ma maison, il y a …
la salle à manger
la salle de séjour
le salon
la cuisine
la salle de bains
la chambre
un lit
un téléphone
une console

Saying where things are (Area 7)

dans/sur/sous

Numbers up to 70

0 zéro	*7 sept*	*14 quatorze*	*21 vingt et un*
1 un	*8 huit*	*15 quinze*	*30 trente*
2 deux	*9 neuf*	*16 seize*	*31 trente et un*
3 trois	*10 dix*	*17 dix-sept*	*40 quarante*
4 quatre	*11 onze*	*18 dix-huit*	*50 cinquante*
5 cinq	*12 douze*	*19 dix-neuf*	*60 soixante*
6 six	*13 treize*	*20 vingt*	*70 soixante-dix*

Classroom language and rubrics

Pour vos devoirs …

Copiez vos devoirs.

Faites l'exercice à la page …

C'est pour lundi.

Apprenez le vocabulaire à la page …

C'est pour un contrôle, vendredi.

Lisez «X» à la page …

Notes

Main theme of *Unité 3*

Family relationships and home

On-going features of *Unité 3*

The following are introduced gradually in the course of the unit (see TB 64):

- days of the week
- numbers up to 70
- introduction to reading
- use of reading strategies

On-going features of Unité 3

The following are introduced gradually in the course of the unit:

1 The days of the week
and *Quel jour sommes-nous? Aujourd'hui c'est ...*

Each lesson, ask which day it is and teach the class how to answer. Subsequently the name of the day could be written on the board and *Aujourd'hui c'est ...* added in for active use. The remaining days are added in Area 4 and there are two practice tasks on SB 17.

2 Numbers up to 70

Revise the numbers already taught and gradually add in the numbers up to 70. The number games on TB 25 can be used for regular practice.

CM 3/5 also has a practice task on numbers.

3 Introduction to reading

A number of activities and ideas are suggested for the introduction of reading in the course of the unit.

Students should be confident about the pronunciation of new words and structures before they see them in print, especially in the early weeks of learning French. Give plenty of practice in matching classroom objects, pictures, flashcards etc. to words written on the board or on cards.

Practice can gradually be extended from just nouns to include numbers and adjectives and then the questions and answers learnt so far, e.g. those linked with name, age, how you are, where you live and classroom commands.

Word labels

Students could make some large word labels on the computer and stick them on appropriate objects with Blu-tack. Occasionally when the class is not in the room, change some of these round and see how long it takes the class to spot this. From time to time individual students could also be given the chance to change the cards round.

Classroom commands

Similarly students could build up a list of these to be placed on the classroom wall or design their own posters with suitable sketches, clip art or cartoons to show what the commands involve. New commands can be added as they are learnt and special sections or separate posters could be allocated to, say, *Informatique* or *En classe*.

The message game

If writing is to be introduced, this game can be used. Someone writes one of the commands from the list/posters on a slip of paper and gives it to another student, who silently carries out the command. The others have to guess what was written on the paper or identify it on the poster.

Using recorded text to teach reading

Some suggested strategies:

a Students listen to the recording alone first. They then listen again and follow the printed text.

b Students listen to the recording sentence by sentence and then repeat the sentence either together or individually after the recording.

c Students follow the printed text and listen to the recording. The teacher uses the pause button to stop the recording at unexpected moments and students have to supply the next word in the text.

d Students listen to the complete passage while following the text and then read it aloud individually.

e Students read sentences aloud, without listening to the recording. Some of them could be recorded and these could be played back later and compared with the original recording. (Groups of students could record a sentence each and the class could listen to the recordings and decide whose is most like the original

Écoute et parle (Student CD)

Many of the tasks in this section are designed to help students to link the written or printed word with the sounds of French. See SB 150–159 and, for this unit, TB 73–74.

CM 3/1 **READING**

Lire, c'est intéressant

This copymaster is intended to be used before beginning new work on *Unité 3*, but could be used later for revision. It gives practice in:

- reading words/structures met in *Unités 1–2*
- alphabetical order
- working out the meaning of words to be taught in *Unité 3*.

Solutions:

1 Dans la salle de classe

1b, 2e, 3a, 4i, 5j, 6f, 7g, 8h 9c, 10d

2 Serpent

Ten cognates: *table f* (table), *port m* (port), *appartement m* (appartment/flat), *village m* (village), *France f* (France), *café m* (cafe), *cinéma m* (cinema), *football m* (football), *radio f* (radio), *cousin m* (cousin)

3 Dans l'ordre alphabétique

Liste A	**Liste B**	**Liste C**
Angleterre	cahier	sac
deux	calculette	salle de classe
maison	cinéma	salon
porte	cinq	six
rue	console	sofa
ville	crayon	stylo

4 Tu comprends ces mots?

1f, 2g, 3i, 4j, 5c, 6h, 7e, 8a, 9d, 10b

Area 1
Describing the family
Using 3rd person singular
Masculine and feminine articles
SB 14, 1–3
CD 1/22
il/elle s'appelle (+ name)
il/elle a (+ number) *ans*

La famille

PRESENTATION

Introduce orally the family vocabulary, beginning with some of the words from CM 3/1 if used (*mère, père, famille, fille, garçon, frère, sœur, fils*). For visuals to help with this you could use magazine pictures of famous people, e.g. pop or sporting stars, royal family. Allow time for plenty of repetition and play some vocabulary games (see TB 26).

SB 14, 1/22

LISTENING
READING

1 Ma famille

a Speak about the Laurent family using the photos and introduce the recording, incorporating some of the strategies listed above (**Using recorded text** – TB 64). If suitable equipment is available, students can go on to listen to the recorded text several times, with or without the printed version. The recorded text is exactly the same as in the Students' Book.

Ma famille

1 – Je m'appelle Thomas Laurent et j'ai douze ans. Dans ma famille, il y a cinq personnes: mes parents et trois enfants.
2 – Voici mon frère. Il s'appelle Daniel et il a dix ans.
3 – Voici ma sœur. Elle a quatorze ans.
– Je m'appelle Louise et je suis la sœur de Thomas et de Daniel.
4 – Voici ma mère, Madame Claire Laurent.
5 – Voici mon père, Monsieur Jean-Pierre Laurent.

b Students then copy and complete the Laurent family tree.

Solution:

Le père Jean-Pierre — La mère Claire

- La fille Louise 14 ans
- Le fils Thomas 12 ans
- Le fils Daniel 10 ans

SB 14

READING

2 Qui est-ce?

Students read through the statements and, referring back to the text if necessary, decide who is speaking or described each time.

The activity could be corrected orally.

Solution: **1** *Thomas,* **2** *Louise,* **3** *Daniel,* **4** *M. Laurent,* **5** *Louise,* **6** *Mme Laurent,* **7** *M. Laurent,* **8** *Louise*

SB 14

READING
WRITING

3 La famille Laurent

Students complete the description, orally or in writing, using the words in the box. They should read out the full sentence when correcting this task.

Solution: **1** *père,* **2** *mère,* **3** *famille,* **4** *une,* **5** *fils,* **6** *deux,* **7** *frères,* **8** *sœur*

SB 15

GRAMMAR

Dossier-langue
Masculine and feminine

This short explanation is repeated in the fuller item on gender, on SB 20, but should help to get students used to *le* and *la* which they are already meeting quite frequently.

Area 2
Talking more about family relationships
SB 15, 4–6
Au choix SB 128, 1
CM 3/2
CD 1/23
Tu as (As-tu) des frères ou des sœurs?
J'ai (+ brothers/sisters etc.)
Je suis fille/fils unique

Des frères et des sœurs

PRESENTATION

Tell the class you are going to ask them whether they have any brothers and sisters and ask *Tu as (As-tu) des frères ou des sœurs?* with just *Oui* or *Non* for the answers to begin with.

SB 15

READING

4 Une grande famille

This short cartoon introduces the printed version of the question *Tu as des frères ou des sœurs?* and supplies examples of how to answer it.

Talk the class through the cartoon to check it has been understood, e.g.

Voici une fille. Elle dit, 'Tu as des frères ou des sœurs?' Et voici un garçon. Il répond ...
Regarde les photos. Le garçon dit, 'J'ai quatre sœurs' etc.

Write on the board:
Oui, j'ai ... sœur(s).
Oui, j'ai ... frère(s).

Then ask some of the students to answer more fully the question *Tu as des frères ou des sœurs?*, choosing first those you know to have siblings. Eventually teach orally *Non, je suis fille/fils/enfant unique*. Add this to the list on the board, which should be left there as you go on to the next item.

SB 15, 1/23 LISTENING READING

5 Trois familles

First give the class a few minutes to look at the photos and the text below them.

Add to the list on the board *demi-frère, demi-sœur, grand-père/grand-mère/grands-parents*. Ask the class to repeat these words and work out the meaning.

Go through each of the statements with the class, pointing at the relevant words on the board as you say them, e.g.
Voici Talia. Elle est fille unique. Voici Simon. Il est fils unique. Il habite avec sa grand-mère et son grand-père, avec ses grands-parents.

Voici Alice. Elle a un demi-frère et une demi-sœur.

Now use the recording, and incorporate some of strategies listed above (TB 64).

Solution: 1F, 2F, 3V, 4V, 5F, 6F, 7V, 8V, 9V, 10V

Trois familles

1 – Talia, tu as des frères ou des sœurs?
– Non, je suis fille unique.

2 – Et toi, Simon, as-tu des frères ou des sœurs?
– Non, je suis fils unique
– Et tu habites avec ta grand-mère et ton grand-père. C'est ça?
– Oui, j'habite avec mon père, et mes grands-parents.

3 – Et toi, Alice. Tu es enfant unique aussi?
– Non, non. Dans ma famille, il y a aussi mon demi-frère, David, et ma demi-sœur, Erika. Ils sont fantastiques!

The reading task in part **b** is based on the photos and text above, but with the verbs in the third person. It could be done orally as a class activity or as a written task by more able students, working alone.

Au choix SB 128,  SPEAKING

1 Combien?

This activity gives further practice of question and answer work about families and could be done orally in class with all students or used as an extension activity by more able students who could write the answers.

Students could go on to design various different families for each other, using pencil and paper and stick men or, if they have access to multi-media facilities, they could use computer graphics to design a number of families and then change over, answering questions about each other's families.

Solution:

1 *J'ai deux frères et une sœur.*
2 *J'ai une sœur.*
3 *Je suis enfant unique.*
4 *J'ai quatre frères.*
5 *J'ai un frère et une sœur.*
6 *J'ai trois sœurs.*
7 *J'ai un frère.*
8 *J'ai un frère et deux sœurs.*

SB 15 WRITING

6 À toi!

This can be done at the simplest level, with everyone just writing their own answer and eventually learning the corrected version. (Students could refer to the *Sommaire* for spelling.)

Alternatively, it could be expanded, with students writing a fuller description of their family, perhaps including sketches or photos.

CM 3/2,  SPEAKING WRITING

La famille Techno

This is an information-gap activity, based on a family tree. Students work in pairs, asking questions in turn to complete the ages of the people on their allocated family tree.

Fun with Texts

For extra practice students could use *Fun with Texts* to do a text-reconstruction activity. This could be based on the *famille Laurent*, their own family, the *famille Techno* (CM 3/2) or the *famille Corpuscule* (SB 16).

Area 3
Possessive adjectives
SB 16, 1–3
mon, ma, mes
ton, ta, tes

My and your

PRESENTATION

Begin by teaching *mon* and *ma*, *ton* and *ta* orally, e.g. by picking up classroom objects and saying *Voici mon crayon. Où est ton crayon?/C'est ta gomme, ça? Oui, c'est ma gomme?* etc.

Go round the class 'stealing' possessions from students. When you have assembled a pile of these, ask students *C'est ton crayon/ta gomme/etc?* They can only claim their possessions back by correctly saying *C'est mon crayon* etc.

Gradually extend this type of activity to include some plurals, *tes cahiers, mes livres* etc.

When most students are getting the idea, move on to the explanation on SB 16.

SB 16 GRAMMAR

Dossier-langue
How to say 'my' and 'your'

Get the class to read through the explanation and see if they have worked out the rule and understood it, first by getting one or two of them to explain it to the class, then asking the whole class to work in pairs and explain the rule to each other.

For practice, divide the class in half, one team being 'my' and one 'your'. When you say a French word, perhaps also holding up an object, the members of each team take it in turns to say, e.g. *mon stylo/ta règle/mes affaires* etc. The teams should take it in turns to answer first and the winner is the first to get, say, 20 points for correct answers.

SB16 **GRAMMAR**

1 La famille Corpuscule

Talk about this unusual family, using the illustrations and getting students to repeat the names of the family, preferably in short sentences, e.g.
Voici la famille Corpuscule. C'est une famille de Vampires.
Voici le père. Il s'appelle Tombô. Voici la mère. Elle s'appelle Draculine etc.

Then move on to the task which involves supplying the correct possessive adjective.
Voici Désastre. Il présente sa famille. Complète la description pour Désastre.

The missing possessive adjectives can then be supplied orally or as a written task.

Solution: **1** *Ma*, **2** *mes*, **3** *Mon*, **4** *Ma*, **5** *Mon*, **6** *Ma*, **7** *mes, mes*

SB 16 **GRAMMAR**

2 Des questions utiles

Students supply the correct adjective: *ton*, *ta* or *tes*.

This could be an oral exercise or the answers could be written and checked orally.

Solution: **1** *Ton*, **2** *Ta*, **3** *Tes*, **4** *Ton*, **5** *ton*, **6** *Ton*, **7** *ta*, **8** *tes*

SB 16 **GRAMMAR**

3 Tu as tes affaires?

Further practice of the two possessive adjectives. Draw students' attention to the colour-coding (masculine objects in blue and feminine ones in red).

Students could do this task orally in pairs changing over roles half way through. More able students could then write the answers as consolidation (just possessives + noun).

Solution:

1. *ta trousse – ma trousse*
2. *ta règle – ma règle*
3. *ton livre – mon livre*
4. *tes cahiers – mes cahiers*
5. *tes crayons – mes crayons*
6. *ton ordinateur – mon ordinateur*
7. *ton stylo – mon stylo*
8. *ta gomme – ma gomme*
9. *ton classeur – mon classeur*
10. *ton sac – mon sac*

Area 4
Days of the week

SB 17, 4–5
CD 1/24–25
Quel jour sommes-nous?

Days **PRESENTATION**

By now most of the days will have been introduced, so begin by revising these and teaching any not yet encountered.

Students might be interested in the names of the days and their Latin origins. If told that *dies* is the Latin for day, they will probably find it easy to spot the link with *di*, appearing as a prefix or suffix in all the French words for the days.

SB 17, 1/24 **LISTENING** **WRITING**

4 La semaine

This is a very simple task to link the spoken and written forms. Students listen to the recording and make a list of the days. The words are recorded in the correct order and the written form is supplied in the box.

La semaine

lundi, mardi, mercredi, jeudi
vendredi, samedi, dimanche

SB 17, 1/25 **LISTENING**

5 Quel jour sommes-nous?

This time students hear the question *Quel jour sommes-nous?* and write down the correct letter to indicate the answers.

Solution: **1e, 2a, 3b, 4f, 5d, 6e, 7g, 8c**

Quel jour sommes-nous?

1 – Quel jour sommes-nous?
– C'est jeudi.

2 – Quel jour sommes-nous?
– C'est lundi.

3 – Quel jour sommes-nous?
– C'est samedi aujourd'hui.

4 – Quel jour sommes-nous?
– Aujourd'hui, c'est mercredi.

5 – Quel jour sommes-nous?
– C'est vendredi aujourd'hui.

6 – Quel jour sommes-nous?
– Je pense que c'est jeudi. Oui, c'est ça. C'est jeudi.

7 – Quel jour sommes-nous?
– Aujourd'hui? Euh, ah oui, c'est mardi.

8 – Quel jour sommes-nous?
– Aujourd'hui, c'est dimanche! Fantastique, non!

Area 5
Saying who things belong to

SB 17, 6

C'est le/la (+ noun) *de* (+ name)

C'est le/la ... de ... PRESENTATION

Introduce this structure by going round the classroom and picking up objects, saying, e.g.
Voici la règle de Martin, et ça, qu'est-ce que c'est?
C'est le stylo de Linda.
C'est le crayon de David. Vrai ou faux?

Use some games for practice, e.g

1 Put a few of the objects in a box. Take one out and hold it behind your back. The students have to guess what it is and who it belongs to, e.g. *C'est la règle de Chantal?*
2 **Je touche ...** (See TB 26.)
3 **Je pense à quelque chose**, played as usual, but with each person guessing using the construction *C'est le livre de Caroline* etc. (See TB 26.)
The choice of objects could be limited in order to stop one person's turn from going on interminably.

SB 17 **GRAMMAR**

!

This new structure is presented in a box as a reminder.

SB 17 **READING**

Dani

Give the class time to read through the cartoon strip and work out the story. Then ask them some questions, on similar lines to those in the exercise which follows, e.g. *Regardez le baladeur. C'est le baladeur de Dani? Non? C'est le baladeur de son frère? Oui, c'est ça.*

SB 17 **PRACTICE**

6 Dani et son frère

Students can now do this task, writing down which is the true statement in each pair. The task can be corrected orally, with students reading out the full sentence each time, e.g.
*Regardez **a**. C'est le baladeur de Dani? Oui? Non?*

*Et regardez **b**. C'est le baladeur de son frère. C'est vrai? Oui, c'est vrai.*

Solution: 1b, 2b, 3b, 4b, 5a, 6b

Area 6
Describing rooms in the house

SB 18, 1–3
FC 5–6, 13–17, 20
CD 1/26–27

Où est?
Qu'est-ce qu'il y a?
il y a ...

FC 5–6, 13–17 **PRESENTATION**

On parle de la maison

Using the flashcards of the house and flat, revise:
Tu habites où?
J'habite ...

Qu'est-ce que c'est?
C'est une maison/un appartement.

Then present and practise the names of the rooms in the house by question and answer work using the flashcards.

For practice, any of the flashcard games could be played (TB 27). A useful one here is 'Guess which room it is' or 'Guess which room it isn't', e.g.

– *Ce n'est pas la cuisine?*
– *Vrai.*
– *Ce n'est pas la salle à manger?*
– *Faux, c'est la salle à manger. Regarde!*

Gradually expand this to include the word *pièce* and objects or items of furniture which appear in the rooms., e.g. revise *table, chaise, télévision, radio, ordinateur, lecteur de CDs, magnétophone* and add *lit, téléphone, console*.

SB 18, 1/26, FC 20 **SPEAKING READING LISTENING**

1 La maison de la famille Laurent

First get the class to look at the plan of the house and talk briefly about the rooms, e.g.

La salle à manger, c'est numéro ...?
Numéro 1, c'est quelle pièce? C'est le salon.
Et voici la cuisine. Regardez. Dans la cuisine il y a une radio etc.

Use flashcard 20 to teach *le chat*.

1 As the class listens to the recording, hold up cards for the correct rooms as they are mentioned, pointing to rooms on the plan and to items of furniture etc. either on the flashcards or on the plan.
2 Using the recording and Students' Book texts together, incorporate some of the strategies listed above (**Using recorded text**, TB 64).
3 Ask questions about the plan, introducing *Qu'est-ce qu'il y a?* and *Il y a ...* and gradually train the class to answer and then ask each other these, e.g.
a – *C'est le salon?*
– *Oui, c'est le salon./Non, c'est la salle à manger.*
b – *Il y a une table/une radio/un lit dans la salle à*

manger/la cuisine/la chambre de Louise? Oui ou non?

c – *Où est le lecteur de CDs/l'ordinateur?*
– *Dans la chambre de Louise/de Thomas et Daniel etc.*

d – *Qu'est-ce qu'il y a dans la chambre de Louise?*
– *Dans la chambre de Louise, il y a un lit, un chat et un lecteur de CDs.*

4 Finally play the recording again and this time let the class listen without the printed text.

La maison de la famille Laurent

Voici notre maison et notre jardin.
Dans la maison, il y a sept pièces: le salon, la salle à manger, la cuisine, la salle de bains et trois chambres.
Dans la chambre de mes parents il y a un lit et un magnétophone.
Dans la chambre de mes frères, il y a deux lits et une console.
Il y a une télévision dans le salon et aussi dans les chambres de mes parents et de mes frères.
Il y a aussi un téléphone dans la chambre de Maman et Papa.
Dans la salle à manger, il y a une table et cinq chaises.
Dans la cuisine, il y a une radio et un téléphone.
Dans ma chambre, il y a mon lecteur de CDs, mon ordinateur – et, regardez, sur mon lit, il y a mon chat, Mimi!

SB 18, 1/27 **LISTENING**

2 C'est quelle pièce?

This is a listening task based on the plan of the house but this time with no supporting printed text. Teach *ici*, if not already known.

Solution:

1 5 *(la chambre de T et de D)*
2 7 *(la chambre de L)*
3 4 *(La chambre de M. et Mme L)*
4 1 *(le salon)* or 5 *(la chambre de T et de D)*
5 7 *(la chambre de L)*
6 3 *(la cuisine)*
7 5 *(la chambre de T et de D)*
8 1 *(le salon)* or 4 *(La chambre de M. et Mme L)*
9 2 *(la salle à manger)*

C'est quelle pièce?

Exemple:
1 Thomas: Il y a deux lits dans notre chambre. Tu écris 5.

1 Thomas: Il y a deux lits dans notre chambre.
2 Louise: Regarde mon chat sur le lit!
3 Mme L: Voici le téléphone, et il y a aussi un magnétophone à cassettes et une télévision.
4 Mme L: Il y a une télévision dans cette pièce aussi.
5 Louise: J'écoute des CDs ici – voici le lecteur de CDs.
6 Mme L: Il y a une radio ici, et moi, j'écoute la radio.
7 Thomas: Et voici notre ordinateur – c'est fantastique!
8 Thomas: Où est mon frère? Il n'est pas dans notre chambre. Ah oui, il est ici – il regarde la télévision.
9 Mme L: Il y a une table et cinq chaises dans la pièce.

SB 18 **READING**

3 Les pièces

This is a straightforward reading task, matching two halves of each sentence. Correct it orally, to give practice in reading out the complete sentences.

Solution: 1b, 2i, 3g, 4h, 5e, 6a, 7d, 8c, 9f 10j

Area 7
Prepositions – *dans, sur, sous*
SB 19, 4–5
CM 3/3
Au choix SB 128, 2–4
CD 1/28–29

Où est ...? **PRESENTATION**

There are a variety of ways to teach and practise these three prepositions, e.g. with classroom objects, piling them up, putting them in, on or under things and asking questions beginning with *Où est ...?* At first supply the answers too, then get the class to answer. Eventually students can ask and answer similar questions. The small diagram on SB 19 serves as a reminder of the meaning of the three words.

Several oral games will be useful for practising these prepositions, e.g. *Qu'est-ce qu'il y a dans la boîte?* (see TB 26).

SB 19, 1/28 **READING** **LISTENING**

4 Notre chambre

Students look at the picture of the boys' room and could talk about it briefly with the teacher. They then listen to Thomas describing the room and guess which is his side.

After this first hearing, go through the whole item more thoroughly using the printed text. Use listening and reading strategies as appropriate (see TB 64).

Ask questions about the picture, e.g. *Où sont les livres de Thomas?/Où est le lit de Daniel? – Voici/Voilà ... Où est le sac à dos?/Qu'est-ce qu'il y a dans la trousse?* etc.

Notre chambre

Je suis Thomas Laurent, et Daniel est mon petit frère.
Voici notre chambre et voici notre console, avec les jeux électroniques et les manettes.

Voici mes affaires. Mes livres sont sur la table, et mes crayons sont dans la boîte. Mon stylo est sur le cahier et mes classeurs sont sous la table. Et voici mon baladeur.

Mais voici les affaires de mon frère Daniel.

Où est le sac à dos? Ah oui, il est sur le lit! Dans le sac, il y a une règle et des livres. Et qu'est-ce qu'il y a sous le lit? Voilà! Le baladeur de Daniel est sous le lit. Et voici la trousse de Daniel – elle est sur la chaise. Et qu'est-ce qu'il y a dans la trousse? Regardez! Il y a une gomme dans la trousse, mais les crayons et le stylo sont sous la chaise!

SB 19 **READING WRITING**

5 Dans la chambre

Students just have to supply the word *sur*, *sous* or *dans* to complete these sentences. Most are given in the text, but one or two have to be discovered through the picture of the bedroom. The answers should be checked orally afterwards, with students reading aloud each completed sentence in full.

Solution: **1** *dans,* **2** *sur,* **3** *dans,* **4** *sur,* **5** *dans, sur,* **6** *dans,* **7** *sous,* **8** *sur*

More questions and answers on the same lines could be used to consolidate the new vocabulary and should also serve to introduce students to the use of the pronouns *il* and *elle*.

Follow-up

CONSOLIDATION

The following copymaster and *Au choix* activities present a selection of differentiated activities which could be used here to consolidate work on rooms in the house, prepositions and expressing possession.

CM 3/3 **READING WRITING**

À la maison

This is a non-expendable support worksheet which serves as useful consolidation for both household vocabulary and prepositions. It is suitable for all.

Solutions:

1 Mots et images

a *la chambre des parents* **b** *la salle de bains*
c *la chambre des enfants* **d** *la cuisine*
e *le salon* **f** *la salle à manger*

2 C'est quelle pièce?

1a, 2d, 3f, 4e, 5c, 6c

3 C'est quel mot?

1 *sur,* **2** *sur,* **3** *dans,* **4** *sur une chaise*

AU CHOIX SB 128, 1/29 **LISTENING WRITING**

2 La maison de la famille Lambert

This task is suitable for most students. Students listen to the recording and complete the text. This could be done as an oral exercise with students of lower ability.

Solution: **1** *maison,* **2** *chaises,* **3** *table,* **4** *salle à manger,* **5** *salon,* **6** *la télévision,* **7** *un,* **8** *les,* **9** *la,* **10** *de*

La maison de la famille Lambert

Voici la maison et le jardin de la famille Lambert.
Dans la cuisine, il y a trois chaises et une table.
Mme Lambert est dans la salle à manger.
Anne-Marie Lambert est dans le salon. Elle regarde la télévision.
Dans la chambre de Christophe Lambert, il y a un lit et aussi les affaires de Christophe.
Voici la salle de bains.

AU CHOIX SB 128 **WRITING**

3 Où est l'ordinateur?

This task is suitable for more able students.

Solution:

L'ordinateur est dans la cuisine.
La table est dans la chambre.
Le lit est dans le salon.
La chaise est sous le lit.
Le sac à dos est sur le lit
La télé avec les manettes est dans la salle de bains.

AU CHOIX SB 128 **WRITING**

4 Jeu de mémoire

This task could be done now or later for consolidation. It brings together work on the rooms of the house and also revises possession. Students study the pictures on SB 18–19 before trying to identify the objects, using the substitution table to help them give the answers.

Draw attention to the table and also use the example to check that everyone knows what to do. The task could be done in writing and checked back orally.

Solution:

1 *C'est la radio de la famille Laurent.*
2 *C'est le lit de Thomas.*
3 *C'est le stylo de Daniel.*
4 *C'est la trousse de Daniel.*
5 *C'est le baladeur de Thomas.*
6 *C'est le chat de Louise.*
7 *C'est le sac à dos de Daniel.*
8 *C'est le lecteur de CDs de Louise.*

Optionally, this task could be followed by more oral questions about the objects shown, practising *C'est le* (+ noun) *de* (+ name).

Some students may be able to cope with the alternative structure *C'est à qui? C'est à* (+ name) – see *Grammaire 3.3* (SB 161). This could be done first with the teacher asking questions, then with some students making up similar questions about the objects shown or about things in the classroom, e.g.

– *Le baladeur, c'est à Louise?*
– *Non.*

- *C'est à qui?*
- *C'est à Simon.*
- *Et ce cahier, c'est à James?*
- *Oui.*
- *Ah oui, c'est le cahier de James* etc.

Area 8
The singular paradigm of the verb *être*
SB 19, 6
CD 1/30
FC 13–17

FC 13–17 PRESENTATION SPEAKING

Être

As all parts of the singular of *être* have occurred naturally in the text of this unit, this seems an appropriate place to provide some explanation and practice, although the full paradigm will be taught and practised in *Unité 5*.

A good way to provide some oral practice, linked with the present topic, would be to use the flashcards for the rooms, giving them to students and asking questions, e.g.
- *Où es-tu?*
- *Je suis ...*
- *Où est Richard? Il est dans la cuisine?*
- *Non, il est dans la salle à manger* etc.

SB 19, 1/30 LISTENING READING SPEAKING

6 Samedi

Students look at the pictures, then listen to the recording with the text.

Next, go through the text with the class, commenting on where everyone is and asking questions such as *Où est Louise? Ah, voilà, elle est dans sa chambre* etc.

Finally, students could read the conversation aloud in groups of four, perhaps recording some of them.

Samedi

- Où est Louise? Je pense qu'elle est dans sa chambre. Louise, tu es dans ta chambre?
- Oui, Maman. Je suis ici. J'écoute des CDs.
- Et Thomas? Il est dans sa chambre aussi?
- Je suis dans le salon. Je regarde la télé.
- Très bien. Mais où est Daniel? Daniel, tu es dans ta chambre?
- Oui, Maman, je suis dans ma chambre. Je range mes affaires.
- Tu ranges tes affaires!!
- Oui, Maman. C'est bien, non? ... Maman, il y a le carnaval en ville, et moi, j'adore les carnavals ...!

SB 19 GRAMMAR

Dossier-langue
Être – to be

Go through this brief explanation with the class and get them to complete the singular paradigm, finding the words in the conversation above (Task 6).

Area 9
Gender
SB 20, 1–2
CM 3/4
Grammar in Action 1, page 3

C'est un/une ... PRESENTATION

Begin with brief oral work asking about classroom objects etc., e.g. *Qu'est-ce que c'est? C'est une gomme. C'est masculin ou féminin?*

SB 20 GRAMMAR

1 Masculin ou féminin?

Draw the class's attention to the words in the box and make the point that words other than the definite and indefinite article show if a noun is masculine or feminine.

Students then work on writing the two lists of nouns, showing their gender and their meaning.

Solution:

masculin		*féminin*	
français	***anglais***	***français***	***anglais***
un livre	a book	*ta gomme*	your rubber
un crayon	a pencil	*ma calculette*	my calculator
ton ami	your friend	*ta chaise*	your chair
un ordinateur	a computer	*l'amie*	the (girl)friend
le cartable	the satchel	*une table*	a table
le baladeur	the personal stereo		
mon grand-père	my grandfather		

SB 20 GRAMMAR

Dossier-langue
Masculine and feminine

By now students have met all the articles and several possessive adjectives and pronouns, so this item really serves as a reference table bringing the main examples together.

The table ...
- sets out more fully the link between *un* and *le/une* and *la* (already mentioned on SB 12)
- includes *l'* +vowel
- mentions the use of the pronouns *il* and *elle* to mean 'it'
- explains that gender applies to things as well as people in French.

If some students are not too clear about any of these points, give them more examples, either now or before using the explanation, e.g.

Voici un stylo. (Write *un stylo* on the board.)

C'est le stylo de Vivienne, oui? (Write *le stylo* under *un stylo*.)

Put the pen in a box, or any other suitable place.

Bon, le stylo de Vivienne est dans la boîte. Il est dans la boîte. (Write *il* under *le*.)

Coloured chalks or pens could be used to highlight masculine and feminine words.

Continue in the same way using feminine objects and with words beginning with a vowel, so that students can see the pattern.

SB 20 — READING, GRAMMAR PRACTICE

2 Où est?

This task involves matching the correct pronoun (*il* or *elle*) with a masculine or feminine noun.

Solution: 1c, 2a, 3d, 4b, 5f, 6e

Un/Une

As follow-up, play this game to practise gender discrimination.

Half the class is the masculine team and half the feminine. The teacher asks a member of each team in turn *Est-ce que tu as* (+ object)? or *Tu as* (+ object)?

The first team must only answer *Oui, j'ai* (+ object) to masculine nouns and the other team to feminine nouns, otherwise remaining silent. The team loses a point if they make a mistake. When one team has lost five points the other has won.

CM 3/4 — GRAMMAR PRACTICE

Masculin, féminin

This gives practice of gender and is suitable for all.

There is a built-in incline of difficulty, so less able students may need help with Tasks 3 and 4.

Solutions:

1 Les mots féminins

The following should be underlined: *la famille, la cuisine, une demi-sœur, la chambre, la mère, la télévision, la radio, la grand-mère, une règle*

2 5-4-3-2-1

5 *un frère, une demi-sœur, le père, la mère, la grand-mère*
4 *la télévision, un ordinateur, un magnétophone, la radio*
3 *la cuisine, la chambre, le salon*
2 *vendredi, dimanche*
1 *un cinéma*

3 Dans l'ordre alphabétique

5 mots masculins	**5 mots féminins**
l'animal	*la ferme*
le jardin	*la grand-mère*
le lecteur de CDs	*la maison*
l'ordinateur	*la rue*
le sac	*la sœur*

4 Les blancs

This is an open-ended task.

GRAMMAR IN ACTION 1, PAGE 3 — CONSOLIDATION

Masculine and feminine

This provides consolidation of the work on gender and could be done now, for homework or extra practice, or used later for revision.

Area 10
Further activities and consolidation
SB 20, 3, SB 21
CM 3/5–3/9
Écoute et parle SB 152, 7, 1–8
Student CD 1/16–23
CD 1/31–34

SB 20, — WRITING

3 À toi

This is an open-ended writing activity, with some help given. Students of lower ability will need more guidance, but the task should be a good opportunity for the more able to show what they can do.

This is also a good chance to work on a computer using, e.g. the house description text reconstruction activity from *Fun with Texts*.

This could be based on the text from *La maison de la famille Laurent* (SB 18) or *Notre chambre* (SB 19). This text could provide a model for the students' own work. Suitable *Fun with Texts* options would be: Text salad, Scrambler or Copywrite.

Invente des phrases

For more practice in sentence construction, students could use a grid similar to the one below. The addition of clip art images (by teacher or students) is a good way to make this exercise meaningful rather than just random phrases.

J'ai	un ordinateur.		sur	la table.
	une radio.			le lit.
	un baladeur.	Il est		la chaise.
Voici	un chat.		sous	mon sac.
	le cartable de Daniel?	Elle est		ma chambre.
	l'ami de Thomas?			le salon.
Où est	la maison de Louise?		dans	la rue.

SB 21

Vocabulaire de classe

Students match up the French and English instructions as usual and should add the words to their vocabulary lists and electronic phrase book (see TB 40).

Solution: 1c, 2e, 3b, 4h, 5f, 6g, 7a, 8d

SB 152, TB 74, SCD 1/22 — LISTENING

7 Vocabulaire de classe

This task in *Écoute et parle* is linked to the above task and could be done now or later for revision.

CM 3/5 **SUPPORT**

Jeux de vocabulaire

This sheet gives practice of numbers, class instructions and some key questions and answers.

Solutions:

1 Les numéros

a *vingt-huit,* **b** *soixante-deux,* **c** *quarante-quatre,* **d** *quatorze,* **e** *cinquante,* **f** *trente-cinq*

2 En classe

1d, 2g, 3e, 4b, 5a, 6f, 7c

3 Les contraires

1d, 2a, 3c, 4e, 5f, 6b

4 Questions et réponses

1b, 2d, 3e, 4a, 5c

SB 21, CM 3/6

Sommaire

As usual, this page is also on copymaster for filing or sticking in students' exercise books.

SB 152, SCD 1/16–23 INDEPENDENT LISTENING

Écoute et parle – Unité 3

1 Les sons français

Solution: **è: (a) 1c, 2b, 3d, 4a**
qu: (a) 1d, 2a, 3c, 4e, 5b

Les sons français

La lettre è

a 1 lève-toi
2 mère
3 près
4 frère

b père
très
après
chère

Les lettres qu

a 1 quarante
2 quel
3 que
4 qu'est-ce que c'est?
5 qui

b quelle
quand
quatre
question
quatorze

2 Des phrases ridicules

Des phrases ridicules

Mon père et ma mère préfèrent les desserts de mon frère.

Quelles sont les quinze questions que Quasimodo pose aux quiches?

3 C'est quel mot?

Solution: **1b, 2b, 3a, 4a, 5b, 6a**

C'est quel mot?

1 je, j'ai, j'ai
2 j'ai, j'aime, j'aime
3 je, j'aime, je
4 trois, toi, trois
5 la, pas, pas
6 fils, fille, fils

4 C'est anglais ou français?

Solution: **(b) 1F, 2A, 3F, 4F, 5A, 6F, 7A, 8F**

C'est anglais ou français?

a 1 *conversation,* conversation
2 *nation,* nation
3 *instruction,* instruction
4 *description,* description

5 *rat,* rat
6 *Robert,* Robert
7 *restaurant,* restaurant
8 *rare,* rare

b 1 conversation
2 *nation*
3 instruction
4 description

5 *rat*
6 Robert
7 *restaurant*
8 rare

5 C'est quel nombre?

Solution: **1a** 30, **2a** 60, **3b** 31, **4b** 70, **5a** 59, **6b** 13

C'est quel nombre?

1 trente
2 soixante
3 trente et un
4 soixante-dix
5 cinquante-neuf
6 treize

6 Et après?

Solution: **1** *mercredi,* **2** *vendredi,* **3** *dimanche,* **4** *mardi,* **5** *jeudi,* **6** *samedi*

Et après?

1 mardi
2 jeudi
3 samedi
4 lundi
5 mercredi
6 vendredi

7 Vocabulaire de classe

Solution: 7, 5, 8, 6, 2, 4, 1, 3

Vocabulaire de classe

Regarde la page 21. Écoute le CD et écris le nombre de chaque instruction dans l'ordre du CD.

C'est pour un contrôle, vendredi.

C'est pour lundi.

Lisez «X» à la page trente.

Apprenez le vocabulaire à la page vingt-cinq.

Copiez vos devoirs.

Faites l'exercice à la page vingt.

Pour vos devoirs …

Écoutez la cassette.

8 Une conversation

Une conversation

a Écoute les questions et réponds pour Dominic.

– Bonjour! Où habites-tu? (pause)
– J'habite à Aberdeen, en Écosse.
– Tu as des frères ou des sœurs? (pause)
– Oui, j'ai un frère et une sœur.
– Ton frère, comment s'appelle-t-il? (pause)
– Il s'appelle Duncan.
– Quel âge a-t-il? (pause)
– Il a huit ans.
– Ta sœur, comment s'appelle-t-elle? (pause)
– Elle s'appelle Lucie.
– Quel âge a-t-elle? (pause)
– Elle a trois ans.

b Écoute les questions et réponds pour toi.

– Bonjour! Où habites-tu?
– (pause)
– Tu as des frères ou des sœurs?
– (pause)

Épreuve – Unités 1–3

These worksheets can be used for an informal test of listening, reading and writing or for extra practice, as required.

For general notes on the *Épreuves*, see TB 20.

CM 3/7, 1/31–34 **INFORMAL ASSESSMENT LISTENING**

Épreuve: Écouter

As the first item of each task is given as an example, each task is effectively out of 5, giving a total of 20 marks for the listening test.

A Des affaires scolaires (NC 1)

Solution: 1b, 2f, 3e, 4d, 5a, 6c (mark /5)

Des affaires scolaires

Voici des affaires scolaires:
1 Regarde la trousse – c'est ma trousse.
2 Et voici un cartable. C'est le cartable de Suzanne.
3 Et où sont les cahiers? Ah oui, voici les cahiers.
4 Voici une console. C'est ma console.
5 Et voilà mes crayons. Il y a douze crayons.
6 Et où est ma règle? Ah oui, voici ma règle!

B C'est moi! (NC 2)

Solution: boxes ticked as follows: **1** *Sophie*, **2** *12 ans*, **3** alone, **4** house, **5** bedroom with walkman in it, **6** Mum in dining room (mark /5)

C'est moi!

1 Salut! Je m'appelle Sophie.
2 J'ai douze ans.
3 Je suis enfant unique.
4 J'habite dans une maison.
5 Voici ma chambre et voici mon baladeur.
6 Et voici ma mère dans la salle à manger.

C C'est quelle phrase? (NC 2)

Solution: 1a, 2a, 3b, 4b, 5b, 6b (mark /5)

C'est quelle phrase?

Exemple: 1a

1a Voici Michel avec ses deux sœurs.
b Voici Michel avec ses deux frères.
2a Voici Marie avec son demi-frère.
b Voici Marie avec sa demi-sœur.
3a Il y a un cahier sur la table.
b Il y a un cahier sous la table.
4a Voici une photo de mes grands-parents avec ma sœur et moi.
b Voici une photo de mon grand-père avec ma sœur et moi.
5a Voici une ville. Elle est près de Paris.
b Voici un village. Il est près de Calais.
6a Dans la cuisine, il y a une table et trois chaises. Il y a aussi une radio.
b Dans la cuisine, il y a une petite table et deux chaises. Il y a aussi un téléphone.

D Je pense à quelque chose (NC 3)

Solution: **1b, 2e, 3a, 4c, 5f, 6d** (mark /5)

Je pense à quelque chose

– Je pense à quelque chose. Qu'est-ce que c'est?
– C'est un crayon?
– Non, ce n'est pas ça.
– Ce sont des gommes?
– Non, non. Ce n'est pas ça.
– Je sais, je sais – c'est une calculette.
– Non, ce n'est pas une calculette.
– Ce sont des livres?
– Des livres? Non, ce n'est pas ça.
– Zut ... qu'est-ce que c'est, alors? C'est une règle – c'est correct?
– Non, non. Ce n'est pas correct.
– Alors, c'est un baladeur?
– Oui, fantastique! C'est un baladeur!

CM 3/8 **READING**

Épreuve: Lire

There are three reading tests, effectively out of 6, 7 and 7, giving a total of 20 marks.

A Notre maison (NC 1)

Solution: **1g, 2e, 3d, 4f, 5b, 6a, 7c** (mark /6)

B C'est quelle image? (NC 2)

Solution: **1f, 2d, 3a, 4g, 5e, 6c, 7b, 8h** (mark /7)

C Le télé-quiz (NC 3)

Solution: **1V, 2V, 3F, 4V, 5F, 6V, 7V, 8V** (mark /7)

CM 3/9 **WRITING GRAMMAR**

Épreuve: Écrire et grammaire

There are three writing and grammar tests, effectively out of 6, 6 and 8, giving a total of 20 marks.

A Les mots corrects (NC 1)

Solution: **1** *une maison*, **2** *une ville*, **3** *un village*, **4** *La France*, **5** *une porte*, **6** *des cahiers*, **7** *des livres* (mark /6)

B Les images et les descriptions (NC 2)

Solution:

1e *Voici une fille.*
2b *Voici un garçon.*
3f *Les crayons sont dans la trousse.*
4g *Le livre est sur la table.*
5a *Voici un ordinateur.*
6c *La famille Lebrun.*
7d *La calculette est sous la boîte.* (mark /6)

C Une lettre de Martin (NC 3)

Solution: **1** *suis* (or *m'appelle*), **2** *j'ai*, **3** *J'ai*, **4** *Mon*, **5** *ma*, **6** *as*, **7** *es*, **8** *Mes*, **9** *ta* (mark /8)

SB 22–23 **CONSOLIDATION READING WRITING**

Rappel 1

This section can be used at any point after *Unité 3* for revision and consolidation. It provides reading and writing activities which are self-instructional and can be used by students working indiviudally for homework or during cover lessons.

1 Deux conversations

Solution:

1 – *Bonjour Marc.*
– *Bonjour Suzanne, ça va?*
– *Oui, ça va bien, merci, et toi?*
– *Ça va, merci.*

2 – *Bonjour Lucie*
– *Bonjour David, ça va?*
– *Oui, ça va bien, merci, et toi?*
– *Non, pas très bien. Au revoir David.*
– *Au revoir, Lucie.*

2 Masculin, féminin

Solution:

masculin		féminin	
frère	*mon*	*elle*	*mère*
garçon	*père*	*fille*	*sœur*
il	*ton*	*la*	*ta*
le	*un*	*ma*	*une*

3 Un multi-quiz

Solution: **En France: 1c, 2b, 3a**
Au collège: 4a, 5b, 6c
En famille: 7c, 8c

4 Le jeu des images

Solution: **1b, 2a, 3d, 4i, 5e, 6c, 7f, 8g, 9h, 10j**

5 Des descriptions

This task requires production of vocabulary involving some knowledge of gender and number.

Solution:

1 *une table, une chaise et un livre*
2 *des maisons et un cinéma*
3 *famille, fille, garçons, parents (adultes). La, ans*

6 Les petits mots

This task requires production of articles and possessive adjectives.

Solution: **a 1** *une*, **2** *une*, **3** *ton*, **4** *ta*, **5** *le*, **6** *ton*
b 7 *ma*, **8** *mon*, **9** *ma*, **10** *mon*, **11** *le*

7 Questions et réponses

This is a predominantly open-ended task testing key language from Unités 1–3.

Solution: **1–5** open-ended, **6** *sur la table*, **7** *sous la table*, **8** *sur le livre*, **9** *une maison*, **10** *Oui, c'est le chat de Louise.*

Encore Tricolore 1
nouvelle édition

unité 4 Les animaux

Areas	Topics	Grammar
1	Talking about animals and pets	
2	Describing animals and other things Colours Spelling names	Adjectives (masculine and feminine singular) (D-L SB 25)
3	Asking questions	Using *Est-ce que …?* and other question forms (D-L SB 26)
4		Using the singular paradigm of *avoir* (D-L SB 27)
5	Expressing likes and dislikes	
6		Using *tu* and *vous* (D-L SB 29)
7	Further activities and consolidation	

National Curriculum information

Some students	Levels 2–3
Most students	Level 2
All students	Levels 1–2

Refer also to the information about coverage of 'Knowledge, skills and understanding' (TB 9).

Revision

The vocabulary and structures introduced in *Unités 4–5* are revised in the *Rappel* section following *Unité 5* (SB 48–49, TB 109).

Presse-Jeunesse 1 provides opportunities for reading for pleasure (SB 32–33, TB 91).

Sounds and writing

- *h*, *r*, spotting regular spelling patterns
- using the French alphabet
- spelling names etc. in French
- reading and hearing rhymes – *Presse-Jeunesse* (SB 33)
- see *Écoute et parle* (SB 153, TB 89–90)

ICT opportunities

- beginning a file of personal information (TB 86)
- naming the main parts of a computer (TB 88)

Reading strategies

Using clues to interpret meaning (CM 103)

Assessment

- Informal assessment is in the *Épreuves* at the end of this unit (TB 90).
- Formal assessment is in the *Premier contrôle* at the end of this unit (see TB 200).

Students' Book

Unité 4 SB 24–31

Au choix SB 129 1 (TB 80), 2 (TB 81), 3 (TB 82) SB 130 4 (TB 83), 5 (TB 84), 6 (TB 86)

Écoute et parle SB 153 (TB 89)

Presse-Jeunesse 1 SB 32–33 (TB 91)

Flashcards

1	smiley face
2	sad face
18–26	animals

Additional

Grammar in Action 1, pages 4–7

CDs

1/35–49

Student CD 1/24–30

Student CD 2/22–24

Copymasters

4/1	*Les animaux* [mini-flashcards/support] (TB 79)
4/2	*Les animaux de mes amis* [extension: vocabulary practice/dictionary work] (TB 81)
4/3	*Questions et réponses* [speaking/writing] (TB 87)
4/4	*À l'ordinateur* [ICT] (TB 88)
4/5	*C'est moi!* [support] (TB 86)
4/6	*Tu comprends?* [independent listening] (TB 88)
4/7	*Sommaire* (TB 89)
4/8	*Épreuve: Écouter* (TB 90)
4/9	*Épreuve: Lire* (TB 91)
4/10	*Épreuve: Écrire et grammaire* (TB 91)
103	*Presse-Jeunesse 1* (TB 91)
109–114	*Premier contrôle* (TB 200)

Language content

Animals and pets (Area 1)

Est-ce que tu as un animal à la maison?
Oui, j'ai un chat/chien/etc.
un chat
un cheval
un chien
un cochon d'Inde
un hamster
un lapin
un oiseau
un perroquet
une perruche
un poisson (rouge)
une souris
une tortue

Describing animals and other things, especially colour and size (Area 2)

De quelle couleur est-il/elle?	*Il/Elle est gris(e).*
Est-ce qu'il/elle est gros(se)?	*Il/Elle est gros(se).*
Il/Elle est comment?	*Il/Elle est petit(e).*

Les couleurs (Area 2)

noir	*noire*
brun	*brune*
blanc	*blanche*
gris	*grise*
vert	*verte*
bleu	*bleue*
rouge	
orange	
jaune	
multicolore	

La taille (Area 2)

Il est (très) grand.
Elle est (assez) grande.

petit	*petite*
gros	*grosse*
énorme	*énorme*

Other qualities (Area 2)

Il est méchant.
Elle est méchante.
Il est mignon.
Elle est mignonne.

Likes/dislikes/preferences (Area 5)

Est-ce que tu aimes …?

♡	*J'aime …*
♡ +	*(Oui), j'aime beaucoup …*
♡♡	*J'adore …*
♡ ✔	*Je préfère …*
♡ –	*(Non), je n'aime pas beaucoup …*
✗	*(Non), je n'aime pas …*
✗✗	*Je déteste …*

Classroom language and rubrics

Écoutez bien.
Copiez ces mots.
Lève-toi.
Viens ici.
Répétez après moi.
Écris ton nom.
Vérifiez vos réponses.
Lis à haute voix.
Chantez!
Regardez le tableau.

Ongoing activities

The French alphabet and *Comment ça s'écrit?* are taught throughout *Unité 4* (see TB 78).

Students begin to build up a self-description file which can be extended in subsequent units (see TB 86).

On-going feature of Unité 4

The French alphabet

In the course of this unit the French alphabet should be taught. The suggested order is as follows:

- The class repeats a few letters at a time – ask them to spot the 'catches' as they arise (e/i, g/j etc.).
- Gradually work up to the whole alphabet using such strategies as stopping and seeing if the class or one group can go on alone, dividing the class into two or more groups and 'conducting' them, moving swiftly from one group to another, one group carrying on as the other leaves off.
- Teach students to spell their names and introduce *Comment ça s'écrit?*
- Help the class to get used to asking the teacher to spell any word they are not sure of.
- Practise spelling a few words regularly and perhaps play a spelling game, e.g.
  Ton nom s'écrit comme ça?
  The teacher, and later one of the class, spells out someone's name in French. Anyone who thinks their name is being spelt should stand up. If the wrong person stands up or the person named fails to stand up, they lose a point. If the person named stands up, they have the next turn at spelling a name.

The introduction of the French alphabet could be linked with ICT, providing a good opportunity to explore the keyboard, which would be useful for those students with poor keyboard skills.

The most basic activity is *Trouve la touche*. Dictate spellings or phrases by saying, for example, *Tapez 'd', tapez 'e', tapez 'u', tapez 'x' – Qu'est-ce que ça écrit?*

1/43, SB 29, TB 34–35 — **LISTENING SPEAKING**

Chantez! L'alphabet

The alphabet song (SB 29) is usually a popular way of practising the alphabet and could be introduced now or left until later in the unit.

See TB 87 for the text of the song and refer also to the notes on using the songs (TB 33).

Area 1
Talking about animals and pets

CD 1/35
FC 18–26
Écoute et parle SB 153, 5
Student CD 1/28

hamster, chien, chat, lapin, poisson (rouge), cheval, souris, perruche, perroquet, cochon d'Inde

FC 18–26 — **PRESENTATION**

Est-ce que tu as un animal à la maison?

Using the flashcards, teach the names of these pets, introducing them a few at a time, using repetition and then adding the question *Qu'est-ce que c'est?*

Eventually write the words on the board for a game of *Effacez!* or *Je pense à un animal*.

Start some simple copy-writing with a game of *Loto*, in which students write down the names of three animals and the teacher or another pupil acts as caller.

1/35 — **LISTENING**

Sondage

This *Sondage* introduces the question *Est-ce que tu as/vous avez un animal à la maison?*, but, apart from making sure it is understood, do not spend much time on it, as it will be explained and practised later in the unit. The main purpose is to get students used to hearing the new words and linking them to the printed version. Students copy down the list (see **Solution**) and add a tick by each animal as it is mentioned, checking at the end to see how many of each animal there are.

Solution: *Total: 3 chiens, 3 chats, 1 cochon d'Inde, 2 hamsters, 2 poissons, 2 souris, 1 lapin, 1 perruche*

Sondage

- Est-ce que tu as un animal à la maison?
- Oui, j'ai un chien. Il s'appelle Tom.
- Est-ce que tu as un animal à la maison?
- Oui, j'ai un lapin et deux poissons.
- Et toi, tu as un animal à la maison?
- Oui, j'ai un hamster et un chien.
- Est-ce que vous avez un animal à la maison, Madame?
- Oui, un chat et un chien. J'adore les animaux!
- Et vous, Monsieur, est-ce que vous avez un animal?
- Moi, oui, un chat, un grand chat, et ma fille a un hamster.
- Excusez-moi, Madame, mais est-ce que vous avez un animal à la maison?
- Oui, oui. J'ai un petit chat et une perruche.
- Et vous les garçons, vous avez des animaux à la maison?
- Moi, non. Ma mère n'aime pas les animaux. Mais mon ami Luc a un cochon d'Inde et deux souris.
- C'est vrai, Luc?
- Oui, oui, c'est ça.

SB 153, TB 89, SCD 1/28 — **LISTENING**

5 Comment ça s'écrit?

For further practice in spelling animal vocabulary, students could do this *Écoute et parle* task from the Student CD. (See TB 89.)

Area 2
Describing animals and other things

SB 24–25, 1–5
CD 1/36–37
FC 18–26
CM 4/1, 4/2
Au choix SB 129, 1–3
Écoute et parle SB 153, 4
Student CD 1/27
Grammar in Action 1, page 4

adjectives (masc. and fem. singular)
colours (see SB 25)

FC 18–26 **PRESENTATION**

Les couleurs

Teach colours with objects previously learnt, e.g. *Voilà un stylo: il est noir* and the animal flashcards, e.g. *Voilà un lapin, il est blanc et gris.* Introduce *De quelle couleur est-il/elle?*, teach the class to answer it, and gradually encourage students to ask each other about colours, using masculine nouns only to start with.

Masculine/feminine agreement

When the class is using the colours with confidence, introduce the feminine forms orally.

Explain that most adjectives (colours, describing words) change when they are used with feminine nouns. Demonstrate the change in sound, by describing the colour of feminine classroom objects, e.g. *boîte, table, gomme, règle.*

Les couleurs dans l'ordre

You could use this game for practising colours now or later for extra practice and consolidation.

Each pair or group has a set of coloured pencils or felt-tip pens etc. One student says the colours quickly while another has to arrange the pencils in the correct order, changing the positions as instructed.

CM 4/1 **MINI-FLASHCARDS SUPPORT**

Les animaux

This is an expendable support sheet for practising animal vocabulary. Students copy the names of the animals onto the correct square and colour in the animals according to the instructions. These could, if wished, be stuck onto card, cut up and used as mini-flashcards for pair or group practice (see suggestions for games and mini-flashcards TB 27–28).

SB 24 **READING SPEAKING**

1 Grand Concours National

Ask students if they can guess the words *concours national* and *finalistes.*

Talk about the animals in the photos, introducing the words *grand/gros* and *petit* and referring to classroom objects etc. to emphasise the meaning.

Refer to the note at the bottom of SB 24 about the use of *grand* and *gros.*

Tell the class to read through the six descriptions of the animals and do the simple task, matching the descriptions with the photos.

Solution: 1c, 2a, 3e, 4f, 5b, 6d

This could be checked orally, e.g.

Numéro 2, c'est Minnie. C'est quelle photo?

Further oral work could be based on the photos and descriptions, e.g.

Est-ce que Minnie est blanche/grise/noire?
Le hamster, comment s'appelle-t-il?
Est-ce que Samba est gros ou petit?
Est-ce que le lapin s'appelle Minou?
Il est noir et blanc. C'est Samba?

SB 24, 1/36 **SPEAKING LISTENING**

2 Vote, vote, vote!

a Ask students, *Tu préfères quel animal?* After a few oral answers, ask everyone to write their vote on a slip of paper as indicated.

b Add up the votes to find the class results – extra number practice can be given by getting the class to count out each animal's score aloud. Sort the votes into separate piles for each animal and give out the piles to individual students.
Alors qui a les votes pour Minou? Suzanne? Bon, comptez les votes avec Suzanne! ... Très bien – sept votes pour Minou etc.

c Play the first part of the recording – but only as far as Dodu – so that the class can listen to the order in which the six finalists are mentioned and jot down the correct letters or the names.

Solution: **1c** *(Samba),* **2a** *(Minnie),* **3d** *(Minou),* **4e** *(Flic),* **5f** *(Carotte),* **6b** *(Dodu)*

Then play the rest of the recording so that the class can compare their results with those of the national competition.

Solution: **1** *Minou, le chat,* **2** *Samba, le chien,* **3** *Flic, le petit hamster*

Vote, vote, vote!

Bonsoir, bonsoir! Voici des résultats importants – les résultats du Grand Concours National. Il y a six finalistes: Samba, un gros chien adorable; Minnie, la petite souris blanche; le chat Minou; puis un petit hamster qui s'appelle Flic; Carotte, un lapin noir et blanc; et un cochon d'Inde qui s'appelle Dodu.
Et finalement, voici les résultats.
Le premier prix ... c'est pour Minou, le chat.
Alors, Minou a gagné le concours, le grand concours national!
Le deuxième prix ... c'est pour Samba, le chien.
Alors, Samba est numéro deux.

Et finalement, numéro trois ... c'est Flic – oui, Flic, le petit hamster, a gagné le troisième prix. Félicitations à tous les animaux, et bonsoir!

AU CHOIX SB 129 **READING WRITING**

1 Une histoire de chats

This task gives practice with adjectives and feminine agreements. Either work through it step-by-step with the whole class, or reserve it for more able students, who should be able to manage it on their own.

Introduce the words *mignon/mignonne* and *méchant/méchante*, e.g.

Regardez Mimi. Elle est mignonne, non?
Et voilà Minette.Elle est mignonne aussi, elle n'est pas méchante. (Write the words on the board.)

Next, the class reads through the story, first silently, then aloud. Ask them some questions, e.g.

Est-ce que César est jaune?
Est-ce que Mimi est grosse?
Est-ce que Minette est mignonne?
Est-ce que César est le chat de Monsieur Lenoir?
Est-ce que tu préfères Mimi ou César?

Eventually students can complete the sentences at the end of the story.

More able pupils might like to act the story or make up another playlet based on the same idea.

Solution: **1** *César,* **2** *Mimi,* **3** *Géant,* **4** *Minette,* **5** *César/Géant,* **6** *Mimi*

SB 25 **READING WRITING**

3 C'est à qui?

This task practises recognition of colours. The maze puzzle is not quite as straightforward as might at first appear. Although students should have no trouble in tracing the owners of each animal by using the lines, they will have to look carefully to distinguish between the actual pets, since the puzzle includes three birds, two fish and two horses, all of different colours.

Make sure everyone is clear what has to be done, e.g.
Regardez l'oiseau bleu et vert – il est mignon, non?
Mais il est à qui?
Suivez la ligne ... voilà – il est à Magali.
Maintenant, regardez les descriptions des animaux ...
Numéro 1, l'oiseau bleu et vert ... c'est ça.

Students can note down their answers by just putting the number and the name of the owner or they can write out the whole sentence for practice. In either case, answers could be checked orally, with the full sentences being read out. See TB 70 for explaining the construction *c'est à* (+ name) if not already done.

Solution: **1** *Christophe,* **2** *Magali,* **3** *Séverine,* **4** *Isabelle,* **5** *M. Garnier,* **6** *Séverine,* **7** *Jean-Pierre,* **8** *Jean-Pierre*

For further practice, this item could be followed by some true or false statements or questions, made up by the teacher or by students, e.g.
Est-ce que M. Garnier a un poisson? Jean-Pierre a un poisson rouge, orange et vert. C'est vrai?

SB 25 **GRAMMAR**

Dossier-langue Adjectives – how to describe animals in French

This provides an explanation of the agreement of adjectives (singular only). In the course of *Unités 1–5*, plurals are introduced receptively, but not fully explained until *Unité 5*.

Tell the class to look at the description of the dog and the mouse, spot the differences in the spelling of the words *noir, blanc, petit* and *mignon* which describe them and work out and explain the reason for these.

Ask students to read aloud the masculine and feminine forms of the adjectives listed, perhaps with one side of the class saying the feminine form and the other the masculine, changing over from time to time.

SB 153, TB 89, SCD 1/27 **LISTENING**

4 C'est quel mot?

The difference in sound of the masculine and feminine forms of the adjective can be demonstrated by this listening discrimination practice. (See *Écoute et parle*, TB 89.)

SB 25 **GRAMMAR**

4 Des adjectifs

This task gives routine practice of masculine and feminine forms of common adjectives and produces a useful table that students can refer to later.

Solution:	*masculin*	*féminin*
colours	*noir*	*noire*
	brun	**1** *brune*
	gris	**2** *grise*
	blanc	*blanche*
	jaune	*jaune*
	rouge	**3** *rouge*
size	*gros*	*grosse*
	grand	*grande*
	petit	**4** *petite*
	énorme	**5** *énorme*
nasty	*méchant*	*méchante*
nice	*mignon*	*mignonne*

SB 25 **WRITING**

5 Jean-Pierre et ses animaux

Practice in writing adjectives with the correct agreement. Remind students not just to look for the word with the right meaning, but also to pick the correct masculine or feminine agreement.

Solution: **1** *petit, noir,* **2** *grande, blanche,* **3** *gros, rouge, orange, blanc,* **4** *grosse, noire, mignonne*

Follow-up **CONSOLIDATION**

The following activities present a selection of differentiated games and tasks which could be used here to consolidate work on animals and adjectives.

Un jeu: Le message secret

Each student writes a 'secret message' on a piece of paper and signs it. The message is an instruction to draw and colour an animal (the message can be sensible or 'silly'), e.g. *Dessine un gros chien blanc et noir./Dessine trois chats, un bleu, un vert et un orange.*

Some messages might contain more detail, e.g.
Dessine Georges. C'est un cochon d'Inde. Il est noir.
Dessine Lulu. C'est une souris. Elle est blanche et très mignonne.
Dessine Noiraud. C'est un chien. Il est gros – et il est très méchant.

The messages are folded, pooled and given out at random.

The person receiving each message must carry out the instruction correctly and show it to the teacher (or group leader) to prove that it has been understood.

To make further use of these drawings and descriptions, after students have written their names on the back, the papers could be pinned up or laid on tables around and numbered. They could then be used as a matching game in which students have to match up the descriptions with the drawing which resulted.

CM 4/2 **EXTENSION**

Les animaux de mes amis

Some students could work on this copymaster while some of the more able do the *Au choix* tasks.

This copymaster gives further practice of descriptive vocabulary and some dictionary practice with the names of animals.

Some students might need help with the final task.

Solutions:

1 Complète les mots

1 *chien,* **2** *poisson,* **3** *souris,* **4** *perroquet,* **5** *tortue,* **6** *oiseau,* **7** *cheval,* **8** *lapin*

2 C'est utile, le dictionnaire

canard (m)	duck
canari (m)	canary
chameau (m)	camel
chat (m)	cat
chauve-souris (f)	bat
cheval (m)	horse
chien (m)	dog
chimpanzé (m)	chimp
cochon d'Inde (m)	guinea pig

3 Les animaux de mes amis

1 *petite,* **2** *grande,* **3** *blanc,* **4** *noir,* **5** *mignon,* **6** *gris,* **7** *méchant,* **8** *vert*

Au choix SB 129, 1/37, **LISTENING**

2 Chat perdu

Teach *perdu*, demonstrating perhaps by putting a pencil under a book:
J'ai perdu mon crayon, où est mon crayon?.
Ah, voilà mon crayon. J'ai trouvé mon crayon.

Then talk a bit about the advert and photograph, introducing the expression *Il est comment?*, e.g.
Regardez le chat. Il est comment?
Il est gros ou petit?
De quelle couleur est-il?
Mais le chat dans la photo est perdu, non?
Mais Mme Robert a trouvé le chat? Alors il est à qui?
Écoutez les conversations au téléphone.Est-ce que le chat est à Mme Duval, à Claire Martin ou à François Léon?

Play the three telephone conversations, stopping after each one to let the class compare the details with the photo, perhaps asking some questions, e.g.
Il est comment, le chat de Mme.Duval? Il est petit ou gros? Il est blanc?

At the end of the recording, take a vote by show of hands to see who the class thinks owns the cat (*François*).

Chat perdu

– Allô. C'est Mme Robert?
– Oui.
– Je m'appelle Mme Marie Duval. J'ai perdu mon chat et ...
– Ah bon. Il est comment, votre chat?
– Eh bien, il est noir, complètement noir, et il est très gros.

– Allô.
– Allô. Je m'appelle Claire Martin et j'ai perdu mon petit chat, Tigre.
– Bonjour Claire. Il est comment, ton Tigre.
– Oh, il est adorable! Il est fantastique!
– Oui, oui, mais il est comment? Il est gros ou petit? Il est de quelle couleur?
– Ben, blanc, il est blanc, mais brun aussi, et noir, et jaune aussi. Enfin, il est de toutes les couleurs, mais surtout blanc.
– Et il est gros?
– Oh oui. Il est très, très gros. Il mange beaucoup. Il est énorme!

– Allô. C'est Mme Robert?
– Oui, oui, c'est moi. Je suis Mme Robert.
– Alors, Madame, je pense que vous avez trouvé notre chat. Le chat dans la photo – c'est notre chat, Magique!
– Ah bon. Il est comment, Magique?
– Il n'est pas très gros, mais il n'est pas très petit. Il est gris, blanc et noir, avec les pattes blanches.
– Et toi, comment t'appelles-tu?
– Moi, je m'appelle François Léon.

Possibilities for further exploitation of this task:

1 Students could listen again to the recording and try to complete the descriptions of the three cats:
Le chat de Mme Duval est ...
Le chat de Claire est ...
Le chat de François est ...

2 Groups of (able) students could make up similar telephone calls. One student could draw or write a description of a cat and the others could 'phone in' and try to claim it.

3 A word processor or text-reformulation and graphics package, could be used for descriptions and pictures of pets.

AU CHOIX SB 129, — WRITING

3 Des animaux

Students write simple descriptions of the animals illustrated.

As follow-up, a computer could be used for reconstructing texts describing pets, using *Gapkit 2*. This allows the teacher to create a gapped text with images or sounds.

Alternatively, use a word-processing package with clip art images of pets. Students then have to match up text with images.

Animal posters: Students can draw or use clip art to produce posters with pictures and descriptions of the animals, e.g. use specialist drawing or painting packages such as *Paintbrush* or *Corel Draw*.

Teach students how to add text labels to their pictures.

Perhaps give the students a time limit and ask them to draw and label an animal in that time – sometimes this produces amusing results!

GRAMMAR IN ACTION 1, PAGE 4 — GRAMMAR

Using adjectives – singular

These self-explanatory tasks give further straight-forward practice in describing animals etc. and would be useful for homework, or could be used later for consolidation.

Area 3
Asking questions
SB 26, 1–3
Au choix SB 130, 4
CD 1/38–39
Using *Est-ce que …?* and other question foms

PRESENTATION
GRAMMAR

Asking questions

Using flashcards, ask some questions, e.g.
C'est un chat? (Oui/Non.)
Est-ce que c'est un oiseau? (Non, c'est un animal.)

Then ask students about their pets, e.g.
Est-ce que tu as un chat, Katie?
Harry, est-ce que tu as un animal à la maison?

SB 26 — PRESENTATION

Est-ce que tu as un animal à la maison?

Use the two cartoons to show how to answer, e.g.

Voici une question:
Est-ce que tu as un animal à la maison?
Lucie répond, «J'ai un perroquet.»
David répond, «J'ai une tortue.»

In the course of the next few lessons, make sure all students have a turn at answering this question themselves. Those who have no pets could just answer *Non*, but could be encouraged to say something about someone else's pet, e.g. … *mais mon ami(e)* (+ name) *a un chien,* etc.

SB 26, 1/38 — LISTENING

1 Trois interviews

Students look at the questions about the three interviews and listen to the recording. Pause the recording so that students can write *Oui* or *Non* after each question.

Solution:

Jean-Paul	**a** *Oui*	**b** *Oui*	**c** *Non*
Charlotte	**a** *Non*	**b** *Oui*	**c** *Non*
Mme Bernard	**a** *Oui*	**b** *Non*	**c** *Oui*

Trois interviews

Conversation 1

– Salut, Jean-Paul! Est-ce que tu as un animal à la maison?
– Oui, j'ai un chien – il s'appelle Pirate.
– Est-ce qu'il est gros ou petit?
– Il est très gros et complètement noir – très, très noir.

Conversation 2

– Bonjour, Charlotte.
– Bonjour.
– Est-ce que tu as un animal à la maison, Charlotte?
– Non, Monsieur, mais mon frère a un animal. C'est un hamster.
– Tu n'aimes pas les animaux, toi?
– Ce n'est pas ça, Monsieur. J'aime les animaux, mais notre famille habite dans un appartement à Paris.
– Ah bon, je comprends.

Conversation 3

– Bonjour, Mme Bernard.
– Bonjour, Monsieur.
– Est-ce que vous habitez ici, dans ce village?
– Oui, oui. C'est ça. J'habite ici avec mon mari, à la ferme.
– Est-ce que vous avez beaucoup d'animaux?
– Bien sûr, Monsieur. Il y a beaucoup d'animaux sur notre ferme. C'est très bien. J'adore les animaux.

SB 26 — GRAMMAR

Dossier-langue
Asking questions

Go through this brief explanation with the class asking

them to look at all the questions in *Trois interviews* to see how they all begin with *Est-ce que* …

Make sure that students have really understood that just by putting *Est-ce que* … at the beginning of a sentence, you can turn that sentence into a question.

They could then practise turning more sentences into questions, e.g.

Charlotte habite en France.
Maman est dans la maison.
La radio est dans la cuisine.
Martin/Sandra est le frère/la sœur de Nicole.

Consolidation

This can be developed into a pair or team activity with one pupil making a statement and another turning it into a question. Students should be told to confine their statements to information about other people and things so they avoid such nonsensical questions as *Est-ce que je suis un garçon?* etc.

Some of the questions could be written down on slips of paper and then re-used, one student picking out a question at random and another answering it. Students should be helped to see that most of the answer is often the same as the question without the *Est-ce que* …

Au choix SB 130 — **CONSOLIDATION SPEAKING/WRITING**

4 Des questions

Students use the substitution table to help them make up six more questions.

Grammar in Action 1, page 6 — **WRITING**

This full page practice on the use of *Est-ce que* … would be useful for homework or for revision.

Asking questions

SPEAKING

Before moving on to the next task, which includes other common question forms, revise the questions already learnt by playing a chain question game. One student asks someone a question and if it is answered correctly, the second student asks a question of a third person etc.

Students could refer back to *Unité 3* for ideas.

SB 26 — **READING SPEAKING**

2 Questions et réponses

This includes some of the most common question and answer forms. Students match up the question and answer pairs. These could be checked orally with the whole of each question and answer being read aloud.

Solution: 1d, 2a, 3c, 4b, 5e, 6h, 7g, 8f

SB 26, — **SPEAKING**

3 Inventez des conversations

The two conversations (and variations) bring together the work on questions and answers about animals and should be practised orally in pairs.

Follow-up

The next two activities can be used to consolidate work on much of the material covered so far.

1/39 — **LISTENING**

On parle à Grégory et à Roseline

This optional item gives practice in listening to conversations containing a variety of questions. Students should listen to the interviews two or three times and then give as much information about each person as they can remember.

They could also work in groups, and after each hearing, each group in turn could try to add another piece of information, e.g.

Il s'appelle Grégory/Il habite à La Rochelle.

This could continue until no new information can be added. The last group to make a statement wins.

On parle à Grégory et à Roseline

1 – Bonjour. Tu t'appelles comment?
– Je m'appelle Grégory Charpentier.
– Tu as quel âge, Grégory?
– J'ai onze ans.
– Est-ce que tu habites à La Rochelle?
– Oui, j'habite à La Rochelle.
– Est-ce que tu as des animaux à la maison?
– Oui, j'ai un lapin.
– Comment s'appelle-t-il?
– Il s'appelle Chouchou.
– Comment ça s'écrit?
– C-H-O-U-C-H-O-U.

2 – Bonjour. Tu t'appelles comment?
– Je m'appelle Roseline Clément.
– Tu as quel âge, Roseline?
– J'ai seize ans.
– Est-ce que tu as des frères ou des sœurs?
– Oui, j'ai un frère, Olivier. Il a quatorze ans.
– Est-ce que tu as des animaux?
– Non, mais mon frère a un chien.
– Comment s'appelle-t-il, le chien de ton frère?
– Il s'appelle Bianco – B-I-A-N-C-O.
– Il a quel âge, Bianco?
– Il a trois ans.

Jeu de cartes

Groups of students make sets of cards on which are written or printed questions, e.g.

Imagine un animal. Qu'est-ce que c'est?
De quelle couleur est-il?
Comment s'appelle-t-il?

These could be dealt at random, using cards from several sets, and students asked to write down the answers to the questions, according to each card they receive.

Area 4
Singular paradigm of *avoir*
SB 27, 4–6
Au choix SB 130, 5
CD 1/40

As-tu un animal? PRESENTATION

Ask some of the questions already introduced, especially those containing part of *avoir*, e.g.

As-tu un animal? Quel âge a-t-il?
Et toi, quel âge as-tu?
Qui a un animal/oiseau?
Richard, tu as un chien, non? etc.

SB 27, WRITING

4 À toi!

Students should now be able to write (and perhaps record) a short description of one of their own or a friend's pets, using the models supplied here.

This would be a good activity for classes with access to a multi-media facility. If writing on a computer or word processor, they could start with some prompts, e.g.

Animal	*J'ai ...*
Nom	*Il/Elle ...*
Age	*Il/Elle a ...*
Couleur	
Gros ou petit	
Méchant ou mignon	

This task can be adapted by giving different levels of support to suit students of varied abilities.

SB 27 GRAMMAR
PRESENTATION

Dossier-langue
Avoir (to have)

Students read through this explanation and, perhaps working in pairs, find the parts of the singular paradigm of *avoir* in the conversation *À toi!*

SB 27, 1/40 LISTENING GRAMMAR

5 C'est quelle phrase?

In this task, students hear short conversations, all including parts of the verb *avoir*. They then have to choose the true statement (a or b) from six pairs of sentences.

If necessary, explain the use of *ne (n') ... pas* in **4b** and **6b**. The negative has been used in specific phrases, such as *je n'aime pas*, and is taught fully in *Unité 9*.

Solution: 1a, 2b, 3a, 4b, 5a, 6b

C'est quelle phrase?

1 – Tu as un perroquet, n'est-ce pas Simon?
– Oui, j'ai un perroquet.

2 – Tu as un frère, Suzanne?
– Oui, j'ai deux frères.

3 – Christophe, est-ce que tu as une amie qui s'appelle Alice?
– Oui, elle s'appelle Alice Bonnard.

4 – Est-ce que tu as une télé dans ta chambre, Sophie?
– Non, mais j'ai un lecteur de CDs et une radio.

5 – J'ai une console dans ma chambre. Tu viens jouer?
– Ah oui, Michel, j'adore les jeux électroniques.

6 – Tu as un ordinateur dans ta salle de classe, Alain?
– Non, mais il y en a beaucoup dans la salle de technologie.

SB 27 SPEAKING WRITING

6 À toi!

Using the substitution table, students make up four sentences and two questions, all containing part of *avoir*. This is an open-ended speaking or writing task.

Au choix SB 130 GRAMMAR SUPPORT

5 Questions et réponses

a Students complete the questions with a part of *avoir*.
b Students complete the answers.
c Students match up the correct question and answer.

Solution:

a **1** *as*, **2** *as*, **3** *as*, **4** *as*, **5** *a*, **6** *as*, **7** *a*, **8** *ai*
b **a** *a*, **b** *ai*, **c** *ai*, **d** *a*, **e** *ai*, *a*, **f** *ai*, **g** *ai*, **h** *a*
c **1h, 2g, 3b, 4e, 5a, 6c, 7f, 8d**

Area 5
Expressing likes and dislikes
SB 28, 1–3
Au choix SB 130, 6
FC 1–2
CD 1/41–42
CM 4/5 (optional)
j'aime (beaucoup), j'adore, je préfère, je déteste

FC 1–2 **PRESENTATION**

Opinions

Ask students for their opinions about animals, their town or school etc., e.g.
Est-ce que tu aimes la ville de Wundover?
Tu aimes beaucoup ton village, c'est vrai?
Est-ce que tu détestes les serpents/les tarentules?
Est-ce ce que tu préfères la radio ou la télé?

For variety, you could indicate which opinion you mean by using Flashcards 1 and 2 or home-made cue cards using the standard symbols (see SB 28).

SB 28, 1/41 **LISTENING READING EXTENSION**

1 Des animaux extraordinaires

This recorded passage contains a few new words, of which the most important is *parce que*. Others, probably guessable, are *extraordinaires*, *par exemple* and *naturellement*.

Adopt some of the suggested strategies for using recorded text to teach reading – see *Unité 3*, TB 64.

Eventually, students can do the True or false? task, in which the emphasis is on likes and dislikes.

Solution: 1V, 2V, 3F, 4F, 5V, 6F, 7V, 8F, 9F, 10F

Further questions could also be asked on this passage, e.g.
Est-ce qu'Éric habite dans un appartement?
Est-ce qu'il aime les chiens et les chats?
Comment s'appelle le chien de Marc?
Qu'est-ce qu'il aime? etc.

Des animaux extraordinaires

Je m'appelle Éric Garnier. J'habite dans une ferme, près de Toulouse. J'aime beaucoup les animaux, mais à la maison, il y a des animaux extraordinaires … par exemple, il y a Télé – c'est le petit chien noir de mon frère, Marc. Il s'appelle Télé parce qu'il adore la télévision.

Et il y a aussi Blanco, le petit chat de Maman. Naturellement, il s'appelle Blanco parce qu'il est blanc. Il déteste la télévision, mais il aime beaucoup la radio et il adore la musique.

Eh bien, Télé aime la télévision, mais Blanco préfère la radio … voilà, c'est très bien … mais non! Ce n'est pas très bien parce qu'il y a aussi Jules et quelquefois, il y a Néron. Jules est le perroquet de ma sœur, Claire. Il est petit et très mignon, mais il n'aime pas la télévision, il n'aime pas la radio et il déteste la musique.

Et Néron, qui est-il? Eh bien … Néron est un gros chien noir et blanc. C'est le chien de mon grand-père et il est très méchant. Il déteste les chats, il déteste les perroquets, il déteste la radio, il déteste la musique et il n'aime pas beaucoup le chien de Marc. Alors, qu'est-ce qu'il aime, Néron? Il aime deux choses … mon grand-père et le football … à la télévision, naturellement! Il adore ça!

SB 28, 1/42 **LISTENING**

2 Des opinions

The beginnings of the sentences listed under each of the names (Daniel, Luc and Mireille) are all ways of expressing a like, dislike or preference.

Students look first at these, then at the second half of the sentences, before listening to the recording and finding the pairs (i.e. both halves of the sentence).

Though quite suitable for class use, this item would be ideal for use with individual listening equipment if available.

Des opinions

1 – Salut Daniel!
– Salut!
– Alors Daniel, est-ce que tu aimes la musique?
– Oui, j'aime la musique.
– Est-ce que tu écoutes souvent la radio?
– Non, je n'aime pas beaucoup la radio. Je préfère la télévision.
– Ah, tu préfères la télévision.

2 – Bonjour Luc.
– Bonjour!
– Luc, est-ce que tu aimes les jeux électroniques?
– Les jeux électroniques? Ah non, moi je déteste ça.
– Et le sport, tu aimes le sport, le tennis, par exemple?
– Oui, oui, j'aime le tennis, mais je préfère le football.
– Ah bon. Tu préfères le football.

3 – Salut Mireille. Ça va?
– Oui, ça va très bien, merci.
– Dis-moi, Mireille, est-ce que tu aimes les animaux, les hamsters, par exemple?
– Non, je n'aime pas beaucoup les hamsters et je déteste les souris.
– Alors, tu détestes les souris.
– Oui, mais j'aime les chiens. J'ai un chien à la maison. Et mon animal favori, c'est le cheval. J'adore les chevaux.

Solution:
Daniel: 1a, 2h, 3f
Luc: 4c, 5g, 6e
Mireille: 7b, 8i, 9d, 10j

SPEAKING EXTENSION

Suggested follow-up activities

Some able students could work in pairs to re-create conversations based on the recording, and some of these could be recorded.

Groups could each work on a different one of the conversations and develop it into a survey asking just one or two of the questions within their limited group and reporting back to the class.

SB 28 **WRITING**

3 À toi!

Using the words in the box to help them, students write their own statements of likes, dislikes and preferences, completing each of the sentences 1 to 7.

As a follow-up activity, show students how to make a similar symbol chart of their own, using hearts and crosses to be found in a number of symbol fonts.

They could then make up their own sheet of likes and dislikes, e.g.
J'adore les chats.
J'aime beaucoup les ordinateurs.
J'aime le français.
Je n'aime pas beaucoup mon frère.
Je n'aime pas les souris.
Je déteste les tarentules.

Au choix SB 130 **READING CONSOLIDATION**

6 Un échange

Students read through the cartoon strip and decide whether the statements are true or false.

Solution: 1V, 2F, 3F, 4V, 5F, 6F, 7F, 8F

CM 4/5 **CONSOLIDATION**

C'est moi!

This could be done now, or at the end of the unit as consolidation. Students complete their self-portrait, filling in the blanks to give name, age, address and an account of their possessions and preferences.

The corrected version of this sheet could be filed for future reference.

CONSOLIDATION

Self-description file: Moi

Students begin a word-processing file that they can add to or update over the course of their study of French, called, for example, *Moi* or *Mon dossier personnel*.

For the moment, they can set up the file and type in the basic sentences they have learned so far (name, age and where they live). Students might also add sections which describe their families and their home, especially their own room, as covered in *Unité 3*.

When complete, the file can be checked for errors using a spell checker if a French spell check facility is available. If not, students could print out their sheets for checking and then carry out the corrections on screen.

As an introductory activity to the self-description file, students could work on text reconstruction activities (e.g. *Fun with Texts*) with a model self-description of a fictional student.

The completed word-processed file should be saved so that it can be added to and revised in subsequent units/years. Depending upon access to computers, this activity can be done in each unit or on a termly or yearly basis. It links well with penpal activities, e-mail or conventional post, since it provides a ready made self-description.

At a later stage, students can use their self-descriptions as a basis for creating their personal web pages.

Note that self-descriptions are an individual activity – if there is only one computer between two some thought needs to be given to organising the activity. If possible, half the class might work on something else. If not, dictation may work well with the 'author' dictating and the partner typing.

Area 6
Using *tu* and *vous*

SB 29, 4
CM 4/3
CD 1/43–44
Grammar in Action 1, page 5

Tu/vous

PRESENTATION

Ask a few individuals questions containing the word *tu*, e.g.
Richard, est-ce que tu aimes les chiens?
Sarah, tu préfères les chiens ou les chats?

Then ask the whole class questions containing *vous*, e.g.
Est-ce que vous aimez les animaux?

Toute la classe, vous préférez les chiens ...(levez la main) ... ou les chats (levez la main)?

Est-ce que vous préférez le sport ou les jeux électroniques? ... Le sport ... (levez la main) ... ou l'ordinateur ... (levez la main)?

When the students have grasped the difference, alternate these two types of questions. When they are ready, students can ask you questions using *vous*, e.g. *Maintenant posez-moi des questions ...*

SB 29 GRAMMAR

4 Qui dit ça?

Students match the correct captions to the cartoons, choosing mainly on the basis of whether *tu* or *vous* is used.

To check answers, ask students to read out the complete captions.

Solution: 1g, 2h, 3c, 4e, 5b, 6d, 7a, 8f

SB29 GRAMMAR

Dossier-langue
You

Ask the class to look at the cartoon captions and spot the two different words for 'you' and explain when each is used.

If this seems unclear, do some more oral work, as above.

Go through the brief explanation with the students and, to check if they have understood it, ask them to explain the rule to each other in English.

Students then link the rule with the examples from the cartoons.

Solution: **1 e** or **b, 2 c** or **e, 3 d, 4 g,**
5 a, f, g, or **h, 6 a, f, g,** or **h**

CM 4/3, WRITING SPEAKING CONSOLDATION

Questions et réponses

If preferred, this copymaster could be used for more able students only, and as an alternative to CM 4/5 which is easier.

Some students might need help with the first section, *Deux interviews*, in which they compile the complete conversation script, using questions from the box.

When they have completed the two conversations, students can read them aloud in parts, and some could be recorded.

Solution:

1 Deux interviews
A a1, b9, c5, d3, e10, f4
B g8, h7, i11, j9, k12, l13

The second section, *Conversations au choix*, involves throwing a dice or choosing questions in turns and answering from a choice of suggestions or with invented answers.

Demonstrate this process first, using two able students.

The questions and answers from the first section could also be used in a team game (see TB 25–29).

EXTENSION

If the class has access to computers, they could work in pairs and make up similar conversations to those in *Deux interviews*. They could then set these either to each other or to another pair.

GRAMMAR IN ACTION 1, PAGE 5 CONSOLIDATION

Using *tu* or *vous*

This page of the *Grammar in Action* book would provide further practice and could be used for homework or later for revision.

Follow-up

From now on encourage students to ask the teacher questions for a few minutes in most lessons, so that they have plenty of practice in using the *vous* form when addressing an adult.

SB 29, TB 33, TB 34–35, 1/43–44 LISTENING SPEAKING

Chantez! L'alphabet

A song to teach or practise the alphabet which could be introduced now or at some other point in the unit. See the introduction to this unit (TB 78) and the notes on using the songs (TB 33). The score is on TB 34–35.

L'alphabet

Moi, je sais l'alphabet.
Écoute, est-ce que c'est bon?
ABCDEFGH …
Ça continue comment?
Moi, je sais l'alphabet.
Écoute, est-ce que c'est bon?
ABCDEFGH
IJKLMNOP …
Ça continue comment?
Moi, je sais l'alphabet.
Écoute, est-ce que c'est bon?
ABCDEFGH
IJKLMNOP
QRSTUVW …
Ça continue comment?
Moi, je sais l'alphabet.
Écoute, est-ce que c'est bon?
ABCDEFGH
IJKLMNOP
QRSTUVW
XYZ …
Ça continue comment?
Idiote, c'est tout, c'est bon!
ABCDEFGH
IJKLMNOP
QRSTUVW
XYZ

Area 7
Further activities and consolidation

SB 30, 1–2, SB 31
Écoute et parle SB 153, 6, 1–7
Student CD 1/24–30; Student CD 2/22–24
CD 1/45–49
CM 4/4, 4/5 (if not already used), **4/6–4/10**

SB 30, PRACTICE SPEAKING

1 Combien d'animaux?

Students identify the number of different pets in the picture. Able students can write out their replies in full. Others can just write the number in figures and their answers can be checked orally.

Solution: **1** *3 hamsters,* **2** *4 chiens,* **3** *1 oiseau,* **4** *2 chats,* **5** *1 souris,* **6** *2 poissons,* **7** *1 lapin*

2 La chasse à l'intrus PRACTICE

In addition to spotting the odd word, more able students could explain why it is the odd one, e.g.
1 *Les autres sont des jours de la semaine.*

Note: this is not possible for 9 or 10.

Solution: **1** *vingt,* **2** *oui,* **3** *une maison,* **4** *un garçon,* **5** *gros,* **6** *la cuisine,* **7** *une tortue,* **8** *Paris,* **9** *treize,* **10** *quinze*

SB 30 SOUNDS AND WRITING

! é (e with an acute accent)

Students read through this note about the acute accent and try spelling the words aloud. This could form part of a Spelling Bee or another spelling game linked with the *Sommaire*, SB 31. (See TB 29.)

SB 30, ICT/EXTENSION

Students list words containing é and type them out on the computer. Some students may need to be shown how to obtain this symbol using the ALT key and the short cut menu.

CM 4/4, ICT

À l'ordinateur

This would be a suitable time for students to complete this worksheet on computer vocabulary which could be filed for future reference.

Solutions:

1 Voici un ordinateur
CD-ROM – *un cédérom*, keyboard – *le clavier*, floppy disk – *une disquette*, screen – *l'écran m*, printer – *l'imprimante f*, computer – *un ordinateur*, mouse – *la souris*, keys – *les touches f pl*

2 Acrostiche

1 (down): **ordinateur**

2 t**o**uches
3 sou**r**is
4 cé**d**érom
5 clav**i**er
6 écra**n**
7 imprim**a**nte
8 disque**t**te
9 travaill**e**r
10 s**u**rfer
11 tape**r**

SB 31, SB 153, TB 90, SCD 1/29

Vocabulaire de classe

Students decide if one person or the whole class is being addressed. They also write the English for each of the classroom commands.

Solution: **1** *classe* – Listen carefully. **2** *classe* – Copy these words. **3** *élève* – Stand up. **4** *élève* – Come here. **5** *classe* – Repeat after me. **6** *élève* – Write your name. **7** *classe* – Check your answers. **8** *élève* – Read aloud. **9** *classe* – Sing! **10** *classe* – Look at the board.

There is a task for this item on Student CD 1, *Écoute et parle* (see TB 90).

CM 4/6, SCD 2/22–24 INDEPENDENT LISTENING

Tu comprends?

1 Ma chambre

Students colour in the picture according to the recorded instructions.

Ma chambre

Voici ma chambre.
1 Mon lit est bleu.
2 Sur mon lit, il y a un classeur jaune et un livre brun.
3 Près de mon lit, il y a une chaise rouge.
4 Près de la table, il y a une chaise blanche.
5 La table est noire.
6 Mon ordinateur est sur la table. L'ordinateur est vert.
7 Puis il y a la porte. La porte est blanche.

2 Où sont les animaux?

Students draw a line from each animal to show which room it is in.

Où sont les animaux?

Aujourd'hui, il y a beaucoup d'animaux dans l'appartement. Le chat est dans la chambre de mes parents. Le poisson rouge est dans la salle de bains. La tortue est dans la salle de séjour. Le chien est dans ma chambre. Le perroquet est dans la cuisine et le lapin est dans la salle à manger.

3 Qu'est-ce que c'est?

Students write down the words dictated on the recording and spot the odd one out (4 – *calculette*).

Qu'est-ce que c'est?

1 d-i-m-a-n-c-h-e
2 m-e-r-c-r-e-d-i
3 v-e-n-d-r-e-d-i
4 c-a-l-c-u-l-e-t-t-e
5 l-u-n-d-i
6 j-e-u-d-i

SB 31, CM 4/7 **READING CONSOLIDATION**

Sommaire

A summary of the vocabulary and structures of the unit. Students could make up a wordsearch to set to each other, using the lists of animals and colours for reference. The summary could also form the basis of a Spelling Bee.

The copymaster is identical to the *Sommaire* on SB 31, and is especially useful for homework in situations where it is not possible for students to take their textbooks home.

SB153, SCD 1/24–30 **INDEPENDENT LISTENING SOUNDS AND WRITING**

Écoute et parle – Unité 4

1 Les sons français

Solution: **h: (a) 1d, 2c, 3a, 4e, 5f, 6b**
r: (a) 1d, 2a, 3b, 4f, 5e, 6c

Les sons français

La lettre h

a 1 hôpital
2 hiver
3 Henri
4 haut
5 hôtel
6 héros

b habite, heure, histoire, homme, huit

La lettre r

a 1 riche
2 Roland
3 résiste
4 risque
5 refuse
6 rat

b revoir, rouge, radio, rue, réponds

2 Des phrases ridicules

Des phrases ridicules

Huit hamsters habitent en haut de l'hôtel en hiver.

Le rat, dans une rage, rentre avec la radio dans le garage.

3 C'est anglais ou français?

Solution: (b) 1A, 2F, 3A, 4F, 5F, 6A, 7F, 8A

C'est anglais ou français?

a 1 *hockey,* hockey
2 *hamster,* hamster
3 *horizon,* horizon
4 *horrible,* horrible
5 *possible,* possible
6 *article,* article
7 *nature,* nature
8 *village,* village

b 1 *hockey*
2 hamster
3 *horizon*
4 horrible
5 possible
6 *article*
7 nature
8 *village*

4 C'est quel mot?

Solution: **1a, 2b, 3b, 4a, 5a, 6b**

C'est quel mot?

1 blanc, blanche, blanc
2 vert, verte, verte
3 petit, petite, petite
4 grand, grande, grand
5 gris, grise, gris
6 gros, grosse, grosse

5 Comment ça s'écrit?

Solution: **(a)** See transcript. **(b) 5** *(dimanche)*

Comment ça s'écrit?

1 c-h-a-t
2 c-h-e-v-a-l
3 t-o-r-t-u-e
4 s-o-u-r-i-s
5 d-i-m-a-n-c-h-e
6 l-a-p-i-n

6 Vocabulaire de classe

Solution: 6, 1, 8, 4, 5, 10, 9, 7, 2, 3

Vocabulaire de classe

Regarde la page 31. Écoute le CD et écris le nombre de chaque instruction dans l'ordre du CD.

Écris ton nom.
Écoutez bien.
Lis à haute voix.
Viens ici.
Répétez après moi.
Regardez le tableau.
Chantez!
Vérifiez vos réponses.
Copiez ces mots
Lève-toi.

7 Une conversation

Une conversation

Écoute les questions et réponds comme indiqué.

– Est-ce que tu aimes les animaux?
(pause)
– Oui, j'aime les animaux.
– Est-ce que tu as un animal à la maison?
(pause)
– Oui, j'ai un chien.
– Comment s'appelle-t-il?
(pause)
– Il s'appelle Caspar.
– Comment ça s'écrit?
(pause)
– Ça s'écrit C-A-S-P-A-R.
– Il a quel âge?
(pause)
– Il a quatre ans.

Épreuve – Unité 4

These worksheets can be used for an informal test of listening, reading and writing or for extra practice, as required. For general notes on administering the *Épreuves*, see TB 20.

CM 4/8, 1/45–48 **INFORMAL ASSESSMENT LISTENING**

Épreuve: Écouter

A Les animaux (NC 1)

Solution: b, c, e, d, f, a (mark /5)

Les animaux

1 Voici mon chien. C'est mon chien.
2 Et voici mon chat. C'est mon chat.
3 Et voilà ma souris. Elle est blanche, ma souris.
4 J'ai aussi un cochon d'Inde. C'est Dodu, mon cochon d'Inde s'appelle Dodu.
5 Puis voici ma perruche. C'est ma perruche bleue.
6 Et voilà mon lapin. Le lapin s'appelle Pierrot.

B Comment ça s'écrit? (NC 2)

You may wish to point out that these are all proper names and that number 4 is two words.

Solution: See transcript. (mark /5)

Comment ça s'écrit?

1 V-a-n-i-l-l-e
2 C-a-r-o-t-t-e
3 M-i-n-o-u
4 L-a R-o-c-h-e-l-l-e
5 P-a-r-i-s
6 B-l-a-n-c-o

C C'est quelle image? (NC 2)

Solution: 1a, 2b, 3a, 4a, 5b, 6b (mark /5)

C'est quelle image?

1 – Est-ce que tu as un animal à la maison?
– Oui, j'ai un oiseau. C'est une perruche. Regarde, elle est dans sa cage.
2 – Est-ce que tu as un animal, David?
– Oui, j'ai des poissons. J'ai trois poissons rouges.
3 – Voici mon cheval. Il est super, non?
– Oui, oui. Il est complètement blanc. Il est fantastique, ton cheval!
4 – Regarde! Dans la boîte, il y a deux petits hamsters.
– Ah oui, ils sont mignons, tes petits hamsters! Tu as des lapins aussi?
– Non, je n'ai pas de lapins.
5 – Attention! Ton chat est sur la table!
– Oh non! Maman! Minou est sur la table!
6 – Voici ton prix. C'est un cédérom sur les animaux.
– Oh, merci beaucoup. J'aime beaucoup les cédéroms, et j'adore les animaux.

D Un sondage – Aimez-vous les chiens? (NC 3)

Solution: 1a, 2b, 3c, 4a, 5d, 6a (mark /5)

«Aimez-vous les chiens?» Un sondage

1 – Tu aimes les chiens?
– Oui, j'aime les chiens.
2 – Qu'est-ce que vous préférez, Mademoiselle, les chiens ou les chats?
– J'adore tous les animaux. J'adore les chiens.
3 – Est-ce que vous aimez les chiens, Monsieur?

- Non, pas beaucoup. Enfin, non, je n'aime pas les animaux.

4 – Est-ce que tu aimes les chiens, Linda?
- Bien sûr. J'ai deux chiens et je les aime.

5 – Tu aimes les chiens, Richard?
- Ah non. J'aime les chats, mais je déteste les chiens. Ils sont souvent méchants!

6 – Monsieur, on pose des questions sur les chiens. Est-ce que vous aimez les chiens?
- Euh, les chiens, oui, ça va. Oui, oui, j'aime les chiens, mais je préfère les chats – les chats sont plus indépendants.

CM 4/9 **READING**

Épreuve: Lire

A Les animaux et les couleurs (NC 2)

Solution: **1** black cat, **2** green bird, **3** blue and orange parrot, **4** grey mice, **5** red and yellow fish (mark /7: 1 mark per colour)

B C'est quelle description? (NC 2)

Solution: **1b, 2a, 3a, 4a, 5a, 6b** (mark /5)

C Chez la famille Marchadier (NC 3)

Solution: **1V, 2V, 3V, 4F, 5V, 6F, 7F, 8V, 9F** (mark /8)

CM 4/10 **WRITING GRAMMAR**

Épreuve: Écrire et grammaire

A Un serpent (NC 1)

Solution: *un chien, une perruche, un chat, un cheval, un poisson, une tortue, un perroquet* (mark /6)

B Masculin ou féminin (NC 1)

Solution: **1** *petit,* **2** *mignonne,* **3** *grande,* **4** *jolie,* **5** *blanche,* **6** *grand,* **7** *gros* (mark /6)

C Des questions (NC 3)

Solution: Open-ended task (mark /8: 1 mark for correct question, 1 mark for correct *tu* or *vous* form)

SB 32–33, CM 103, 1/49 **READING**

Presse-Jeunesse 1

These pages provide reading for pleasure. They can be used alone or with the accompanying copymaster. See the notes on TB 17.

CM 103 **READING STRATEGIES**

1 Lire – c'est facile

This is the first of a series of short sections covering reading strategies. Similar items feature on each of the *Presse-Jeunesse* copymasters, and it is suggested that students cut them out and stick them in their exercise books for reference.

SB 32, CM 103

Henri ou Henriette

Solutions:

A **1** adopt, **2** RSPCA, **3** keep, **4** alas/unfortunately, **5** open, **6** closes/shuts, **7** *a* disaster, **8** *a* hedgehog
B **1** *un chat,* **2** *la cuisine,* **3** *une cage,* **4** *la porte,* **5** *le poisson*
C **1, 7, 2, 8, 10, 3, 9, 5, 4, 6**

SB 33, CM 103, 1/49 **SOUNDS AND WRITING**

Deux comptines

These items are at the end of CD 1.

Solution: **1b, 2c, 3d, 4f, 5a, 6e**

Deux comptines

Un, deux, j'ai pondu deux œufs
«Un, deux, j'ai pondu deux œufs»,
dit la poule bleue.
«Un, deux, trois, j'en ai pondu trois»,
répond l'oie.
«Quatre, cinq, six, sept, j'en ai pondu sept»,
s'écrie la poulette.
«Huit et neuf, qu'il est beau, mon œuf!»

Le Pont Neuf
Un, deux, trois, quand il fait froid,
Quatre, cinq, six, comme exercice,
Sept, huit, neuf, sur le Pont Neuf,
Dix, onze, douze, chantons ce blues:
Un, deux, trois, quand il fait froid.

SB 33, CM 103

Flash-Web

Solutions:

Les Extra-terrestres

1 *deux,* **2** *un, une,* **3** *Vénus,* **4** *frère,* **5** *le père,* **6** *la mère,* **7** *Katie*

Internet et les extra-terrestres

circulaire – circular, *communiquer* – to communicate, *explorer* – to explore, *gigantesque* – gigantic, *identifier* – to identify, *message* – message, *possible* – possible, *signal* – signal, *solution* – solution, *télescope* – telescope

Encore Tricolore 1
nouvelle édition

unité 5 Des fêtes et des festivals

Areas	Topics	Grammar
1	Months of the year Asking for and giving the date	
2		Present tense of *être* (D-L SB 37)
3	Discussing important events in the year Understanding and giving greetings	
4	Talking about some clothes	Plural of nouns (D-L SB 40)
5	Talking about birthdays and presents	
6	Describing presents	Agreement of adjectives (singular and plural) (D-L SB 44)
7		Present tense of *avoir* (D-L SB 45)
8	Further activities and consolidation	

National Curriculum information

Some students	Level 3
Most students	Levels 2–3
All students	Levels 1–2

Refer also to the information about coverage of 'Knowledge, skills and understanding' (TB 9).

Revision

The vocabulary and structures introduced in *Unités 4–5* are revised in the *Rappel* section following this unit (SB 48–49, TB 109).

Sounds and writing

- *ou* and *u*
- introduction to liaison (*nous avons*)
- see *Écoute et parle* (SB 154, TB 106–107)

ICT opportunities

- looking up information on French Internet sites (TB 95)
- sending a virtual greetings card (TB 98, 207–208)

Reading strategies

Use of a dictionary to interpret meaning. Introduction of *C'est utile, le dictionnaire* (SB 39, 41) which becomes a regular feature from this point onwards.

Assessment

- Informal assessment is in the *Épreuves* at the end of this unit (TB 107–108).
- Formal assessment is in the *Deuxième contrôle* following *Unité 7* (TB 201).

Students' Book

Unité 5 SB 34–47

Au choix SB 131 1 (TB 95), 2 (TB 97), 3 (TB 98), 4 (TB 99) SB 132 5 (TB 100), 6 (TB 101), 7 (TB 103)

Écoute et parle SB 154 (TB 106)

Rappel 2 SB 48–49 (TB 109)

Flashcards

1 smiley face
13–17 rooms
18–26 animals etc.
11, 27, 41, 43, 45, 100 (for clothing)

Additional

Grammar in Action 1, pp 12, 17

CDs

2/1–11
Student CD 1/32–37
Student CD 2/25–27

Copymasters

5/1 *Des dates* [speaking: pairwork] (TB 95)
5/2 *être* [grammar] (TB 97)
5/3 *Des vêtements* [mini-flashcards/support] (TB 99)
5/4 *Jeux de vocabulaire* [support] (TB 102)
5/5 *Des cadeaux et des vêtements* [reading/speaking/writing] (TB 102)
5/6 *Une lettre pour dire «merci»* [grammar: adjectival agreement] (TB 103)
5/7 *avoir* [grammar] (TB 104)
5/8 *Tu comprends?* [independent listening] (TB 105)
5/9 *Sommaire* (TB 106)
5/10 *Épreuve: Écouter* (TB 107)
5/11 *Épreuve: Lire* (TB 108)
5/12 *Épreuve: Écrire et grammaire* (TB 108)

Language content

The date (Area 1)

Le combien sommes-nous?
C'est le trente août.
C'est quand, le concert/le match?
C'est le mardi premier juin.
C'est quand, ton anniversaire?
C'est le dix-neuf juillet.
Quelle est la date de ton anniversaire?
Mon anniversaire est le quinze mars.

Months (Area 1)

janvier
février
mars
avril
mai
juin
juillet
août
septembre
octobre
novembre
décembre

Events in the year (Area 1)

le jour de l'An
la Fête Nationale
Pâques
Noël
le Mardi gras

Greetings (Area 3)

Bonne année
Joyeuses Pâques
Joyeux Noël
Bon anniversaire
Bonne fête

Clothes (Area 4)

baskets (f pl)
casquette (f)
chaussette (f)
chaussure (f)
cravate (f)
jogging (m)
jupe (f)
pantalon (m)
robe (f)
short (m)
pull (m)
T-shirt (m)

Talking about presents (Area 5)

Voici un petit cadeau pour toi/vous.
C'est très gentil.
Merci beaucoup.
De rien.
Qu'est-ce qu'on t'a offert?
On m'a offert des vêtements.

Classroom language and rubrics

Écris le mot qui manque.
Trouve le bon dessin.
Choisis le bon mot.
Complète les phrases.
Lis le résumé.
Note la bonne lettre.
C'est vrai ou faux?
Écris les verbes dans ton cahier.
Changez les mots en couleur.

Area 1
Months of the year
Asking for and giving the date

SB 34–35, 1–6
Au choix SB 131, 1
CD 2/1
CM 5/1

Quel jour sommes-nous? C'est quelle date? C'est quand, ...? C'est le ...

Numbers **REVISION**

Revise the numbers 1–31 orally, perhaps using some of the number games (see TB 25).

Days of the week **REVISION**

Revise the days of the week, e.g.

a by writing some days on the board but missing some out – students read them out and fill in the blanks;

b by playing *Loto* with four days written on a piece of paper. This game can be extended or varied by having, say, four days and four numbers between 1 and 10 (see TB 25, 28).

Months **PRESENTATION**

Next, teach the months orally, then write these on the board. This works well in batches of three months at a time. Various games could be played to practise the months, e.g. *Chef d'orchestre, Effacez!, Loto, Pelmanism* (see TB 25–30).

For extra practice, use a French calendar, if available, or refer to the list of months on the board. Point to one and say *C'est* (+ month), *oui ou non?* to elicit *Oui, c'est* (+ month) if correct, or *Non, c'est* (+ correct month).

Teach *premier* and *dernier*, e.g.
Le premier mois, c'est ...? Le dernier mois, c'est novembre? Non, le dernier mois, c'est décembre.

The full date **PRESENTATION**

Teach and practise the full date orally and eventually in written form, starting from today's date. Then point to the first day of several months on the calendar, or jot down some dates in figures, to practise *le premier* before going on to other full dates. Give plenty of practice, e.g. by dictating some to be written down in figures, writing dates on the board and getting individuals to supply the date of the days before and after. *Effacez!* would be a good game to play; with the dates written in figures on the board. (See TB 26 for this and other games to practise the date.)

SB 34–35, 2/1 **LISTENING**

1 C'est quelle date?

Students should have a look at the fourteen dates, before listening to the recording. They then note down which date is linked with each conversation.

Solution: **1h, 2a, 3i, 4j, 5n, 6d, 7k, 8g, 9f, 10c, 11e, 12l**

C'est quelle date?

1 – C'est quand, l'anniversaire de Christophe?
– C'est lundi, le 17 juillet.

2 – Salut.
– Salut. Ça va?
– Oui, ça va.
– Tu vas au grand match de football, Marseille contre Saint-Étienne?
– C'est quand, le match?
– C'est samedi, le 20 janvier.
– Oui, je veux bien.

3 – Hé, Françoise, tu vas au concert?
– C'est quand le concert?
– C'est vendredi, le 11 août.
– Le onze août, hmm ... je ne sais pas.

4 – Salut, Pascale. Tu vas à la surprise-partie chez Roland?
– Non ... c'est quand?
– C'est samedi, le 15 septembre.

5 – Le film au Club des Jeunes, c'est quand?
– Le film sur la vie des animaux? C'est mercredi, le 13 décembre.

6 – C'est quand, le match de rugby?
– C'est dimanche, le neuf mars.

7 – Salut Chantal. Il y a un bon concert à l'Olympia. Tu as vu l'affiche?
– Non. C'est quand?
– C'est jeudi, le 18 octobre.

8 – La fête de la musique, c'est quand, cette année?
– C'est le 21 juin. C'est un samedi.
– Excellent! J'adore ça!

9 – C'est quand, la Fête des Mères?
– C'est dimanche, le 25 mai.

10 – Mardi gras, c'est quand cette année?
– C'est le 15 février.

11 – Alexandre, c'est quand, ta fête?
– C'est le 22 avril.

12 – Sylvie, c'est quand ta fête?
– Ma fête, c'est le cinq novembre. Le cinq novembre, c'est la Sainte-Sylvie.

SB 34 **WRITING**

2 Des dates importantes

Students complete the dates with the correct month.

Solution: **1** *février,* **2** *février,* **3** *octobre,* **4** *août,* **5** *janvier,* **6** *décembre,* **7** *mai*

SB 34, SPEAKING/WRITING

3 C'est quand?

One student asks for the date of an event and the other replies by referring to the calendar slips. If preferred, it could be done as a written task.

Solution:

1 *C'est le 15 février.*
2 *C'est le 21 juin.*
3 *C'est le cinq novembre.*
4 *C'est le neuf mars.*
5 *C'est le 17 juillet.*
6 *C'est le 15 septembre.*

As follow-up, students could ask each other in turn the date for other events, e.g.

– *Le concert à l'Olympia, c'est quand?*
– *C'est le dix-huit octobre.*

SB 34 WRITING

4 Les jours de la semaine

Students supply the missing vowels in order to write out the days correctly. They are listed in order.

SB 34 EXTENSION

Students may remember from *Unité 3* that the two letters are *di*.

SB 35 READING

5 Bonne fête

This short reading passage gives some background information about the traditional practice of naming French children after saints and celebrating the saint's day as their *fête*.

For further information about saints' days, see TB 31 and TB 207.

When students have read the text, they should find the *fêtes* for the names listed and answer the questions orally and/or in writing.

If students enquire why *la* is used with the names of masculine saints, point out that *la Saint-Olivier* is short for ***la fête** de Saint Olivier*.

Solution: **1** *le 18 octobre,* **2** *le 25 mai,* **3** *le 22 avril,* **4** *le 5 novembre,* **5** *le 15 septembre,* **6** *le 13 décembre,* **7** *le 15 février,* **8** *le 6 décembre,* **9** *le 17 juillet,* **10** *le 11 août*

SB 35 READING

!

Students or teachers might use the Internet to research saints' days (see TB 207 for website details). Information can be downloaded for use off-line.

SB 35 WRITING

6 Les mois de l'année

In this short task, students write out several different months.

Solution: **1** *mars,* **2** *avril,* **3** *août,* **4** *novembre,* **5** *janvier,* **6** *décembre,* **7** *mai,* **8** *septembre*

CM 5/1, SPEAKING

Des dates

In this information-gap task, students have to find out details about dates and events.

Au choix SB 131 WRITING

1 L'année prochaine

This task is best done before or near the beginning of a new year. Students consult a calendar and note down the days and dates of significant events, birthdays, Easter etc.

Additional activities

CONSOLIDATION

Jeu: Rendez-vous?

Students should note down two free days in a diary for next week. They then work in pairs to see if they have a free day in common and to see who is first to discover the other person's two free days. They can then play the game again with other partners and continue until they find another person with the same free days as theirs.

Tu es libre le lundi 27 janvier?
Non. Et toi, tu es libre le jeudi 31 janvier?
Oui. Voilà. Alors rendez-vous le jeudi 31 janvier.

The calendar

For information about the origin of the names of months and different kinds of calendars see TB 32.

Area 2
Present tense of *être*

SB 36–37, 1–4
Au choix SB 131, 2
CM 5/2
CD 2/2
FC 13–17
Grammar in Action 1, page 17

FC 13–17 PRESENTATION PRACTICE

Singular paradigm of *être*

Using the flashcards, revise the names of rooms in a house taught in *Unité 3* and use these to revise the singular forms of *être*.

Give the flashcards to individual students and ask *Où es-tu?* for the reply *Je suis dans* (+ room).

After this has been practised several times, revise the third person singular by asking the rest of the class: *Où est-il/elle? Où est* (name)? for the reply *Il/Elle est dans* (+ room).

The singular paradigm could be written on the board for reference at this point.

For more practice, see *Touché-coulé* (TB 26).

Plural paradigm of *être* — PRESENTATION

• ***nous* form**

To present *nous sommes*, say some sentences which relate to the class as a whole, and get students to deduce the meaning, e.g.
Nous sommes dans la salle de classe.
Nous sommes au collège.
Nous sommes à (+ town).
Nous sommes en Angleterre/en Écosse etc.

Write these on the board for a game of *Effacez!* later (see TB 26).

Add *nous sommes* to the paradigm on the board.

• ***vous* form**

Play a 'mind-reading game' (see TB 27). The teacher thinks of a French town from those shown on the map (SB 3). Students have to guess where the teacher is, using *Vous êtes* (+ place). Then two students can consult together to think of a town and the rest of the class have to guess where they are. Continue for about six goes. Then write a few example sentences on the board for a game of *Effacez!* (see TB 26).

Add *vous êtes* to the paradigm.

• ***ils* form**

Collect together several pencils and revise:
Qu'est-ce que c'est?
C'est un crayon.
Il y a combien de crayons? etc.

Then describe them:
Ils sont verts.
Ils sont sur la table.

Choose two other groups of objects, e.g. pens, books, exercise books, and get the class to think of a few ways to describe them.

Once the class is thoroughly clear about the meaning, add *ils sont* to the paradigm.

• ***elles* form**

The *elles* form can then be presented in a similar way, using *gomme, boîte, règle*. Eventually add it to the paradigm.

Paradigm of *être*

Once you have completed the paradigm of *être* on the board, use it for a version of *Effacez!* now or after using the *Dossier-langue* (SB 37). Make up sentences, using one of the forms, and choose a student to point to or rub out the form used.

After a few parts of the verb have disappeared, replace them, getting members of the class to spell out the missing words to someone else, who writes them in the gap.

Where possible, get students to make up further sentences themselves.

SB 36, 2/2 — **LISTENING**

1 Le Mardi gras

This presents examples of all forms of *être* in context. Explain *déguisé* and *les deux méchantes sœurs* and write these on the board, e.g.
'Déguisé', qu'est-ce que c'est en anglais?
Et 'les deux méchantes sœurs' de Cendrillon?

Students should then listen to the recording and choose the correct answer, **a** or **b**.

Solution: 1b, 2b, 3a, 4a, 5b, 6a, 7b, 8a

Le Mardi gras

– Bonjour. Je m'appelle Luc. Aujourd'hui, c'est le 15 février.
– Oui, c'est mardi 15 février et c'est Mardi gras.
– Nous sommes à la discothèque pour une grande soirée Carnaval.
– C'est très amusant. Beaucoup de personnes à la discothèque sont déguisées.
– Regarde le garçon là-bas. Il est déguisé comme Dracula.
– Et moi, je suis déguisée comme un perroquet.
– Voilà les deux méchantes sœurs de Cendrillon. Vous êtes bien déguisées! Qui êtes-vous?
– Tu ne sais pas? Nous sommes Anne-Marie et Suzanne. Nous sommes bien comme les deux méchantes sœurs, non?
– Oui, vous êtes excellentes.
– Mais regarde le fantôme là-bas. Qui est-ce?
– C'est Sébastien?
– Non, ce n'est pas Sébastien.
– Alors, c'est Olivier. C'est toi, Olivier? Tu es le fantôme?
– Oui, c'est moi – je suis le fantôme.

SB 36 — **READING**

2 C'est qui?

This gives further examples of the verb *être* in use. Students read through the introduction and speech bubbles in order to identify the people in fancy dress.

Solution: **1** *Coralie,* **2** *Luc,* **3** *Sébastien,* **4** *Olivier,* **5** *Roseline,* **6** *Christophe,* **7** *Jean-Pierre,* **8** *Anne-Marie et Suzanne*

SB 37 — **GRAMMAR**

Dossier-langue
Être (to be – I am, you are etc.)

This explains the complete paradigm of *être*.

If not done earlier, write the paradigm of *être* on the board and use it for a game of *Effacez!* (see TB 26). Alternatively it could be written with some gaps and the class have to read it out, filling in the gaps.

SB 37 GRAMMAR

3 C'est moi!

Students match the subject with the correct part of the verb.

Solution: 1g, 2h, 3d, 4c, 5i, 6a, 7f, 8e, 9b

SB 37 GRAMMAR

4 Des photos

Students complete the comments on the photos with parts of *être*. This can be done orally or by writing the complete part of *être*.

Solution: **1** *Vous êtes,* **2** *je suis,* **3** *Tu es,* **4** *Nous sommes,* **5** *je suis,* **6** *Il est,* **7** *Ils sont,* **8** *Elles sont,* **9** *Coralie est,* **10** *Roseline est*

CM 5/2 GRAMMAR PRACTICE

This provides further practice in using *être* and can be used at any time after the full paradigm has been presented.

Solutions:

1 Où est tout le monde?
1 *êtes,* **2** *suis,* **3** *est,* **4** *sommes,* **5** *sont,* **6** *est,* **7** *est*

2 Questions
1 *sommes,* **2** *est,* **3** *es,* **4** *sont,* **5** *Es,* **6** *est,* **7** *êtes,* **8** *est*

3 Réponses
a *suis,* **b** *suis,* **c** *est,* **d** *sont,* **e** *est,* **f** *est,* **g** *est,* **h** *sommes*

4 Trouve les paires
1g, 2f, 3b, 4d, 5a, 6e, 7h, 8c

AU CHOIX SB 131 CONSOLIDATION

2 Notre famille

This task provides further practice of the different parts of *être*.

Solution: **1** *Notre famille est,* **2** *je suis,* **3** *Mon anniversaire est,* **4** *Il est,* **5** *Elle est,* **6** *es-tu,* **7** *Il est,* **8** *Il est,* **9** *nous sommes,* **10** *mes parents sont,* **11** *ils ne sont pas*

GRAMMAR IN ACTION 1, PAGE 17 GRAMMAR

Using the verb être – to be

This provides further practice of *être*, if needed, but includes some unfamiliar vocabulary, e.g. *libres, ce soir, ce matin, à l'heure* etc. It might be best to use this later (perhaps in *Unité* 8) for revision.

Area 3
Discussing important events in the year
Understanding and giving greetings

SB 38–39, 1–5
Au choix SB 131, 3
CD 2/3

SB 38, 2/3 LISTENING READING

1 L'année en France

First play the recording without the text, and stop after each section to bring out the main points. Then play the complete passage with the class following the text in their books.

Use the illustrations to help students to understand the information about each event and explain aspects the students might not know about, in English if necessary, e.g. *La Fête des Rois*.

L'année en France

1. Le premier janvier, c'est le jour de l'An. On dit «Bonne année» à des amis.
2. Le six janvier, c'est la Fête des Rois. Nous mangeons un gâteau spécial ce jour-là. Le gâteau s'appelle la galette des rois.
3. Au mois de février, il y a le Mardi gras. On mange des crêpes.
   Dans certaines villes, comme à Nice par exemple, il y a un grand carnaval.
4. Le premier avril, on fait des poissons d'avril. Ça, c'est amusant!
5. En mars ou en avril, il y a Pâques. On mange des œufs en chocolat ... et aussi des lapins et des poules en chocolat. Hmm, c'est bon. J'aime bien le chocolat.
6. Puis en mai, il y a la Fête des Mères. Les enfants donnent une carte ou des fleurs à leur mère.
7. Et le 14 juillet, c'est la Fête Nationale. Il y a un défilé dans la rue. Et le soir, il y a souvent un feu d'artifice.
8. Au mois d'août, c'est les vacances. Ça, c'est bien.
9. Au mois de septembre, c'est la rentrée. La nouvelle année scolaire commence.
10. Enfin, il y a Noël. La fête de Noël commence le 24 décembre. Nous allons à l'église. Nous chantons des chants de Noël. Le Père Noël apporte des cadeaux aux enfants. On dit «Joyeux Noël» à tous.

SB 39 DICTIONARY PRACTICE

2 C'est utile, le dictionnaire

Students look up words from Task 1 and find out translations and genders, using the glossary.

Solution:

cadeau m = present	*fleur m* = flower
défilé m = procession	*œuf m* = egg
église f = church	*poule f* = hen
feu d'artifice m = firework	

SB 39 WRITING

3 C'est quel mois?

Check that students know the greetings for each of the main festivals, e.g.
Qu'est-ce qu'on dit à Noël/Pâques/pour le nouvel an?
On dit «Joyeux Noël/Joyeuses Pâques/Bonne année».

The pronoun *on* is used in Tasks 3 and 4. Briefly explain its meaning here. It is taught more fully in *Unité 6*.

Solution: **1** *en mars ou en avril,* **2** *en février ou en mars,* **3** *en janvier,* **4** *en décembre,* **5** *en juillet,* **6** *en janvier,* **7** *en janvier*

SB 39, SPEAKING

4 C'est quelle fête?

One student reads out a description of the event and the other has to guess the *fête*.

Solution: **1** *Noël,* **2** *Mardi gras,* **3** *Pâques,* **4** *la Fête Nationale,* **5** *la Fête des Mères,* **6** *Noël,* **7** *la Fête des Rois*

SB 39 READING

5 Des cartes pour toutes les fêtes

Students link greetings with appropriate *fêtes*.

Solution: 1c, 2d, 3a, 4b, 5f, 6g, 7e

CONSOLIDATION

Virtual greetings cards

This task could be done at any point in *Unité 5*. A virtual greetings card in French can be sent via numerous websites (see TB 207 for more details). This would work well as an early e-mail or Internet activity. A card could be sent to friends in other classes, family or students from link schools.

As an example, the teacher could send the class a virtual greetings card in advance.

Au choix SB 131 READING EXTENSION

3 Des annonces

Students read material based on events linked to festivals and decide whether the statements are true or false. As an extension activity, students could correct the false sentences.

Solution: **1F** *C'est à Pâques.* **2V, 3F** *C'est vendredi, samedi et lundi.* **4F** *C'est le 14 juillet.* **5V, 6V, 7F** *C'est le 17, le 18 et le 19 décembre.*

Area 4
Talking about some clothes
Using the plural form of nouns

SB 40–41, 1–4
CM 5/3
Au choix SB 131, 4–5
CD 2/4–5
Écoute et parle SB 154, 3
Student CD 1/31
FC (optional) **11, 27, 41, 43, 45, 100**
(or others showing clothing)

une jupe, une robe, un pantalon, un pull, un T-shirt, une cravate, un jogging, un short, des chaussettes, des chaussures, des baskets, une casquette

FC 11, 27, 41, 43, 45, 100 ETC. PRESENTATION

Clothing vocabulary

Teach some of the above clothing vocabulary by describing what you and students are wearing or by describing the clothing of the people illustrated on the flashcards, e.g.

11 *Le garçon de café porte une cravate (noire).*

27 *Le garçon porte une casquette (bleue), un T-shirt (vert), un short (bleu) et des chaussures (noires).*

41 *La fille porte un pull (brun), un pantalon (bleu) et des chaussettes (blanches).*

43 *La fille qui regarde les oranges porte une robe (rose).*

45 *La fille porte une jupe (rouge), un pull (vert) et des chaussures (noires).*

100 *Le garçon porte un T-shirt (rouge), un short (marron) et des baskets (blanches).*

Additional flashcards for clothing can be made by using pictures from magazines, particularly of well-known personalities. The Internet also provides a ready source of photographs of famous people. You can make good visuals if you have access to a colour printer. See procedures outlined in the introductory ICT section for finding pictures on the Internet, copying and printing images (TB 21–24).

Appropriate visuals can be distributed to students who have to describe one or more item of clothing worn by the person illustrated.

SB 40, READING SPEAKING

1 Des vêtements

This presents the written form of the new vocabulary. The pictures can be used first for an oral task, done as a pairwork or class activity, e.g.
1 *Qu'est-ce que c'est? Un pantalon.*

The words could also be written on the board for a game of *Effacez!* (TB 26).

Students should then write out a list of the new clothing vocabulary in their exercise books, referring to the shapes for help. They could also add them to their electronic phrase book if they have one (TB 40).

SB 40 **GRAMMAR**

Dossier-langue
Plurals

Several plural words have already been introduced in previous units, but this table summarises the basic plural forms.

After students have read through the explanation, ask them to form plurals orally, using known vocabulary, e.g. *un livre, un stylo, une balle, le garçon, la fille, le chien, l'appartement, un T-shirt, une chaussette* etc.

Emphasise that the plural does not normally sound any different from the singular in French (unlike in English).

SB 154, TB 106, SCD 1/31 **LISTENING READING WRITING**

3 Les sons français

This *Écoute et parle* task gives further practice of plural sounds and liaison (see TB 106).

SB 41, 2/4 **LISTENING**

2 On parle des vêtements

a First revise colours by asking questions about the clothes worn by the people illustrated, e.g. *Qui porte une jupe? De quelle couleur est la jupe? Qui porte un pantalon gris?* etc.

Students then listen to these short descriptions and identify the people speaking.

Solution: **1** *Thomas,* **2** *Lucie,* **3** *Julie,* **4** *Luc,* **5** *Claire,* **6** *Marc*

On parle des vêtements

1. Pour le voyage à La Rochelle, je porte un short vert et un T-shirt jaune … et je porte ma nouvelle casquette bleue.
2. Moi, je vais à Paris, alors je porte un pull bleu, une jupe grise et des chaussures noires.
3. Pour le voyage à Toulouse, je porte un jogging bleu et un T-shirt rouge et je porte mes nouvelles chaussures blanches.
4. Alors, moi, je vais dans les Alpes, où il fait froid. Je porte un pantalon noir et deux pulls – un est gris, l'autre est rouge. Et je porte des chaussettes rouges aussi.
5. Pour le voyage à Bordeaux, je porte une robe verte et des chaussures vertes aussi. Et je prends un pull blanc avec moi.
6. Pour aller à Strasbourg, je porte un pantalon gris et un pull bleu et mes baskets. J'ai aussi une cravate bleue, mais elle est dans ma poche!

b As an extension to the *Vrai ou faux?* activity, students could also correct the false statements.

Solution:

1F *Marc porte un pantalon gris.*
2F *Claire porte une robe verte.*
3F *Thomas porte un short vert.*
4V
5F *Luc porte des chaussettes rouges.*
6V
7F *Julie porte un T-shirt rouge.*
8V
9F *Marc a une cravate bleue.*
10V

c In this gap-fill activity students write down the appropriate items of clothing.

Solution:

1. *pulls, pull, rouge*
2. *pantalon, chaussettes*
3. *robe, chaussures*
4. *jaune, short, casquette*
5. *jogging, T-shirt, chaussures*
6. *gris, bleu, cravate*

Describing clothing **SPEAKING**

For further practice of the new vocabulary and colours, play a chain game where each student describes one item of clothing that they are wearing and then names a fellow student, e.g.
Je porte des chaussures noires. Philippe.
Je porte un pantalon gris. Suzanne … etc.

CM 5/3 **MINI-FLASHCARDS/SUPORT**

Les vêtements

These mini-flashcards can be used here for consolidation and support to practise clothing vocabulary or in Area 6 to practise adjectival agreement. See TB 28 for suggestions for use.

AU CHOIX SB 131, 2/5 **WRITING LISTENING**

4 Des vêtements pour le week-end

a Students write out a list of the clothing shown.

Solution:

1. *un jogging noir*
2. *un T-shirt jaune*
3. *un pull gris*
4. *des chaussettes vertes*
5. *des chaussures (des baskets) blanches*
6. *un short rouge*
7. *une casquette brune*
8. *un pantalon bleu*

b Students then listen to the recording and note the difference in colour of six of the clothes.

Solution:

Dans la conversation, …
1. *le T-shirt est bleu,*
2. *le pull est rouge,*
3. *les chaussettes sont grises,*
4. *le short est blanc,*
5. *la casquette est verte,*
6. *le pantalon est noir.*

Des vêtements pour le week-end

– Qu'est-ce que tu prends comme vêtements pour le week-end à Strasbourg?
– Bon, euh, je prends mon jogging noir et mon T-shirt bleu.
– Tu prends un pull aussi?
– Oui, je prends mon pull rouge.
– Tu prends tes chaussettes vertes?
– Non, je prends mes chaussettes grises. Je prends aussi mon short blanc.
– Ton short blanc et ta casquette?
– Oui, je prends ma casquette verte.
– Tu prends un pantalon aussi?
– Oui, je prends mon pantalon noir et mes baskets. Voilà, c'est tout.

SB 41 **GRAMMAR**

3 C'est au pluriel?

Students find five words in the plural.

Solution: **2** *les fenêtres,* **3** *les baskets,* **6** *des chaussures,* **7** *mes animaux,* **10** *des casquettes*

SB 41 **DICTIONARY PRACTICE**

4 C'est utile, le dictionnaire

In this task, students find the plural form as well as the gender and the English translation and write the words in alphabetical order.

Solution:

bateau, bateaux (m) = boat
chapeau, chapeaux (m) = hat
château, châteaux (m) = castle
gâteau, gâteaux (m) = cake
grand-mère, grands-mères (f) = grandmother
oiseau, oiseaux (m) = bird
petit-fils, petits-fils (m) = grandson

SB 41 **EXTENSION**

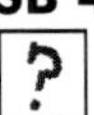

Two words which are plural in English but singular in French are *un pantalon* (trousers) and *un short* (shorts).

Au choix SB 132 **GRAMMAR WRITING**

5 Des cadeaux par deux

Solution: *deux balles de tennis, deux calculettes, deux classeurs, deux stylos, deux trousses, deux sacs (de sport), deux cédéroms*

Area 5
Talking about birthdays and presents

SB 42–43, 1–5
CD 2/6–7
CM 5/4, 5/5
Au choix SB 132, 6

C'est quand ton anniversaire? C'est ...
Voici un petit cadeau pour toi/vous.
C'est très gentil. Merci beaucoup.
De rien.
Qu'est-ce qu'on t'a offert? On m'a offert ...

SB 42 **PRESENTATION**

Idées cadeaux

This presents a selection of gifts which are used for various activities. Read through the names of the gifts to familiarise students with the pronunciation.

SB 42, 2/6 **LISTENING**

1 Vous cherchez un cadeau?

Students listen to the recording and note down the letter for each of the eight items mentioned.

Solution: **1a, 2b, 3d, 4e, 5h, 6j, 7m, 8o**

Vous cherchez un cadeau?

C'est l'anniversaire d'un ami? Vous cherchez un cadeau un peu spécial? Nous avons sélectionné pour vous un grand choix de cadeaux de toutes sortes:
Pour les enfants qui aiment s'amuser, surtout le 1er avril, il y a des souris en plastique et même une tarentule en plastique.
Pour les jeunes à l'école, le matériel scolaire est nécessaire et utile – mais ça peut être amusant aussi. Nous avons, par exemple, une trousse en forme de carotte et un crayon énorme.
Pour les personnes qui sont toujours devant l'ordinateur, il y a un grand choix de tapis d'ordinateur.
Pour les jeunes qui aiment les vêtements, il y a des casquettes de tous les styles.
Pour les sportifs, il y a des balles de tennis amusantes.
Et pour toutes les personnes qui aiment la musique, il y a un grand choix de CDs.

SB 42 **READING**

2 La légende

This presents the written form of each gift. Students should note down the letter for each item listed.

Solution: **1m, 2l, 3p, 4c, 5j, 6n, 7o, 8g, 9k, 10e, 11a, 12f, 13h, 14b, 15d, 16i**

SB 43

SPEAKING
WRITING

3 C'est pour offrir

Students choose an appropriate gift for each person.

For support, this could be done orally first, with suggestions from the class written on the board. The task could then be completed in writing.

Solution:

1. *Pour Henri, une tarentule (ou une souris) en plastique.*
2. *Pour Daniel, une calculette.*
3. *Pour Claire, un crayon géant.*
4. *Pour Karim, une bande dessinée.*
5. *Pour Lucie, des balles de tennis.*
6. *Pour Sanjay, un ballon de football.*
7. *Pour Elodie, des chaussettes fantaisie ou un T-shirt.*
8. *Pour Luc, un tapis d'ordinateur ou un cédérom.*

Memory game

PRACTICE

At any suitable point in this area, the class could play a memory game. They look at the selection of gifts in *Idées cadeaux*, close their books and try to recall as many items as possible. To help jog memories, the initial letter of the items could be written on the board.

Dates

REVISION

Quickly revise dates and ask a few able students the date of their birthday.

SB 43, 2/7

LISTENING

4 L'anniversaire de Marc

This conversation is used initially for listening comprehension and then as a model for three dialogues which students practise in pairs. Explain *une raquette de tennis* if necessary.

Solution: 1a, 2c, 3a, 4b, 5c

L'anniversaire de Marc

– Salut, Marc!
– Salut, Claire!
– C'est quand, ton anniversaire?
– C'est aujourd'hui, le premier février.
– Ah! Bon anniversaire. Quel âge as-tu?
– Aujourd'hui, j'ai treize ans.
– Qu'est-ce qu'on t'a offert?
– On m'a offert un T-shirt et une raquette de tennis.
– Il est de quelle couleur, le T-shirt?
– Il est vert.
– Et la raquette?
– Elle est noire.
...
– Bon anniversaire, Marc!
– Salut, Daniel!
– Voici un petit cadeau pour toi.
– C'est très gentil. Une bande dessinée! Merci beaucoup.
– De rien.

PRESENTATION

C'est quand, ton anniversaire?

Remind students of the way in which Claire asked Marc when his birthday was. Then ask a few students *C'est quand, ton anniversaire?*

Eventually develop this into a chain game where each person asks someone else the date of their birthday.

SPEAKING
WRITING

Un sondage

It might be interesting to conduct a birthday survey, to see how many students have their birthday in each month and whether any two or more students have a birthday on the same day.

Students could be divided into four groups and each group asked to collate the results for the people in their group. This could then be reported back to the class as a whole, e.g.

Dans notre groupe, il y a (number) *personnes qui ont un anniversaire au mois de* ... etc.

Or students could work in pairs to find out the date of their partner's birthday and could then report back this information to a group leader or the teacher, e.g.
Robert, c'est quand ton anniversaire?
C'est le 18 janvier.

Qui a un anniversaire au mois de janvier?
L'anniversaire de Robert est le 18 janvier.

The results could be put on a bar graph or database, showing the distribution of birthdays throughout the 12 months. This could be done using ICT.

PRACTICE
SPEAKING

On m'a offert ...

A chain game with an ever increasing list of presents could be played using vocabulary for suitable presents. These could include classroom items, pets and other vocabulary learnt in earlier units as well as the items and clothes taught in this unit.

SB 43,

SPEAKING

5 Inventez des conversations

This consists of three sections from the above conversation, with options for alternative details. Students practise one or more sections according to ability. Able students could do all three sections together.

AU CHOIX SB 132

WRITING

6 Les chaussettes de Jacques

Students write out the missing words in the picture strip.

Solution: **1** *Bon,* **2** *cadeau,* **3** *merci,* **4** *anniversaire,* **5** *beaucoup,* **6** *gentil,* **7** *rien,* **8** *petit,* **9** *chaussettes,* **10** *rouge,* **11** *aime*

CM 5/4 SUPPORT READING WRITING

Jeux de vocabulaire

This consists of four vocabulary tasks based on the themes of the unit so far and could be used as an alternative to the other tasks by students who need more support.

Solutions:

1 Mots mêlés

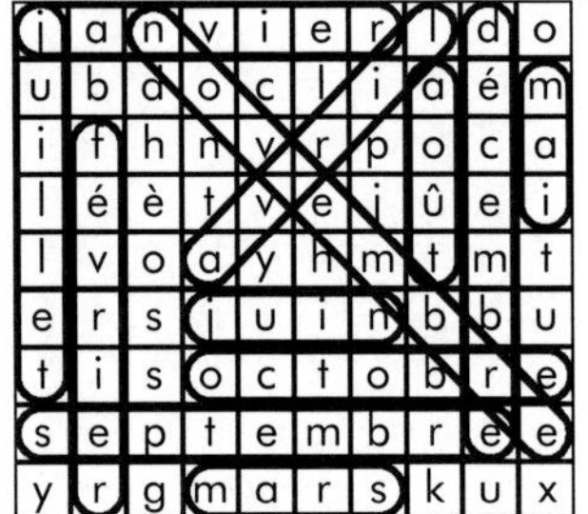

2 Sept vêtements

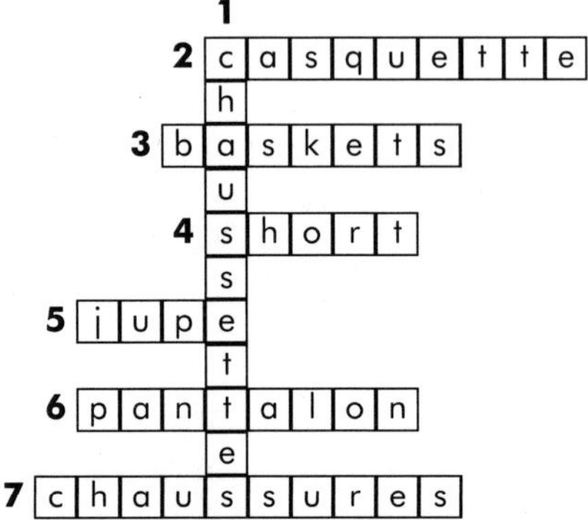

3 Qu'est-ce qu'on dit?
1d, 2a, 3e, 4f, 5b, 6c

4 Un jour important

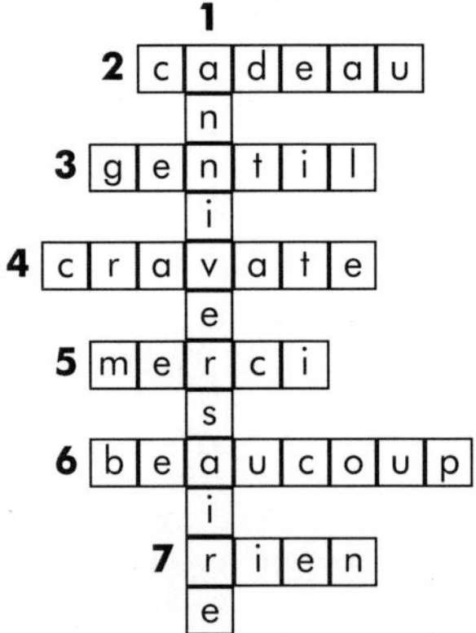

CM 5/5 READING SPEAKING WRITING

Des cadeaux et des vêtements

This copymaster provides consolidation, if needed, for all students.

1 Questions et réponses

This involves matching questions and replies.

Solution: 1e, 2d, 3a, 4f, 5b, 6c

2 Conversations au choix

This provides a framework for a short conversation and could be used in pairs in class or written out for homework. The 'presents' have been chosen to be appropriate for both sexes and this has involved adding one item, which should be easy to understand, but may need to be explained beforehand: *une robe de chambre*.

3 Qu'est-ce qu'il y a dans la valise?

This provides practice of the plural forms of clothing and colours and would be best done after the next area (Area 6).

Solution: *Il y a deux T-shirts, deux tricots, deux pantalons, deux cravates, deux chaussures et deux jupes.*

Area 6
Describing presents
Agreement of adjectives (singular and plural)

SB 44–45, 1–4
Au choix SB 132, 7
CM 5/6
Grammar in Action 1, page 12
FC 1

FC1 REVISION PRESENTATION

Adjectives

Briefly revise adjectives which have already been taught, e.g. colours, *petit*, *grand*. Teach *content* (using FC 1) and *nouveau/nouvelle*.

SB 44 READING

1 Des cadeaux de Noël

Students match up written descriptions with packages.

Solution: 1c, 2a, 3d, 4e, 5b

SB 44 GRAMMAR

Dossier-langue
Using adjectives (singular and plural)

Remind students what an adjective is by writing some examples on the board and asking *Trouvez des adjectifs*, e.g.

- *Les chaussettes sont bleues.*
- *Les chaussures sont grandes.*
- *Les souris sont petites.*

Students could reply orally or could underline the adjective.

Then go through the *Dossier-langue*, pronouncing the examples so that students realise that the final *-s* is not pronounced.

SB 44 GRAMMAR

2 Merci pour les cadeaux

Students choose the appropriate adjective ending.

Solution: **1** *électroniques,* **2** *rouges,* **3** *intéressant,* **4** *contente,* **5** *petits,* **6** *utiles,* **7** *verte,* **8** *élégantes,* **9** *nouveau,* **10** *musicale*

SB 44 GRAMMAR

3 Cherche des adjectifs

Remind students about the plural endings, e.g. *Quand l'adjectif est au pluriel, il y a un -s ou un -x à la fin du mot.*

Solution: (possible examples on SB 44) *blancs, blanches, bons, bonnes, électroniques, élégantes, français, françaises, grands, grandes, musicales, nouveaux, nouvelles, petits, rouges, utiles, vertes*

SB 44 GRAMMAR

!

Encourage students to learn irregular adjectives in phrases, preferably ones they have invented themselves.

SB 45 WRITING

4 Combien d'animaux

Students write sentences using the plural forms of animals and corresponding adjectives of size and colour.

Solution:

1 *Il y a deux cochons d'Inde noirs.*
2 *Il y a trois chats noirs.*
3 *Il y quatre lapins blancs.*
4 *Il y a deux gros chiens.*
5 *Il y a cinq petites souris brunes.*
6 *Il y a trois perroquets verts.*
7 *Il y a six poissons rouges.*
8 *Il y a quatre hamsters jaunes.*
9 *Il y a cinq perruches bleues.*

AU CHOIX SB 132 WRITING

7 Une lettre illustrée

a Students complete the 'thank you' letter by writing the names of the presents (and colours, if possible).

Solution: **1** *la bande dessinée,* **2** *un T-shirt bleu,* **3** *un short blanc,* **4** *une casquette rouge,* **5** *une raquette de tennis,* **6** *des chaussettes bleues,* **7** *des balles de tennis,* **8** *un (petit) chien*

b For extension, students write a similar letter, describing four presents received.

GRAMMAR IN ACTION 1, PAGE 12 GRAMMAR

Singular and plural – nouns, adjectives

This provides additional practice and consolidation of the singular and plural and could be used by students working independently.

CM 5/6 GRAMMAR EXTENSION

Une lettre pour dire «merci»

The letter provides further practice of adjectival agreement for able students and could be used for extension here or later in the course for revision.

Solutions:

1 La lettre

Les mots corrects sont: fantastique, magnifiques, gris, jaune, rouge, noires, petit, verte, énorme, petite, bleues, blanc, gros, brun, blanc, petite, blanche, intelligent

2 Trouve les erreurs

1 *Dominique déteste le groupe "Citron Pressé". aime/adore*
2 *C'est la fête de Dominique. l'anniversaire*
3 *Il a sept cadeaux. dix*
4 *Parmi ses cadeaux, il a des chaussures vertes. noires*
5 *Dominique a une sœur et un beau-frère. frère*
6 *Tigre est un lapin. chat*
7 *Il est noir et blanc. brun*
8 *C'est un animal stupide. intelligent*

3 5-4-3-2-1

5 any five from: *gris, jaune, rouge, noir, vert, bleu, blanc, brun*
4 *un pantalon, un T-shirt, des chaussures, des chaussettes*
3 any three from: *fantastique, magnifique, petit, énorme, gros, intelligent*
2 *un frère, une sœur*
1 any from: *un crayon, une trousse, un stylo*

Area 7
Present tense of *avoir*
SB 45, 5, SB 46, 1–3
FC 18–26
CM 5/7
Classroom objects or clothing

REVISION PRESENTATION

Singular paradigm of *avoir*

Using a collection of classroom objects or clothing, revise the singular paradigm of *avoir*, e.g. *Moi, j'ai une gomme, un livre etc.*

Distribute the objects to students and ask *(Nom), qu'est-ce que tu as?* for the reply *J'ai ... (une gomme/un livre).*

Then ask another student *Est-ce que (nom) a … (une gomme/un livre)?* for the reply *Oui/Non, il/elle a …*

Write the singular paradigm on the board.

Alternatively, ask about personal possessions, perhaps including some ridiculous ones for fun, e.g. *Est-ce que tu as un baladeur/un ordinateur/un perroquet/une tarentule/un dragon/un éléphant dans ta chambre?*

Home-made flashcards could be used to illustrate some of the more unusual possessions.

FC 18–26 **PRESENTATION**

Plural paradigm of *avoir*

To present the *nous* and *vous* forms, ask four able students to come to the front, and say they represent *la famille Lafitte*. Give each pupil two animal flashcards.

Explain to the rest of the class that the Lafittes have lots of pets, and the class have to ask them questions about them, e.g. *Est-ce que vous avez un chien?*

The student with the appropriate flashcard should reply *Oui, nous avons un chien* and show the appropriate flashcard.

Add the *nous* and *vous* forms to the paradigm on the board then make up some sentences about the Lafittes, using the *ils* form, e.g.
Ils ont beaucoup d'animaux.
Ils ont un chien, un cheval, un chat, des lapins.

Then complete the paradigm on the board.

Make up sentences using the present tense of *avoir* and get students to point to the form used and/or to repeat the sentences. Alternatively, make this into a game of *Effacez!* (TB 26).

SB 45

Dossier-langue
Avoir (to have)

This sets out the full paradigm of *avoir* for easy reference.

SB 45 **READING WRITING**

5 Un message de Nicole

This message presents all parts of the verb *avoir* and provides the vocabulary for the first part of the task.

Solution:

a 5 *adjectifs:* any five from: *petit, mignon, blancs, brun, grand, grise, nouveau, électronique*
4 *animaux:* any four from: *un hamster, deux lapins, un cochon d'Inde, un chien, une chatte*
3 *meubles: un lit, une table, une chaise*
2 *membres de la famille: des frères, une sœur,*
1 *appareil électrique:* any one from: *un baladeur, un ordinateur*

b Able students could write a similar message, perhaps to send by e-mail to another class in the UK or in France.

SB 46 **GRAMMAR WRITING**

1 Des cadeaux

Students follow the lines to find the correct present for each person.

Solution:

1 *Mme Lambert a une robe.*
2 *M. Lambert a une cravate.*
3 *Moi, j'ai des baskets/des chaussures.*
4 *Toi, Christophe, tu as un jogging.*
5 *Les filles, vous avez des T-shirts.*
6 *Nous avons des pulls.*
7 *Les deux frères ont des casquettes.*
8 *Les deux sœurs ont des chaussettes.*

SB 46 **GRAMMAR**

2 Chez nous

Students choose the correct part of the verb *avoir* from three options.

Solution: **1** *Nous avons,* **2** *nous avons,* **3** *Nous avons,* **4** *vous avez,* **5** *j'ai,* **6** *ma sœur a,* **7** *mes frères ont,* **8** *tu as*

SB 46 **GRAMMAR**

3 Une conversation

Students give the correct part of *avoir* to match the subject.

Solution: **1** *as-tu,* **2** *J'ai,* **3** *j'ai,* **4** *tu as,* **5** *j'ai,* **6** *je n'ai pas,* **7** *Ma sœur a,* **8** *J'ai,* **9** *Il a,* **10** *vous avez,* **11** *nous avons,* **12** *Nous avons*

CM 5/7 **GRAMMAR PRACTICE**
This provides further practice of *avoir*, if required.

1 avoir – to have

Students complete the paradigm for future reference.

Solutions:

2 En classe
1e, 2f, 3d, 4a, 5c, 6b

3 Des questions et des réponses
a **1** *as,* **2** *as,* **3** *ont,* **4** *a,* **5** *avez,* **6** *a*
b **a** *ont,* **b** *a,* **c** *a,* **d** *avons,* **e** *ai,* **f** *ai*
c **1e, 2f, 3a, 4b, 5d, 6c**

4 Mots croisés

Area 8
Further activities and consolidation

SB 46, 4–5, SB 47
Écoute et parle SB 154, 6, 1–7
CM 5/8–5/12
CD 2/8–11
Student CD 1/33–37
Student CD 2/25–27

SB 46, 2/8 LISTENING/READING

4 Des cadeaux pour Suzanne

This provides further practice of the language used when giving or receiving presents. When students have listened to the recording, ask a few general or *vrai/faux* questions, e.g.

1 *C'est la fête de Suzanne.*
2 *Suzanne a 15 ans.*
3 *On lui a offert beaucoup de livres.*
4 *Les parents de Suzanne lui ont offert un CD.*
5 *Suzanne a beaucoup de CDs de Citron Pressé.*

Then students listen again and complete the *résumé*.

Solution: **1** *janvier,* **2** *l'anniversaire,* **3** *quinze,* **4** *cadeaux,* **5** *CDs,* **6** *parents,* **7** *aime,* **8** *favori,* **9** *beaucoup*

Des cadeaux pour Suzanne

– Aujourd'hui, c'est le vendredi vingt-neuf janvier. C'est l'anniversaire de Suzanne. Elle a quinze ans. On sonne à la porte.

...

– Bonjour, Suzanne. Bon anniversaire!
– Salut Marie. Merci.
– Voici un petit cadeau pour toi.
– Oh merci! C'est très gentil. Mais qu'est-ce que c'est? Oh, un CD! Formidable. Mon groupe préféré! Merci beaucoup.
– De rien.

...

– Salut Suzanne! Bon anniversaire!
– Salut Jean-Luc.
– Voici un petit cadeau.
– Oh merci. C'est très gentil, Jean-Luc. Un CD! Merci beaucoup.
– C'est ton groupe favori, n'est-ce pas?

...

– Bon anniversaire, Suzanne.
– Bonjour Catherine.
– Voilà un petit cadeau pour toi. C'est un CD.
– Oh merci. Citron Pressé!
– Tu aimes bien le groupe Citron Pressé, n'est-ce pas?

...

– Bon anniversaire, Suzanne. Voici un cadeau pour toi.
– Oh merci. C'est un CD?
– Oui, c'est un CD. C'est bien ton groupe favori?
– Oui, j'aime beaucoup ce CD! Merci!

...

– Voici le cadeau de Papa et moi ... Bon anniversaire, Suzanne.
– Oh Maman! C'est très gentil, mais ...
– Tu n'aimes pas le CD, Suzanne?
– Si, maman, mais regarde ...

Chain game with presents SPEAKING

Play a game where one student mentions one item they received for their birthday or Christmas and the next student has to go one (or more!) better and says they have received any number (greater than one) of the same item, e.g.

Pour mon anniversaire, on m'a offert un lapin.

Pour mon anniversaire, on m'a offert neuf lapins.

With able students, adjectives could be included, e.g. *vingt lapins noirs*.

SB 46 WRITING

5 À toi

Students write a list of six names, birthdays and presents.

SB 47, SB 154, TB 107, SCD 1/36 LISTENING

Vocabulaire de classe

This list gives some of the rubrics used in the Students' Book. They are also recorded in random order on the Student CD (see TB 107).

Solution: **1e, 2g, 3c, 4a, 5f, 6h, 7b, 8i, 9d**

CM 5/8, SCD 2/25–27 INDEPENDENT LISTENING

Tu comprends?

1 C'est quand?

The first task could be used at any time after completion of Area 1.

Solution: **1** *août,* **2** *juin,* **3** *avril,* **4** *mai,* **5** *mars,* **6** *octobre*

C'est quand?

1 – C'est quand, le film sur les animaux?
– C'est le six août.
– Le six août, alors.

2 – C'est quand, le concert de musique?
– C'est le 19 juin.
– Ah bon, c'est le 19 juin.

3 – C'est quand, la fête d'anniversaire?
– C'est le 21 avril.
– Le 21 avril, c'est ça?
– Oui.

4 – Le match de basket, c'est quand?
– C'est le 14 mai.
– Le 14 mai, alors.

5 – La soirée Carnaval, c'est quand?
– C'est le 2 mars.
– Le 2 mars, bon.

6 – Le feu d'artifice, c'est quand?
– C'est le 28 octobre.
– Le 28 octobre, alors.

2 Catherine

This practises clothing and colours and can be used at any time after Area 3.

Solution: yellow T-shirt, red jumper, blue skirt, grey shoes, black baseball cap

Catherine

– Qu'est-ce que tu portes pour la fête, Catherine?
– Moi, je porte un T-shirt jaune avec un pull rouge et une jupe bleue. J'ai des chaussures grises et je porte aussi une casquette noire.
– Alors, un T-shirt jaune avec un pull rouge et une jupe bleue, des chaussures grises et une casquette noire.

3 Des cadeaux de Noël

For use after Area 4 or later.

Solution: 1f, 2d, 3a, 4c, 5h, 6b, 7e, 8g

Des cadeaux de Noël

1 – Qu'est-ce que c'est? Ah, une cassette vidéo. C'est bien, j'adore ce film.
2 – Qu'est-ce que tu as?
– Une raquette de tennis. C'est fantastique, j'aime bien le tennis.
3 – Et toi?
– Des jeux de stratégie en cédérom. C'est excellent.
4 – Mmm, une boîte de chocolats. Délicieux.
5 – Moi, j'ai des balles de tennis. Ça, c'est toujours utile.
6 – Qu'est-ce que c'est?
– Un livre, ah, une bande dessinée – j'aime bien ça.
7 – Et toi, qu'est-ce que tu as?
– Un ballon de football.
8 – Et moi, j'ai un nouveau stylo noir. Regarde, il est très chic.

SB 47, CM 5/9

Sommaire

A summary of the main vocabulary and structures of the unit.

SB 154, SCD 1/33–37 SOUNDS AND WRITING

Écoute et parle – Unité 5

Most of these tasks can be used at any appropriate time during the unit. Tasks 3 and 5 fit in with Area 4 (plural forms and clothing) and Task 7 is best used at the end of the unit, when all the language has been practised.

1 Les sons français

Solution: u: (a) 1b, 2e, 3d, 4a, 5c
ou: (a) 1e, 2b, 3c, 4d, 5a

Les sons français

Le son u

a **1** utile
2 Lulu
3 jupe
4 du
5 pur

b rue, sud, sur, tu, judo

Le son ou

a **1** trousse
2 joue
3 août
4 tout
5 nous

b vous, où, douze, joues, groupe

2 Des phrases ridicules

Des phrases ridicules

Tu mets une jupe et du sucre dans la rue?
Douze souris rouges jouent à Toulouse.

3 Les sons français

Solution: 1a z, **b** –, **2a** –, **b** z, **3 a** –, **b** z, **4 a** –, **b** z, **5a** –, **b** z, **6a** z, **b** –

Les sons français

La lettre s

1 a mes animaux
b mes livres

2 a tes lapins
b tes amis

3 a les chaises
b les enfants

4 a des garçons
b des insectes

5 a tes chevaux
b tes oiseaux

6 a les hôtels
b les chats

4 C'est quel mot?

Solution: 1a, 2b, 3a, 4a, 5b, 6b

C'est quel mot?

1 sous, sur, sous
2 rue, tu, tu
3 nous, tout, nous
4 tout, tu, tout
5 douze, du, du
6 pur, sur, sur

5 Comment ça s'écrit?

Solution: (b) 3 *(chien)*

Comment ça s'écrit?

a 1 j-u-p-e
2 r-o-b-e
3 c-h-i-e-n
4 p-a-n-t-a-l-o-n
5 b-a-s-k-e-t-s
6 c-h-a-u-s-s-e-t-t-e-s

6 Vocabulaire de classe

Solution: 7, 5, 9, 2, 1, 8, 3, 4, 6

Vocabulaire de classe

Regarde la page 47. Écoute le CD et écris le nombre de chaque instruction dans l'ordre du CD.

C'est vrai ou faux?
Lis le résumé.
Changez les mots en couleur.
Trouve le bon dessin.
Écris le mot qui manque.
Écris les verbes dans ton cahier.
Choisis le bon mot.
Complète les phrases.
Note la bonne lettre.

7 Une conversation

Une conversation

Écoute les questions et réponds comme indiqué.

– Salut! C'est quand ton anniversaire?
(pause)
– C'est aujourd'hui.
– Quel âge as-tu?
(pause)
– J'ai treize ans.
– Qu'est-ce qu'on t'a offert?
(pause)
– Un T-shirt et un CD.
– Il est de quelle couleur, le T-shirt?
(pause)
– Il est rouge.

Épreuve – Unité 5

These worksheets can be used for an informal test of listening, reading and writing or for extra practice, as required. For general notes on administering the *Épreuves*, see TB 20.

CM 5/10, 2/9–11 **INFORMAL ASSESSMENT LISTENING**

Épreuve: Écouter

A Les vêtements (NC 1)

Solution: 1e, 2d, 3a, 4f, 5c, 6g, 7b (mark /6)

Les vêtements

1 J'ai un short. Voici mon short.
2 Je porte un jogging. J'aime bien ce jogging.
3 Sylvie porte une robe. Elle est jolie, la robe.
4 Marc a une cravate. La cravate est dans sa poche.
5 – Où sont mes baskets?
– Tes baskets sont ici.
6 Lucie porte une jupe. La jupe est grise.
7 – Où sont mes chaussettes?
– Voici tes chaussettes.

B C'est quelle date? (NC 2)

Solution: 1c, 2b, 3g, 4f, 5a, 6d, 7e (mark /6)

C'est quelle date?

1 – Richard, c'est quand, ta fête?
– Ma fête, c'est le trois avril.
– Ah bon, la Saint-Richard, c'est le trois avril.

2 – Pâques, c'est quand cette année?
– Le dimanche de Pâques, c'est le 29 mars.
– Alors, c'est le 29 mars.

3 – Tu vas au match de football, Lille contre Strasbourg?
– Je ne sais pas. C'est quand?
– C'est le trois octobre.
– Le trois octobre, alors oui, je veux bien.

4 – Il y a un bon concert à La Rochelle, tu sais?
– Ah bon, c'est quand?
– C'est le 13 novembre.
– Le 13 novembre? Bon, je vais voir.

5 – Isabelle, c'est quand ta fête?
– La Sainte-Isabelle, c'est le 22 février.
– Ah bon, alors, ta fête, c'est le 22 février.

6 – C'est quand le film sur le Canada?
– C'est le cinq juin.
– Ah bon, le cinq juin. Et c'est au club des jeunes, non?
– Oui, c'est ça.

7 – Quelle est la date de ton anniversaire?
– Mon anniversaire? C'est le 18 février.
– Le 18 février, bon.

C Des cadeaux (NC 2)

Solution:

1 **a** *petit*
2 **b** *vert*
3 **b** *rouge*
4 **b** *amusant*
5 **a** *mignon*
(mark /8: 1 mark for correct present, 1 mark for adjective; ignore misspellings)

Des cadeaux

1. On m'a offert un petit lapin. Oui, un petit lapin.
2. Alors, moi, on m'a offert un sac de sport. Un sac de sport vert – c'est bien, ça. J'adore le sport.
3. Et moi, on m'a offert des chaussures. Des chaussures rouges – j'aime bien la couleur rouge.
4. On m'a offert une bande dessinée. C'est très amusant. J'adore les BDs.
5. Alors moi, on m'a offert un chien. Il est mignon, mon chien. J'adore les chiens.

CM 5/11 **INFORMAL ASSESSMENT READING**

Épreuve: Lire

A Pierre (NC 2)

Students will need coloured pencils for this task. If these are not available, they could write the appropriate colour by each item in English.

Solution: red T-shirt, green jumper, grey trousers, black shoes, yellow cap, brown sports bag (mark /6)

B Les fêtes (NC 2)

Solution: **1b, 2e, 3a, 4d, 5f, 6c, 7g, 8h** (mark /7)

C Une conversation (NC 3)

Solution: **1d, 2g** (allow **h**)**, 3h** (allow **g**)**, 4f, 5b, 6e, 7c, 8a** (mark /7)

CM 5/12 **INFORMAL ASSESSMENT WRITING GRAMMAR**

Épreuve: Écrire et grammaire

A C'est quand? (NC 1)

Solution: **1** *avril,* **2** *janvier,* **3** *février,* **4** *juillet,* **5** *décembre* (mark /4)

B Une liste de cadeaux (NC 1)

Solution: Give one mark each for any five of the following presents that are reasonably appropriate and spelt recognisably: *(un cédérom), une cravate, un pull, un livre, une bande dessinée (BD), des baskets, une raquette de tennis, un T-shirt, une cassette vidéo, un stylo* (mark /5)

C À la maison (NC 1)

Solution: **1** *Nous avons,* **2** *Mes frères ont,* **3** *vous avez,* **4** *Nos deux chiens sont,* **5** *Le chat est,* **6** *Nous sommes* (mark /5)

D Un message électronique (NC 3)

Solution: (mark /6: 2 marks for correct date, 2 marks for each present correctly described)

SB 48–49 **REVISION CONSOLIDATION**

Rappel 2

This section can be used at any point after *Unité* 5 for revision and consolidation. It provides reading and writing activities which are self-instructional and can be used by students working individually for homework or during cover lessons.

SB 48

1 5-4-3-2-1

Solution:

5 *blanc, jaune, noir, rouge, vert*
4 *un cochon d'Inde, un hamster, un serpent, une tortue*
3 *une cravate, une jupe, une robe*
2 *grand, mignon*
1 *Pâques*

SB 48

2 Chasse à l'intrus

Solution:

1. *une carte – les autres sont des choses à manger*
2. *une chaussure – les autres sont des animaux*
3. *un lapin – les autres sont des vêtements*
4. *une cravate – les autres sont des affaires scolaires*
5. *bleu – les autres sont des mois*
6. *méchant – les autres sont des jours de la semaine*
7. *mardi – les autres sont des nombres*
8. *petit – les autres sont des jours de la semaine*
9. *le perroquet – les autres sont des pièces*
10. *ma maison – les autres sont des membres de la famille*

SB 48

3 Masculin, féminin

Solution:

masculin	***féminin***
un cadeau	*une cassette*
un gâteau	*une gerbille*
un oiseau	*une gomme*
	une salle
	une trousse
	une ville

SB 48

4 Ça commence avec c

Solution:

une calculette	*des chaussettes*
un cartable	*des chaussures*
une carte d'anniversaire	*un cheval*
une casquette	*un chien*
une cassette	*un classeur*
un cédérom	*un cochon d'Inde*
une chaise	*des crayons*

SB 49

5 L'année en France

Solution:

1. *janvier*
2. *juin*
3. *mars, avril*
4. *avril*
5. *mai*
6. *février, mars*
7. *juillet*
8. *décembre*
9. *août*
10. *septembre*
11. *octobre*
12. *novembre*

SB 49

6 Beaucoup de cadeaux

Solution:

1. *Le pull est vert.*
2. *Le sac est gris.*
3. *La casquette est rouge.*
4. *Les chaussettes sont jaunes.*
5. *Les baskets sont noires.*
6. *Les chaussures sont blanches.*
7. *Les hamsters sont bruns.*
8. *Le perroquet est bleu, vert et jaune.*
9. *La trousse est bleue.*
10. *Les stylos sont rouges.*

SB 49

7 Questions et réponses

Solution:

a **1** *ton*, **2** *ton*, **3** *ta*, **4** *ta*, **5** *tes*, **6** *tes*
b **1** *ma*, **2** *Mes*, **3** *Mon*, **4** *mes*, **e** *Ma*, **f** *Mon*
c **1c, 2f, 3e, 4a, 5b, 6d**

SB 49

8 Charles

Solution:

1. *Je suis*
2. *Mon père est, ma mère est*
3. *J'ai*
4. *J'ai*
5. *Mon frère a*
6. *Il est*
7. *Ma sœur a*
8. *Elle est*
9. *Nous avons*
10. *Ils sont, ils sont*
11. *Mes amis sont*
12. *Nous sommes*

Encore Tricolore 1
nouvelle édition

unité 6 Qu'est-ce que tu fais?

Areas	Topics	Grammar
1	Talking about the weather	
2	Talking about the temperature and seasons	
3		Numbers 0–100, letters and accents (D-L SB 53)
4	Talking about sport	Present tense of *jouer* (D-L SB 55)
5	Talking about other leisure activities	Other *-er* verbs (D-L SB 57)
6	Talking about weather and leisure activities	The pronoun *on* (D-L SB 60)
7	Further activities and consolidation	

National Curriculum information

Some students	Level 3
Most students	Levels 2–3
All students	Levels 1–2

Refer also to the information about coverage of 'Knowledge, skills and understanding' (TB 9).

Revision

The vocabulary and structures introduced in *Unités 6–7* are revised in the *Rappel* section following *Unité 7* (SB 78–79, TB 147).

Presse-Jeunesse 2 provides opportunities for reading for pleasure (SB 63–65, TB 129)

Sounds and writing

- ê; nasal vowels *am, an, em, en* and *on*
- further work on endings of words
- see *Écoute et parle* (SB 155, TB 125)

ICT opportunities

- typing French accents on the computer (TB 117)
- looking at weather details on Internet (TB 113)
- using the table facility to create a personal verb table (TB 119)
- text reconstruction (TB 122)

Reading strategies

Reading for detail and for gist – two different comprehension techniques (CM 104)

Assessment

- Informal assessment is in the *Épreuves* at the end of this unit (TB 127).
- Formal assessment is in the *Deuxième contrôle* following *Unité 7* (TB 201).

Students' Book

Unité 6 SB 50–62

Au choix SB 133 1 (TB 113), 2 (TB 115), 3 (TB 116), 4 (TB 120) SB 134 5 (TB 122), 6 (TB 123), 7, 8 (TB 124)

Écoute et parle SB 155 (TB 125)

Flashcards

27–33 Weather

34–42 Activities

CDs

2/12–27

Student CD 1/38–44

Student CD 2/28–31

Additional

Grammar in Action 1, pp 8–11

Copymasters

6/1 *Le temps et les saisons* [mini-flashcards/support] (TB 113, 115)

6/2 *La France en été et en hiver* [consolidation] (TB 116)

6/3 *La météo* [speaking: information gap] (TB 116)

6/4 *Les chiffres* [support] (TB 117)

6/5 *Taper les accents français* [ICT] (TB 117)

6/6 *Tom et Jojo* [grammar: verbs] (TB 121)

6/7 *Les verbes* [grammar] (TB 122)

6/8 *Des cartes postales* [extension] (TB 124)

6/9 *Tu comprends?* [independent listening] (TB 124)

6/10 *Sommaire* (TB 125)

6/11 *Épreuve: Écouter* (TB 127)

6/12 *Épreuve: Lire* (TB 128)

6/13 *Épreuve: Écrire et grammaire* (TB 128)

104 *Presse-Jeunesse 2* (TB 129)

Language content

The weather (Areas 1, 2)

Quel temps fait-il?

Il fait	*beau.*	*Il y a*	*du brouillard.*
	chaud.		*du soleil.*
	froid.		*du vent.*
	mauvais.	*Le ciel est bleu.*	
Il pleut.		*Il neige.*	

The seasons (Area 2)

le printemps	*au printemps*
l'été (m)	*en été*
l'automne (m)	*en automne*
l'hiver (m)	*en hiver*

Numbers 70–100 (Area 3) and some minus numbers, e.g.

70	*soixante-dix*	*–5*	*moins cinq*
71	*soixante et onze*	*–10*	*moins dix*
72	*soixante-douze*		
80	*quatre-vingts*		
81	*quatre-vingt-un*		
82	*quatre-vingt-deux*		
90	*quatre-vingt-dix*		
91	*quatre-vingt-onze*		
92	*quatre-vingt-douze*		
100	*cent*		

Sports (Area 4)

jouer au	*badminton*	*basket*
	golf	*hockey*
	football	*rugby*
	tennis	*tennis de table*
	volley	

Other activities (Area 5)

Qu'est-ce que tu fais?
Qu'est-ce que tu fais, le week-end, normalement?
Qu'est-ce que tu fais quand il fait mauvais?
Je reste à la maison.

Je regarde	*une vidéo.*
	un film.
	la télévision.
J'écoute	*de la musique.*
	la radio.

Je chante.
Je danse.
Je dessine.
Je range ma chambre.
Je joue à la console.
Je travaille.
Je joue/travaille sur l'ordinateur.
Je surfe sur le Net.
Je regarde mes messages électroniques.
Je tape des messages.
Je téléphone à un(e) ami(e).
Je retrouve mes amis.
Je discute avec mes amis.
On joue aux jeux électroniques.
On joue aux cartes.
On joue au Monopoly.

Some regular -er verbs (Area 5)

adorer	*écouter*	*rentrer*
aimer	*entrer*	*rester*
arriver	*habiter*	*surfer*
chercher	*jouer*	*taper*
cliquer	*penser*	*téléphoner*
détester	*regarder*	*travailler*

Classroom language and rubrics

Je n'ai pas de stylo.
Je ne comprends pas.
Je ne sais pas.
Je voudrais un livre, s'il vous plaît.
Qu'est-ce que c'est en anglais?
Comment ça s'écrit?
Répétez la question, s'il vous plaît?
C'est masculin ou féminin?

On-going activities

Weather record

Once the main weather expressions have been taught in Area 1, students could keep a personal record of the weather conditions for a fortnight or so, by writing down a brief daily description in French, perhaps with the appropriate symbol. After Area 2, they could also record the temperature, if there is a school thermometer.

Verb tables

This unit is particularly suited to the development of personal verb tables using the table facility of a word processor (see TB 40).

Area 1
Talking about the weather
SB 50, 1–3
Au choix SB 133, 1
CD 2/12
FC 27–33
CM 6/1 (optional)
Quel temps fait-il?
Il fait chaud/froid/beau/mauvais.
Il pleut/neige. Il y a du soleil/vent/brouillard.

FC 27–33 **PRESENTATION**

Introduction to weather

Using the flashcards, teach the following expressions. A mime of appropriate gestures, e.g. shivering, wiping brow, should help to make the meaning clear.

Quel temps fait-il?

Il fait chaud/froid.

Il pleut/neige.

Il y a du soleil/vent/brouillard.

For *il fait beau*, use the sunny flashcard.

For *il fait mauvais*, use a combination of two or more of the rain, cold, foggy and windy flashcards.

Use some games (see TB 26–27) to practise these expressions, e.g. *Effacez!* (where students point to or take the flashcard) and *Jeu de mémoire* (Kim's game).

BACKGROUND INFORMATION

Climate in France

Some teachers might like to refer to a map of France (SB 3, 50) and talk briefly about the climate in France (in English, if wished), mentioning such things as:

- the Mediterranean climate, with hot summers and mild winters, fruit such as peaches and grapes growing outside and people eating outdoors a lot;
- the Alps, where there is often snow for five months of the year, making skiing a popular sport;
- the Mistral, and how houses are built with no windows on the side it blows from;
- the effect of the warmer climate on people's homes – houses have shutters to keep out the strong sunlight, tiled floors in the kitchen to keep the house cool, fitted carpets are generally less common.

SB 50 **PRESENTATION** **READING**

1 Le temps en France

Introduce the French weather map, checking that the symbols are clearly understood and referring to the *Légende*.

La France est un grand pays. Dans le nord de la France, il fait mauvais. À Lille il pleut. À Dieppe il y a du brouillard. À Strasbourg, il fait froid.

Mais à La Rochelle, il fait beau. Il y a du soleil.

Et dans les Alpes, à Grenoble, quel temps fait-il? Est-ce qu'il pleut? Est-ce qu'il fait chaud?

Et à Nice? Et à Bordeaux? etc.

Students then complete the *vrai/faux* task. As an extension task, students could correct the wrong weather descriptions.

Solution: **1F** (*Il fait mauvais.*)**, 2V, 3F** (*Il fait chaud.*)**, 4V, 5F** (*Il y a du brouillard.*)**, 6F** (*Il fait beau.*)**, 7V, 8F** (*Il fait froid.*)

SB 50, 2/12 **LISTENING**

2 On téléphone à Suzanne

Explain the context of the recording, e.g.

Suzanne est à La Rochelle, mais beaucoup de ses amis sont en vacances.
Ils téléphonent à Suzanne – mais où sont-ils et quel temps fait-il?

a Students listen to the recording and note down the towns mentioned.

b They listen again and note down the weather using the letter abbreviations shown in the *Légende*.

When checking the answers, expand what students say, if necessary, e.g.

Alors, la première personne qui téléphone à Suzanne, c'est qui? (Jean-Pierre.)

Oui, c'est Jean-Pierre. Et où est-il? (Grenoble.)

Oui, il est à Grenoble dans les Alpes. Et quel temps fait-il dans les Alpes? (Il neige.)

Solution:
1 a *Grenoble,* **b N, F**
2 a *Nice,* **b C**
3 a *Lille,* **b M, P**
4 a *Toulouse,* **b B, F**
5 a *Paris,* **b M, P**
6 a *Rennes,* **b F, Br**
7 a *La Rochelle,* **b C, S**

On téléphone à Suzanne

Suzanne Lambert est à La Rochelle, mais beaucoup de ses amis sont en vacances.

1 – Allô!
– Salut Suzanne. C'est Jean-Pierre à l'appareil.
– Ah, Jean-Pierre, où es-tu?
– Je suis à Grenoble, dans les Alpes. Je fais du ski. C'est formidable!
– Ah bon. Et quel temps fait-il là-bas?
– Il neige et il fait froid.

2 – Allô!
– Bonjour Suzanne. C'est Mireille à l'appareil.
– Salut, Mireille. Où es-tu?
– Je suis à Nice. Je suis en vacances avec ma famille.
– C'est bien. Quel temps fait-il à Nice?
– Oh, il fait chaud, très chaud.

3 – Salut Suzanne. C'est Luc.
– Bonjour Luc. Ça va? Où es-tu?
– Oui, ça va. Je suis chez mes grands-parents à Lille.
– À Lille? Et quel temps fait-il là?
– Bof. Il fait mauvais et il pleut. Moi, je reste à la maison.

4 – Bonjour! C'est Stéphanie à l'appareil.
– Bonjour Stéphanie. Es-tu en vacances aussi?
– Oui, je passe une semaine chez des amis à Toulouse.
– Et quel temps fait-il là?
– Il fait beau, en général, mais la nuit, il fait froid.

5 – Salut, Suzanne. C'est Coralie.
– Ah, bonjour Coralie. Où es-tu?
– Je suis à Paris avec mon père.
– Paris, c'est bien, n'est-ce pas?
– Oui, Paris est bien, mais il ne fait pas beau ici. Aujourd'hui, il fait mauvais et il pleut.

6 – Suzanne, c'est toi? C'est Sébastien à l'appareil.
– Tiens, bonjour Sébastien. Où es-tu?
– À Rennes. Je passe une semaine chez mon cousin qui habite à Rennes.
– Et est-ce qu'il fait beau à Rennes?
– Non. Il fait froid et il y a du brouillard. Et à La Rochelle? Quel temps fait-il à La Rochelle?
– Oh, à La Rochelle, il fait chaud, il y a du soleil. C'est magnifique!

SB 50 **SPEAKING/WRITING**

3 Quel temps fait-il?

Students refer to the table or the map to complete the weather descriptions.

Solution:

1 *À Dieppe, il y a du brouillard.*
2 *À Strasbourg, il fait froid.*
3 *À Paris, il fait mauvais.*
4 *À Nice, il fait chaud.*
5 *À Toulouse, il y a du soleil.*
6 *À Grenoble, il neige*
7 *À Lille, il pleut.*

AU CHOIX SB 133 **WRITING EXTENSION**

1 Quel temps fait-il?

This task provides further practice of writing weather descriptions.

Solution:

1 *À Brighton, il fait mauvais.*
2 *À Exeter, il fait chaud.*
3 *À Bristol, il y a du soleil.*
4 *À Bangor, il y a du vent.*
5 *À Dublin, il y a du vent.*
6 *À Belfast, il fait beau.*
7 *À Glasgow, il fait froid.*
8 *À Aberdeen, il neige.*
9 *À Leeds, il y a du brouillard.*
10 *À Manchester, il pleut.*
11 *À Ipswich, il fait beau.*

CM 6/1 **MINI-FLASHCARDS SUPPORT**

Le temps et les saisons

The first task can be used now or the complete worksheet can be used later, after the seasons have been taught (see TB 115). When students have completed the captions, the cards can be cut up and used for various activities (see TB 28).

Additional activities

Weather symbols and names of towns **SPEAKING**

Divide the class into two groups. The students in group A each draw a simple weather symbol or write a letter denoting the weather (see *Légende* SB 50) on a piece of paper or card. To ensure that all nine weather conditions are covered, ask them first to say a different weather description in turn, referring them to SB 50, if necessary. The students in group B each write the name of a town anywhere in the world on a piece of paper.

The weather cards and the town cards are collected in, shuffled and put in two piles. A student chooses a card from each pile and states what the weather is like in the town selected, e.g. *À New York, il pleut.*

Weather forecasts **PRACTICE SPEAKING**

The weather symbol cards or the mini-flashcards can be used with a large map of France (or Britain) to talk about the weather. This could be done first by the teacher, but later by students, e.g.

Quel temps fait-il aujourd'hui en France (en Grande-Bretagne)?

Eh bien, à Paris (à Londres), il fait chaud.
(Card showing hot weather is pinned or stuck on Paris or London.)

Il fait chaud aussi à La Rochelle (à Brighton).

Mais à Lille (à Leeds), il fait mauvais et il pleut.

Students can visit websites to discover the actual weather today in La Rochelle or other French towns. *Yahoo! France* has a good selection of French towns (see TB 207–208).

Students could update their electronic phrase books with weather terms and maybe find one or two new ones from the web visit. It is important to follow up the search with a question and answer session, e.g.

Quel temps fait-il aujourd'hui en France?

Students: *À La Rochelle/Bordeaux/Lille (etc.), il …*

Area 2
Talking about the temperature and seasons

SB 51, 4–7, SB 52, 1–3
Au choix SB 133, 2–3
CD 2/13–16
FC 27–33
CM 6/1, 6/2, 6/3
il fait chaud/froid
le printemps/au printemps; l'été/en été; l'automne/en automne; l'hiver/en hiver

Numbers 0–40

REVISION

Revise numbers 0–40 orally using one of the number games, e.g. *Continue!, Comptez comme ça!, Effacez!* (see TB 25–26).

SB 51

PRESENTATION
PRACTICE

4 Les températures

Look at the thermometer and teach *assez chaud, assez froid* and *moins* (+ number). A simplified thermometer could perhaps be drawn on the board, e.g.

Quand il fait 35 degrés, est-ce qu'il fait froid?
Non, il fait chaud.

Est-ce qu'il fait assez chaud?
Non, il fait très chaud.

Et quand il fait moins cinq degrés, est-ce qu'il fait chaud? etc.

Introduce the table of temperatures to the class, using the example to show what to say.

Students could then practise this orally in pairs.

For further practice, a list of towns (perhaps including some local or well known ones) could be written on the board, each with a different temperature.

Give the name of the town or the temperature, or invite a volunteer to do so.

A student then has to give the other item and prompt the next student, and so on, e.g.

Teacher: *Strasbourg.*
Student A: 9 *(degrés). Paris …*
Student B: 18 *(degrés).* Londres …

This is more fun if there is a time limit of, say, five seconds for each reply.

SB 51, 2/13

LISTENING
EXTENSION

5 Voici la météo

Teach *parapluie* and write it on the board. The recording could be played with pauses after each town for students to note down their answers. To make it easier, students could work in pairs or the class could be divided into two groups. One pair or group just notes down the weather, and the other notes down the temperatures.

Solution:

1 *Paris* **F,** *7°*
2 *Rennes* **P,** *12°*
3 *Bordeaux* **Br,** *13°*
4 *Toulouse* **B,** *19°*
5 *Nice* **C, S,** *21°*
6 *Grenoble* **N,** *–4°*
7 *Strasbourg* **V,** *5°*
8 *Lille* **M,** *8°*
9 *Dieppe* **Br, P** *9°*

Voici la météo

– Bonjour, Mesdames et Messieurs.
Aujourd'hui, c'est le cinq mars. Est-ce qu'il va faire beau aujourd'hui? Écoutons la météo avec Daniel Dubois.

– Eh bien, voici la météo.
Commençons par la capitale. À Paris, il fait froid pour la saison; la température est de sept degrés.
Dans l'ouest de la France, à Rennes, il pleut. Alors, prenez votre parapluie si vous êtes à Rennes. La température à Rennes est de douze degrés.
À Bordeaux, sur la côte Atlantique, il y a du brouillard. Température: treize degrés.
Dans le sud de la France, il fait beau. À Toulouse, il fait beau et la température est de dix-neuf degrés. Alors, du beau temps à Toulouse.
Et à Nice et partout dans la région méditerranéenne, le ciel est bleu. Il y a du soleil et il fait chaud. Température: vingt et un degrés.
Par contre, à Grenoble et dans les Alpes, il neige. C'est bien pour les skieurs, mais la température est de moins quatre degrés.
À Strasbourg et dans l'est de la France, il y a du vent. Oui, du vent assez fort et la température à Strasbourg est de cinq degrés.
Passons maintenant au nord du pays. À Lille, il fait mauvais en général. Température: huit degrés.
Et à Dieppe, sur la côte nord, il y a du brouillard et il pleut. Température maximum de neuf degrés.

Weather activities

SPEAKING
PRACTICE (OPTIONAL)

1 Tu fais la météo

Prepare a set of cards, each with a number (including some minus ones) to denote temperatures and use these with the weather and town cards made earlier. Students select a town card, a weather card and a temperature card from each of the three piles and give a description of the weather.

2 Consequences

Each student has a piece of paper and writes the name of the town at the top. The paper is folded over and passed to another student, who adds a weather symbol. The paper is folded again and passed on to a third student who writes a number for the temperature.

The next student unfolds the paper and reads the weather forecast according to the prompts.

SB 51, **SPEAKING**

6 Inventez des conversations

This is based on a short conversation about the weather. Further conversations could be made up using the consequences idea above.

SB 51 **READING**

7 La météo aujourd'hui

Teach *nord* and *sud* by referring to towns on the map, e.g.

Lille est dans le nord de la France.
Nice est dans le sud de la France.
Et Dieppe? Et Toulouse?

Then ask students to look at the weather map (SB 50) and read the weather descriptions to work out which is the correct description. This can be done as a group activity, with each group looking at one description in order to find out whether it is the correct one or not.

The noun *pluie*, which is used here (rather than *il pleut*) for the sake of authenticity, is explained on the page.

Solution: **2** is the correct description.

SB 51 **EXTENSION**

?

Students who are interested in language could be given other words with the prefix *para-* or *pare-* and asked to work out their meaning, e.g. *paratonnerre*, given that *tonnerre* means thunder (lightning conductor); *parachute* (what does *chute* mean in French?); *un pare-brise* (windscreen); *un pare-choc* (car bumper); *un pare-étincelle* (fireguard).

FC 27–33 OR SB 52 **PRESENTATION**

Seasons

Teach the names of the seasons and practise related weather conditions, using the flashcards or the picture in the Students' Book, e.g.

Il y a quatre saisons dans l'année: le printemps, l'été, l'automne et l'hiver.

Au printemps, il fait beau quelquefois et il y a du soleil.

En été, il fait chaud et le ciel est bleu.

En automne, il y a du vent et quelquefois, il y a du brouillard.

Et en hiver, quel temps fait-il en hiver?

SB 52 **PRESENTATION PRACTICE**

1 Les saisons

This presents the names of the seasons and some related vocabulary, e.g. *le ciel, la pluie, quelquefois*. Students complete the sentences describing typical weather for each season.

Solution: **1** *beau,* **2** *soleil,* **3** *pleut,* **4** *chaud,* **5** *bleu,* **6** *vent,* **7** *brouillard,* **8** *froid,* **9** *mauvais,* **10** *neige*

Follow-up activities **SPEAKING**

1 Le temps ... la saison

Working in pairs, one student says a weather phrase. The other person has to complete the sentence with an appropriate season, e.g.

Student A: *Il pleut ...*
Student B: *... en hiver.*

2 Chain game

One student says a season and a weather condition and the next student has to repeat this and add another appropriate weather condition up to a maximum of three or four, e.g.

En hiver/automne, il pleut et il y a du brouillard ... et il y a du vent ... et il fait froid.

or

En été, il fait chaud et il y a du soleil ... et le ciel est bleu ... et il fait beau.

CM 6/1 **MINI-FLASHCARDS SUPPORT/CONSOLIDATION**

Le temps et les saisons

This can be used now, if not used earlier in Area 1. See TB 28 for ideas on using the mini-flashcards.

SB 52 **READING**

2 Quel temps!

This task gives practice in understanding more expressions linked to the weather. Check that students understand the use of *quel(le)* (here meaning 'what awful') in *quel temps, quel vent, quelle pluie*.

Solution: **1b, 2e, 3a, 4c, 5d**

AU CHOIX SB 133 **WRITING EXTENSION**

2 Les quatre saisons

This gives practice in using *souvent* and *quelquefois* with weather and seasons.

SB 52, **WRITING**

3 À toi!

A brief description of the local weather throughout the year could be prepared on the board, by taking suggestions from students, and then copied out. Some students may be able to do this task independently. The text could be used for a text reconstruction exercise, perhaps using *Fun with Texts*.

SB 52, TB 37, 2/14–15 LISTENING SPEAKING

Chantez! Le premier mois

The song can be used at any convenient point in the unit. For notes on using songs, see TB 33. The photocopiable score is on TB 37.

Chantez! Le premier mois

Le premier mois, c'est janvier.
Nous sommes en hiver.
Il neige beaucoup en février,
En mars, il fait mauvais.

Au mois d'avril, il pleut, il pleut.
Nous sommes au printemps.
Il fait très beau au mois de mai,
La météo dit: beau temps!

Et puis c'est juin, et juillet, août.
Nous sommes en été.
Il fait très chaud pour les vacances,
Ma saison préférée.

Au mois de septembre, la rentrée.
Octobre, c'est l'automne.
Du brouillard pendant novembre.
Oh! qu'est-ce qu'il fait du vent!

Le dernier mois, on fête Noël.
Nous sommes en décembre.
Il fait très froid, mais moi, j'ai chaud –
Je reste dans ma chambre!

SB 52 EXTENSION

?

Explain that *en* is used before a vowel (or 'mute h'), because *au* + vowel would be more difficult to say.

CM 6/2 READING WRITING

La France en été et en hiver

This task gives further practice of weather and temperatures. It can be used here or later for revision.

Solution:

2 L'hiver

À Paris, il y a du brouillard. Température cinq degrés.
À La Rochelle, il y a du vent. Température six degrés.
À Toulouse, il pleut. Température sept degrés.
À Nice, il fait beau. Température huit degrés.
À Grenoble, il neige. Température deux degrés.
À Strasbourg, il fait froid. Température trois degrés.

CM 6/3 SPEAKING

La météo

In this information-gap activity, students exchange details about the weather in different towns in order to complete a weather map.

Au choix SB 133, 2/16 LISTENING EXTENSION

3 La météo

Students listen to a radio broadcast about events and weather in the UK and note down the details.

Solution: **a** *il fait froid,* **b** *6,* **c** *rugby,* **d** *(il y a du) vent,* **e** *10,* **f** *football,* **g** *il fait beau,* **h** *12,* **i** *hockey*

La météo

– Ce week-end, il y a des matchs importants en Angleterre, en Écosse et au pays de Galles. Alors, quel temps fait-il là-bas ce week-end, Robert Legrand?

– Oui, eh bien, ce week-end le temps est assez variable. À Cardiff, par exemple, où il y a le grand match de rugby, la France contre le pays de Galles, il fait froid. La température est de 6 degrés.

– Oh, à Cardiff, il fait froid. Alors, bon courage à tous les supporters de l'équipe de France. Et à Birmingham?

– À Birmingham, il y a du vent assez fort, alors, là, il ne fait pas beau non plus. Oui, à Birmingham, il y a du vent pour le match de football cet après-midi ... mais la température est de 10 degrés – alors, une température normale pour la saison.

– Hmm, du vent à Birmingham. Et en Écosse?

– Eh bien, à Édimbourg, pour le grand match international de hockey, il fait beau. Alors, si vous allez à Édimbourg pour le match de hockey, vous avez de la chance – il fait beau. La température est de 12 degrés.

– Très bien, du beau temps à Édimbourg. Merci, Robert.

Area 3
Numbers 0–100, letters and accents
SB 53, 4–7
CD 2/17
Écoute et parle SB 155, 1
Student CD 1/38
CM 6/4, 6/5

REVISION PRESENTATION

Numbers 0–100

Use some of the number games to revise numbers 0–70 and to teach 71–100, e.g. *Continue!*, *Comptez comme ça!*, *Effacez!* (TB 25–26).

SB 53 READING

4 La tombola

Check that students can recognise and name the prizes illustrated.

They then match the written form of the numbers with the figures to identify each prize.

Solution: **1** *un ordinateur de poche,* **2** *un stylo,* **3** *une trousse,* **4** *des crayons,* **5** *un CD,* **6** *une calculette,* **7** *un poisson rouge,* **8** *un classeur,* **9** *une BD,* **10** *un sac à dos*

CM 6/4 **SUPPORT**

Les chiffres

These four tasks practise numbers.

1 C'est la loterie

Solution: 1d, 2f, 3b, 4e, 5i, 6h, 7j, 8a, 9g, 10c

2 Un message secret

Solution: ~~SEPT~~ RENDEZ-VOUS ~~ONZE~~ CE ~~TREIZE~~ SOIR ~~DOUZE~~ AU ~~QUATORZE~~ CAFÉ ~~SEIZE~~

3 Continue comme ça

For an extension activity, students could make up similar sequences.

Solution: **1** *huit,* **2** *sept,* **3** *douze,* **4** *quarante,* **5** *cent,* **6** *quatre-vingts*

4 Calcule

Solution: **1** *neuf,* **2** *quinze,* **3** *treize,* **4** *seize,* **5** *dix-huit,* **6** *onze,* **7** *sept,* **8** *douze,* **9** *quatre-vingt-un,* **10** *quatre-vingts,* **11** *douze,* **12** *huit*

The alphabet **REVISION**

Revise the alphabet orally, playing various games, e.g. *Effacez!*, *Continue!* etc. (TB 25–26).

SB 53, **SPEAKING**

5 C'est quel mot?

This task provides revision of the alphabet and other general vocabulary from *Unités 1–6*.

Students work in pairs and take it in turns to ask and answer questions.

Some students could make up additional questions for use in a pair or team game.

Solution: (suggestions) **1** *avril, août,* **2** *le basket, le badminton,* **3** *la cuisine, la chambre,* **4** *dimanche,* **5** *écouter, écrire, entrer,* **6** *février,* **7** *grand, gros,* **8** *hiver,* **9** *jaune,* **10** *un lapin,* **11** *Noël,* **12** *un pantalon, un pull*

SB 53 **GRAMMAR**

Dossier-langue
Les accents

This gives details of the three main accents: *accent aigu* (acute), *accent grave* and *accent circonflexe* (circumflex).

Divide the class into three groups and allocate a different accent to each group. They see how many words they can find with their accent on in a given time. To check, they read out the words in turn, with everyone listening (and perhaps repeating the words) to see how the pronunciation links up with the accent.

CM6/5, **WRITING READING**

Taper les accents français

This task provides details and practice for typing letters with accents on a computer. It can be used at any convenient point.

Look at the codes and explain how accents can be produced on your system if it is different.

1 Mots et images

Solution: **1** *un café,* **2** *un cinéma,* **3** *une règle,* **4** *une fenêtre,* **5** *une télévision,* **6** *un magnétophone,* **7** *une vidéo,* **8** *un cédérom,* **9** *un téléphone,* **10** *un zéro*

2 C'est quel mot?

Solution: **1** *âge,* **2** *Où,* **3** *près,* **4** *numéro de téléphone,* **5** *fête,* **6** *écoutes,* **7** *à,* **8** *préféré*

3 Invente des phrases

Students have the opportunity to write a few sentences of their own, following the example if they want.

SB 155, TB 125, SCD 1/38 **LISTENING SOUNDS AND WRITING**

1 Les sons français

This *Écoute et parle* task gives practice in the pronunciation of ê (see TB 126).

SB 53 **PRACTICE**

6 Les accents

In this task students have to group together words with the same accent.

Solution:

a *accent aigu: été, équipe, téléphone*
b *accent grave: mère, où, là*
c *accent circonflexe: gâteau, vêtements, août*

SB 53, 2/17 **SOUNDS AND WRITING LISTENING**

7 Comment ça s'écrit?

Students should write down the letters and identify the words.

Comment ça s'écrit?

1 p-è-r-e
2 é-n-o-r-m-e
3 h-ô-t-e-l
4 r-è-g-l-e
5 a-o-û-t
6 m-é-t-é-o
7 g-â-t-e-a-u
8 F-r-é-d-é-r-i-c

Area 4
Talking about sport
Present tense of *jouer*
SB 54–55, 1–6
CD 2/18
FC 37–42

SB 54, FC 38–40 **PRESENTATION**

Les sports

First teach *le tennis de table, le basket* and *le volley* using the flashcards.

Then introduce the photographs on SB 54 orally first, before writing the names of the eight sports on the board for easy reference, e.g.

Voilà un groupe de jeunes.

On fait beaucoup de sports.

Claire et Thomas jouent au volley. Le volley, qu'est-ce que c'est en anglais? C'est 'volleyball'.

On joue beaucoup au volley en France, et ici?

Est-ce que Claire et Thomas jouent au tennis?

Non, ils jouent au …

Et Sophie, elle joue au volley?

Paul et Yannick jouent à quel sport?

Qui joue au basket? etc.

SB 54, 2/18 **LISTENING**

1 Au club de sports

This task brings together the eight sports and the different forms of *jouer* which are explained and practised later in the area. Students note down the correct photo for each speaker.

Solution: 1a, 2d, 3b, 4f, 5h, 6g, 7e, 8c

Au club de sports

1 – Bonjour Claire, bonjour Thomas. Qu'est-ce que vous faites aujourd'hui?
– Bonjour. Comme il fait beau, nous jouons au volley.

2 – Et Marc, est-ce qu'il joue avec vous?
– Non, Marc joue au basket.

3 – Et toi, Simon, tu joues au tennis, non?
– Oui, moi, je joue au tennis.

4 – Tu aimes le sport, Ibrahim?
– Oui, j'adore le sport, je joue au hockey aujourd'hui.

5 – Est-ce que Jonathan et Nicole jouent au hockey aussi?
– Non, ils jouent au badminton.

6 – Et vous, Daniel et Luc, vous jouez au tennis de table, non?
– Oui, nous jouons au tennis de table.

7 – Et Sophie, elle joue avec vous?
– Non, Sophie joue au golf.

8 – Et Paul et Yannick, ils jouent au football, je suppose.
– Oui, ils jouent au football.

SB 54 **READING**

2 C'est faux!

This task presents the third person form, singular and plural and should be done orally first. Point out that the 3rd person singular and plural sound identical, even though they are spelt differently.

Solution:

1. *Marc joue au basket.*
2. *Claire et Thomas jouent au volley.*
3. *Ibrahim joue au hockey.*
4. *Paul et Yannick jouent au football.*
5. *Simon joue au tennis.*
6. *Sophie joue au golf.*
7. *Daniel et Luc jouent au tennis de table.*
8. *Jonathan et Nicole jouent au badminton.*

Chain game **SPEAKING**

Play a quick class game, such as a cumulative list of sports or a game where each person has to mention a different sport, referring to the list on the board if necessary, e.g.
Je joue au tennis, et toi, (student A)*?*
Je joue au tennis et au football, et toi, (student B)*?* etc.

For other vocabulary games, see TB 26.

SB 54, **SPEAKING**

3 Inventez des conversations

Students practise in pairs making up short conversations about sport.

SB 54 **GRAMMAR**

!

A reminder of the construction *jouer au* with sports.

SB 55, **GRAMMAR**

Dossier-langue
Jouer – to play (a regular *-er* verb)

This sets out the present tense of *jouer*, with key points that apply to all verbs. More work is done on *-er* verbs in Area 5, with another key *Dossier-langue* on SB 57. However, it is a good idea to establish the idea of the paradigm and the standard pattern with just one verb.

Write the verb on the board and give plenty of practice rubbing off a few endings at a time or removing the stem or the pronoun from some parts and asking students to replace them. This could be played in teams, with students taking turns to rub out or fill in missing parts. Similar practice could be given using an OHT and covering bits up or with computer software.

GRAMMAR

Making a verb table

Students could use the table facility on their computers to create their own verb table of *jouer* and add other verbs to it as they progress through the course (see ICT notes, TB 40).

SB 55 GRAMMAR PRACTICE

4 Ils jouent bien?

This task gives practice in selecting the correct part of the verb from three options.

Solution: **1** *Je joue,* **2** *Tu joues,* **3** *Ma fille joue,* **4** *Nous jouons,* **5** *Vous jouez,* **6** *Ils jouent*

SB 55 GRAMMAR PRACTICE

5 Du sport pour tous

In this task, students have to add the correct part of *jouer* and the correct sport. Check that the symbols are understood.

Solution:

1 *vous jouez au volley*
2 *nous jouons au basket*
3 *tu joues au badminton*
4 *je joue au badminton*
5 *il joue au hockey*
6 *ma sœur joue au hockey*
7 *mon frère joue au rugby*
8 *tes parents jouent au tennis*
9 *ils jouent au tennis*
10 *mon grand-père joue au golf*

FC 37, 41, 42 PRESENTATION

Vous n'aimez pas le sport?

Present the words for a few activities (with *jouer*) for non-sporty people, e.g.

Moi, je ne suis pas sportif/sportive, je joue aux cartes.

Mon frère n'est pas sportif, il joue aux jeux électroniques/sur l'ordinateur.

Mes enfants/parents ne sont pas sportifs, ils jouent à la console.

Quelquefois, nous jouons tous au Monopoly.

SB 55 WRITING

6 À toi!

Prepare this task in class with volunteers writing suggestions on the board to help students who need more support.

Area 5
Talking about other leisure activities
Other -*er* verbs

SB 56–57, 1–5, 58–59, 1–6,
SB 60, 1
Au choix SB 133, 4, SB 134, 5–6
CD 2/19–22
Écoute et parle SB 155, 5
Student CD 1/42
CM 6/6, 6/7
FC 34–36, (37–42)
Grammar in Action 1, pages 8–11

FC 34–36, (37–42) PRESENTATION PRACTICE

Introduction

Teach *Qu'est-ce que tu fais?* and use this to prompt answers in the first person, e.g.

Je regarde la télévision.

J'écoute la radio/de la musique.

Je travaille.

Then play some miming or flashcard games (see TB 27–28), using different persons of the verb. The flashcards using *jouer* can also be used for further practice.

SB 56, 2/19 LISTENING

1 À la maison

Students listen to the conversation and choose the correct answers.

Solution: **1a, 2c, 3a, 4b**

À la maison

Aujourd'hui, c'est mercredi. Il fait mauvais et il pleut. Christophe arrive chez Marc.

– Salut Marc!

– Salut Christophe! Ça va?

– Non, ça ne va pas. Il pleut. Qu'est-ce que tu fais?

– Moi, j'écoute des disques. Et toi, tu aimes la musique?

– Non, je n'aime pas ça.

– Tu aimes la radio?

– Non, je n'aime pas ça.

– Tu aimes le tennis de table?

– Non, je n'aime pas ça.

– Tu préfères la télé?

– Oui, qu'est-ce qu'il y a?

– Il y a un film de Tom et Jojo.

– Ah, chouette! J'aime bien ça.

SB 56, 2/20 LISTENING READING

2 Un film de Tom et Jojo

This presents several examples of verbs of action. Students listen to the recording and follow the text.

Un film de Tom et Jojo

Jojo est une souris. Elle pense à quelque chose.
C'est le fromage.
Tom est un chat. Il pense à quelque chose.
C'est Jojo.
Voilà le fromage. Voilà Jojo.
Jojo mange le fromage.
Voilà Tom. Tom entre dans la cuisine.
Tom chasse Jojo. Est-ce qu'il mange Jojo?
Jojo entre dans le salon.
Tom saute sur Jojo. Il attrape Jojo?
Aïe!! Non, il n'attrape pas Jojo.
Tom chasse Jojo dans la salle de bains. Il saute ...
Pouf! Non! Il n'attrape pas Jojo dans la salle de bains.
Jojo rentre dans la cuisine.
Voilà le fromage! Mais voilà Tom!
Et voilà Butch! Butch arrive.
Butch n'aime pas Tom.
Il chasse Tom ...
... et Jojo mange le fromage.

SB 56 READING

3 C'est faux!

Students now correct seven mistakes in the summary of the *Tom et Jojo* story.

Solution:

1 *Jojo est une ~~tortue~~ souris.*
2 *Tom est un ~~cheval~~ chat.*
3 *Tom entre dans la ~~maison~~ cuisine.*
4 *Jojo entre dans le ~~jardin~~ salon.*
5 *Tom chasse Jojo dans la salle ~~à manger~~ de bains.*
6 *Jojo rentre dans la ~~chambre~~ cuisine.*
7 *Jojo mange le ~~chocolat~~ fromage.*

SB 57 GRAMMAR PRACTICE

4 Où est le verbe?

This task provides practice in identifying the verb in a sentence.

Solution: **1** *écoute,* **2** *habites,* **3** *clique,* **4** *parle,* **5** *surfons,* **6** *aimez,* **7** *cherchent,* **8** *détestent*

SB 57 GRAMMAR

Dossier-langue
Regular -*er* verbs

The pattern of regular -*er* verbs is applied here to other verbs. Use the example of the flower – the stem remains the same whilst the flower has different petals – just like the stem of a verb, which doesn't change whilst the endings do.

To reinforce the importance of learning the endings, explain to students that they can use these to form the present tense of all verbs in French which end in -*er* (except *aller*) and prove it by giving them one or two verbs they have never used before, e.g. *porter*.

Stress that, whilst the spelling changes for some endings, the pronunciation of all the parts is the same except for the *nous* and *vous* forms.

Play some simple verb games for practice (see TB 28).

SB 155, TB 126, SCD 1/42 SOUNDS AND WRITING INDEPENDENT LISTENING

5 Quel son est différent?

This *Écoute et parle* listening discrimination task is based on verbs and could be used at any convenient point after the verb paradigm has been taught (see TB 126).

GRAMMAR

See the earlier suggestion about creating individual verb tables (TB 119, TB 40). If the class have started with *jouer*, they can now add other verbs. The verbs could be colour-coded so that it is obvious which part is the stem and which are the endings.

Practice of verbs

There are a number of tasks to practise verbs and the teacher can select those that are most appropriate for the class. It is not necessary to do them all and some could be used later for revision. In addition, there are several ideas for verb games in Section 2 (TB 28).

Au choix SB 133 CONSOLIDATION

4 Devant la télé

This task gives practice in writing out different parts of the verb *regarder* and provides consolidation for all students.

Solution: **1** *regardes,* **2** *regarde,* **3** *regardent,* **4** *regardez,* **5** *regardent,* **6** *regardons,* **7** *regarde,* **8** *regardent,* **9** *regarde,* **10** *regardent,* **11** *regarde*

SB 57, 2/21 LISTENING

5 Pendant les vacances

Introduce this item by referring to the opening dialogue, e.g.

On va écouter des personnes qui parlent des vacances.
Par exemple, voici François. Il aime les vacances et il adore le camping.
Maintenant, écoutez le CD et trouvez les paires.

Play the conversations, pausing after each one for students to match up the two parts of the sentences, or play the whole recording twice, with shorter pauses. If used in a language laboratory, this task could be done on an individual basis.

Correct the task as a class activity, with students reading out the complete sentences as well as giving the matching numbers and letters.

Solution: **1b, 2c, 3a, 4e, 5d, 6g, 7j, 8f, 9h, 10i**

11 Pendant les vacances

1 – François, tu aimes les vacances?
– Bien sûr.
– Et qu'est-ce que tu fais pendant les vacances?
– Je fais du camping avec mes amis. J'adore le camping.

2 – Et toi, Christine, qu'est-ce que tu fais?
– J'habite à La Rochelle, avec ma famille et en été, nous passons beaucoup de temps au soleil.

3 – Jean-Marc et Sandrine, qu'est-ce que vous aimez faire pendant les vacances?
– Ça dépend. En hiver, nous aimons faire du ski.

4 – Et en été, qu'est-ce que vous faites?
– En été, nous restons à la maison et nous invitons des amis à la maison.

5 – M. et Mme Duval, qu'est-ce que vous faites pendant les vacances?
– Eh bien, au mois de juin, il y a la Fête de la Musique. Alors nous écoutons toutes sortes de musique.

6 – Et votre fille, Mathilde, chante dans un groupe, non?
– Oui, c'est ça. Notre fille, Mathilde, chante dans un groupe ici.

7 – Salut, Nicolas et Isabelle. Qu'est-ce que vous faites pendant les vacances?
– Comme nous habitons à la ferme, nous restons ici, normalement. Ma sœur, Isabelle, et moi, nous travaillons à la ferme avec mon père.

8 – Tu aimes les animaux, Isabelle?
– Ah oui, j'aime beaucoup les animaux.

9 – Et qu'est-ce que tu fais, le soir, Nicolas?
– Le soir, je joue au football avec mes amis.

10 – Et quand il pleut?
– Quand il pleut, je joue sur l'ordinateur.

SB 58 **READING**

1 Les frères, c'est difficile!

This letter can be used here or later with the related tasks in *Au choix* (SB 134, tasks 5–6, TB 122–123).

Check that students have understood the main points by asing a few questions, e.g.

Comment s'appelle le frère d'Alain? (Henri)
Quel âge a Henri? (4 ans)
Henri, est-il méchant ou mignon?
Qu'en pense Alain?
Qu'en pense sa mère?
Et qu'en pensez-vous/penses-tu?

a For support, this could be prepared orally and the missing words written on the board in random order.

Solution: **1** *frère*, **2** *chambre*, **3** *méchant*, **4** *saute*, **5** *dessine*, **6** *mange*, **7** *écoute*, **8** *travaille*, **9** *chante*, **10** *danse*

b This task involves recognition of a range of verbs, including parts of *avoir* and *être*.

Solution: Any ten verbs from the following: *J'ai, Il s'appelle, Il a, il partage, Il est, Il saute, il dessine, il écoute, il mange, je travaille, il chante, il danse, je raconte, elle dit, il est, il est, pensez-vous*

SB 58 **GRAMMAR PRACTICE**

2 Des correspondants

This straightforward task, in which students choose the correct part of the verb for *je* or *tu*, can be used for support while more able students work on *Les frères, c'est difficile!* and the tasks in *Au choix*.

Solution: **1** *J'habite*, **2** *J'adore*, **3** *Je joue*, **4** *Je regarde*, **5** *Je cherche*, **6** *Tu habites*, **7** *Tu aimes*, **8** *Tu parles*, **9** *Tu cherches*, **10** *Tu as*

CM 6/6 **VOCABULARY/GRAMMAR PRACTICE**

Tom et Jojo

1 Un petit lexique

Students write down the English meanings of some regular -*er* verbs.

Solution:

adorer	to love	*entrer*	to come/go in
aimer	to like	*manger*	to eat
arriver	to arrive	*penser*	to think
chasser	to chase	*regarder*	to look at/watch
chercher	to look for	*rentrer*	to return
détester	to hate	*sauter*	to jump

2 Tom et Jojo

Practice of the *il* and *je* forms of a range of -er verbs.

Solution: **1** *cherche*, **2** *pense*, **3** *regarde*, **4** *entre*, **5** *chasse*, **6** *saute*, **7** *rentre*, **8** *arrive, chasse*, **9** *mange*, **10** *déteste*, **11** *aime*, **12** *adore*

SB 58 **GRAMMAR PRACTICE** **READING**

3 Les Paresseux

This gives practice of the *nous* and *ils* forms of regular -er verbs.

Solution: **1** *nous organisons*, **2** *les Paresseux surfent*, **3** *nous jouons*, **4** *les Paresseux regardent*, **5** *nous dansons*, **6** *ils écoutent*, **7** *nous travaillons*, **8** *ils restent, ils consultent*, **9** *nous chantons*, **10** *ils écoutent*, **11** *nous fêtons*

The task could be followed by some question and answer work, e.g.

Est-ce que les Paresseux jouent au tennis?
Et les Actives, est-ce qu'ils jouent?
Et dans ta famille, vous jouez au tennis ou vous regardez le tennis à la télé?

WRITING

The story *Les Paresseux* could be used as a text reconstruction activity. *Fun with Texts* would be suitable software for creating a file for this, using the completed text, i.e. with the first person plural endings. Suitable *Fun with Texts* options would be Text Salad, Prediction and Copywrite, in that order. Cloze could also be used, but the file would need to be set up with the verb forms clozed out.

SB 59 **GRAMMAR PRACTICE**

4 Le week-end

This task gives practice of all forms of the present tense with a range of *-er* verbs.

Solution: **1** *Je prépare,* **2** *Tu chantes,* **3** *Il déteste,* **4** *Elle travaille,* **5** *Nous surfons,* **6** *Vous travaillez,* **7** *Ils aiment,* **8** *Elles regardent*

CM 6/7 **GRAMMAR**

Les verbes

This provides further practice of the present tense of *-er* verbs for use now or later for revision.

Solution:

1 Puzzle

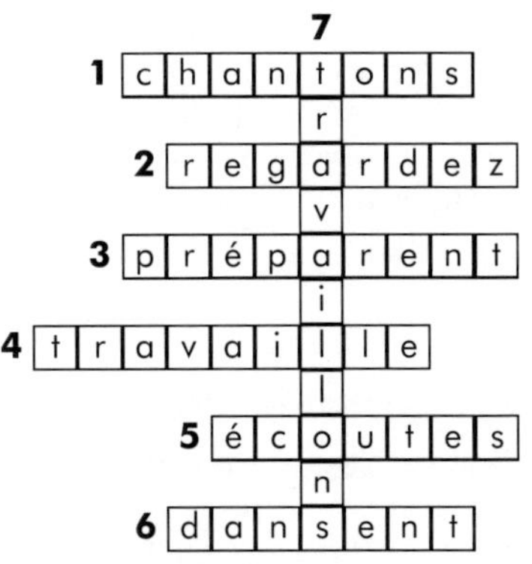

2 Qu'est-ce qu'on dit?

1 *joue,* **2** *travailles,* **3** *prépare,* **4** *joue,* **5** *dansons,* **6** *aimez,* **7** *regardent*

SB 59, 2/22 **LISTENING**

5 Deux interviews

This listening task provides some examples for students to use in their own conversations when they carry out the pairwork task which follows.

Solution: **a 1b, 2a, 3b, 4a, 5a, 6b**
b 1c, 2a, 3d, 4e, 5b

Deux interviews

Interview a

– Bonjour. Comment t'appelles-tu?
– Je m'appelle Anne.
– Est-ce que tu aimes le sport, Anne?
– Non, je n'aime pas le sport.
– Qu'est-ce que tu fais, normalement, le week-end?
– Ça dépend. Quelquefois, je retrouve des amis. Nous discutons ensemble. Nous écoutons de la musique.
– Et quand tu n'es pas avec tes amis, qu'est-ce que tu fais?
– Alors, je joue à la console ou je regarde une vidéo.

Interview b

– Et toi, comment t'appelles-tu?
– Je m'appelle Marc.
– Et qu'est-ce que tu fais, normalement, le week-end, Marc?
– Eh bien, moi, j'adore le sport. Alors, je joue au football avec des amis. Quelquefois, je joue au tennis dans le parc.
– Et quand il fait mauvais, qu'est-ce que tu fais?
– Quand il fait mauvais, je regarde du sport à la télé.
– Est-ce que tu aimes la musique?
– Non, je n'aime pas beaucoup la musique.

SB 59, **SPEAKING WRITING**

6 Une question importante

In this activity students ask each other questions about week-end activities. For some students this will be sufficient. Able students could write down the details, transferring from the first to the third person.

SB 60 **WRITING**

1 Des phrases au choix

Students practise using different parts of the verb to write a range of silly sentences, generated randomly.

AU CHOIX SB 134 **READING**

5 Une lettre de Françoise

This is a letter in response to the letter from Alain (SB 58, **1** *Les frères, c'est difficile!*), in which a girl writes about similar problems with a younger sister.

a This is a *vrai ou faux* task. For extension, students could correct the false statements.

Solution: **1V, 2F** *(Elle a une sœur.)* **3V, 4F** *(Elle a sept ans.)* **5V, 6F** *(Sophie porte les vêtements de Françoise.)* **7V**

b Students complete a summary of the letter. For support the missing words could be written in jumbled order on the board.

Solution: **1** *sœur,* **2** *Elle,* **3** *chambre,* **4** *pulls, chaussures,* **5** *écoute, danse* **6** *travaille,* **7** *jouent*

Au choix SB 134 **WRITING**

6 Une petite sœur difficile

Students write a similar letter about a difficult younger sister.

Solution: **1** *ai, Elle, travaille, mange,* **2** *joue,* **3** *dessine,* **4** *regarde*

Grammar in Action 1, pages 8–11 **GRAMMAR**

Regular -*er* verbs

Further practice material to be used at any suitable point. Pages 8 and 9 practise the singular; pages 10 and 11 practise all parts of regular -*er* verbs.

Area 6
Talking about weather and leisure activities
The pronoun *on*
SB 60–61, 2–6
Au choix SB 134, 7–8
CD 2/23
FC 27–33, 34–42 (optional)
CM 6/8

SB 60 **PRESENTATION GRAMMAR**

Dossier-langue *On*

La fête de la musique has become very popular in France in recent years and it takes place in June, during the nearest weekend to *la Saint-Jean-Baptiste* (one of several saints in the calendar called Jean).

This short article includes several examples of the pronoun *on*. Ask students to read the article, then ask questions about it, e.g.

Qu'est-ce qu'on fait à la fête de la musique?
Est-ce qu'on chante/danse/joue des instruments/ écoute de la musique?
C'est quand, la fête? etc.

Explain that *on* is used a lot in French and can be translated in different ways (one, they, we, you, people in general etc.).

SB 60, **GRAMMAR PRACTICE**

2 Des fêtes

Students practise making up sentences using *on*.

The table for this task could be made into a computer-based phrase-generation activity using a word processor (see TB 40).

SB 60, 2/23 **LISTENING**

3 Au téléphone

These two conversations bring together the themes of weather and leisure activities.

a Students listen to the recording then find the correct words in the box to complete the sentences.

Solution: **1** *Bordeaux,* **2** *basket,* **3** *beau,* **4** *maison (La Rochelle),* **5** *mauvais,* **6** *chambre*

b In this task, students have to answer questions in French.

Solution: **1** *Max,* **2** *Nicole,* **3** *Max,* **4** *Nicole,* **5** *Il fait très froid.*

Au téléphone

a Suzanne et Luc

– Allô.
– Salut Suzanne. C'est Luc à l'appareil.
– Ah bonjour, Luc. Ça va?
– Oui, ça va bien. Je suis à Bordeaux.
– Ah bon, et qu'est-ce que tu fais là?
– Je suis avec l'équipe de basket. Nous jouons un match aujourd'hui.
– Et est-ce qu'il fait beau?
– Oui, il fait beau, mais pas très chaud. C'est bien. Et toi, qu'est-ce que tu fais aujourd'hui?
– Ben, ici à La Rochelle, il fait très mauvais. Alors, je reste à la maison et je range ma chambre.

b Nicole et Max

– Allô.
– Bonjour Nicole. C'est Max à l'appareil.
– Ah bonjour, Max. Ça va?
– Oui, merci. Et toi?
– Oui, ça va bien.
– Qu'est-ce que tu fais aujourd'hui?
– Je travaille sur l'ordinateur. Je regarde mes e-mails et je tape des messages.
– Mais on joue au tennis dans le parc. Tu aimes le tennis? Viens jouer avec nous.
– Merci, mais il fait très froid aujourd'hui. Je préfère rester à la maison.

SB 61 **READING WRITING**

4 Une carte postale

Students choose the appropriate words to complete the postcard.

Solution: **1** *avril,* **2** *passons,* **3** *mauvais,* **4** *il,* **5** *nous,* **6** *regardent,* **7** *joue,* **8** *prépare*

CM 6/8 PRACTICE

Des cartes postales

This provides further practice of weather, leisure and verbs for use here or later for revision.

1 À lire

Solution:

1 *un mois – une semaine*
2 *août – octobre*
3 *beau – mauvais*
4 *volley – tennis de table*

2 À compléter

Solution:

Bordeaux, le 12 avril
Nous passons un week-end dans un hôtel ici.
C'est pour fêter l'anniversaire de mon père.
Il fait chaud. Il y a du soleil. C'est fantastique.
Aujourd'hui, nous jouons au tennis.
À bientôt,
Alex

3 À écrire

Students can now write their own postcards based on the details given.

SB 61 WRITING

5 À toi!

Students write a short postcard describing the weather and one or more activities.

For support, this could be done as a class activity with suggestions written on the board.

FC 27–42 SPEAKING

Le temps et les loisirs

Use the flashcards to practise combining weather descriptions and appropriate activities, e.g.

Il pleut. Qu'est-ce que (nom) fait?

Il/Elle reste à la maison et il/elle regarde la télé etc.

SB 61, SPEAKING

6 Inventez des conversations

Students practise conversations about the weather and related activities.

Au choix SB 134 WRITING

7 Ça dépend du temps

An open-ended task, in which students complete the sentences with an appropriate activity.

Au choix SB 134 WRITING

8 Mon journal de vacances

Students describe the weather and an activity on two different days in the holidays.

Area 7
Further activities and consolidation

SB 61–62
Écoute et parle SB 155, 6, 1–7
Student CD 1/38–44
Student CD 2/28–31
CD 2/24–27
CM 6/9–6/13

This area brings together a selection of items using the themes and language of the unit. They can be used in any order and all are optional.

SB 61, SB 155, TB 127, SCD 1/43 LISTENING

Vocabulaire de classe

The French instructions are recorded in a different order in the *Écoute et parle* task (see TB 127).

Solution: 1d, 2h, 3a, 4b, 5e, 6g, 7c, 8f

CM 6/9, SCD 2/28–31 INDEPENDENT LISTENING

Tu comprends?

1 Les numéros de téléphone

Solution:

le cinéma Rex:	*03.24.13.42.50*
le café Robert:	*03.15.56.37.60*
le collège:	*03.39.68.12.41*
La famille Laurent:	*03.75.80.16.23*

Les numéros de téléphone

1 – Tu as le numéro de téléphone du cinéma Rex?
– Oui, le voilà. C'est zéro trois, vingt-quatre, treize, quarante-deux, cinquante.
– Alors, je répète: zéro trois, vingt-quatre, treize, quarante-deux, cinquante.

2 – Le numéro du café Robert, qu'est-ce que c'est?
– C'est zéro trois, quinze, cinquante-six, trente-sept, soixante. Je répète: zéro trois, quinze, cinquante-six, trente-sept, soixante.

3 – Le numéro du collège, qu'est-ce que c'est?
– C'est: zéro trois, trente-neuf, soixante-huit, douze, quarante et un.
– Alors, je répète: zéro trois, trente-neuf, soixante-huit, douze, quarante et un.

4 – Vous avez le numéro de téléphone de la famille Laurent?
– Oui, le voilà. C'est zéro trois, soixante-quinze, quatre-vingts, seize, vingt-trois. Je répète: zéro trois, soixante-quinze, quatre-vingts, seize, vingt-trois.

2 La météo

Solution: 1b, 2b, 3a, 4a, c, 5b, a, 6b, b

La météo

– Bonjour Mesdames et Messieurs. Aujourd'hui, c'est jeudi quinze janvier. Il fait froid. Est-ce que ça va continuer, Claire Artaud?

– Oui, en effet, il fait froid et il va continuer à faire froid dans toute la France. La température est de trois degrés. À Paris, il pleut et il y a du vent.

– Alors de la pluie et du vent à Paris. Et dans les Alpes, est-ce qu'il y a de la neige?

– Oui, dans les Alpes, il y a de la neige et il y a du brouillard aussi. Alors, faites très attention, si vous êtes en montagne.

– Alors, dans les Alpes, de la neige et du brouillard. Et le beau temps, est-ce qu'il y a du beau temps aussi?

– Oui, dans l'ouest, à Bordeaux, il y a du soleil et il fait assez beau, mais il fait toujours froid.

– Alors, voilà, pour trouver le beau temps, il faut aller à Bordeaux. Merci, Claire.

3 Comment ça s'écrit?

Solution: 4 (*cahier*) is the odd word out.

Comment ça s'écrit?

1 c-h-a-n-t-e-r
2 j-o-u-e-r
3 a-i-m-e-r
4 c-a-h-i-e-r
5 é-c-o-u-t-e-r
6 p-r-é-p-a-r-e-r
7 t-r-a-v-a-i-l-l-e-r

4 Un sondage sur le sport

Solution:

	bad'ton	*basket*	*hockey*	*football*	*tennis*	*volley*
1 *Anne*					✔	✔
2 *Marc*		✔		✔		
3 *Nicole*						✔
4 *Paul*	✔		✔			
5 *Lucie*	✔				✔	✔
6 *Robert*				✔		
Total	*2*	*1*	*1*	*2*	*2*	*3*

Le sport le plus populaire est: le volley

Un sondage sur le sport

1 – Bonjour Anne. Est-ce que tu fais du sport?
– Oui, je fais beaucoup de sport. Je joue au volley et je joue au tennis.

2 – Bonjour Marc. Est-ce que tu aimes le sport?
– Oui, j'aime le sport. Je joue au football et au basket.

3 – Bonjour Nicole. Est-ce que tu aimes le sport aussi?
– Non, pas beaucoup, mais je joue au volley quelquefois.

4 – Tu es Paul, non?
– Oui, c'est moi.
– Alors, Paul, est-ce que tu fais du sport?
– Oui, je fais beaucoup de sport. Je joue au badminton et au hockey. J'aime ça.

5 – Lucie, est-ce que tu aimes le sport?
– Le sport? Oui, j'adore le sport.
– Qu'est-ce que tu fais, comme sports?
– Je joue au badminton et au tennis et je joue au volley aussi.

6 – Et toi, Robert, est-ce que tu aimes le sport?
– Un peu. Je joue au football quelquefois, mais c'est tout.

SB 62, CM 6/10

Sommaire

A summary of the main vocabulary and structures in the unit.

SB 155, SCD 1/38–44 INDEPENDENT LISTENING SOUNDS AND WRITING

Écoute et parle – Unité 6

1 Les sons français

Solution: ê: (a) 1b, 2c, 3a
ɑ̃: (a) 1d, 2c, 3f, 4a, 5e, 6b
ɔ̃: (a) 1c, 2a, 3d, 4b, 5e

Les sons français

La lettre ê

a 1 pêche
2 prêt
3 arrête

b êtes, être, fête, fenêtre

Le son ɑ̃

a 1 ensemble
2 enfant
3 cent
4 janvier
5 différent
6 camping

b camp, dans, trente, entre, blanc

Le son ɔ̃

a 1 ton
2 oncle
3 concours
4 nation
5 melon

b concert, question, pantalon, non, sont

2 Des phrases ridicules

Des phrases ridicules

La pêche s'arrête à la fenêtre pour voir la fête.
Mon oncle, Léon, entend souvent son cochon, Néron, manger du melon.

3 C'est anglais ou français?

Solution: (b) 1F, 2F, 3A, 4F, 5A, 6F, 7A, 8F

C'est anglais ou français?

a 1 *danger,* danger
2 *excellent,* excellent
3 *intelligent,* intelligent
4 *incident,* incident
5 *nature,* nature
6 *table,* table
7 *imagination,* imagination
8 *important,* important

b 1 danger
2 excellent
3 *intelligent*
4 incident
5 *nature*
6 table
7 *imagination*
8 important

4 Comment ça s'écrit?

Solution: (b) 4 *(automne)*

Comment ça s'écrit?

a 1 j-a-n-v-i-e-r
2 f-é-v-r-i-e-r
3 j-u-i-l-l-e-t
4 a-u-t-o-m-n-e
5 a-o-û-t
6 d-é-c-e-m-b-r-e

5 Quel son est différent?

Solution: **1b**, *-er, -ez,* **2b**, *-es, -ent,* **3c**, *-ent, -e,* **4a**, *-ez, -er,* **5c**, *-e, -ent,* **6c**, *est, es*

Quel son est différent?

1 a écouter
b écoutes
c écoutez

2 a cliques
b cliquez
c cliquent

3 a travaillent
b travaille
c travaillons

4 a regarde
b regardez
c regarder

5 a aime
b aiment
c aimons

6 a est
b es
c êtes

6 Vocabulaire de classe

Solution: 5, 3, 8, 1, 4, 2, 7, 6

Vocabulaire de classe

Regarde la page 61. Écoute le CD et écris le nombre de chaque instruction dans l'ordre du CD.

Comment ça s'écrit?
Je ne comprends pas.
Je voudrais un livre, s'il vous plaît.
C'est masculin ou féminin?
Qu'est-ce que c'est en anglais?
Je ne sais pas.
Répétez la question, s'il vous plaît?
Je n'ai pas de stylo.

7 Une conversation

Une conversation

Écoute les questions et réponds comme indiqué.

– Salut, c'est Nicole. Ça va?
(pause)
– Oui, ça va bien.
– Quel temps fait-il?
(pause)
– Il fait froid et il neige.
– Et qu'est-ce que tu fais?
(pause)
– J'écoute de la musique.

Épreuve – Unité 6

CM 6/11, 2/24–26 **INFORMAL ASSESSMENT LISTENING**

Épreuve: Écouter

A Le temps et les saisons (NC 1)

Solution: 1i, 2e, 3h, 4f, 5g, 6d, 7b, 8a, 9c
(mark /4: $^1/_2$ mark per correct item)

Le temps et les saisons

1 – Il neige.
– Ah oui, il neige.

2 – Il fait chaud.
– Pff, comme il fait chaud.

3 – Il y a du vent.
– Oui, quel vent.

4 – Il pleut.
– Oui, il pleut beaucoup.

5 – Il fait froid.
– Oui, il fait très froid.

6 – Il y a du brouillard.
– Oui, il y a du brouillard.

7 – C'est l'hiver.
– On est en hiver.

8 – Moi, je préfère le printemps. Le printemps, c'est ma saison préférée.

9 – Il y a du soleil.
– Oui, j'adore le soleil.

B À la maison (NC 2)

Solution:

	musique	ord'teur	cartes	dessiner	télé	console
1 *Sanjay*			✔			
2 *Claire*				✔		
3 *Jonathan*						✔
4 *Magali*					✔	
5 *Daniel*	✔					
6 *Sika*		✔				

(mark /5)

À la maison

1 – Qu'est-ce que tu fais quand il fait mauvais, Sanjay?
– Moi, je joue aux cartes avec mes amis.
– Tu joues aux cartes. C'est bien.

2 – Et toi, Claire, qu'est-ce que tu fais?
– Moi, je dessine. J'aime beaucoup dessiner.

3 – Jonathan, qu'est-ce que tu fais, normalement, quand tu es à la maison?
– Je joue à la console. J'adore les jeux électroniques.
– Alors, toi, tu joues à la console.

4 – Et toi, Magali, qu'est-ce que tu fais?
– Moi, je regarde la télévision.
– Tu regardes la télévision.

5 – Et toi, Daniel, qu'est-ce que tu fais quand il fait mauvais?
– J'écoute de la musique sur mon baladeur. J'adore la musique.

6 – Et toi, Sika, qu'est-ce que tu fais à la maison?
– Je travaille sur l'ordinateur. J'écris des messages électroniques à mes amis.
– Alors, toi, tu travailles sur l'ordinateur.

C Une interview (NC 3)

Solution:
Nom: *Hér<u>iot</u>* (1 mark)
Prénom: *Claire*
Adresse: *<u>81</u> rue Saint-Pierre* (1 mark)
Numéro de téléphone: *<u>13</u> <u>67</u> <u>90</u> <u>75</u> <u>42</u>* (5 marks)
Sports préférés: hockey ✔; volley ✔ (2 marks)
Autres loisirs: drawing ✔; listening to music ✔ (2 marks)
(mark /11: the name *Claire* is given and is not awarded a mark)

Une interview

– Bonjour. Comment t'appelles-tu?
– Je m'appelle Claire Hériot.
– Hériot. Comment ça s'écrit?
– H-É-R-I-O-T.
– Alors, c'est H-É-R-I-O-T.
– C'est exact.
– Et ton adresse, Claire?
– Alors, mon adresse, c'est quatre-vingt-un, rue Saint-Pierre.
– Quatre-vingt-un, rue Saint-Pierre. Très bien. Et ton numéro de téléphone?
– Mon numéro de téléphone est 13, 67, 90, 75, 42.
– Alors, je répète, c'est 13, 67, 90, 75, 42. Et quels sont tes sports favoris?
– Mes sports favoris sont le hockey et le volley.
– Alors, tes sports favoris sont le hockey et le volley. Très bien. Et est-ce que tu as d'autres loisirs, à part le sport?
– Oui, j'écoute souvent de la musique et je dessine.
– Bon, tu écoutes de la musique et tu dessines. Très bien. Merci, Claire.

CM 6/12 **READING**

Épreuve: Lire

A Des activités (NC 1)

Solution: **1f, 2e, 3h, 4b, 5c, 6g, 7d, 8a**
(mark /7)

B Samedi (NC 2)

Solution: **1c, 2g, 3d, 4e, 5a, 6b, 7f**
(mark /6)

C Une lettre de Bordeaux (NC 3)

Solution: **1F, 2V, 3V, 4F, 5V, 6V, 7V, 8F**
(mark /7)

CM 6/13 **WRITING** **GRAMMAR**

Épreuve: Écrire et grammaire

A Le temps (NC 1)

Solution: **1** *mauvais,* **2** *beau,* **3** *chaud,* **4** *froid*
(mark /3)

B Quel temps fait-il? (NC 1)

Solution: **1** *Il neige.* **2** *Il pleut.* **3** *Il y a du soleil.* **4** *Il y a du vent.* **5** *Il y a du brouillard.*
(mark /4)

C À Dieppe (NC 1)

Solution: **1** *passe,* **2** *habitent,* **3** *travaille,* **4** *jouons,* **5** *aimes,* **6** *chantent,* **7** *rentrez*
(marks/6)

D Une carte postale (NC 3)

Solution: (mark /7: 1 mark for each meaningful sentence + 2 marks for style/accuracy)

SB 63–65, CM 104, 2/27 READING EXTENSION

Presse-Jeunesse 2

These pages provide reading for pleasure. They can be used alone or with the accompanying copymaster. See the notes on TB 17.

CM 104

2 Lire – c'est facile! READING STRATEGIES

This is the second of the series of short articles teaching reading strategies. Similar items feature on each of the Presse-Jeunesse copymasters, and it is suggested that students cut them out and stick them in their exercise books for reference.

SB 63, CM 104

Tom et Jojo

The copymaster task practises gist comprehension of this cartoon story.

Solution:

1 *adore*
2 *il n'y a pas de fromage*
3 *il y a du fromage*
4 *n'est pas*
5 *n'est pas*
6 *est*
7 *Jojo*

SB 63, CM 104

Flash-Web

The copymaster task encourages students to read for more specific detail.

Solution: 1V, 2V, 3V, 4F, 5F, 6V, 7F, 8V

SB 64, CM 104

Le sais-tu?

Solution: **1** *la crêche,* **2** *la bûche de Noël,* **3** *Père Noël,* **4** *Saint Nicolas*

SB 64–65, CM 104

Un correspondant extraordinaire

Students can read the picture story for enjoyment. The copymaster task gives practice in extracting the main points of the story.

Solution: 1, 4, 2, 7, 3, 6, 8, 5

SB 65, 2/27 LISTENING

Encore une comptine

This counting rhyme is recorded at the end of *Unité 6*.

1, 2, 3

1, 2, 3,
lève-toi!
4, 5, 6,
mets ta chemise grise,
7, 8, 9,
ton short neuf,
10, 11, 12,
puis ta veste rouge.

SB 65

Poisson d'avril

A cartoon about an April fool.

Encore Tricolore 1
nouvelle édition

unité 7 Une ville de France

Areas	Topics	Grammar
1	Places in a town	
2	Asking for tourist information	
3	Asking for directions Asking if places are far away	
4	Understanding directions and information about distance	
5	Saying where you are going	*au, à la, à l', aux* (D-L SB 73)
6		Present tense of *aller* (D-L SB 74)
7	Saying where things are	Prepositions (see SB 75)
8	Further activities and consolidation	

National Curriculum information

Some students	Level 3
Most students	Levels 2–3
All students	Levels 1–2

Refer also to the information about coverage of 'Knowledge, skills and understanding' (TB 9).

Revision

The vocabulary and structures introduced in *Unités 6–7* are revised in the *Rappel* section following this unit (SB 78–79, TB 147).

Sounds and writing

- nasal vowels (*in, im, ain; un, um*)
- intonation – raising one's voice at the end of a sentence
- see *Écoute et parle* (SB 156, TB 144)

Assessment

- Informal assessment is in the *Épreuves* at the end of this unit (TB 145).
- Formal assessment is in the *Deuxième contrôle* following *Unité 7* (TB 201).

ICT opportunities

- looking up La Rochelle and other French towns on websites (TB 143)
- sending a virtual postcard (TB 133)
- making a brochure about a French town, using DTP or word processing (TB 143)
- using a phrase generator (see TB 40, 141)

Students' Book

Unité 7 SB 66–77

Au choix SB 135 1, 2 (TB 134), 3 (TB 137)
SB 136 4 (TB 137), 5 (TB 138)
SB 137 6 (TB 138), 7 (TB 139), 8 (TB 141)

Écoute et parle SB 156
Rappel 3 SB 78–79 (TB 147)

Flashcards

1–2	happy/sad face
3, 8–12	town
43–55	places in a town

CDs

2/28–40

Student CD 1/45–52

Student CD 2/32–34

Copymasters

7/1	*Une ville de France* [mini-flashcards/support] (TB 132, 142)
7/2	*En ville* [support] (TB 133)
7/3	*C'est quelle direction?* [consolidation] (TB 139)
7/4	*Où va-t-on?* [grammar: *à*, *au* etc.] (TB 140)
7/5	*aller* [grammar] (TB 141)
7/6	*C'est où?* [grammar: prepositions] (TB 142)
7/7	*Un plan à compléter* [speaking: information gap] (TB 143)
7/8	*Tu comprends?* [independent listening] (TB 143)
7/9	*Sommaire* (TB 144)
7/10	*Épreuve: Écouter* (TB 145)
7/11	*Épreuve: Lire* (TB 146)
7/12	*Épreuve: Écrire et grammaire* (TB 146)
115–120	*Deuxième contrôle* (TB 201)

Additional

Grammar in Action 1, pp 13–15

Language content

Talk about places in a town (Area 1)

auberge de jeunesse (f)
banque (f)
cathédrale (f)
camping (m)
collège (m)
école (f)
église (f)
gare (f)
hôpital (m)
marché (m)
musée (m)
l'office de tourisme (m)
parc (m)
parking (m)
piscine (f)
place (f)
poste (f)
bureau de poste (m)
restaurant (m)
tour (f)

Ask for information (Area 2)

Avez-vous un dépliant sur la ville, s'il vous plaît?
une liste des hôtels,
une brochure,
un plan de la ville,
Est-ce qu'il y a une piscine ici?
Qu'est-ce qu'il y a à voir
à faire à La Rochelle?

Ask for directions (Area 3)

Pardon, Monsieur/Madame/Mademoiselle.
Pour aller au parc, s'il vous plaît?
à la poste,
à l'église,
aux magasins,
en ville,
Est-ce qu'il y a un café près d'ici?
une banque
des toilettes
C'est loin?

Understand and give directions to a French person (Areas 3–4)

C'est à gauche.
à droite.
Continuez tout droit.
Prenez la première (1ère) rue à gauche.
la deuxième (2ème) rue à droite.
la troisième (3ème) rue
Tournez à gauche/à droite.

Understand how far away places are (Area 4–5)

c'est tout près
c'est loin
c'est assez loin
ce n'est pas loin
c'est à 50 mètres

Say exactly where places are (Area 7)

C'est devant l'église.
C'est derrière l'église.
C'est entre le cinéma et le café.

Classroom language and rubrics

Travaillez en groupes.
On fait un jeu?
On commence?
Qui commence?
C'est à qui le tour?
C'est à toi.
C'est à moi.
Tu poses une question.
Qui a gagné?
On va demander au prof.

La Rochelle

This unit contains information that will be useful when visiting any French town, but La Rochelle was selected as the setting for several units for a variety of reasons:

- it is an attractive place to visit and a holiday resort, but also very much a working town;
- it combines old and new areas and has both picturesque buildings and modern developments;
- it is big enough to contain many interesting features, but not too big to visit on foot;
- it is easy to reach by rail and road and welcomes school parties!

For information about La Rochelle, see Section 2 (TB 32–33) and the information pages at the end of the book (TB 207–208).

Area 1
Places in a town
SB 66-67, 1-3, SB 68, 1-3
Au choix SB 135, 1-2
CM 7/1, 7/2
CD 2/28
FC 3, 8-12, 43–55
Qu'est-ce qu'il y a à voir? etc.

En ville

PRESENTATION

A large amount of town vocabulary is introduced in Areas 1 and 2 and practised throughout the unit.

- Using flashcards, revise the relevant vocabulary taught in *Unité* 2 (*le café, le cinéma, le port, la rue, la ville*).
- Teach the following (a few at a time): *l'auberge de jeunesse, le camping, l'école, l'église, la gare SNCF, l'hôpital le marché, le musée, l'office de tourisme, la piscine, la poste (le bureau de poste), le restaurant, l'hôtel de ville* (this will need a brief explanation in English to prevent confusion with *hôtel*).
- Ask students to guess the following cognates (writing them on the board): *la banque, la cathédrale, l'hôtel, le parc, le parking* and also *la tour*.
- Teach (or practise, if known already) *vieux/vieille*, e.g. *Vieux, c'est le contraire de moderne – par exemple* ... (quote the names of old and modern buildings).
- Give some question and answer practice, e.g. distribute flashcards, ask *Où est* (+ noun)?
  The student with the appropriate flashcard returns it, saying *Voici* (+ noun).
- Play some flashcard games and spelling games, e.g. *Effacez!* (using flashcards or words), *Je pense à quelque chose dans une ville* etc. (see TB 26–28).
- Revise the French alphabet and dictate the new and old town vocabulary, a word at a time, to students, who write it on the board. The others put up their hand if they think the current 'scribe' makes a mistake. The words on the board could be re-used for practice in spelling or for *Effacez!* (see TB 26).

CM 7/1 **MINI-FLASHCARDS**

Une ville de France

This worksheet could be used now or later. Students could just fill in the words, colour the pictures and stick them in their books, or the sheets could be mounted on card and the completed and coloured cards could be used for additional practice in pairs or groups.

See TB 28 for ideas for using mini-flashcards.

Solution: 1H, 2B, 3F, 4A, 5C, 6D, 7K, 8L, 9J, 10I, 11G, 12E

SB 66–67, 2/28 **LISTENING READING**

1 Voici La Rochelle

Give the class a few minutes to look at the photos, before listening to the recording and following the text.

Then students should work on matching the text with the pictures, either individually or in pairs. Some help may be needed with **4e** and **7f**.

Solution: 1a, 2c, 3k, 4e, 5l, 6d, 7f, 8h, 9b, 10g, 11j, 12m, 13i, 14n

Voici La Rochelle

1 Voici La Rochelle. C'est une ville en France. En été, il fait très beau et beaucoup de touristes visitent la ville.

2 Qu'est-ce qu'il y a à voir à La Rochelle? Il y a le vieux port avec ses trois tours; la Tour Saint-Nicolas, la Tour de la Chaîne et la Tour de la Lanterne. En été, il y a souvent des acrobates et des clowns au vieux port. C'est très amusant.

3 Le matin, il y a un grand marché aux poissons près d'ici.

4 Il y a une cathédrale et l'église Saint-Sauveur.

5 Il y a des parcs, comme le parc Frank Delmas.

6 Et il y a beaucoup de musées.

7 Voici l'hôtel de ville.

8 La place de Verdun est une grande place dans le centre-ville.

9 Les touristes vont à l'hôtel, au camping ou à l'auberge de jeunesse.

10 Les vieilles rues à arcades sont très jolies.

11 Il y a deux piscines.

12 En été, on fait beaucoup de sports nautiques.

13 Et bien sûr, il y a beaucoup de bons restaurants.

14 Et au mois de juillet, il y a un grand festival de musique – Les Francofolies.

C'est quelle photo?

PRACTICE

The teacher or a student could say something about one of the photos and the class has to identify the correct photo, e.g.

Ça, c'est le vieux port. (Photo c.)

Voici l'hôtel de ville. C'est joli, non?

Ça, c'est le parc.

Ce que j'aime bien à La Rochelle, c'est les musées.

Moi, j'adore aller au marché aux poissons, le matin.

Ça, c'est l'église Saint-Sauveur.

En été, j'aime bien aller à la piscine.

Moi, j'aime les petits magasins dans les rues à arcades.

SB 67 **WRITING**

2 Qu'est-ce que c'est?

Students write out the words with the missing vowels. They can all be found in the captions to the photos.

Solution: **1** *le musée,* **2** *le port,* **3** *le parc,* **4** *le marché,* **5** *la cathédrale,* **6** *le camping,* **7** *le restaurant*

SB 67, **PRACTICE**

3 Français-anglais

Students match up some of the new town vocabulary with the English meaning.

They could add the words to their vocabulary books or electronic word lists.

Solution: 1g, 2c, 3e, 4f, 5d, 6a, 7h, 8b

SB 68 **READING**

1 Photo-quiz

An easy matching activity, which could be done orally with more able students.

Solution: **1** *une tour,* **2** *le marché,* **3** *une église,* **4** *un musée,* **5** *l'hôtel de ville,* **6** *un restaurant,* **7** *une rue,* **8** *une piscine*

SB 68 **READING WRITING**

2 Des cartes postales

Students choose the correct words to complete the postcards.

Solution:

A **1** *l'auberge de jeunesse,* **2** *ville,* **3** *port,* **4** *tours,* **5** *musées,* **6** *chaud,* **7** *piscine*

B **1** *passons,* **2** *camping,* **3** *touristes,* **4** *beau,* **5** *marché,* **6** *parc,* **7** *restaurant*

SB 68 **WRITING**

3 À La Rochelle

Students match the symbols and the words on the signpost.

More able students could omit this and, instead, do *Au choix*, Task 1 (see TB 134).

Solution: **1** *l'école,* **2** *la poste,* **3** *le supermarché,* **4** *la banque,* **5** *le parking,* **6** *la gare,* **7** *l'auberge de jeunesse,* **8** *l'hôpital,* **9** *l'office de tourisme,* **10** *l'hôtel de ville*

Follow-up activities

WRITING

Virtual postcard

Students could send a virtual postcard (see details on TB 207).

PRACTICE

Qu'est-ce qu'il y a à La Rochelle?

This could be done as an individual or a group activity. Students look back at the photos on SB 66–67 for a few minutes, then close their books and try to recall as many different places as possible. This can be built up as a cumulative list on the board. Prompt as necessary. It can also aid memory recall to give initial letters, e.g. *des m…, le p…, des r…* etc.

CM 7/2 **SUPPORT**

En ville

This copymaster contains word games practising town vocabulary.

While some students are doing these games, more able students could do the first two tasks in *Au choix* (SB 135).

Solutions:

1 Un panneau

1 POSTE	MARCHÉ **6**
2 CAMPING	MUSÉE **7**
3 PARC	HÔTEL **8**
4 PORT	PARKING **9**
5 PISCINE	GARE **10**

2 Dans l'ordre alphabétique

1. *auberge de jeunesse* = youth hostel
2. *brochure* = leaflet
3. *cinéma* = cinema
4. *église* = church
5. *gare* = station
6. *hôpital* = hospital
7. *magasin* = shop
8. *office de tourisme* = tourist information
9. *piscine* = swimming pool
10. *tour* = tower

3 Mots mêlés

a

c	a	t	h	é	d	r	a	l	e
i	f	o	x	c	y	e	o	j	l
n	i	u	q	o	t	s	u	e	r
é	l	r	w	l	i	t	î	s	p
m	u	s	é	e	l	a	l	u	a
a	s	d	g	y	i	u	e	c	r
v	i	l	l	e	s	r	n	l	k
x	e	l	i	y	t	a	l	j	i
q	p	i	s	c	i	n	e	i	n
p	r	u	e	t	a	t	o	u	g

b *cathédrale (f)* = cathedral
parking (m) = car park
cinéma (m) = cinema
église (f) = church
tour (f) = tower
musée (m) = museum
école (f) = school
piscine (f) = swimming pool
restaurant (m) = restaurant
ville (f) = town
rue (f) = street
île (f) = island

Au choix SB 135 **WRITING**

1 À La Rochelle

Students complete the publicity material.

Solution: **1** *ville,* **2** *vieux,* **3** *tours,* **4** *vieilles,* **5** *rues,* **6** *très,* **7** *musées,* **8** *poisson,* **9** *cartes,* **10** *magasins*

Au choix SB135 **DICTIONARY PRACTICE**

2 C'est utile, le dictionnaire

This item gives additional town vocabulary to be looked up and listed with genders and translation.

Solution:

1 *auberge (f)* = inn
2 *gare routière (f)* = bus station
3 *marché aux fleurs (m)* = flower market
4 *poste de police (m)* = police station
5 *caserne de pompiers (f)* = fire station
6 *plage (f)* = beach
7 *centre sportif (m)* = sports centre
8 *château (m)* = castle, palace
9 *marché aux poissons (m)* = fish market
10 *crêperie (f)* = café/restaurant specialising in pancakes

Area 2
Asking for tourist information
SB 69, 4–5
CD 2/29
Avez-vous (+ noun)?

Tourist offices **PRESENTATION**

Explain briefly about the importance and prevalence of tourist offices in France, and, using the pictures on SB 69, explain what you can obtain there, asking the class to repeat the words.

SB 69, 2/29 **LISTENING**

4 À l'office de tourisme

Students listen to these short conversations at the tourist office and note down the letter by each item requested.

Solution: **1f, 2b, 3d, 4c, 5a, 6e**

À l'office de tourisme

1 – Bonjour Madame. Avez-vous une liste des campings, s'il vous plaît?
– Oui, voilà, Madame.

2 – Bonjour Madame, avez-vous un plan de la ville, s'il vous plaît?
– Bien sûr, Monsieur. Voilà.
– Merci beaucoup, Madame.
– De rien, Monsieur.

3 – Bonjour Madame. Avez-vous une liste des musées, s'il vous plaît?
– Oui, voilà, Madame.

4 – Bonjour Madame. Avez-vous un dépliant sur la ville?
– Ah, oui, Monsieur. Voici un dépliant sur La Rochelle.

5 – Bonjour Madame. Avez-vous une liste des hôtels, s'il vous plaît?
– Oui, voilà, Madame.

6 – Bonjour Madame. Avez-vous une liste des restaurants, s'il vous plaît?
– Oui, voilà, Monsieur.

SB 69, **SPEAKING**

5 Inventez des conversations

Choose two volunteers to read the conversation aloud, one to play the tourist and one to play the assistant. Read out the list of alternatives available, then invite two different students to read the conversation in an adapted form. Students then practise similar conversations in pairs, using the various alternatives listed.

Area 3
Asking for directions
Asking if places are far away
SB 69, 6–7, SB 70, 1–3
FC 8–12, 43–55
CD 2/30–31
Pour aller à …?
Est-ce qu'il y a … près d'ici? C'est loin?

SB 69, 2/30 **LISTENING**

6 Les touristes à La Rochelle

Before doing the task in the Students' Book, play the recording and ask students to pick out the key phrase for asking the way which occurs in each one. When they have spotted *Pour aller …?* write it on the board.

Then refer them to the Students' Book and play the recording again, so that they can match the pictures to the destinations.

Solution: **1d, 2c, 3e, 4a, 5g, 6f, 7b, 8h, 9j, 10i**

Les touristes à La Rochelle

1 Pardon, Monsieur. Pour aller au restaurant Serge, s'il vous plaît?

2 Pardon, Madame. Pour aller à la gare, s'il vous plaît?

3 Pardon, Monsieur. Pour aller à l'office de tourisme, s'il vous plaît?

4 Pardon, Mademoiselle. Pour aller à la piscine, s'il vous plaît?

5 Pardon, Monsieur. Pour aller au port, s'il vous plaît?
6 Pardon, Madame. Pour aller en ville, s'il vous plaît?
7 Pardon, Monsieur. Pour aller à l'hôtel de ville, s'il vous plaît?
8 Pardon, Mademoiselle. Pour aller au parc Frank Delmas, s'il vous plaît?
9 Pardon, Monsieur. Pour aller au marché, s'il vous plaît?
10 Pardon, Madame. Pour aller au cinéma Dragon, s'il vous plaît?

SB 69 **VOCABULARY PRACTICE**

7 En ville

This is one of a series of three similar word games throughout the unit.

Solution (possible words)**:**

c – *un camping, un cinéma, une cathédrale*
m – *un marché, un musée, un magasin*
g – *une gare*

SB 70 **SPEAKING**

1 Pour aller ...?

Use the substitution table and symbols to provide practice in asking the way to various places. (All the nouns used here are masculine, one of them is plural.)

Solution:

1 *Pour aller au centre-ville, s'il vous plaît?*
2 *Pour aller au musée, s'il vous plaît?*
3 *Pour aller au parc, s'il vous plaît?*
4 *Pour aller au marché, s'il vous plaît?*
5 *Pour aller au cinéma, s'il vous plaît?*
6 *Pour aller au port, s'il vous plaît?*
7 *Pour aller au restaurant, s'il vous plaît?*
8 *Pour aller au supermarché, s'il vous plaît?*
9 *Pour aller aux magasins, s'il vous plaît?*
10 *Pour aller au café, s'il vous plaît?*

FC 8–12, 43–55 **SUPPORT**

Flashcard games

If students need extra practice of the structure Pour aller au ...? use flashcards to cue further questions or play some games, e.g.

1 Flashcard chain-game

Students are issued with flashcards or mini-flashcards depicting places in a town (about three of each card will be needed).

The teacher starts by asking *Pour aller au ...?* The students holding those cards then have to stand up, and the first to do so asks the next question.

2 Flashcard noughts and crosses

Stick nine 'town' flashcards to the board. Students play this in two teams, with each team asking the way to a place (*Pour aller au ...?*) in turn. The card representing the place is then removed and replaced with a cross or a nought. The object of the game is to get three in a row.

SB 70, 🎧 2/31, FC 8–12, 43–55 **PRESENTATION LISTENING READING**

2 C'est loin?

Before using this recording of three young visitors to La Rochelle, teach the expressions *Est-ce qu'il y a ... près d'ici?* and *C'est loin?*, perhaps using flashcards.

a Let the class listen to the sequence of three conversations once, without the text, just to get the gist of what happens.

Then go through the three conversations, with the text, encouraging students to ask in French if there is anything they don't understand. See notes on using recordings with printed text (TB 64).

Students eventually practise reading the conversations aloud, in groups of six (three students, three passers-by).

🎧 C'est loin?

Hassan et ses amis, Alain et Caroline, passent les vacances à La Rochelle. Ils arrivent à la gare de La Rochelle. C'est le cinq juillet et il fait très chaud.

– Pardon, Madame. Le centre-ville, c'est loin?
– Le centre-ville? Oui, c'est loin!
– Est-ce qu'il y a un autobus?
– Oui, prenez l'autobus numéro 1 devant la gare.
– Merci, Madame.
– De rien.

Les trois amis arrivent au centre-ville. Ils descendent de l'autobus place de Verdun.

– Maintenant – un plan de la ville!
– Bonne idée!
– Pardon, Monsieur, est-ce qu'il y a un office de tourisme près d'ici?
– L'office de tourisme? Oh, c'est loin! C'est sur le Quai du Gabut.
– C'est où, ça?
– C'est près de la mer et c'est assez près de la gare.
– C'est près de la gare, oh non! Ça alors!
– Zut alors! L'office de tourisme est très loin!
– Ouf! Il fait très chaud, n'est-ce pas?
– Oui, c'est vrai. Alors, on cherche un café?
– Bonne idée. ... Pardon, Madame. Est-ce qu'il y a un café près d'ici?
– Bien sûr! Il y a le café de la Paix dans la rue Chaudrier – ce n'est pas loin.

b Students find the errors in these sentences and correct them.

Solution:

1 ~~janvier~~ *juillet*
2 ~~froid~~ *chaud*
3 ~~piscine~~ *gare*
4 ~~port~~ *centre-ville*
5 ~~l'auberge de jeunesse~~ *l'office de tourisme*
6 ~~cathédrale~~ *gare*
7 ~~marché~~ *café*

SB 70, **SPEAKING**

3 Inventez des conversations

a Using this basic dialogue, students ask each other in turn if different places are far away. The diagrams provide the information.

b Similar practice, but this time, asking if a certain place is nearby.

Chain game **CONSOLIDATION**

To complete this area, play a chain question game, with students asking a different question each time, e.g.

Student A *Le port, c'est loin,* (Student B)?

Student B *Oui/Non/Je ne sais pas. Est-ce qu'il y a un camping près d'ici,* (Student C)? etc.

Area 4
Understanding directions and information about distance

SB 71, 4–8, SB 72, 1–2
Au choix SB 135–137, 3–7
CM 7/3
FC 8–12, 43–55
CD 2/32–36

à gauche, à droite, tout droit
premier(ère), deuxième, troisième
c'est à (+ distance)

FC 8–12, 43–55 **PRESENTATION**

À gauche, à droite, tout droit

To introduce the expressions *à gauche*, *à droite* and *tout droit*, draw three arrows on the board pointing to the left, right and straight on. Hold or attach flashcards on the left and right, and talk about them, e.g.

Où est le cinéma?
Le cinéma est à gauche.
La piscine est à droite.

Repeat this, and introduce *tout droit*.

Gradually encourage students to ask and answer the questions and add:
Pour aller au cinéma, s'il vous plaît?
Tourner à gauche etc.

Some students in this age group are not too confident, even in English, about the concepts of left and right, and they may need extra practice in reacting quickly to *gauche* and *droite*.

2/32 **LISTENING**

C'est où?

This optional listening task could be used before students start Task 4.

Students write down the numbers 1 to 8 in their books and listen to find out whether the places mentioned are to the right, to the left or straight on. They can write their answers in English or draw arrows.

Solution: **1** left, **2** straight on, **3** right, **4** straight on, **5** left, **6** right, **7** straight on, **8** right

C'est où?

1 – Pardon, Madame, la piscine, c'est où, s'il vous plaît?
– C'est à gauche, Monsieur.

2 – La cathédrale, c'est où, s'il vous plaît?
– C'est tout droit.

3 – L'hôtel de ville, c'est loin, Monsieur?
– Non, c'est tout près, c'est à droite.

4 – Pour aller au supermarché, s'il vous plaît?
– C'est tout droit, Madame.

5 – Où est le camping, s'il vous plaît, Monsieur?
– C'est là-bas, à gauche.

6 – Où est l'hôpital, s'il vous plaît, Madame.
– C'est ici, à droite, Monsieur.

7 – Le vieux port, c'est loin, Madame?
– Non, c'est tout droit.

8 – Pour aller au marché, s'il vous plaît?
– C'est là-bas, à droite, Madame.

SB 71 **PRACTICE**

4 À gauche ou à droite?

This provides practice based on photographs of actual signs in La Rochelle.

Solution: **1** *à gauche,* **2** *à gauche,* **3** *à droite,* **4** *à gauche,* **5** *à gauche,* **6** *à droite,* **7** *à gauche,* **8** *à droite,* **9** *à droite,* **10** *à gauche*

PRESENTATION

Premier(ère), deuxième, troisième

Introduce the idea of *premier/première, deuxième, troisième*, first for comprehension only, for example by describing where students are sitting in class (*au premier/deuxième rang* etc.), or line them up in a queue and ask *Qui est premier/deuxième/troisième?*

Regardez le plan **PRESENTATION**

Draw a simple sketch on the board or on OHT, with one road running vertically, crossed by three horizontal roads (see below):

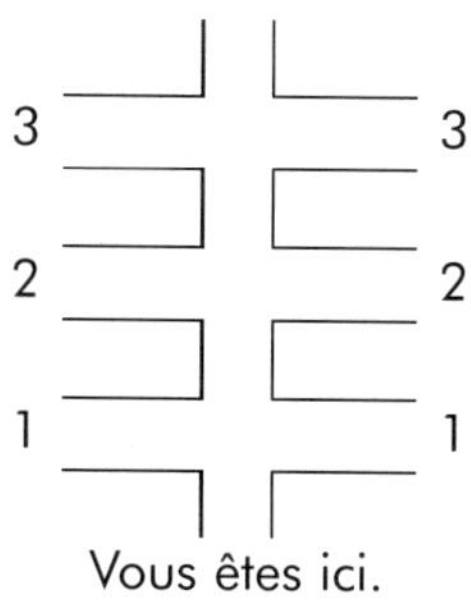

Use this to demonstrate simple directions, e.g.

Prenez la première/deuxième/troisième rue à droite/gauche.
Continuez/Allez tout droit.

Give instructions to students, who trace the route with their finger or a ruler, and later choose students to direct each other.

SB 71, 2/33 **LISTENING**

5 Pardon, Monsieur

This is a multiple-choice exercise for students to practise understanding simple directions.

There is an incline of difficulty in this exercise so students might need to listen to items 4–6 several times. Ideally they could work at their own pace if equipment is available.

Solution: 1c, 2a, 3b, 4c, 5b, 6a

Pardon, Monsieur

1 – Pardon, Monsieur. Pour aller à la poste, s'il vous plaît?
– Prenez la deuxième rue à gauche, Madame.

2 – Pardon, Monsieur. Pour aller au marché, s'il vous plaît?
– Prenez la première rue à droite.

3 – Pardon, Monsieur. Pour aller au parc Frank Delmas, s'il vous plaît?
– Allez tout droit Madame.

4 – Pardon, Madame. Est-ce qu'il y a une banque près d'ici?
– Mais oui. Il y a la Banque de France dans la rue Réaumur. Continuez tout droit, puis c'est la première rue à droite.
– Merci, Madame. Alors, c'est tout droit, puis la première rue à droite.

5 – Pardon, Mademoiselle. Est-ce qu'il y a un café près d'ici?
– Mais oui, Monsieur. Vous avez le café de la Poste. C'est tout près. Prenez la première rue à droite.
– Merci, Mademoiselle.

6 – Pardon, Monsieur. Est-ce que l'hôpital est près d'ici?
– Oui, Madame. Pour aller à l'hôpital, vous continuez tout droit, tout droit.. C'est à deux cents mètres. L'hôpital est au coin de la rue Saint-Louis.

SB 71 **(LISTENING) READING**

6 Par ici!

a First use the map to give instructions to students, who can imagine that they are tourists following the directions and discover where they are going, e.g. *Prenez la première rue à gauche. Puis c'est tout droit. Où êtes-vous? (À la poste.)*

b Using the map students have to match up the correct question with the correct directions in the book.

Solution: 1b, 2d, 3a, 4c, 5e

SB 135–136

Au choix

There are several tasks in *Au choix* which could be done either now or later, for extension.

AU CHOIX SB 135, 2/34,  **READING LISTENING SPEAKING**

3 Deux conversations

This task is useful for all students.

a Students complete the two conversations.

b They listen to the recorded version to check their answers.

c They practise the conversations in pairs.

Solution: **a1** *à la piscine; aller; droit; deuxième; gauche; Merci; loin*

a2 *château; tout droit; la première rue à gauche; Merci; loin*

Deux conversations

1 – On va à la piscine?
– Oui, d'accord.
– Pardon, Monsieur, pour aller à la piscine, s'il vous plaît?
– Continuez tout droit, puis prenez la deuxième rue à gauche. Descendez la rue et voilà!
– Merci Monsieur. C'est loin?
– Non, c'est tout près.

2 – Pardon, Madame, pour aller au château, s'il vous plaît?
– Continuez tout droit, puis prenez la première rue à gauche.
– Merci Madame. C'est loin?
– Oui, c'est assez loin.

AU CHOIX SB 136 **READING EXTENSION**

4 Les musées, c'est intéressant!

a Dictionary practice – students guess or look up words which appear in the museum publicity material.

Solution:

1	in motion	**7**	famous
2	a model	**8**	an automaton, robot
3	a boat	**9**	veteran cars
4	century	**10**	floating
5	life on board	**11**	sound and light (type of display or show)
6	a battle	**12**	open

b In this part students read the museum publicity material and do the true or false activity

Solution: 1V, 2V, 3V, 4F, 5V, 6V, 7F, 8F, 9V, 10F

c Now they correct the statements which were untrue.

Solution:

4 *Pour voir les automates, on va au Musée des Automates.*
7 *Le Musée Maritime est ouvert tous les jours.*
8 *Le Musée Grévin est sur le Vieux Port.*
10 *Le musée flottant s'appelle le Musée Maritime.*

Au choix SB 136, 2/35 **LISTENING**

5 Où sont-ils?

Students listen to the conversations and write simple sentences saying where each speaker is. Less able students could just jot down the letter for the appropriate museums (in numbers 3, 4, 5 and 7).

For support, write the destinations in jumbled order on the board.

Solution:

1. *Luc est à la gare.*
2. *M. Dupont est à l'office de tourisme.*
3. *Nicole est au Musée des Automates.*
4. *Le guide est au Musée Maritime.*
5. *Daniel et ses frères sont au Musée des Modèles réduits.*
6. *Mme Martin est au marché/dans un magasin.*
7. *Le professeur et Charlotte sont au Musée Grévin.*
8. *Les amis sont au cinéma.*

Où sont-ils?

1 – Le train pour La Rochelle, c'est quand?

2 – Je voudrais un plan de la ville, s'il vous plaît, et un dépliant sur les musées.

3 – Regarde les automates en mouvement – c'est fantastique, non?

4 – Ce musée est unique – c'est un musée flottant.

5 – Regardez les petits trains en mouvement. Ils sont très amusants, non?

6 – Je voudrais un T-shirt rouge, comme ça, s'il vous plaît, et une paire de chaussettes rouges aussi.

7 – Tu aimes l'histoire?
– Ça dépend. Mais ce musée de l'histoire de La Rochelle est assez intéressant.

8 – Tu aimes les films historiques?
– Non, pas beaucoup. Allons voir ce film comique – j'adore les comédies.

Au choix SB 137, **SPEAKING**

6 C'est où?

Students work in pairs making up short conversations, based on the three rows of signposts to places in a town.

Some students could start straight away. Others could prepare for this by each writing four or five questions and then putting them to each other in turns.

Distance **PRESENTATION**

Extend the idea of distance, introduced so far just by *loin* and *près*, by speaking about your own locality and using such expressions as
(Place) *est très loin/près d'ici, c'est à* (number) *mètres/kilomètres.*

Revise key numbers, e.g. 5, 50, 100.

SB 71, 2/36 **LISTENING**

7 C'est à ...?

Students listen and write down the correct distance, e.g. in shortened form – 50m, 100km.

Solution: **1** *à 2km,* **2** *à 100m,* **3** *à 50m,* **4** *à 50m,* **5** *à 5km,* **6** *à 1km*

C'est à ...?

1 – Pardon, Monsieur. Pour aller au port, s'il vous plaît? C'est loin?
– Oui, c'est assez loin. C'est à deux kilomètres. Prenez l'autobus numéro 1 de la place de Verdun.

2 – Pardon, Madame. Pour aller à la piscine? C'est loin?
– Non, ce n'est pas loin. C'est à cent mètres. C'est tout près du parc.

3 – Pardon, Monsieur. Pour aller à l'hôpital? C'est loin?
– Non, c'est tout près. Continuez tout droit. C'est à 50 mètres.

4 – Pardon, Mademoiselle. Pour aller à l'église Saint-Sauveur, s'il vous plaît? C'est loin?
– Non, ce n'est pas loin. C'est à 50 mètres.

5 – Pardon, Monsieur. Pour aller au camping, s'il vous plaît?
– Pour aller au camping, c'est loin. C'est à cinq kilomètres d'ici.

6 – Pardon, Madame. Pour aller à la cathédrale, s'il vous plaît?
– C'est assez loin. C'est à un kilomètre d'ici. Prenez l'autobus jusqu'à la place de Verdun.

SB 71 **VOCABULARY PRACTICE**

8 En ville

This can be done at any odd moment or for homework.

Solution (possible words)**:**

p – *la poste, la piscine, le parc, le parking, la place*
e – *une église, une école*
b – *une banque*

SB 72 **PRACTICE**

Un plan de la ville

This plan of an imaginary town could be the basis for a range of activities, in addition to the tasks actually included in the book. Students could begin by having a good look at the details of the town and some simple oral practice could be based on it, e.g. asking each other questions beginning *Où est* (+ building)?

Replies could be *Voici* (+ building), perhaps including a street name, e.g. *dans la rue de l'Église*.

This can eventually be built up into harder oral work after the printed tasks have been done. Students could work in pairs, deciding on a starting point and asking for and giving directions in turns to other places in the town.

SB 72 **READING**

1 Le centre-ville

Students read the statements and check on the plan to see if they are true or false.

Solution: 1F, 2V, 3F, 4F, 5F, 6F, 7F, 8V, 9V, 10F

SB 72 **PRACTICE**

2 Questions et réponses

Students look at the plan and decide on the correct distances from *la place du Marché*, writing **a**, **b**, **c** or **d** as set out in the shapes to the right of the questions.

Solution: 1c, 2b, 3c, 4d, 5b, 6b, 7a, 8b (other answers possible, depending on students' perception of what is near or far)

AU CHOIX SB 137, **SPEAKING EXTENSION**

7 Le guide, c'est toi!

Students work in pairs, giving directions from the tourist office. They take turns to act as the tourist or the guide.

CM 7/3 **SUPPORT**

C'est quelle direction?

This provides easier practice of understanding directions using a simpler plan. It could be used as a supplement to or a substitute for the map and tasks on SB 72. The final task is slightly more challenging than the first two.

Solutions:

1 Une petite ville

A 1V, 2F, 3V, 4F, 5V, 6V, 7F, 8V

B 1 *première*, **2** *première*, **3** *deuxième*, **4** *deuxième*, **5** *troisième*, **6** *troisième*, **7** *gauche*, **8** *droite*

2 Pour arriver chez moi

En sortant de la gare tourne à gauche, puis prends la deuxième rue à droite et continue tout droit. (c'est la rue de l'Église). Notre maison est à gauche. C'est le numéro 5, près de l'église. Ce n'est pas loin.

Area 5
Saying where you're going
Using the preposition *à* etc.

SB 73, 3–5
CM 7/4
FC 43–55
Grammar in Action 1, page 13

FC 43–55 **PRESENTATION**

Où vas-tu?

Using the flashcards, demonstrate how to say where you are or where you're going, using *à*, *au*, *à la*, *à l'* and *aux* (which could be written on the board with suitable nouns).

Distribute the flashcards to students, saying *Où vas-tu?*

They reply *À la banque* or *J'arrive à la banque*, then they return the flashcard.

SB 73 **READING**

3 Questions sur la ville

This short quiz includes many examples of the preposition *à* in use.

Solution: 1a, 2c, 3c, 4b, 5a, 6c

SB 73 **GRAMMAR**

Dossier-langue
Au, à la, à l', aux

This summarises the different forms of *à*. Ask students to find other examples shown on the page, e.g. in the quiz above.

SB 73, , **SPEAKING READING**

4 On va en ville?

This short dialogue provides practice of the preposition *à*. Students read it through silently first to find out what happens. Then they practise it in pairs, changing the destinations etc., using the substitution table (*Pour t'aider*) to help them.

This could also be used for a text reconstruction exercise.

SB 73 **WRITING**

5 Où vont-ils?

This gives practice in using the correct form of *à* with places in a town. It also introduces different parts of the present tense of *aller*, as preparation for the next area.

Solution: **1** *au concert,* **2** *à la piscine,* **3** *à la poste,* **4** *à l'église,* **5** *au camping,* **6** *au collège*

GRAMMAR IN ACTION 1, PAGE 13 **GRAMMAR**

Using *au, à la, à l', aux*

Further practice of *à*, *au* etc.

CM 7/4 **GRAMMAR**

Où va-t-on?

Extra practice of *à*, *au* etc.

Solutions:

1 La semaine de Charles
1 *au cinéma,* **2** *au parc,* **3** *à la plage,* **4** *à la piscine,* **5** *aux magasins,* **6** *à l'auberge de jeunesse,* **7** *au lit*

2 Où vont-ils?
1 *au camping,* **2** *à la gare,* **3** *à la poste,* **4** *au restaurant,* **5** *à l'hôpital,* **6** *à la plage*

Area 6
Present tense of *aller*
SB 74, 1–2, SB 75, 3
Au choix SB 137, 8
CD 2/37
CM 7/5
FC 43–55
Grammar in Action 1, page 14

FC 43–55 **PRESENTATION**

Using the present tense of *aller*

Students have already used parts of *aller* in the course of the unit. Revise the different pronouns and their meanings (*je, tu, il, elle, nous, vous, ils, elles*).

See how many of the parts of *aller* the class can produce from memory or by looking at earlier pages.

Gradually build up the whole verb on the board, e.g. using the flashcards, ask students:
Où vas-tu? for the reply *Je vais …*
Où va-t-il/elle? (Il/Elle va…)

SB 74 **GRAMMAR**

Dossier-langue
Aller (to go)

Students first read through the introductory sentences, then look at the pictures and spot the different parts of *aller*. Build the verb up bit by bit on the board from the parts they find.

Check that students understand the idea of the paradigm, regular and irregular verbs, and remember that nouns are followed by the third person of the verb etc.

Go through all the note with the class, perhaps seeing if they can explain the points made to each other, as a useful way of getting them to organise their own thoughts.

Give them an opportunity of asking anything they don't understand before going on to the next task, *Coralie est au lit*.

Suggest that they add this verb to their personal verb table (see TB 40, TB 119).

SB 74, 2/37 **LISTENING GRAMMAR**

1 Coralie est au lit

Students practise the third person of *aller* singular and plural.

a Students listen to the recording and note down the letter, indicating who goes where. When this is checked orally, they should supply the full sentences – they have to choose the correct part of *aller* to complete each sentence.

Solution: **1c** *va,* **2f** *va,* **3d** *va,* **4a** *va,* **5e** *vont,* **6b** *vont/vont*

b As an extension, students listen again to the recording and write down with whom each person goes out.

Solution:

1 *Sébastien va avec son cousin.*
2 *Luc va avec son frère.*
3 *Anne-Marie va avec sa mère.*
4 *Vincent va avec ses cousins.*
5 *Stéphanie va avec Mireille.*
6 *Christophe va avec Jean-Pierre.*

Coralie est au lit

– Allô!
– Salut Coralie. Ça va?
– Ah, bonjour Sébastien. Non, ça ne va pas. Je suis au lit. Où vas-tu aujourd'hui?
– Je vais au cinéma avec mon cousin.
– Ah oui. Alors, au revoir.
– Au revoir Coralie.
…
– Allô, oui?
– Bonjour Coralie.
– Ah, bonjour Luc. Qu'est-ce que tu fais ce soir? Tu viens chez moi?
– Oh, Coralie, je suis désolé, mais moi, je vais au parc avec mon frère – il y a un match de football.
– Ah bon. Alors, au revoir Luc.
– Au revoir.
…

- Salut Coralie. C'est moi, Anne-Marie.
- Ah, bonjour Anne-Marie, tu viens me voir?
- Alors ... non. Je suis désolée, mais je vais aux magasins avec ma mère. Je vais te téléphoner ce soir, ça va?
- Ah, oui, oui, oui. Ça va!

...

- Bonjour Coralie. C'est Vincent ici.
- Ah oui, Vincent. Je me suis cassé la jambe, tu sais. Tu viens me voir?
- Mais non, Coralie. Je vais au Musée Maritime avec mes cousins. Je suis désolé!
- Moi aussi! Au revoir Vincent.

...

- Salut Coralie. C'est Stéphanie ici.
- Bonjour Stéphanie. Qu'est-ce que tu fais?
- Ben, je suis avec Mireille. Nous allons au Club des Jeunes. Tu viens?
- Ah non. Je suis au lit. Je me suis cassé la jambe.
- Ça alors! Quel désastre! Alors, au revoir Coralie.
- Au revoir!

...

- Bonjour, Coralie. C'est Christophe. Je vais à la discothèque avec Jean-Pierre. Nous allons au Plaza. Tu viens?
- Mais Christophe, moi, je me suis cassé la jambe!
- Oh pardon, Coralie. Je suis désolé!

...

- Coralie reste au lit, elle regarde la télé, elle dessine ... mais ça ne va pas. Elle n'est pas contente.
- Zut alors! J'ai beaucoup d'amis, ils sont gentils, mais où sont-ils? ... Mais qu'est-ce que c'est?
- Salut Coralie!
- Surprise, surprise!
- Voilà, c'est nous!
- Oh, salut, bonjour ... ça alors – mais c'est fantastique!

SB 74 — **GRAMMAR / PRACTICE**

2 Allez! allez! allez!

Practice in matching up the correct pronouns with the different parts of *aller*.

Solution: 1h, 2e, 3c, 4a, 5b, 6g, 7d, 8f

SB 75, — **SPEAKING / WRITING**

3 Le week-end

Remind the class of the difference between the two words for 'you' and which parts of *aller* go with each.

After they have had time to look at the table, ask questions using *Où vas-tu le samedi?* and also *Où allez-vous?* and help them to make up some answers orally before they write their own six sentences.

If access to a computer is available, the table on SB 75 can be used as a 'phrase generator' (see TB 40). Students could work on it in small groups, seeing which group can make the most sentences in, say, ten minutes.

CM 7/5 — **GRAMMAR**

aller

This sheet provides practice of *aller* in the context of a cartoon strip.

1 aller – to go

Check that the paradigm has been correctly completed before students work on the comic strip, or ask students to check it themselves in *Grammaire* (SB 164).

2 Une erreur

Solution: **1** *vais,* **2** *va,* **3** *va,* **4** *va,* **5** *allons,* **6** *vas,* **7** *vont,* **8** *va,* **9** *allons,* **10** *allez*

GRAMMAR IN ACTION 1, PAGE 14 — **GRAMMAR**

Using the verb *aller* – to go

This provides further practice of *aller*, if required.

AU CHOIX SB 137, — **GRAMMAR / SPEAKING**

8 Ah non!

Students complete the conversation with the correct part of *aller* and the correct form of the preposition *à*. They could then practise this short sketch in pairs, with some of them perhaps recording it.

Solution: **1** *vais à la,* **2** *vais au,* **3** *allons à la,* **4** *vais au,* **5** *va aux; vas,* **6** *va au; vais au,* **7** *allons ... au*

Area 7
Saying where things are

SB 75, 4–6, SB 76, 1–2
Écoute et parle SB 156, 8
Student CD 1/52
7/1
FC 43–55
Grammar in Action 1, page 15
devant, derrière, entre

FC 43–55, CM 7/1 — PRESENTATION

Where?

Teach *devant*, *derrière* and *entre* by describing where students are sitting and where things are in the classroom.

Use the flashcards for various places in a town. Prop them against the board or hold them one behind another and describe where certain places are, e.g.
La piscine est derrière le parc.
L'hôtel est entre la poste et le cinéma.

Next practise in groups with the mini-flashcards (CM 7/1). See TB 28 for instructions for using mini-flashcards to play Pelmanism.

SB 75 — GRAMMAR PRESENTATION

4 Dans la rue

Start with some oral work on the illustration, e.g.
Où est le café? Entre le supermarché et …?

Then students can work on the true/false task.

Solution: **1F, 2V, 3F, 4V, 5F, 6F, 7F, 8V, 9F, 10V**

SB 75 — GRAMMAR PRACTICE

5 Où?

This item is for further practice of *entre*, *devant* and *derrière* and revision of the prepositions *sur*, *dans* and *sous* learnt earlier.

Solution: **1** *entre*, **2** *derrière*, **3** *sur*, **4** *sous*, **5** *devant*, **6** *sur*, **7** *entre*, **8** *dans*

WRITING

6 À toi!

This an optional task based on the previous one. Using some of the ideas in *Où?*, students could produce cartoons involving prepositions, perhaps using clip art. Some of these could be combined to make a Cloze type task to be set to other groups (see ICT section, TB 41 for information about Cloze tasks).

SB 76, — SPEAKING

1 Inventez des conversations

Students make up conversations in pairs using the basic conversation and the substitution table.

SB 156, TB 145, SCD 1/52 — INDEPENDENT LISTENING

8 Une conversation

Similar questions and answers for use in conversations can be practised with the recording in *Écoute et parle* (see SB 156 and TB 145). Alternatively, this can be used at the end of this area.

Grammar in Action 1, page 15 — GRAMMAR

Using prepositions (1)

This offers practice of prepositions with a range of vocabulary.

SB 76 — VOCABULARY

2 En ville

This is the last of the inserts testing town vocabulary.

Solution: (possible words)

h – *l'hôpital, l'hôtel, l'hôtel de ville*
r – *un restaurant, une rue*
t – *une tour*

SB 76 — EXTENSION

?

This short item reminds students of the grave accent which makes the difference between the verb *a* and the preposition *à*.

Area 8
Further activities and consolidation

SB 76–77
CM 7/6–7/12
Student CD 2/32–34
Écoute et parle SB 156, 7, 1–8
Student CD 1/45–52
CD 2/38–40

CM 7/6 — GRAMMAR

C'est où?

This worksheet can be used for further practice of prepositions or for revision later.

Solutions:

1 Un petit lexique

a	*dans*	in
b	*derrière*	behind
c	*entre*	between
d	*sur*	on
e	*sous*	under
f	*devant*	in front of

2 Attention! Le vétérinaire arrive!

A **1V, 2V, 3F, 4V, 5F, 6F, 7V, 8F**
B **1** *devant*, **2** *entre*, **3** *sur*, **4** *sous*, **5** *dans*, **6** *sous*
C This is an open-ended task.

CM 7/7, SPEAKING WRITING

Un plan à compléter

This copymaster provides extra oral practice of places in the town.

Cut the sheet in half so that one partner has a complete plan. The other student acts as a tourist and asks questions to fill in the missing places on their plan. The pair could change roles after three turns.

The completed plans could be used for further question and answer practice including prepositions, e.g.

Où est le cinéma?

Entre le parking et le marché.

Une ville de France

Students could make a brochure of a French town or city using information and images from appropriate websites (see TB 207–208). Specify that pupils should only download one or two images to avoid taking too long.

The text and images from the web should be copied to a publishing program or word processor. The text etc. could be designed in three columns in landscape format. It could be printed back to back and folded into a leaflet.

Alternatively, DTP could be used for this activity, incorporating clip art illustrations as well.

SB 76, SB 156, TB 145, SCD 1/51

Vocabulaire de classe

Students match up the words as usual.

Solution: 1j, 2c, 3f, 4d, 5i, 6b, 7e, 8a, 9h, 10g

There is listening and speaking practice of these phrases in *Écoute et parle* (see TB 145).

CM 7/8, SCD 2/32–34 INDEPENDENT LISTENING

Tu comprends?

1 Qu'est-ce que c'est?

Simple practice, matching town vocabulary with pictures or symbols.

Solution: 1b, 2j, 3h, 4i, 5e, 6g, 7f, 8d, 9a, 10c

Qu'est-ce que c'est?

Nous sommes en ville.

1 – Voici la poste. C'est la poste principale.

2 – Où est l'hôtel de ville?
– L'hôtel de ville est ici.

3 – Et voilà la cathédrale. Elle est superbe, la cathédrale, non?

4 – Pardon, je cherche l'office de tourisme.
– L'office de tourisme est par là.

5 – Où est la piscine, s'il vous plaît?
– La piscine? Là-bas, à droite.

6 – Est-ce qu'il y a des toilettes par ici?
– Des toilettes? Oui, voilà les toilettes.

7 – Pour aller au centre-ville, c'est par là?
– Le centre-ville? Oui, c'est par là.

8 – Le camping, c'est loin?
– Le camping? Non, ce n'est pas loin.

9 – Est-ce que la gare est près d'ici?
– La gare? Oui, c'est près d'ici.

10 – Est-ce que l'auberge de jeunesse est loin d'ici?
– L'auberge de jeunesse? Oui, c'est assez loin.

2 C'est quelle direction?

Choosing directions to match each conversation.

Solution: 1b, 2c, 3d, 4a, 5e, 6f

C'est quelle direction?

1 Tournez à gauche.
2 Continuez tout droit.
3 Prenez la première rue à gauche.
4 Tournez à droite.
5 Prenez la première rue à droite.
6 Prenez la deuxième rue à gauche.

3 Où vas-tu?

Following directions and giving the destinations.

Solution: 1c *à l'hôtel Royal,* **2a** *au parc,* **3f** *aux toilettes,* **4d** *au supermarché,* **5b** *à la piscine,* **6e** *au théâtre,* **7g** *à l'auberge de jeunesse*

Où vas-tu?

1 Allez tout droit et prenez la deuxième rue à droite.
2 Allez tout droit et prenez la deuxième rue à gauche. Puis c'est à gauche.
3 Allez tout droit et tournez à droite. C'est la première rue à droite.
4 Allez tout droit et prenez la première rue à gauche. C'est devant vous.
5 Tout droit, tout droit, puis prenez la troisième rue à droite.
6 Allez tout droit, puis prenez la deuxième rue à gauche et c'est à votre droite.
7 Allez tout droit, puis prenez la deuxième rue à gauche, puis la première rue à droite.

SB 77, CM 7/9

Sommaire

A summary of the main language and structures of the unit, also on copymaster for ease of reference.

SB 156, SCD 1/45–52 **INDEPENDENT LISTENING SOUNDS AND WRITING**

Écoute et parle – Unité 7

1 Les sons français

Solution: ɛ̃ **: (a) 1d, 2c, 3a, 4b**
œ̃ **: (a) 1c, 2b, 3d, 4a**

Les sons français

Le son ɛ̃

a 1 américain
2 magasin
3 impossible
4 coin

b lapin
train
important
intéressant

Le son œ̃

a 1 Verdun
2 brun
3 trente et un
4 parfum

b un
lundi
vingt et un
humble

2 Une phrase ridicule

Une phrase ridicule

Cinquante et un lapins bruns rentrent dans leur coin à Verdun.

3 Anglais ou français?

Solution: (b) 1F, 2F, 3A, 4F, 5A, 6F, 7F, 8A

Anglais ou français?

a 1 *cousin*, cousin
2 *train*, train
3 *influence*, influence
4 *impossible*, impossible
5 *camp*, camp
6 *parent*, parent
7 *Paris*, Paris
8 *absent*, absent

b 1 cousin
2 train
3 *influence*
4 impossible
5 *camp*
6 parent
7 Paris
8 *absent*

4 C'est quel mot?

Solution: 1a, 2b, 3a, 4a, 5b, 6a

C'est quel mot?

1 un
une
un

2 brun
brune
brune

3 cousin
cousine
cousin

4 ont
sont
ont

5 lampe
camp
camp

6 train
vin
train

5 C'est une question?

Solution: 1b, 2a, 3b, 4b, 5a, 6b

C'est une question?

1 a La piscine, c'est loin.
b La piscine, c'est loin?
2 a Le parc, c'est près d'ici?
b Le parc, c'est près d'ici.
3 a C'est un cahier.
b C'est un cahier?
4 a Nicole aime le sport.
b Nicole aime le sport?
5 a Marc chante dans le concert?
b Marc chante dans le concert.
6 a Ils vont à la gare.
b Ils vont à la gare?

6 Et après?

Solution: **1** *février,* **2** *mai,* **3** *juillet,* **4** *septembre,* **5** *décembre,* **6** *mars,* **7** *juin,* **8** *novembre*

Et après?

1 janvier
2 avril
3 juin
4 août
5 novembre
6 février
7 mai
8 octobre

7 Vocabulaire de classe

Solution: 3, 6, 9, 8, 2, 4, 1, 10, 5, 7

Vocabulaire de classe

Regarde la page 76. Écoute le CD et écris le nombre de chaque instruction dans l'ordre du CD.

On commence?
C'est à toi.
Qui a gagné?
Tu poses une question.
On fait un jeu?
Qui commence?
Travaillez en groupes.
On va demander au prof.
C'est à qui le tour?
C'est à moi.

8 Une conversation

Une conversation

Pose des questions comme indiqué, puis écoute la question pour vérifier et écoute la réponse.

1 – Je peux vous aider?
(pause)
– Le centre-ville, c'est loin?
– Non, ce n'est pas très loin. Continuez tout droit.
(pause)

2 – Est-ce qu'il y a un supermarché près d'ici?
– Oui, il y a un supermarché, rue de l'église.
(pause)

3 – Pour aller à la piscine, s'il vous plaît?
– Prenez la première rue à gauche.
(pause)

4 – Où est le camping, s'il vous plaît?
– Oh, c'est loin – c'est à trois kilomètres d'ici.
(pause)

5 – Est-ce qu'il y a un autobus?
– Oui, l'autobus numéro quatre va au camping.

Épreuve – Unité 7

CM 7/10, 2/38–40 **INFORMAL ASSESSMENT LISTENING**

Épreuve: Écouter

A Un plan de la ville (NC 1)

Solution: 1b, 2a, 3f, 4c, 5d, 6e, 7h, 8g (mark /7)

Un plan de la ville

Regardez le plan. Voici ma ville. Elle est assez petite.

1 Voici la place. C'est la place centrale.
2 Et voici la piscine. J'aime bien aller à la piscine.
3 Et ici, c'est un restaurant. C'est un très bon restaurant.
4 Voilà la banque. Regardez, la banque est là.
5 Puis il y a un supermarché – voici le supermarché.
6 Et voici la poste. Là, c'est la poste.
7 Et voilà l'église. C'est l'église Saint-Pierre.
8 Et la gare est ici. Voici la gare SNCF.

B C'est loin? (NC 2)

Solution: 1P, 2L, 3P, 4L, 5P, 6P, 7P, 8L (mark /7)

C'est loin?

1 – Est-ce que l'hôtel de ville est près d'ici?
– Oui, oui, c'est tout près.

2 – L'église Saint-Jean, c'est loin?
– Oui, c'est assez loin.

3 – L'auberge de jeunesse, c'est près d'ici?
– L'auberge de jeunesse? Oui, c'est à dix minutes d'ici.

4 – Je cherche le camping «Bon séjour». C'est près d'ici?
– Le camping? Ah non, il est à cinq ou six kilomètres de la ville.

5 – Je vais au parc aujourd'hui. Tu viens?
– Oui, je viens. Ce n'est pas loin.

6 – Où est l'hôpital, s'il vous plaît? C'est urgent!
– C'est tout près. Tournez à gauche et voilà l'hôpital.

7 – Je voudrais un plan de la ville.
– Alors, allez à l'office de tourisme.
– À l'office de tourisme?
– Oui, c'est tout près.

8 – Où allez-vous?
– Je vais à la cathédrale.
– À la cathédrale? Mais c'est très loin!

C Le guide, c'est toi! (NC 2)

Solution: **1c, 2a, 3b, 4g, 5d, 6e, 7f** (mark /6)

Le guide, c'est toi!

1. Comment s'appelle cette église?
2. Est-ce qu'il y a un marché ici?
3. Est-ce qu'il y a des musées?
4. La grande place, comment s'appelle-t-elle?
5. Le festival de musique, c'est quand?
6. Qu'est-ce qu'il y a à voir au vieux port?
7. Je cherche un plan de la ville.

CM 7/11 **READING**

Épreuve: Lire

A C'est où? (NC 2)

Solution: **1 ←, 2 →, 3 ↑, 4 ←, 5 ←, 6 ↑, 7 →** (mark /6)

B Le jeu des définitions (NC 2)

Solution: **1g, 2e, 3a, 4d, 5f, 6b, 7c, 8h** (mark /7)

C Des vacances de Christelle (NC 3)

Solution: **1b, 2a, 3h, 4e, 5d, 6g, 7c, 8f** (mark /7)

CM 7/12 **WRITING GRAMMAR**

Épreuve: Écrire et grammaire

A En ville (NC 1)

This is an open-ended task. (mark /4)

B C'est où, exactement? (NC 1)

Solution: **1** *entre,* **2** *entre,* **3** *devant,* **4** *derrière,* **5** *derrière* (mark /4)

C Où va-t-on? (NC 2)

Solution:

1 *Je vais à l'église.*
2 *Je vais à l'école.*
3 *Nous allons à la piscine.*
4 *Tous mes amis vont au stade.* (mark /6)

D Des destinations (NC 3)

This is an open-ended task. (mark /6)

SB 78–79 **REVISION/CONSOLIDATION**

Rappel 3

This section can be used at any point after *Unité 7* for revision and consolidation. It provides reading and writing activities which are self-instructional and can be used by students working indiviudally for homework or during cover lessons.

SB 78

1 Au contraire

Solution: 1e, 2g, 3a, 4f, 5h, 6d, 7c, 8b

SB 78

2 Les mots en escargot

Solution:

a *église, gare, hôpital, poste, banque, tour*
b *printemps*

SB 78

3 Chasse à l'intrus

Solution:

a **1** *du sport,* **2** *travailler,* **3** *février,* **4** *un homme,* **5** *derrière,* **6** *méchant,* **7** *l'ami,* **8** *le printemps*

b
1 *Les autres sont des descriptions du temps.*
2 *Les autres sont des nombres.*
3 *Les autres sont des verbes.*
4 *Les autres sont des bâtiments.*
5 *Les autres sont des nombres.*
6 *Les autres sont des prépositions.*
7 *Les autres sont des saisons.*
8 *Les autres sont des sports.*

SB 78

4 Quel temps fait-il?

Solution:

1 *Il y a du soleil.* (**c**)
2 *Il fait froid.* (**a**)
3 *Il pleut.* (**d**)
4 *Il y a du brouillard.* (**b**)
5 *Il neige.* (**e**)
6 *Il fait chaud.* (**f**)

SB 78

5 Masculin, féminin

Solution:

masculin	***féminin***
un bureau	*une brochure*
un camping	*une chaussette*
un bateau	*une chaussure*
un parking	*une calculette*
un tableau	

SB 79

6 À la maison

Solution: **1** *neige,* **2** *reste,* **3** *téléphone,* **4** *travailles,* **5** *écoute,* **6** *dessine,* **7** *préparons,* **8** *rangez,* **9** *jouent,* **10** *regardent*

SB 79

7 Où est le lapin?

Solution:

1 *Il est entre les livres.*
2 *Il est sur l'ordinateur.*
3 *Il est sous la chaise.*
4 *Il est derrière la radio.*
5 *Il est dans la boîte.*
6 *Il est devant la télévision.*

SB 79

8 Le week-end

Solution: 1c, 2d, 3b, 4e, 5h, 6g, 7a, 8f

SB 79

9 À toi

This is an open-ended task.

SB 79

10 Tom et Jojo en ville

Solution: **1** *ville,* **2** *aux,* **3** *au,* **4** *à l',* **5** *à la,* **6** *à la,* **7** *chasse,* **8** *va,* **9** *tourne,* **10** *tout droit,* **11** *au,* **12** *tombe*

Encore Tricolore 1
nouvelle édition

unité 8 Une journée scolaire

Areas	Topics	Grammar
1	Telling the time (full hours)	
2	Telling the time (quarter and half hours)	
3	Telling the time (all expressions)	
4	Describing a typical day	*manger, commencer* (D-L 84)
5	Talking about school subjects and opinions	
6		Possessive adjectives (singular): *mon, ma, mes; ton, ta, tes* (D-L 87); *son, sa, ses* (D-L 88)
7		Possessive adjectives (plural): *notre, nos; votre, vos* (D-L 89); *leur, leurs* (D-L 90)
8	Further activities and consolidation	

National Curriculum information

Some students	Level 3+
Most students	Levels 2–3
All students	Levels 1–2

Refer also to the information about coverage of 'Knowledge, skills and understanding' (TB 9).

Revision

The vocabulary and structures introduced in this unit are revised in the *Rappel* section following *Unité 9* (SB 108–109, TB 181).

Presse-Jeunesse 3 offers opportunities for reading for pleasure (SB 93–95, TB 165)

Sounds and writing

- *c* (soft c and hard c); *ch, ph* and *th*
- see *Écoute et parle* (SB 157, TB 163–164)

ICT opportunities

- contact with other schools via e-mail (TB 154)
- creating a database based on results of a questionnaire (TB 153)
- producing school timetable on computer (TB 155)
- using graphics software to produce a graph of favourite subjects (see TB 156)

Reading strategies

Only use the dictionary as a last resort – a summary of techniques to try out first, e.g. using clues such as cognates, key words, prefixes and suffixes (CM 106).

Assessment

- Informal assessment is in the *Épreuves* at the end of this unit (TB 164).
- Formal assessment is in the *Troisième contrôle* following *Unité 10* (TB 203). There are also alternative tasks following *Unité 9* (TB 206).

Students' Book

Unité 8 SB 80–92
Au choix SB 138 1 (TB 152), 2 (TB 154), 3, 4 (TB 158)
SB 139 5, 6, 7 (TB 159)
SB 140 8 (TB 161)
Écoute et parle SB 157 (TB 163)
Presse-Jeunesse SB 93–95 (TB 165)

Flashcards

73, 75, 76, 84, 87 (optional)
Breakfast items

Additional

Grammar in Action 1, pp 16, 19, 20, 31, 35

CDs

3/1–13
Student CD 2/1–7, 35–38

Copymasters

8/1	*Quelle heure est-il?* [mini-flashcards/support] (TB 152)
8/2	*Quelle journée!* [support] (TB 152)
8/3	*Qui est-ce?* [speaking: information gap] (TB 154)
8/4	*La page des jeux* [support] (TB 156)
8/5	*La vie scolaire* [extension] (TB 156)
8/6	*Conversations au choix* [speaking] (TB 157)
8/7	*Mon, ton, son* [grammar] (TB 158)
8/8	*Jeux de vocabulaire – informatique* [ICT] (TB 161)
8/9	*Tu comprends?* [independent listening] (TB 162)
8/10	*Sommaire* (TB 162)
8/11	*Épreuve: Écouter* (TB 164)
8/12	*Épreuve: Lire* (TB 165)
8/13	*Épreuve: Écrire et grammaire* (TB 165)
105–106	*Presse-Jeunesse 3* (TB 165)

Language content

The time (Areas 1–3)

Quelle heure est-il?

Il est une heure/deux heures/trois heures ...

... cinq
... dix
... et quart
... vingt
... vingt-cinq
... et demie
... moins vingt-cinq
... moins vingt
... moins le quart
... moins dix
... moins cinq

Il est midi — *Il est minuit*
Il est midi et demi — *Il est minuit et demi*

Time of day (Area 4)

le matin *l'après-midi* *le soir* *la nuit*

A typical day (Area 4)

une journée typique
Le matin, je prends mon petit déjeuner à ...
J'arrive au collège à ...
Les cours commencent à ...
À midi, je mange à la cantine / des sandwichs.
Je rentre à la maison à ...
Je commence mes devoirs à ...
Le soir, nous mangeons à ...
Je vais au lit à .../Je me couche à ...

Mealtimes (Area 4)

un repas
le petit déjeuner — *le déjeuner*
le goûter — *le dîner*

School subjects (Area 5)

anglais (m)
dessin (m)
EPS (éducation physique et sportive) (f)
français (m)
géographie (f)
histoire (f)
informatique (f)
maths (f pl)
musique (f)
sciences (f pl)
sport (m)
technologie (f)

Giving opinions (Area 6)

C'est	*très*	*amusant.*
	assez	*difficile.*
	un peu	*ennuyeux.*
		facile.
		intéressant.
		utile.
C'est	*nul.*	
	super.	
	sympa.	

Classroom language and rubrics

Trouve le mot qui ne va pas.
Trouve l'image qui correspond.
Quelle est la réponse correcte?
Trouve un mot qui commence avec c.
Change les mots soulignés.
Invente un dessin amusant.
Relis la lettre.
Choisis le bon mot dans la case.
Écoute le CD pour vérifier.
Remplis la grille.

On-going activities

School life in France

A typical school day and a series of e-mail messages from a school in France are a feature of this unit from Area 4 onwards.

At an appropriate point after this, it would be useful to give some background information about school life in France, perhaps in contrast with students' own school life, mentioning points such as: own clothing rather than school uniform, length of day, length of lessons, school on Saturday mornings, absence of religious education etc.

Another possibility would be a brainstorming session at the end of the unit, where students pool what they have found out about school life in France.

Teaching the time

It has proved to be a good long-term strategy to space out the teaching of the time, giving practice at each stage, as this helps to avoid confusion later on. Once the time has been taught, remember to ask two or three students the time at some point in every lesson.

Area 1
Telling the time (full hours)

SB 80, 1–2
CD 3/1
Teaching clock (optional)
Quelle heure est-il?
Il est … heures/midi/minuit

Number games

REVISION

First play some games to revise the numbers up to sixty in both spoken and written form, e.g. *Et après?*, *Loto*, *Avancez et reculez* (see TB 25–26).

PRESENTATION
SOUNDS AND WRITING

Quelle heure est-il? Il est … heures/midi/minuit

One way of teaching the time is to use a home-made or commercially produced clock face with moveable hands. Alternatively, for those used to digital clocks, make two sets of number flashcards, (00–12 to begin with, adding 05, 10, 15, 20, 25, 30, 35, 40, 45, 50, 55, 00 for Areas 2 and 3).

Start by teaching the hours involving numbers that do not change in pronunciation, i.e. 4, 5, 7, 8 and 11.

Then add 2, 3, 6 and 10. Ask the class to listen for the *z* sound before *heures*. Students who have worked on *Écoute et parle, Unité 5* (SB 154) may recall that this is called liaison and occurs before a vowel – here the *h* is silent, so it is as if the word begins with *e*.

Next, teach 9 and 1, *midi* and *minuit* and then put them all together.

The hours

PRACTICE

First use choral repetition to practise all the times around the clock, then use the game *Avancez et reculez*, with the class telling the time, going backwards or forwards as indicated. Move on to ask different students random times. Finally, individuals could move the clock hands or hold up the digital number cards and ask the class *Quelle heure est-il?*

Further activities

PRACTICE

1 Dictate times (whole hours) and ask the class to write them down in figures. Teach the format *3h* – useful later for reading times on notices etc.
2 Dictate times to individual students, who write them on the board in figures. This can then be followed by a short game of *Effacez!* using the same numbers (see TB 26).
3 Ask the class to write down six different times in figures and use this for *Loto* (see TB 25).
4 Pairwork activity: students think of a time and write it down without their partner seeing it. They then take it in turns to guess which time each person has written. The first to guess correctly wins, and then they start again.

SB 80, 3/1 **LISTENING**

1 C'est à quelle heure?

Students listen to the recording and write down, in figures, the time mentioned in each conversation.

Solution: **1** *à 3h,* **2** *à 8h,* **3** *à 2h,* **4** *à 9h,* **5** *à 10h,* **6** *à 11h,* **7** *à midi,* **8** *à minuit*

C'est à quelle heure?

1 – Salut, Guy!
– Salut, Jean-Claude. Tu vas au match de football?
– Oui.
– C'est à quelle heure?
– Le match commence à trois heures.

2 – Qu'est-ce que tu fais ce soir, Monique?
– Je vais au cinéma. Il y a un bon film.
– Ça commence à quelle heure?
– À huit heures.

3 – Christophe, à quelle heure est-ce que tu joues au tennis avec Marc?
– À deux heures.

4 – Bonjour Anne-Marie. C'est Jean-Claude à l'appareil. Écoute, il y a une surprise-partie chez Robert samedi soir.
– Ah, chouette! C'est à quelle heure?
– Ça commence à neuf heures.

5 – Maman, tu vas en ville ce matin?
– Oui, j'y vais à dix heures.

6 – Quand est-ce que papa va en ville?
– Il va aux magasins à onze heures, puis il va jouer au golf.

7 – Vous allez en ville ce matin?
– Oui, nous allons en ville, et à midi, nous allons au restaurant. Tu viens avec nous au restaurant?
– Oui, je veux bien. À midi, alors.

8 – Le supermarché est ouvert jusqu'à quelle heure, le vendredi?
– Le vendredi, c'est ouvert jusqu'à minuit.

À quelle heure?

SPEAKING

Write the question *C'est à quelle heure?* on the board and then list a number of events, e.g. *le film, le concert, le match, la visite au musée.*

Ask students to make up questions and to prompt replies with the homemade 'time' flashcards or clock or by writing an appropriate time on the board.

SB 80 **SPEAKING**
WRITING

2 Le week-end

This task combines practice of times with revision of places.

Solution: **1** *à midi,* **2** *à huit heures,* **3** *à onze heures,* **4** *à une heure,* **5** *à neuf heures,* **6** *à quatre heures,* **7** *à dix heures,* **8** *à sept heures,* **9** *à deux heures,* **10** *à minuit*

Area 2
Telling the time (quarter and half hours)
SB 81, 3–4
CD 3/2
Teaching clock (optional)
Il est … heures et quart/moins le quart/et demie

Quarter and half hours

PRESENTATION PRACTICE

Revise the hours and then teach these new times using a clock face or number cards: *Il est … heures et quart/moins le quart/et demie.*

Give plenty of oral practice using games like *Avancez et reculez*, with the class telling the time every quarter of an hour, going backwards or forwards as indicated (see TB 25).

Dictate some of the times to students, who draw on the board the corresponding clock faces. Write the times in words beside each clock face and ask the class to read them aloud. Then rub off the hands in the clock faces and ask individual students to come out and draw them in again. Eventually, the class could copy down the times in their books and add the appropriate clock faces.

The times and clocks on the board can also provide further practice if used for *Effacez!* (TB 26). Different students read out the times and members of competing teams rub the figures out.

SB 81, 3/2 **LISTENING**

3 Rendez-vous à quelle heure?

Explain *une horloge* (large clock or clock tower). *La grosse horloge* is a well-known site in La Rochelle.

Students listen to the conversations and write down the time (in figures) of each meeting.

Solution: **1** *à 2h30,* **2** *à 11h,* **3** *à 3h15,* **4** *à 4h 45,* **5** *à 7h30,* **6** *à 1h30,* **7** *à 8h15,* **8** *à 8h,* **9** *à 10h15,* **10** *à 10h30*

Rendez-vous à quelle heure?

1 – On va en ville, samedi?
– Oui, je veux bien. À quelle heure?
– À deux heures et demie?
– D'accord. Alors rendez-vous sous la grosse horloge à deux heures et demie.

2 – Tu es libre ce matin? On va au musée?
– Oui, d'accord. À onze heures?
– Oui, d'accord. Alors, rendez-vous devant le musée à onze heures.

3 – On va au marché cet après-midi?
– Oui, d'accord.
– Alors, rendez-vous derrière la cathédrale à trois heures et quart.
– À trois heures et quart, d'accord.

4 – On va au café, après?
– Oui, d'accord.
– Alors, rendez-vous au café à cinq heures moins le quart.
– À cinq heures moins le quart, d'accord.

5 – On va au cinéma ce soir?
– Oui, je veux bien. À quelle heure?
– À sept heures et demie?
– D'accord. Alors, rendez-vous devant le cinéma à sept heures et demie.

6 – On joue au tennis cet après-midi?
– Oui, je veux bien.
– Alors, rendez-vous dans le parc à une heure et demie.
– D'accord, à une heure et demie, dans le parc.

7 – Tu es libre vendredi? On va à Bordeaux?
– À Bordeaux? Oui, je veux bien.
– Alors, rendez-vous à la gare à huit heures et quart.
– Bon, à huit heures et quart, à la gare.
– C'est ça. À vendredi alors.

8 – On va au restaurant ce soir?
– Oui, bonne idée. À quelle heure?
– À huit heures.
– Alors rendez-vous devant le restaurant à huit heures.
– C'est ça. À ce soir.

9 – On va à la piscine ce matin?
– Oui, d'accord.
– Alors, rendez-vous devant la piscine à dix heures et quart.
– D'accord, à bientôt.

10 – Tu vas au supermarché, ce matin?
– Oui, à dix heures et demie.
– Alors, rendez-vous au supermarché à dix heures et demie.

SB 81, **SPEAKING**

4 Inventez des conversations

Students should now be able to make up similar conversations in pairs to arrange a meeting place and time.

Area 3
Telling the time (all expressions)

SB 81, 5
Au choix SB 138, 1
CM 8/1, 8/2
Grammar in Action 1, page 16
Il est … heures (moins) cinq/dix/vingt/vingt-cinq

Times past the hour — PRESENTATION

Times past the hour should now be taught: *Il est … heures cinq/dix/vingt/vingt-cinq*. Practise through various clock games, such as clock *Loto*, *Avancez et reculez* and *Effacez!* (TB 25–26). When asking questions, use *Quelle heure est-il?* and *Il est quelle heure?* to familiarise students with both expressions.

Times to the hour — PRESENTATION

Introduce times to the hour: *Il est … heures moins cinq/dix/vingt/vingt-cinq*. Practise them separately and then with the rest of the times, using games as before.

On-going practice

From now on, spend a short time in each lesson of this unit, dictating some times which students take down in figures and then read back. This can gradually be taken over by the students themselves or developed as a pairwork or group activity, with able students writing the times out in full.

SB 81 — **PRACTICE**

5 Quelle heure est-il?

This task uses a range of different clock faces to give practice in reading a full range of times.

Solution:

1. *Il est sept heures moins dix.*
2. *Il est midi/minuit vingt-cinq.*
3. *Il est cinq heures vingt.*
4. *Il est sept heures moins vingt-cinq.*
5. *Il est onze heures.*
6. *Il est huit heures moins vingt.*
7. *Il est neuf heures vingt-cinq.*
8. *Il est midi/minuit moins le quart.*

CM 8/1 — **MINI-FLASHCARDS SUPPORT**

Quelle heure est-il?

Students draw in the hands so the clock face shows the correct time. When completed, the worksheet can be stuck on to card, cut up and used as a set of mini-flashcards. With two or more sets, various games can be played in pairs, e.g. dominoes and Pelmanism (see TB 28). Students have to give the correct time on a matching pair of cards before they can keep them.

CM 8/2 — **SUPPORT**

Quelle journée!

This worksheet could be used by students needing support, whilst others do the task in *Au choix*. The tasks link time with places in a town.

Solutions:

A
1. *À huit heures, …*
2. *À dix heures vingt, …*
3. *À onze heures cinq, …*
4. *À midi et demi, …*
5. *À deux heures moins vingt-cinq, …*
6. *À trois heures et demie, …*
7. *À six heures et quart, …*
8. *À huit heures moins le quart, …*

B 1b, 2c, 3a, 4b, 5c, 6b, 7a, 8b

Au choix SB 138 — **EXTENSION**

1 Mlle Dupont

This task provides revision of times and *à* with places in a town.

Solution:

1. *À six heures, elle va à la poste.*
2. *À sept heures et demie, elle va au collège.*
3. *À huit heures et quart, elle va à la piscine.*
4. *À neuf heures vingt, elle va au café.*
5. *À dix heures moins cinq, elle va au parc.*
6. *À dix heures vingt-cinq, elle va à la gare.*
7. *À midi moins vingt, elle va à l'hôtel.*
8. *À midi, elle va au cinéma.*
9. *À une heure et demie, elle va au restaurant.*
10. *À dix heures et quart, elle va au lit.*

Grammar in Action 1, page 16 — **GRAMMAR**

Telling the time

This provides graded practice of all times.

Area 4
Describing a typical day

SB 82-83, 1–5, SB 84, 1–2
Au choix SB 138, 2
CD 3/3
CM 8/3
FC 73, 75, 76, 84, 87 (optional)
la journée, le matin, l'après-midi, le soir, la nuit

Time of day — REVISION PRESENTATION

Revise *la journée, le matin, l'après-midi, le soir* and teach *la nuit* perhaps by drawing a diagram on the board, representing *la journée*, and dividing it into parts shown by time ranges, e.g. 7h00–12h00, 12h01–18h00, 18h01–23h00; 23h01–6h59.

Teach and practise *le repas, le petit déjeuner, le déjeuner, le goûter, le dîner*, e.g.
Le matin, on prend le petit déjeuner; à midi, on prend le déjeuner; l'après-midi, on prend le goûter et le soir, on prend le dîner.

Write the new vocabulary on the board for reference and/or for a game of *Effacez!* (TB 26).

FC 73, 75, 76, 84, 87 (OPTIONAL) PRESENTATION PRACTICE

Food

Flashcards can be used to present and practise *du pain, du beurre, de la confiture, du jus d'orange, un chocolat chaud*. These are used in the following item, but are not taught for active use until *Unité 9*.

SB 82, 3/3 PRESENTATION LISTENING READING

1 Une journée typique

Students listen to the recording and follow the text in their books.

Ask some questions to check comprehension, e.g.
C'est la journée d'un élève français, non?
Comment s'appelle-t-il?
C'est une journée scolaire ou c'est dimanche?
Qu'est-ce qu'il fait pendant la journée? Il va au parc? Il va au collège?
Et quand il rentre à la maison, qu'est-ce qu'il fait? Il joue au football? Il travaille? Il joue sur l'ordinateur?
etc.

Une journée typique

– Olivier parle d'une journée scolaire.

– Le matin, je me lève à sept heures.
Je prends mon petit déjeuner à sept heures et demie. Je mange du pain avec du beurre et de la confiture et je bois du jus d'orange.
Je quitte la maison à huit heures et j'arrive au collège à huit heures vingt.
Les cours commencent à huit heures et demie.
J'ai quatre cours, le matin.
À dix heures et demie, il y a la récréation du matin. Ça dure dix minutes.
À midi, je mange à la cantine. Puis je vais dans la cour avec mes copains. Quelquefois, nous jouons au football.
L'après-midi, nous commençons à deux heures.
J'ai cours jusqu'à quatre heures moins dix. Puis je rentre à la maison.
Pour mon goûter, je mange un sandwich et je bois un chocolat chaud.
À six heures, je commence mes devoirs.
Le soir, nous mangeons à sept heures. Après le dîner, je continue à travailler.
Puis, je regarde la télé, j'écoute de la musique ou je joue sur l'ordinateur.
Et à neuf heures, je me couche.

SB 83 READING PRACTICE

2 La journée d'Olivier

Students match up the events in Olivier's school day with the correct times.

Solution: 1f, 2a, 3e, 4b, 5i, 6g, 7h, 8c, 9j, 10d

SB 83 READING

3 Une journée en semaine

This task practises mealtimes and time of day.

Solution: **1** *matin,* **2** *petit déjeuner,* **3** *cours,* **4** *déjeuner,* **5** *après-midi,* **6** *goûter,* **7** *devoirs,* **8** *soir,* **9** *dîner*

SB 83,  SPEAKING

4 Un questionnaire

Before interviewing their partner, students should write down their own answers to the questions. Some questions could be asked of the whole class, e.g. *Combien de personnes quittent la maison à sept heures du matin? Qui arrive au collège à huit heures?* etc.

Students just write the times of each answer. If fuller answers are required, revise how the verb would need to be written in the third person and write some examples on the board to help.

For extension work, the teacher could ask questions involving the third person, e.g. *Ton/Ta partenaire quitte la maison à quelle heure?* etc.

Create a database of the class based on the questionnaire. The finished product, entered onto a spreadsheet, could look like this:

Nom	quitte la maison	arrive au collège	mange	rentre	commence les devoirs	mange le soir	va au lit
John	7.40am	8.30am	cantine	4.40pm	5.00pm	6.30pm	9.00pm
Mary	8.20am	8.45am	sandwichs	4.25pm	7.30pm	5.30pm	9.30pm
Sam	8.30am	8.50am	sandwichs	4.30pm	5.30pm	7.00pm	10.00pm
Lesley	8.05am	8.40am	sandwichs	4.45pm	6.00pm	8.00pm	10.30pm
Ian	8.30am	8.50am	cantine	4.30pm	8.45pm	6.00pm	10.00pm
Daljit	8.25am	8.30am	sandwichs	4.15pm	4.30pm	8.30pm	11.30pm
Sean	8.45am	8.50am	cantine	4.45pm	9.00pm	6.00pm	11.00pm
Philroy	8.00am	8.10am	cantine	4.15pm	7.00pm	5.45pm	10.30pm
Terry	7.45am	8.20am	cantine	4.45pm	8.00pm	7.00pm	9.45pm
Octavia	8.30am	8.50am	sandwichs	4.35pm	8.00am	7.30pm	9.30pm

Set up the labels in the top row of the table before the lesson. Students can then add their own details. This works well as a paired activity with student A asking the questions, student B giving the answer, which student A then types in. They then reverse roles. In this way, each pair will have completed two rows. If a single computer in the classroom is used, the next pair then complete the next two rows. If working in a network, some work will be needed to combine the data from each machine. This could be done by the ICT co-ordinator or by an ICT literate pupil.

Once the data is complete, there is much scope for oral work based on the raw data on screen or in print out and it is also possible to compute averages and charts to supplement the work and provide material for a classroom display.

SB 83 WRITING

5 À toi!

Students describe their own day or that of a friend, using the information from the questionnaire and following the framework of the earlier tasks.

SB 83 **GRAMMAR**

!

Reflexive verbs are briefly mentioned in connection with *je me lève* and *je me couche*. They are covered in more detail in *Encore Tricolore 2*. Other examples used in *Encore Tricolore 1* which could be mentioned are *je m'appelle, tu t'appelles, il/elle s'appelle; asseyez-vous, levez-vous*.

SB 84 **PRACTICE**

1 Au Sénégal

This task provides practice in using the vocabulary to describe a typical day and presents examples of *manger* and *commencer*.

Solution: **1** *habitent,* **2** *parlent,* **3** *collège,* **4** *cours,* **5** *recréation,* **6** *cantine,* **7** *quatre heures,* **8** *rentrent,* **9** *dîner,* **10** *mange*

SB 84, **GRAMMAR**

Dossier-langue *Manger and commencer*

This explains the slight irregularity in the *nous* form of the present tense of these two -*er* verbs. See if students can find the irregular part of each verb and then give plenty of practice in saying these verbs aloud. Ask students to work out the full paradigm of the verbs listed which follow similar patterns.

Students can enter the new verbs in their electronic verb table, if created earlier (TB 40).

SB 84 **GRAMMAR PRACTICE**

2 Des conversations

Students practise using the different parts of *commencer* and *manger*.

Solution:

a **1** *le film commence, le film commence*
2 *les cours commencent, ils commencent*
3 *Vous commencez, nous commençons*
4 *tu commences, je commence*
b **5** *tu manges, je mange*
6 *Vous mangez, nous mangeons*
7 *on mange, mes amis français mangent*

Au choix SB 138 **READING EXTENSION**

2 Une journée en semaine

Students put the sentences in the correct order to describe a typical school day.

Solution: *Le matin:* **d, b, f, a, e, c**
L'après-midi et le soir: **j, g, i, h, k, l**

CM 8/3, **SPEAKING EXTENSION**

Qui est-ce?

Students work in pairs on this information gap activity to find out details about a person's day in order to identify the person. It would be a good idea for two able students to demonstrate how this works, so everyone understands what is entailed.

Area 5
Talking about school subjects and opinions
SB 85, 3–5, 86, 1–4
CD 3/4–5
CM 8/4, 8/5, 8/6
School subjects
amusant, difficile, intéressant, utile, ennuyeux

Text books etc. **PRESENTATION**

Use some text books for different subjects to teach some of the school subjects. Write a list on the board for a game of *Effacez!*, then write some initial letters on the board and ask volunteers to complete the words, thereby recreating the list.

SB 85 **PRESENTATION**

3 Les matières

Introduce and discuss the symbols to check that these are clearly understood. Students then match the symbols and words and write out a list of school subjects, perhaps with the English equivalent.

Solution: **1** *la géographie,* **2** *la musique,* **3** *l'anglais,* **4** *le français,* **5** *les maths,* **6** *l'histoire,* **7** *la technologie,* **8** *le sport,* **9** *les sciences,* **10** *le dessin,* **11** *l'informatique*

SB 85 **PRESENTATION SPEAKING**

Un message de la France

This is the first in a series of fictional e-mail messages from a class in France. Teach *un emploi du temps* and then use this for oral work, e.g.
Regardez l'emploi du temps. Qu'est-ce qu'on a comme cours, lundi à 8h30? Est-ce qu'on a sciences, lundi? Est-ce qu'on a histoire? etc.

E-mail correspondents

A whole class e-mail exchange is very effective. There is advice on how best to manage this in various publications (see TB 208).

Matching correspondents according to interests can be done as an introductory activity, either within a single class or with two classes. This involves using word processing for students to produce 'pen pal wanted' notices. These are coded to avoid revealing identities. Replies are then sent to the advertisers, again using word processing (see TB 208).

SB 85, 3/4 **LISTENING**

4 C'est quel jour?

Students listen to the recording and decide which day is being referred to.

Solution: **1** *samedi matin,* **2** *lundi après-midi,* **3** *jeudi matin,* **4** *mardi matin,* **5** *mardi après-midi,* **6** *lundi matin,* **7** *vendredi matin,* **8** *vendredi après-midi*

C'est quel jour?

1 Alors, je commence avec français, puis c'est anglais. Puis à dix heures vingt, c'est la récréation, et après la récré, j'ai musique.

2 Après le déjeuner, nous avons technologie. Ça c'est bien, c'est ma matière préférée.

3 Eh bien, nous commençons avec maths. Puis on a anglais. Puis c'est la récré, et après la récré, c'est français et puis informatique.

4 Je commence à huit heures et demie avec français, puis c'est la géographie. Après la récré, nous avons maths, et puis dessin.

5 Après le déjeuner, nous avons un double cours de sciences, puis c'est la récré et après la récré, c'est EPS (éducation physique et sportive).

6 On commence à huit heures et demie avec anglais, puis on a histoire. Après la récréation, on a français et puis maths.

7 D'abord, on a éducation civique. Puis le deuxième cours, c'est français. Après la récréation, on a un double cours de maths.

8 Après le déjeuner, nous avons EPS de deux heures dix jusqu'à quatre heures. Et cette semaine, nous allons à la piscine. Ça, c'est bien.

SB 85, **SPEAKING**

5 On a quelle matière?

Students make up their own conversations with their partners, based on the timetable.

SB 85 **EXTENSION**

?

This short item points out the fact that a noun ending in *-ie* in French often ends in -y in English, e.g. *biologie, géographie, technologie, photographie, économie, fantaisie, comédie* etc.

School timetable

Help students to write out their own timetable in French. This could be done on a computer, using the table facility of word processing software.

J'aime/n'aime pas ça **PRESENTATION**

Practise expressing likes and dislikes in relation to school subjects and introduce some positive and negative adjectives, e.g. *amusant, difficile, intéressant, utile, ennuyeux* etc.

Write these on the board and check that students undertand them before proceeding to the next item.

SB 86, 3/5 **LISTENING**

1 Six élèves

Before playing the recording, dr aw attention to the *Légende* and give students a few minutes to study it in conjunction with the photos and captions.

Students listen to the recording and note down who is speaking each time. Further adjectives of opinion are presented in the recording and can be taught beforehand, if wished. It is not necessary to understand the adjectives in order to do the task.

Solution: **1e** *Sylvie,* **2d** *Thomas,* **3a** *Sika,* **4c** *Marion,* **5f** *Tchang,* **6b** *Philippe*

Six élèves

1 – Quelle est ta matière préférée?
– Les maths, j'adore les maths. C'est très utile et notre prof de maths est très gentil. Il explique tout très bien.
– Est-ce qu'il y a des matières que tu n'aimes pas?
– Oui, je déteste le dessin. C'est ennuyeux.

2 – Et toi?
– Moi, je n'aime pas les maths. Ça, c'est très difficile, mais j'aime le sport. Le sport, c'est super.

3 – Est-ce que tu aimes l'anglais?
– Ah non, je déteste ça. L'anglais, c'est nul.
– Alors, qu'est-ce que tu aimes, comme matières?
– J'aime les sciences. Les sciences, c'est amusant.

4 – Quelle est ta matière préférée?
– Le français, j'adore le français. Je trouve ça très intéressant et c'est facile.
– Est-ce qu'il y a des matières que tu n'aimes pas?
– Oui, je n'aime pas l'histoire. Ce n'est pas intéressant.

5 – Et toi, qu'est-ce que tu aimes, comme matières?
– Moi, j'aime la musique. Oui, la musique, c'est ma matière préférée.
– Et qu'est-ce que tu n'aimes pas?
– Je n'aime pas la technologie.

6 – Et toi, quelle est ta matière préférée?
– L'informatique, j'adore l'informatique. C'est super.
– Et est-ce qu'il y a des matières que tu n'aimes pas?
– Oui, je n'aime pas la géographie. C'est ennuyeux.

SB 86 **PRACTICE**

2 C'est utile, le dictionnaire

Students sort a list of adjectives into positive and negative groups and give the English translations.

Solution:

des opinions positives	***des opinions négatives***
amusant – fun	*difficile* – difficult
super – great	*nul* – rubbish
facile – easy	*ennuyeux* – boring
intéressant – interesting	
utile – useful	
sympa – nice	

SB 86, **SPEAKING**

3 Moi, non

Students make up a short conversation about likes and dislikes and school subjects.

SB 86 **READING**

4 Un message de la France

a Read the message to the class, revising *sondage* and interpreting the graph, e.g.
Combien d'élèves aiment les sciences? C'est une matière très populaire, non?
Et l'anglais, c'est aussi une matière populaire?
Et la géographie – est-ce qu'il y a beaucoup d'élèves qui aiment la géographie?
Non, pour cette classe, la géographie n'est pas populaire. Un élève seulement aime la géographie.
etc.

Students should then summarize the details of the French school sondage.

Solution:

1. *Un élève aime la géographie.*
2. *Deux élèves aiment le français.*
3. *Trois élèves aiment l'histoire.*
4. *Quatre élèves aiment le dessin.*
5. *Cinq élèves aiment la technologie.*
6. *Six élèves aiment les maths.*
7. *Sept élèves aiment l'anglais.*
8. *Huit élèves aiment les sciences.*

b A similar survey could be organised as a class or group activity.

The results of the school survey could be put into a database and made into a graph using appropriate software.

CM 8/4 **SUPPORT**

La page des jeux

Some students could work on this worksheet, while others do CM 8/5.

Solutions:

1 Mots mêlés

1	school	*collège*
2	morning	*matin*
3	afternoon	*après-midi*
4	evening	*soir*
5	night	*nuit*
6	lesson	*cours*
7	meal	*repas*
8	lunch	*déjeuner*
9	canteen	*cantine*
10	homework	*devoirs*

a	p	r	è	s	-	m	i	d	i
é	t	e	-	o	b	a	l	é	r
r	c	p	ê	i	a	t	à	j	o
n	o	a	t	r	t	i	p	e	s
u	u	s	-	m	o	n	f	u	t
i	r	l	c	a	n	t	i	n	e
t	s	c	o	l	l	è	g	e	r
c	a	l	d	e	v	o	i	r	s

2 Où sont les voyelles?

1. *l'informatique*
2. *la musique*
3. *l'éducation physique*
4. *le dessin*
5. *l'histoire*
6. *la géographie*

3 Un serpent

Des opinions positives: utile, amusant, facile.
Des opinions négatives: difficile, nul, ennuyeux.
Le repas est dîner.

4 Un acrostiche

1 technologie
2 histoire
3 sciences
4 français
5 anglais
6 géographie
7 dessin

CM 8/5 **EXTENSION**

La vie scolaire

Solutions:

1 Mots croisés

2 Un jeu

Students invent an acrostic puzzle, using school subjects.

This is a possible solution. Clues should be given in English.

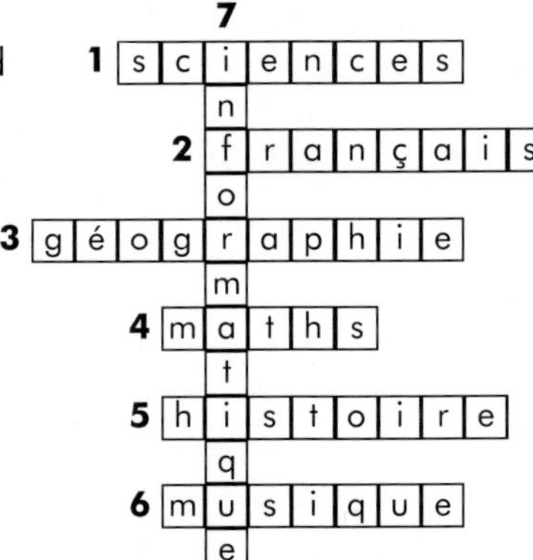

CM 8/6, **SPEAKING**

Conversations au choix

Students make arrangements to meet and give simple opinions about school subjects.

Area 6
Possessive adjectives (singular)
SB 87, 5–7, SB 88, 1–3
Au choix SB 138–139, 3–7
CD 3/6–7
CM 8/7
Grammar in Action 1, pages 19, 20, 31
mon, ma, mes; ton, ta, tes; son, sa, ses
Classroom objects

REVISION PRACTICE

Mon, ma, mes

For revision and practice of *mon, ma, mes,* distribute a few personal items around the classroom, then pretend to look for them, e.g.
Où est mon livre? Est-ce qu'il est sur la table? Ah, voilà mon livre.
(Write *mon livre* on the left of the board.)

Où est ma gomme? Tu as vu ma gomme? Tiens, voilà! Ça, c'est ma gomme.
(Write *ma gomme* in the centre of the board.)

Où sont mes crayons? Ils sont par terre? Non. Eh bien, où sont-ils? Je cherche mes crayons. Ah, voilà mes crayons.
(Write *mes crayons* on the right of the board.)

Continue with other known classroom items or invite able students to join in. Gradually build up a column of masculine words (e.g. *mon cahier, mon cartable, mon classeur*), a column of feminine words (e.g. *ma trousse, ma calculette*) and a column of plural words (e.g. *mes cassettes, mes stylos*). Then check that students remember what *mon, ma* and *mes* mean and when each should be used.

The words on the board can be left for a game of *Effacez!* at the end of the lesson (see TB 26).

It is also a good idea to make a set of dominoes, each domino containing a feminine, masculine or plural noun followed by *mon, ma* or *mes,* e.g.
domino 1: *calculette/mes*
domino 2: *cahiers/mon*
domino 3: *stylo/ma*

Domino 3 would then fit against domino 1, or domino 1 against domino 2, or domino 2 against domino 3.

Ton, ta, tes

REVISION AND PRACTICE

To revise *ton, ta, tes,* go round the class 'stealing' items from various students. Then return them by asking *(Nom), c'est ton cahier?* To reclaim the item, the student has to reply *Oui, c'est mon cahier.*

As a variation, a game can be played where a student collects together six of any classroom objects (pencils, rubbers, rulers etc.) by asking other students *Donne-moi ton crayon, s'il te plaît.* When s/he has collected six, another student is asked to return them to the correct owners, e.g.
(Student A), *c'est ton crayon?*
Oui, c'est mon crayon. Merci! or
Non, ce n'est pas mon crayon.

The student loses a point for each mistake in identifying the owner.

SB 87, 3/6 **LISTENING**

5 Un nouvel élève

This task presents examples of *ton, ta, tes* and *mon, ma, mes.*

Solution:

a *La question qu'on ne pose pas est la question 6.*
b **a** *le basket,* **b** *le sport et l'informatique,* **c** *douze ans,* **d** *l'histoire,* **e** *le 8 juillet*
c **1c, 2e, 3d, 4b, 5a**

Un nouvel élève

– Karim, quel âge as-tu?
– J'ai douze ans.
– Et quelle est la date de ton anniversaire?
– C'est en juillet, le huit juillet.
– Quelle est ta matière préférée?
– Ma matière préférée – bon, l'anglais, c'est utile, mais ce n'est pas ma matière préférée. Ma matière préférée, c'est l'histoire.
– Et quels sont tes passe-temps préférés?
– Mes passe-temps préférés sont le sport et l'informatique. J'adore faire du sport.
– Quel est ton sport préféré?
– Mon sport préféré est le basket.

SB 87 **GRAMMAR**

Dossier-langue
My and your

This explains the use of *mon, ma, mes* and *ton, ta, tes.* Ask students to read it through and to explain what is the key thing to remember about choosing the correct word for 'my' and 'your'.

SB 87 **GRAMMAR PRACTICE**

6 Mes dessins

Students read the letter, then complete the captions to the drawings, using the correct form of *mon, ma, mes.*

Solution:

1 *Voici ma famille – mes parents, mon frère, ma sœur et moi.*
2 *Voici mes animaux – mon chien, mon chat, mon oiseau et ma souris.*
3 *Et voici ma chambre, avec ma guitare, mes livres, mon baladeur et mes cassettes. Et au mur, il y a mon affiche de Londres.*

SB 87, **SPEAKING**

7 Des choses préférées

First ask individual students some of the questions in the box, e.g. *(Nom), quel est ton numéro préféré? Et toi, (nom)?* etc.

Students then work in pairs to ask and answer questions about their favourite things.

Point out that in most cases, the replies should include the definite article, but not in the case of *mois, fête, livre* or *ville*. Suggestions for favourite books could be given in English or translated into French (if fairly simple) and written on the board for future reference.

Au choix SB 138 **CONSOLIDATION WRITING**

3 Mes choses préférées

This task provides further practice of *mon, ma, mes* and favourite things and is suitable for all.

Solution:

a **1** *le douze,* **2** *le noir,* **3** *le samedi,* **4** *le cheval,* **5** *le printemps,* **6** *jouer au tennis et écouter de la musique*
b This is an open-ended task.

Au choix SB 138 **GRAMMAR PRACTICE**

4 Tu aimes mes animaux?

This task provides further practice of *ton, ta, tes*.

Solution: **1** *ton chien,* **2** *Ta souris,* **3** *ton cheval,* **4** *Tes lapins,* **5** *Ton perroquet,* **6** *ton oiseau,* **7** *tes poissons,* **8** *ton hamster,* **9** *ton serpent*

Grammar in Action 1, pages 19–20 **GRAMMAR**

Using *mon, ma, mes*; Using *ton, ta, tes*

Further practice of these possessive adjectives, if required.

SB 88 **WRITING**

1 As-tu une bonne mémoire?

This task presents examples of *son, sa, ses* meaning 'his'.

Solution:

1 *Non, son sport préféré est le basket.*
2 *Non, ses passe-temps préférés sont le sport et l'informatique.*
3 *Non, sa matière préférée est l'histoire.*
4 *Non, son anniversaire est le 8 juillet.*

SB 88 **GRAMMAR**

Dossier-langue
His, her, its

Make sure students understand that the difficulty with this possessive adjective is making the adjective agree with the possession and not with the owner.

SB 88 **GRAMMAR PRACTICE**

2 À la maison

Students practise using *son, sa, ses* to mean 'his' or 'her'.

Solution:

a **1** *ses, sa,* **2** *Ses, sa, sa,* **3** *son, ses,* **4** *son, ses, son,* **5** *son, ses,* **6** *son,* **7** *son, ses,* **8** *son, son, ses,* **9** *son, son,* **10** *ses, sa, son,* **11** *son,* **12** *ses*
b **Luc: 1, 2, 5, 6, 8, 9, 11**
Louise: 3, 4, 7, 10, 12

SB 88, **GRAMMAR PRACTICE**

3 Des machines utiles

a Students practise using *son, sa, ses* to mean 'its'.

Solution: **1** *son stylo,* **2** *ses cahiers,* **3** *sa calculette,* **4** *son crayon,* **5** *sa gomme,* **6** *ses livres,* **7** *sa règle,* **8** *son taille-crayon,* **9** *son dictionnaire*

b Students design a similar machine for sport.

Different machines, along the lines of the above task, could be designed using a desktop publishing programme. The best program to use is the one that the class is familiar with from ICT lessons or other subjects. The facilities needed are:

- clip art
- shapes that can be easily drawn to any size, boxes, circles, triangles etc.
- text that can be added onto the drawing
- freehand draw
- text effects, e.g. text in speech bubbles or word art

It is important to have lots of labels, captions and a title to maximise the language content.

CM 8/7 **SUPPORT**

Mon, ton, son

Some students could work on this worksheet, while others do the tasks in *Au choix*.

This sheet gives further practice of the singular possessive adjectives.

Solutions:

1 Fais des listes
Mots masculins: jour, livre, sport
Mots féminins: matière, saison, ville
Mots féminins (avec voyelle): affiche, amie, équipe
Mots au pluriel: animaux, couleurs, distractions

2 Remplis les blancs
1 *Son livre,* **2** *sa ville,* **3** *Son équipe,* **4** *Ses distractions,* **5** *ton sport,* **6** *ta matière,* **7** *tes couleurs,* **8** *Mes animaux,* **9** *Mon jour,* **10** *Ma saison*

3 Un questionnaire
For support, this can be discussed in class and some suggestions written on the board.

Au choix SB 139 **GRAMMAR EXTENSION**

5 Les vêtements de Sophie

Revise the words for clothing. Students can then do this task which practises *son, sa, ses* meaning 'her' with clothing vocabulary.

Solution:

1. *J'aime son T-shirt rouge.*
2. *Je n'aime pas son short vert.*
3. *Je n'aime pas son sac brun.*
4. *J'aime son pantalon rouge.*
5. *Je n'aime pas sa robe bleue.*
6. *Je n'aime pas ses chaussettes vertes.*
7. *J'aime ses chaussures rouges.*
8. *J'aime son pull rouge.*
9. *Je n'aime pas son pantalon bleu.*
10. *J'aime sa robe rouge.*
11. *Je n'aime pas son T-shirt vert.*
12. *Je n'aime pas sa jupe bleue.*

Au choix SB 139 **GRAMMAR EXTENSION**

6 La chambre de Marc

This task practises *son, sa, ses* meaning 'his' with classroom vocabulary.

Solution: This is an open-ended task.

Au choix SB 139, 3/7 **EXTENSION LISTENING**

7 Deux amies très différentes

This task provides further practice of possessive adjectives, school subjects and opinions.

Solution:

a **1 L, 2 M, 3 M, 4 L, 5 L, 6 M, 7 M, 8 L**
b *Elles aiment l'informatique.*

Deux amies très différentes

- Bonjour, Louise. Ça va?
- Ah oui, ça va très bien. J'ai une nouvelle amie, tu sais. Elle s'appelle Mélanie.
- Ah bon, est-ce qu'elle aime le sport, comme toi?
- Non, elle n'aime pas beaucoup le sport, mais elle adore la musique.
- Mais toi, tu n'aimes pas la musique, non?
- C'est vrai, moi, je n'aime pas beaucoup la musique.
- Est-ce que Mélanie aime les sciences, comme toi?
- Ah non, elle déteste les sciences. Elle trouve ça ennuyeux. Mais elle aime bien l'anglais. L'anglais, c'est sa matière préférée. Elle trouve ça très intéressant.
- Et toi, tu aimes l'anglais, aussi?
- Moi, non. Je n'aime pas l'anglais. C'est difficile.
- Ah bon.
- Mais nous aimons toutes les deux l'informatique. Nous aimons surfer sur le Net, écrire des e-mails et jouer aux jeux électroniques.

Grammar in Action 1, page 31 **GRAMMAR**

Using *son/sa/ses*

This provides further practice of the third person possessive adjectives if required.

> **Area 7**
> **Possessive adjectives (plural)**
> **SB 89, 4–7, SB 90, 1–3**
> **CD 3/8**
> **Grammar in Action 1, page 35**
> *notre, nos; votre, vos; leur, leurs*

SB 89, 3/8 **LISTENING**

4 Au collège

After listening to the recording straight through, students should listen again and note down the missing words. Use the pause button as required.

Solution: **1** *Jules Verne,* **2** *trente-huit,* **3** *la biologie,* **4** *le dessin,* **5** *maths,* **6** *technologie,* **7** *huit heures et demie,* **8** *mercredi,* **9** *samedi*

Au collège

- Nos jeunes reporters, Robert et Cécile, visitent un collège et parlent à deux élèves, Marc et Anne.
- Bonjour Anne et Marc, comment s'appelle votre collège?
- Notre collège s'appelle le Collège Jules Verne.
- Et vous êtes dans quelle classe?
- Nous sommes dans la classe Sixième B.
- Il y a combien d'élèves dans votre classe?
- Il y a trente-huit élèves. C'est beaucoup.
- Oui, c'est vrai. Quelles sont vos matières préférées?
- Moi, j'aime beaucoup la biologie. Notre prof est très sympa.
- Moi, je préfère le dessin. Notre prof de dessin est très amusant.
- En général, est-ce que vos profs sont gentils?
- Oui, en général, ils sont assez gentils. Notre prof de maths, par exemple, est super. Il organise bien ses cours et il explique tout très bien.
- Oui, mais notre prof de technologie est un peu sévère.
- Vos cours commencent à quelle heure, le matin?
- À huit heures et demie, mais on n'a pas cours le mercredi, et le samedi, on finit à midi.

SB 89 **GRAMMAR**

Dossier-langue
Our and your

This sets out the different forms of notre and votre. Students could work in pairs and see how many examples they can find in the interview in a given time, e.g. 5 minutes.

SB 89 **GRAMMAR PRACTICE**

5 Notre voyage scolaire

Students practise using *notre* and *nos*.

Solution: **1** *notre,* **2** *Notre,* **3** *notre,* **4** *notre,* **5** *nos,* **6** *notre,* **7** *nos,* **8** *nos,* **9** *notre*

SB 89 **GRAMMAR PRACTICE**

6 Vos affaires scolaires

Students practise using *votre* and *vos*.

Solution: **1** *votre sac,* **2** *votre gomme,* **3** *vos crayons,* **4** *votre calculette,* **5** *vos classeurs,* **6** *votre trousse,* **7** *vos cahiers/vos livres,* **8** *vos stylos*

SB 89, **WRITING**

7 Un message de la France

This task provides practice in responding to questions about the school, using *notre* and *nos*. The reply could be done using word processing.

SB 90 **READING**

1 Une lettre de Dominique

This letter about French school life includes examples of *leur* and *leurs* in context. Students read the letter and correct mistakes in the sentences which follow it.

Solution:

1. *Lucie et André vont ~~au parc~~ au collège.*
2. *Leur collège est ~~tout près~~ assez loin.*
3. *Leur premier cours est ~~géographie~~ anglais.*
4. *C'est ~~très ennuyeux~~ assez intéressant.*
5. *Leur prof d'anglais est très ~~sévère~~ sympa.*
6. *On a des cours de ~~maths~~ sciences et d'histoire.*
7. *À midi, on mange à la ~~gare~~ cantine.*
8. *L'après-midi, on a ~~dessin~~ technologie et EPS.*
9. *Dominique ~~déteste~~ adore le sport.*

SB 90 **GRAMMAR**

Dossier-langue
Their

This sets out the different forms of *leur*.

SB 90 **GRAMMAR PRACTICE**

2 Une conversation

This task brings together practice of all the plural possessive adjectives.

Solution: **1** *nos grands-parents,* **2** *notre grand-mère,* **3** *vos cousins,* **4** *nos grands-parents,* **5** *Leur maison,* **6** *Leurs chiens* **7** *leur cheval*

SB 90 **GRAMMAR PRACTICE**

3 Deux familles

Students produce sentences describing possession, using *notre*, *nos* and *leur*, *leurs*.

Solution:

1. *Voici notre maison.*
2. *Ça, c'est leur maison.*
3. *Ce sont leurs chats.*
4. *Ce sont nos chats.*
5. *Ça, c'est notre ordinateur.*
6. *Ça, c'est leur ordinateur.*
7. *C'est notre table.*
8. *C'est leur table.*
9. *Ce sont leurs chaises.*
10. *Ce sont nos chaises.*

GRAMMAR IN ACTION 1, PAGE 35 **GRAMMAR**

Using *notre/nos, votre/vos, leur/leurs*

This provides further practice of the plural possessive adjectives if required.

Area 8
Further activities and consolidation
SB 91, 4–6, SB 92
Au choix SB 140, 8
Écoute et parle SB 157, 6, 1–7
CD 3/9–13
Student CD 2/1–7, 35–38
CM 8/8, SB 147–149, CM 8/9–8/13

SB 91 **SUPPORT READING**

4 La journée de Mangetout

Students choose the correct caption from two options for each picture.

Solution: **1b, 2c, 3f, 4g, 5i**

SB 91 **EXTENSION READING**

5 Un frère paresseux

When they have read the letter, students identify the wrong word and find the correct one from a list of words given on the page.

Solution:

a 1 *Pendant les vacances, Charles aime rester ~~au collège~~ au lit.*
2 *Il écoute ~~sa souris~~ sa radio.*
3 *Il ~~mange~~ écoute de la musique.*
4 *Il ~~écrit~~ regarde un magazine.*
5 *Il regarde ~~ses trains~~ ses livres.*

6 *Il reste ~~en classe~~ en pyjama.*
7 *Sa ~~tarentule~~ sœur s'appelle Nicole.*
8 *Elle trouve qu'il est ~~super~~ paresseux.*

b **1** *vacances,* **2** *heures,* **3** *sommes,* **4** *matin,* **5** *midi*

CM 8/8, **WRITING**

Jeux de vocabulaire – informatique

Students could do this worksheet which practises ICT language at any convenient point. They should refer to *À l'ordinateur* (SB 147–149) for help. Some additional help is given with the clues on this worksheet.

Solutions:

1 Un acrostiche

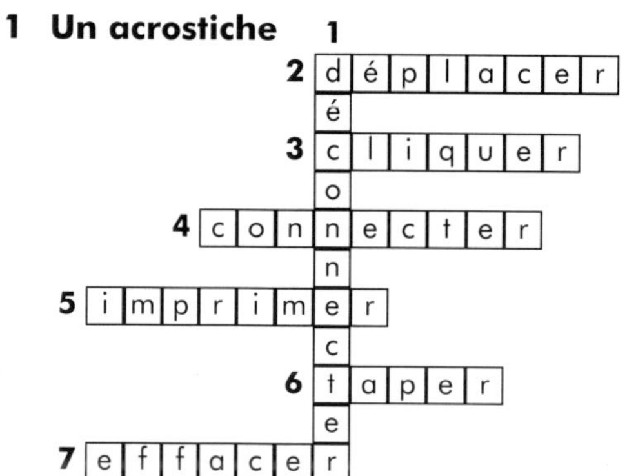

2 Mots croisés

3 À l'ordinateur

1 *allume,* **2** *connecte,* **3** *ouvre,* **4** *tape,* **5** *vérifie,* **6** *sauvegarde,* **7** *imprime,* **8** *ferme,* **9** *déconnecte*

SB 91, **WRITING**

6 Un message à écrire

This task provides practice in writing questions about school life. It could be done as an e-mail, saved and kept for future reference or evidence of ICT work. If the facility has not already been set up, help students to organise their own folders for storing sent e-mails. For students who require more support, a suitable message could be prepared on the board first.

Au choix SB 140,  **EXTENSION READING WRITING**

8 Daniel Laroche

As writing extension, part **b** could be done on a computer. Working together, students could take turns to key in and edit the text before printing out the corrected version of the article.

Solution:

a **1** *février,* **2** *le sport, les maths,* **3** *la musique, le cinéma/les films, le sport,* **4** *Toulouse,* **5** *le tennis, le badminton, le tennis de table,* **6** *le vert,* **7** *seize, huit,* **8** *un frère, une sœur,* **9** *Daniel, Nicole,* **10** *Laroche, Martin*

b *Daniel Laroche, le nouveau champion de ~~judo~~ tennis de table, habite à ~~Bordeaux~~ Toulouse. Il a ~~15~~ 16 ans et la date de son anniversaire est le ~~18 juillet~~ 8 février. Il a un frère et ~~sept~~ deux sœurs. Ses matières préférées sont le sport et ~~l'histoire~~ les maths. Il n'a pas beaucoup de temps libre, mais comme distractions, il aime la musique et le cinéma. Il adore les films ~~historiques~~ comiques. Il préfère la radio à la télévision et sa couleur préférée est le ~~bleu~~ vert.*

SB 92, SB 157, TB 163, SCD 2/6 **LISTENING**

Vocabulaire de classe

Some classroom instructions are summarised here. They are also recorded in random order in the *Écoute et parle* section (see TB 163).

Solution: 1c, 2f, 3j, 4b, 5i, 6e, 7g, 8a, 9h, 10d

SB 93, 3/9–10 **LISTENING SPEAKING**

Chantez! Attention, c'est l'heure!

This rap 'song' practising times appears in the *Presse-Jeunesse* section, but it can be used at any appropriate point in *Unité 8* or later. For notes on using the songs, see TB 33.

Attention, c'est l'heure!

Déjà sept heures moins dix, dix, dix,
Vite, vite, je vais être en retard.
Sept heures et quart je me prépare,
Je quitte la maison, enfin je pars.
Attention, c'est l'heure!

Ça y est, huit heures du mat, matin,
On entre en gare, j'arrive en train.
La cloche sonne à huit heures vingt,
Je suis au collège, tout va bien.
Attention, c'est l'heure!

Enfin midi, j'ai faim, faim, faim,
On va manger à la cantine.
Il est cinq heures, viens Géraldine,
La fin des cours, vive les copines.
Attention, c'est l'heure!

Il est six heures du soir, soir, soir,
Je fais mes devoirs, ouf, ça y est!
Huit heures, on prend tous le dîner,
Et puis, on regarde la télé.
Attention, c'est l'heure!

Besoin d'un bon dodo, dodo,
Très fatigué, je vais au lit.
Eh oui, il est dix heures et demie,
Alors à bientôt, bonne nuit.
Attention, c'est l'heure!

CM 8/9, SCD 2/35–38 INDEPENDENT LISTENING

Tu comprends?

1 Quelle heure est-il?

Solution: **1** *9h00,* **2** *8h00,* **3** *12h00,* **4** *11h30,* **5** *2h15,* **6** *2h45,* **7** *1h30,* **8** *5h15*

Quelle heure est-il?

1 Il est neuf heures.
2 Il est huit heures.
3 Il est midi.
4 Il est onze heures et demie.
5 Il est deux heures et quart.
6 Il est trois heures moins le quart.
7 Il est une heure et demie.
8 Il est cinq heures et quart.

2 Samedi

The language needed for the speaking task in CM 8/3 is incorporated in this dialogue for practice.

Solution: **1** *7h15,* **2a**, **3** *8h20,* **4** *11h00,* **5c**, **6b**, **7** *9h30*

Samedi

– Tu prends le petit déjeuner à quelle heure, le samedi?
– Normalement, je prends le petit déjeuner à sept heures et quart.
– À sept heures et quart? Et qu'est-ce que tu fais le matin?
– Eh bien, le matin, je vais au collège. J'ai cours le samedi matin.
– Ah bon, tu as cours le samedi matin. Les cours commencent à quelle heure?
– À huit heures vingt, comme les autres jours.
– Bon, le collège commence à huit heures vingt. Et les cours se terminent à quelle heure?
– À onze heures. Donc je rentre à la maison à midi.
– Et l'après-midi, qu'est-ce que tu fais?
– Pas grand-chose … je joue sur l'ordinateur, par exemple.
– Et le soir, qu'est-ce que tu fais, le soir?
– Le samedi soir, je regarde la télévision ou une vidéo.
– Et le soir, tu te couches à quelle heure?
– À neuf heures et demie, normalement.

3 Comment ça s'écrit?

Solution: *Le mot qui ne va pas avec les autres est déjeuner* (**2**).

Comment ça s'écrit?

1 d-e-s-s-i-n
2 d-é-j-e-u-n-e-r
3 m-u-s-i-q-u-e
4 h-i-s-t-o-i-r-e
5 a-n-g-l-a-i-s
6 m-a-t-h-s
7 g-é-o-g-r-a-p-h-i-e

4 L'emploi du temps

Solution:

8h	*maths*	*déjeuner*	
9h	*sciences*	*14h*	*français*
récréation		*15h*	*technologie*
10h10	*histoire*	*16h*	*EPS*
11h10	*anglais*		

L'emploi du temps

– Qu'est-ce que tu as comme cours, le lundi?
– Le lundi? Bon, le matin on a quatre cours. On commence avec maths.
– Alors, maths comme premier cours.
– Ensuite, nous avons sciences.
– Alors sciences, puis …
– Puis il y a la récréation.
– Et après la récréation?
– Nous avons histoire.
– Alors, histoire.
– Et ensuite, nous avons anglais.
– Alors, anglais, et puis c'est l'heure du déjeuner, je suppose.
– Oui, alors l'après-midi, on a trois cours. Pour commencer, il y a français.
– Alors, français.
– Puis nous avons technologie.
– Ensuite, technologie, et puis?
– Et puis nous avons EPS, c'est à dire éducation physique et sportive.
– Alors, EPS – et ça, c'est le dernier cours.
– Oui, c'est ça.
– Alors, le lundi, tu as maths, sciences, histoire, anglais, français, technologie et EPS.
– Exactement.

SB 92, CM 8/10

Sommaire

A summary of the main vocabulary and structures of the unit.

SB 157, SCD 2/1–7 SOUNDS AND WRITING

Écoute et parle – Unité 8

1 Les sons français

Solution: c (douce): (a) 1c, 2b, 3a, 4d
c (dure): (a) 1b, 2d, 3a, 4c

Les sons français

La lettre c (douce)

a **1** certainement
2 ça
3 ciel
4 reçu

b garçon, cent, cinq, c'est ça

La lettre c (dure)

a **1** content
2 calculette
3 cage
4 curieux

b café, coin, couleur, cuisine

2 Des phrases ridicules

Des phrases ridicules

Un garçon descend du ciel avec cinq cents citrons. Ça c'est sensationnel!

Coco compte les carottes et les calculettes dans un coin de la cuisine.

3 Et après

Solution: **1** *trente,* **2** *trente-cinq,* **3** *quarante,* **4** *quarante-huit,* **5** *cinquante-deux,* **6** *soixante,* **7** *soixante-douze,* **8** *quatre-vingts,* **9** *quatre-vingt-dix,* **10** *cent*

Et après

1 vingt-neuf
2 trente-quatre
3 trente-neuf
4 quarante-sept
5 cinquante et un
6 cinquante-neuf
7 soixante et onze
8 soixante-dix-neuf
9 quatre-vingt-neuf
10 quatre-vingt-dix-neuf

4 Les sons français

Solution: ch: (a) 1d, 2a, 3c, 4f, 5b, 6e

Les sons français

Les lettres ch

a **1** chic
2 chasse
3 château
4 chocolat
5 chance
6 Chine

b chambre, chez, chat, cherche, chaise, change

Les lettres ph et th

1 pharmacie
2 photo
3 théâtre
4 physique
5 thermomètre
6 phrase
7 théorie
8 Philippe

5 Des phrases ridicules

Des phrases ridicules

Le chat cherche du chocolat dans la chambre du château.

Sur la photo, Philippe apprend la physique dans la pharmacie.

Le terrible Thierry terrifie le théâtre avec ses théories.

6 Vocabulaire de classe

Solution: 10, 2, 5, 1, 6, 8, 4, 9, 7, 3

Vocabulaire de classe

Regarde la page 92. Écoute le CD et écris le nombre de chaque instruction dans l'ordre du CD.

Remplis la grille.
Trouve l'image qui correspond.
Change les mots soulignés.
Trouve le mot qui ne va pas.
Invente un dessin amusant.
Choisis le bon mot dans la case.
Trouve un mot qui commence avec c.
Écoute la cassette pour vérifier.
Relis la lettre.
Quelle est la réponse correcte?

7 Une conversation

Une conversation

a Écoute les questions et réponds comme indiqué.

– Comment s'appelle votre collège?
(pause)
– Il s'appelle le Collège Henri quatre.
– Combien d'élèves est-ce qu'il y a dans votre classe?
(pause)
– Il y a vingt-neuf élèves.
– Quelle est ta matière préférée?
(pause)
– J'adore les sciences. C'est utile.
– Est-ce qu'il y a des matières que tu n'aimes pas?
(pause)
– Oui, je déteste la géographie. C'est difficile.

b Écoute les questions et réponds pour toi.
– Comment s'appelle votre collège?
– (pause)
– Combien d'élèves est-ce qu'il y a dans votre classe?
– (pause)
– Quelle est ta matière préférée?
– (pause)
– Est-ce qu'il y a des matières que tu n'aimes pas?
– (pause)

Épreuve – Unité 8

CM 8/11, 3/11–13 **INFORMAL ASSESSMENT LISTENING**

Épreuve: Écouter

A Quelle heure est-il? (NC 2)

Solution: 1d, 2c, 3b, 4g, 5e, 6a, 7f (mark /6)

Quelle heure est-il?

1 – On va au cinéma, cet après-midi?
– Oui, bonne idée.
– Alors, rendez-vous à deux heures moins le quart?
– À deux heures moins le quart. D'accord.

2 – Quelle heure est-il, s'il vous plaît?
– Il est dix heures et demie.
– Dix heures et demie, merci.

3 – Quand est-ce que Marc et Sophie arrivent à la gare?
– Ils arrivent à trois heures et quart.
– À trois heures et quart, bon.

4 – Quand est-ce que le film commence?
– Il commence à huit heures moins le quart.
– À huit heures moins le quart. Bon.

5 – Le concert commence à quelle heure?
– Il commence à neuf heures et quart.
– À neuf heures et quart, bon, merci.

6 – Les cours se terminent à quelle heure le mercredi?
– Ils se terminent à onze heures.
– À onze heures?
– Oui, c'est ça.

7 – Papa rentre à quelle heure ce soir, maman?
– Il rentre très tard, à minuit.
– À minuit, ah bon.

B On parle des matières (NC 3)

Solution: 1a *difficile*, **2a** *facile*, **3b** *intéressant*, **4c** *ennuyeux*, **5c** *amusant* (mark /8)

On parle des matières

1 – Est-ce que tu aimes la géographie?
– Non, je n'aime pas la géographie.
– Pourquoi?
– Parce que c'est difficile.

2 – Quelle est ta matière préférée?
– La technologie. J'adore la technologie.
– Pourquoi?
– C'est facile.

3 – Tu aimes l'anglais?
– Oui, j'aime beaucoup l'anglais. L'anglais, c'est très intéressant.

4 – Est-ce qu'il y a une matière que tu n'aimes pas?
– Les maths. Je déteste les maths.
– Pourquoi?
– Parce que c'est ennuyeux. Oh, les maths, je trouve ça ennuyeux.

5 – Tu aimes le dessin?
– Oui, j'adore le dessin. Le dessin, c'est amusant.

C Un jour en semaine (NC 2)

Solution: 1 *6h50*, **2** *6h55*, **3** *7h40*, **4** *8h20*, **5** *10h25*, **6** *5h10*, **7** *7h00* (mark /6)

Un jour en semaine

1 – Quand est-ce que tu te lèves, le matin?
– Je me lève à sept heures moins dix.
– À sept heures moins dix.

2 – Et tu prends ton petit déjeuner à quelle heure?
– Je prends mon petit déjeuner à sept heures moins cinq.
– Ah bon, tu prends le petit déjeuner à sept heures moins cinq.

3 – À quelle heure est-ce que tu quittes la maison?
– Je quitte la maison à huit heures moins vingt.
– Alors, à huit heures moins vingt, tu quittes la maison.

4 – Quand est-ce que les cours commencent?
– Les cours commencent à huit heures vingt.

5 – La récréation est à quelle heure?
– À dix heures vingt-cinq.
– La récréation est à dix heures vingt-cinq.

6 – Quand est-ce que tu rentres à la maison?
– Normalement, je rentre à la maison à cinq heures dix.
– Alors, tu rentres à la maison à cinq heures dix.

7 – Et le soir, vous mangez à quelle heure?
– Nous mangeons à sept heures, normalement.
– Alors, vous mangez à sept heures.

ÇM 8/12 **READING**

Épreuve: Lire

A La journée (NC 2)

Solution: 1b, 2c, 3e, 4a, 5d (mark /4)

B Les matières préférées (NC 2)

Solution:

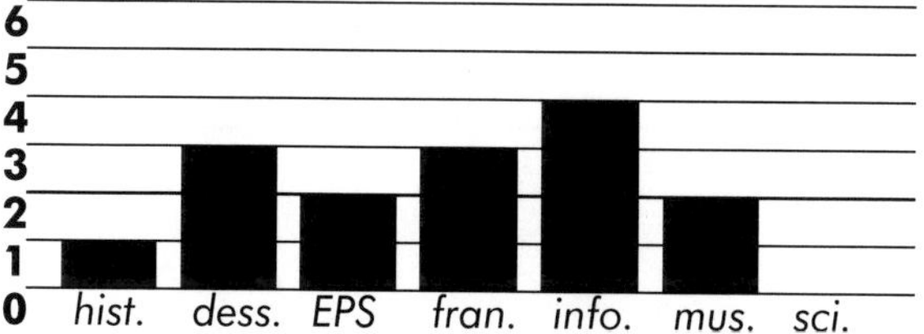

La matière préférée de la classe est l'informatique.
(mark /6: 5 for correct graph, 1 for correct statement)

C Questions et réponses (NC 2)

Solution: 1e, 2d, 3a, 4c, 5b (mark /4)

D Une interview (NC 3)

Solution: 1V, 2F, 3F, 4V, 5F, 6F, 7V (mark /6)

CM 8/13 **WRITING GRAMMAR**

Épreuve: Écrire et grammaire

A Les matières (NC 1)

For more able students, the words in the box could be blanked out.

This is an open-ended task. (mark /6)

B Des conversations (NC 1)

Solution:

a 1 *ton,* **2** *Mon,* **3** *ton,* **4** *Mon,* **5** *ta,* **6** *Ma,* **7** *tes,* **8** *Mes*
b 1 *votre,* **2** *Notre,* **3** *Vos,* **4** *Nos*
c 1 *leur,* **2** *son, son,* **3** *sa, son,* **4** *leurs*
(mark /8: 1/2 mark for each correct word)

C Des questions (NC 3)

This is an open-ended task. (mark /6: 2 marks per correct answer)

SB 93–95, CM 105–106, 🎧 3/9 **READING EXTENSION**

Presse-Jeunesse 3

These pages provide reading for pleasure. They can be used alone or with the accompanying copymaster. See the notes on TB 17.

SB 93, CM 105

Mangetout a des problèmes

The copymaster has a true/false task and a vocabulary building task based on the picture story.

Solution:

A 1V, 2F, 3F, 4F, 5F, 6V, 7V, 8F
B 2 *Mangetout n'est pas content.*
3 *Il décide de chercher des choses intéressantes à manger.*
4 *Il n'aime pas beaucoup ça!*
5 *Au restaurant, il n'y a pas beaucoup à manger.*
8 *Il mange un repas délicieux dans le marché aux poissons.*
C 1b, 2c, 3a, 4e, 5d, 6f

SB 93, TB 161, TB 33, 🎧 3/9 **LISTENING**

Chantez! Attention, c'est l'heure!

This song appears here in the *Presse-Jeunesse* section but can be used at any appropriate point in *Unité 8* or later. It is a rap 'song' practising times. See TB 161 for the text and TB 33 for notes on using the songs.

SB 94

Es-tu un(e) élève modèle?

A personality quiz for fun.

SB 94, CM 105

Le sais-tu?

The copymaster tasks practise reading for more detail.

Solution:

A 1b, 2d, 3g, 4c, 5a, 6e, 7h, 8f
B 1 *par personne,* **2** *la vitamine C,* **3** *nécessaire,* **4** *minéraux,* **5** *du calcium,* **6** *résister,* **7** *originaires de,* **8** *mentionnée,* **9** *l'explorateur,* **10** *un ornement*
C 1 *oranges,* **2** *contient,* **3** *oranger,* **4** *froid,* **5** *bâtiment, hiver,* **6** *manger*

CM 106

3 Lire – c'est facile **READING STRATEGIES**

This third item in the series on reading strategies deals with using clues to avoid looking up too many words in a dictionary.

SB 95, CM 106

Le nouvel élève

The first copymaster task is about reading for gist, whereas the second task requires more detail.

Solution: A 3 is the correct summary.
B 1a, 2b, 3b, 4a, 5a, 6b, 7a, 8b

Encore Tricolore 1
nouvelle édition

unité 9 Mmm – c'est bon, ça!

Areas	Topics	Grammar
1	Describing food and drink for a main meal	
2		The partitive article (*du,de la, de l', des*) (D-L SB 98)
3	Talking about breakfast	
4		The present tense of *prendre* (D-L SB 101)
5	Describing more food and drink	
6	Eating with a family Accepting or declining food	
7	Expressing likes and dislikes Talking about vegetarianism	The negative (D-L SB 105)
8	Further activities and consolidation	

National Curriculum information

Some students	Levels 3–4
Most students	Levels 2–3
All students	Levels 1–2

Refer also to the information about coverage of 'Knowledge, skills and understanding' (TB 9).

Revision

The vocabulary and structures introduced in *Unités 8–9* are revised in the *Rappel* section following this unit (SB 108–109, TB 181).

Sounds and writing

- *oi* and *ai*
- further work on endings of words
- see *Écoute et parle* (SB 158, TB 179)

ICT opportunities

- mentioning problems with ICT equipment (SB 149, TB 177)
- ideas for using text manipulation packages (TB 175–176)
- creating a verb table (TB 171)

Assessment

- Informal assessment is in the *Épreuves* at the end of this unit (TB 180).
- Formal assessment is in the *Troisième contrôle* following *Unité 10* (TB 203). Alternative tasks make it possible to adapt the *Troisième contrôle* to be used at the end of this unit instead of *Unité 10*, if your school prefers to do this, for reporting purposes.

Students' Book

Unité 9 SB 96–107
Au choix SB 141 1 (TB 169), 2, 3 (TB 171), 4 (TB 172)
SB 142 5 (TB 172), 6, 7 (TB 177)
SB 143 8 (TB 178)
Écoute et parle SB 158 (TB 179)
Rappel 4 SB 108–109 (TB 181)

Flashcards

56–89 food and drink
34–42 verbs
43–55 places in town

CDs

3/14–25
Student CD 2/8–15, 39–41

Copymasters

9/1 *On mange et on boit* [mini-flashcards/support] (TB 168)
9/2 *C'est quel mot?* [grammar] (TB 169)
9/3 *Des jeux de vocabulaire* [support] (TB 173)
9/4 *La page des jeux* [extension] (TB 174)
9/5 *À table* [speaking] (TB 175)
9/6 *Ça ne va pas!* [grammar: negative; support] (TB 177)
9/7 *La forme négative* [extension] (TB 177)
9/8 *Tu comprends?* [independent listening] (TB 178)
9/9 *Sommaire* (TB 179)
9/10 *Épreuve: Écouter* (TB 180)
9/11 *Épreuve: Lire* (TB 181)
9/12 *Épreuve: Écrire et grammaire* (TB 181)

121–128 *Troisième contrôle* (including alternative tasks) (TB 203)

Additional

Grammar in Action 1, pp 21–23

Language content

Food and drink for a main meal (Areas 1, 5, 6, 7)

les plats d'un repas
un hors-d'œuvre
le plat principal
le dessert

du fromage
du jambon
de l'omelette (f)
du pâté
de la pizza
du poisson
du potage
du poulet
de la viande

du gâteau
de la tarte aux pommes
un yaourt

Fruit and vegetables (Areas 1, 5, 7)

des légumes (m pl)
des carottes (f pl)
du chou
du chou-fleur
des frites (f pl)
des haricots verts (m pl)
des petits pois (m pl)
des pommes de terre (f pl)
de la salade
une tomate

des fruits (m pl)
une banane
un citron
une fraise
un kiwi
un melon
une orange
une pêche
une poire
une pomme
des raisins

Breakfast (Area 3)

du pain
des croissants (m pl)
du beurre
des toasts (m pl)
de la confiture
de la confiture d'oranges
des céréales (f pl)
du sucre
un œuf
des œufs au bacon (m pl)

Drinks (Areas 1, 3)

des boissons chaudes (f pl)
du café
du thé
un chocolat chaud

des boissons froides (f pl)
de l'eau (f)
de l'eau minérale (f)
de la limonade
du jus de fruit
du lait
du coca
du vin

Accepting and refusing food (Area 6)

Oui, s'il vous plaît.
Oui, je veux bien.
Non, merci.
C'est (très) bon/délicieux.
Encore du ...?
Merci, j'ai assez mangé.

Saying what food and drink you like and dislike (Areas 6, 7)

J'aime (beaucoup) le/la/les ...
Je regrette, mais je n'aime pas beaucoup ça.

Classroom language and rubrics

Ne parlez pas anglais.
Je ne comprends pas ce mot.
Je n'ai pas mon livre.
Je n'ai pas de stylo.
Ce n'est pas difficile.
Je ne trouve pas mon cahier.
Ce n'est pas facile.
Je n'ai pas fini.

On-going activities

Wall display

Students, perhaps working in pairs or small groups, could cut out pictures of food and drink from magazines. (After Area 2, they could label them in French, using the words for 'some').

They could make these into collages or simple wall displays, each featuring a particular meal or category of food, or their own favourite meal. As they learn more vocabulary, they can add to their displays. Several groups could combine to make their display into a complete meal, e.g.
Comme hors-d'œuvre, il y a/je préfère ...
Comme plat principal, il y a ...
Comme légumes, il y a ...
Comme dessert, il y a ...
Comme boisson, il y a ...

Labels, short sentences in French and, perhaps, clip art or other design features could be prepared on the computer and used in these displays.

Brainstorming

Give the class a title, e.g. *le petit déjeuner* or *les légumes*. Working individually or in groups, the class have to think of as many words as possible on that subject in a predetermined time, say two minutes.

Then ask for suggestions and list these on the board.

French food tasting

Brave teachers, or a school French club, could organise a French food-tasting session or a French meal with French bread, cheeses and pâté etc.

Area 1
Describing food and drink for a main meal

SB 96–97, 1–3
CD 3/14
CM 9/1
FC 56–64, 68, 69, 73, 78–79, 81–83
Meals and food items

FC 56–64, 68, 69, 73, 78–79, 81–83 PRESENTATION

Food

Use flashcards to present and practise the following vocabulary: *du jambon, du poulet, de la viande, du poisson, de l'omelette, des pommes de terre, des frites, des carottes, des petits pois, de la salade (verte), du fromage, un yaourt, une pomme, une banane (des fruits), du vin, de l'eau, de la limonade.* Teach also *du melon* and *du pâté* (not on flashcards).

Introduce the words preceded by the correct word for 'some', as this will familiarise the class with the different forms of the partitive article. This is explained fully later and practised throughout the unit.

Ask questions, such as *Qu'est-ce que c'est? Qu'est-ce que tu manges? Qu'est-ce que tu bois?* and prompt replies with the flashcards.

After plenty of oral practice, write some of the words on the board for a game of *Effacez!* later.

The words fall naturally into groups, such as the separate courses (as presented in SB 96-97).

At this stage, students can absorb a lot of vocabulary at once so long as they use it in plenty of enjoyable activities, e.g. *Jeu de mémoire, Morpion* etc. (TB 27).

SB 96 PRESENTATION SPEAKING

Un repas typique

Although a lot of vocabulary is used in the first item, students are not yet expected to know it thoroughly. It is re-used and practised throughout the unit.

Explain that the photos show some things that might be included in a typical meal, although a typical meal would not include all the items shown.

Introduce the photos in the Students' Book and the words for courses – *un hors-d'œuvre, un plat principal, des légumes, un dessert, des boissons*, explaining these, if necessary, and practising the new vocabulary, e.g.
Le numéro neuf, qu'est'ce que c'est? (Des frites.)
Qu'est-ce qu'il y a, comme hors-d'œuvre/desserts/boissons?
Le poulet, c'est un légume?

SB 97, 3/14 LISTENING

1 Trois familles

Students listen to the recording, in which three families discuss what they are eating for their main meal, and then note down the number for each item mentioned.

Solution:
A *les Dubois:* **2, 4, 11, 14, 15, 18, 19**
B *les Martin:* **1, 7, 9, 12, 16**
C *les Lacan:* **3, 6, 8, 10, 13, 17, 18, 20**

Trois familles

Famille A
– Chez la famille Dubois, on mange du pâté, comme hors-d'œuvre. Ensuite, comme plat principal, il y a du poulet avec des petits pois. Puis il y a des yaourts et des fruits. Comme boisson, il y a du vin et de l'eau.

Famille B
– La famille Martin est végétarienne. Alors, pour commencer, ils vont manger du melon. Puis, comme plat principal, on va manger de l'omelette avec des frites. Toute la famille aime ça. Puis, on va prendre de la salade. Et comme dessert, on va manger un gâteau.

Famille C
– Mme Lacan, qu'est-ce que vous mangez aujourd'hui pour le déjeuner?
– Comme hors-d'œuvre, nous mangeons du jambon. Puis, comme plat principal, nous mangeons du poisson, avec, comme légumes, des pommes de terre et des carottes. Ensuite, on va prendre du fromage. Et comme dessert, il y a une tarte aux pommes.
– Et qu'est-ce que vous prenez comme boisson?
– Alors, comme boisson, il y a du vin et, pour les enfants, il y a de la limonade.

SB 97 (VOCABULARY) PRACTICE WRITING

2 Qu'est-ce que c'est?

Students supply the vowels to identify the items. This could be done orally first.

Solution: **1** *de la viande,* **2** *de l'omelette,* **3** *du poulet,* **4** *des petits pois,* **5** *des pommes de terre,* **6** *une banane,* **7** *un yaourt,* **8** *de l'eau,* **9** *du melon*

SB 97 READING

3 Un repas en morceaux

Students join the two parts of each word to find an item of food or drink for each category.

Check the answers orally, with students reading out the complete sentence.

Solution: **1** *jambon,* **2** *poisson,* **3** *carottes,* **4** *salade,* **5** *fromage,* **6** *gâteau,* **7** *limonade*

CM 9/1 MINI-FLASHCARDS SUPPORT/CONSOLIDATION

On mange et on boit

The mini-flashcards can be used for a number of games, e.g. *Le jeu des sept familles, Je pense à quelque chose* etc. (see TB 26–28).

Area 2
The partitive article (*du, de la, de l', des*)

SB 98–99, 1–3
Au choix SB 141, 1
CM 9/2
Grammar in Action 1, page 21

SB 98 READING

1 Chasse à l'intrus

This activity contains many examples of the partitive article. It can be done at a simple level, with students just picking out the word which doesn't match the others; or at a higher level, with students writing the answer and explaining why it doesn't fit the category. For extra help, the 'reasons' could be written in jumbled order on the board.

Solution:

1 *le marché (les autres sont des repas)*
2 *des oranges (les autres sont des légumes)*
3 *de la salade (les autres sont des boissons)*
4 *du fromage (les autres sont des plats)*
5 *du jambon (les autres sont des fruits)*
6 *des frites (les autres sont des desserts)*

SB 98 GRAMMAR

Dossier-langue
Some

Read the reminder and the information in the two tables aloud to the class, stopping to make sure that they know the various words for 'some'. Encourage them to find further examples from earlier in the unit. Emphasise the link between the correct word for 'some' and the gender of the noun.

The explanation of the partitive article here does not include the point that, in French, the word for 'some' is always used, whereas in English it is sometimes omitted, e.g. *Pour le petit déjeuner, je prends du pain et du beurre.* (For breakfast I have bread and butter.) It is left to the teacher to decide whether to explain this, since it might confuse some classes while others will probably take it in their stride.

SB 98 GRAMMAR/READING

2 Trouve les mots

All the answers in this quiz are preceded by the partitive article.

Solution: **1** *du vin,* **2** *du melon,* **3** *de la viande,* **4** *de la salade,* **5** *de l'eau,* **6** *de l'omelette,* **7** *des carottes,* **8** *des pommes*

SB 98 EXTENSION

?

It could be mentioned that vinegar was first 'discovered' when old wine turned sour.

SB 99 READING

3 Mangetout – un bon repas

This picture story reinforces the vocabulary of the unit and includes many examples of the partitive article. When students have read the story, they should look at the items of food illustrated. Revise these orally to check that students recognise them. They then list what Mangetout eats and doesn't eat in the story.

With less able students, do this as a class activity and build up the lists on the board, then re-use them for more oral work or a game of *Effacez!* (TB 26).

For extension, students could study the story for a few minutes and then close their books and try to recall as many items of food as possible from memory.

Solution:

M mange tout ça: du pain (**b**), *de la salade* (**c**), *du gâteau* (**d**), *du fromage* (**e**), *des carottes* (**f**), *du poisson* (**h**), *de la viande* (**j**), *des tomates* (**l**)
M ne mange pas ça: des pommes (**a**), *des frites* (**g**), *de l'omelette* (**i**), *des petits pois* (**k**)

Au choix SB 141 CONSOLIDATION/WRITING

1 Un mélange

Students write the names of food and drink for different courses, with the partitive article.

Solution: **1** *du jambon, du pâté,* **2** *de la viande, de l'omelette,* **3** *des carottes, des oignons,* **4** *des tartes aux fruits, des yaourts,* **5** *de l'eau, du vin,* **6** *des bananes, des oranges*

CM 9/2 GRAMMAR

C'est quel mot?

This copymaster provides practice of genders and the partitive with a slightly wider range of food and drink vocabulary.

1 Masculin/féminin
Practice in identifying genders.

Solution:

a **M**: *un repas, un yaourt, le petit déjeuner, le dîner, le goûter, le poisson;*
F: *une tarte, la pomme, la salade, une banane, la viande, une poire*
b *une boisson (f), le petit pois (m), le légume (m), une banane (f), une carotte (f), un croissant (m), le sandwich (m), le gâteau (m)*

2 Un tableau
Students identify the gender, then complete a grid with the appropriate articles and possessive adjective.

3 Mon repas favori
Productive practice of the above language.

Solution:

1 *Mon repas favori est le goûter. Je mange du pain avec de la confiture ou un fruit et je bois un chocolat chaud ou un jus de fruit.*
2 *Mon repas favori est le dîner. Je prends du pâté et comme plat principal, j'adore le poisson avec des frites et des petits pois. Mon dessert favori est la tarte aux pommes et ma boisson favorite est le coca.*

GRAMMAR IN ACTION 1, PAGE 21 GRAMMAR

Using *du, de la, de l', des*

This provides practice of the partitive but would be best used later in the unit, when more food and drink vocabulary has been taught.

Area 3
Talking about breakfast

SB 100, 1–3
Au choix SB 141, 2–3
CD 3/15–16
FC 69–79, 82–89
Breakfast food and drink

FC 69–79, 82–89 PRESENTATION SPEAKING

Breakfast food and drink

Introduce this topic by saying what you (and other members of the family) eat for breakfast and show the class a flashcard each time one of the items of food and drink is mentioned, e.g.
À sept heures et demie, je prends le petit déjeuner. Je mange du pain avec du beurre et de la confiture. Quelquefois, je mange un fruit, par exemple une banane. Je bois du jus de fruit et un café au lait.

Teach and practise the main items for breakfast, using any appropriate flashcard games (see TB 27).

SB 100, 3/15 PRESENTATION LISTENING

1 Le petit déjeuner

Go through the illustrations, asking students to repeat the names of the items illustrated.

Some things may need a brief explanation in English, e.g. *des tartines, des croissants, Nutella* and the custom of drinking hot chocolate, coffee etc. in a *bol*.

Next students listen to the recording and note down the numbers to indicate each item mentioned after the appropriate name.

Solution:

Nicole – 1, 3, 4 (or **5), 16**
Marc – 9, 7, 13
Claire – 8 (or **1, 3), 6, 15**
Luc – 2, 1, 3, 4 (or **5), 14** (+ **17), 18**
Des touristes – 9, 11, 12, 10, 1, 2, 14, 15

Le petit déjeuner

Nicole
– Normalement, je prends le petit déjeuner à sept heures du matin. Je prends du pain avec du beurre et de la confiture. Comme boisson, je prends un chocolat chaud.

Marc
– Moi, je prends le petit déjeuner à sept heures et quart. Je mange des céréales, par exemple des Corn Flakes, et des toasts et je bois du jus de fruit.

Claire
– Pendant la semaine, je prends le petit déjeuner à huit heures moins le quart. Je mange des tartines, c'est à dire, du pain avec du beurre. Quelquefois, je fais des tartines avec du Nutella. J'aime bien ça. Comme boisson, je prends du thé.

Luc
– Le dimanche, nous prenons le petit déjeuner plus tard, vers huit heures et demie. Nous mangeons souvent des croissants ou du pain avec du beurre et de la confiture. Moi, je bois du café au lait avec du sucre.

Des touristes
– Mes parents travaillent dans un grand hôtel. À l'hôtel, on prépare un petit déjeuner sous forme de buffet pour les touristes. Souvent des touristes mangent des céréales ou des yaourts ou des fruits. Puis ils mangent un œuf à la coque avec du pain ou des croissants. Comme boissons, ils prennent du café ou du thé.

SB 100 PRACTICE READING/WRITING

2 Qu'est-ce qu'on prend?

To check that students understand what is included on each tray, describe the breakfast on one tray and ask students to tell you which one it is (**a–e**), e.g.
Pour le petit déjeuner, il y a des céréales, du toast et du chocolat chaud. (**c**)

Ask the class to suggest what is included on the other trays and list this on the board.

Students then follow the lines to see who eats which breakfast and complete sentences in their books.

Solution:

1 **(d)** *Lucie prend du pain avec du beurre et de la confiture. Comme boisson, elle prend du jus de fruit.*
2 **(c)** *Thomas prend des céréales et du toast et il boit du chocolat chaud.*
3 **(a)** *Sylvie prend un yaourt et du pain/des tartines avec du Nutella. Comme boisson, elle prend du thé.*
4 **(e)** *Le dimanche, Luc mange souvent du pain ou des croissants avec du beurre et de la confiture. Il boit du café avec du lait et du sucre.*
5 **(b)** *Des touristes mangent des céréales ou des yaourts ou des fruits. Puis ils mangent un œuf à la coque avec du pain ou des croissants. Comme boissons, ils prennent du café ou du thé.*

SPEAKING

Pour le petit déjeuner, je prends ...

Play a chain breakfast game with an ever-increasing list of items for breakfast.

SB 100, SPEAKNG/WRITING

3 À toi!

Read out the message and explain about the 'traditional British breakfast'. Ask a few students to suggest possible sentences orally before the class work on their individual replies as suggested in the example.

Different parts of *prendre* are used here and this is explained more fully later in the unit. *Je bois* and *on boit* are used as vocabulary items only, as the verb *boire* is not covered in detail in the unit.

A computer could be used for this activity which could be presented as a real e-mail.

Au choix SB 141 — **EXTENSION DICTIONARY PRACTICE**

2 C'est utile, le dictionnaire

Students list the words in alphabetical order, check the meanings and gender and then use the words to complete sentences.

Solution:

a

chips (m pl)	crisps	*poivre (m)*	pepper
glace (f)	ice cream	*potage (m)*	soup
miel (m)	honey	*sel (m)*	salt
moutarde (f)	mustard	*sucre (m)*	sugar

b **1** *potage,* **2** *chips,* **3** *sucre,* **4** *glace,* **5** *miel,* **6** *sel, poivre* **7** *moutarde*

Au choix SB 141, 3/16 — **LISTENING**

3 Qu'est-ce qu'ils mangent?

First ask the class to look at the drawings and discuss with them what is shown in each picture, using *du, de la* etc.

For support, this can be done as an oral activity. First list the items in each picture on the board, and ask a volunteer to tick them off as they are mentioned. For extension work, this can be done as a written activity.

Later, the recording can be used for further listening practice, with able students noting down the time of each meal then listening again and writing down the other items of food or drink mentioned by each speaker.

Solution: **1** *du pain et du beurre,* **2** *du café (au lait), une orange,* **3** *du poisson et des fruits,* **4** *du potage et des frites,* **5** *un gâteau et du yaourt,* **6** *un sandwich et du coca*

Qu'est-ce qu'ils mangent?

1 Le samedi, je prends le petit déjeuner à huit heures et demie. Je mange du pain avec du beurre, ou un croissant. Je prends un chocolat chaud.

2 Le lundi, je prends le petit déjeuner à sept heures et quart. Je bois du café au lait et je mange une tartine et une orange.

3 À midi et demi, je déjeune. Je prends le déjeuner au collège. Nous mangeons un hors-d'œuvre, puis de la viande ou du poisson et comme dessert, il y a des fruits.

4 Chez nous, le dîner est à huit heures moins le quart. Aujourd'hui, nous mangeons du potage, une omelette au fromage avec des frites et des haricots verts, puis du yaourt.

5 À cinq heures, mon petit frère prend le goûter. Il mange un gâteau ou du yaourt. Il boit de la limonade.

6 Mon père déjeune en ville. Il n'a pas le temps de manger un grand repas, alors il prend un sandwich et un dessert, et il boit de la limonade ou du coca.

Area 4
The present tense of *prendre*
SB 101, 4–6
Au choix SB 141–142, 4–5
CD 3/17
Grammar in Action 1, page 22
Meals

SB 101 — **PRESENTATION READING**

4 Les repas en France

Revise the names of all meals, e.g. *Le matin, on prend quel repas? Et à midi, et le soir? Quand les enfants rentrent à la maison, ils prennent souvent quelque chose à manger et à boire, ça s'appelle ...?*

This short quiz presents most parts of the verb *prendre*.

Solution: **1c, 2b, 3c, 4a, 5c**

SB 101, — **GRAMMAR**

Dossier-langue *Prendre*

Check that students understand the more common meaning of *prendre* – to take.

If students have compiled an individual verb table using a table facility on the computer, *prendre* could be added at this point (see TB 40).

SB 101, — **SPEAKING**

5 Un jeu

This could be used on several occasions, featuring different meals and foods.

Students who are not good at writing could draw pictures of the food and drink they choose or use some of the mini-flashcards made from CM 9/1.

SB 101 — **GRAMMAR**

6 Questions et réponses

Using the verb *prendre*, students have to first complete questions, then replies, then match them up.

Solution: **1** *vous prenez,* **2** *On prend,* **3** *on prend,* **4** *tu prends,* **5** *tes amis prennent*

a *Je prends,* **b** *ils prennent,* **c** *On prend,* **d** *Nous prenons,* **e** *nous prenons*

1e, 2c, 3d, 4a, 5b

Au choix SB 141 **GRAMMAR**

4 Des phrases mélangées

For further practice of *prendre*, students unjumble these sentences.

Solution:

1 *Le matin, je prends un bon petit déjeuner.*
2 *Qu'est-ce que tu prends pour le petit déjeuner?*
3 *Je prends le train pour aller au collège.*
4 *Pour la gare, prenez la première rue à droite.*
5 *À midi, je prends des sandwichs.*
6 *Beaucoup d'élèves prennent le déjeuner à la cantine.*
7 *Nous prenons de l'eau comme boisson.*

Au choix SB 142, 3/17 **LISTENING/READING EXTENSION**

5 On gagne des prix

This task involves the use of prendre in a different context. Introduce the item, referring to the picture in the Students' Book, e.g.

Radio Jeunesse a organisé un grand jeu et une équipe de six personnes a gagné le premier prix. Il y a six prix individuels. Il y a un bon (voucher) *pour un repas pour quatre personnes au restaurant Max, il y a un baladeur et un lecteur de CDs. Il y a un cédérom et il y a des billets pour le Parc Astérix (un parc d'attractions près de Paris) et des billets pour un grand match de football.*

Il y a six personnes et six prix. Alors, voilà la question: qui prend chaque prix?

Students then read through the details and make an intelligent guess about who chooses each prize. They note down their answers and then listen to the recording to check them.

Finally students can make their own choice from the prizes on offer and give a simple reason.

Solution:

a **1f, 2c, 3a, 4e, 5b, 6d**
b **1** *Coralie prend le repas.*
2 *Mireille prend le lecteur de CDs.*
3 *Stéphanie prend le baladeur.*
4 *Sébastien prend le cédérom.*
5 *Luc prend les billets pour le match.*
6 *Christophe prend les billets pour le Parc Astérix.*

On gagne des prix

– Bonsoir, salut! Ici Radio Jeunesse! Il est huit heures du soir. Ce soir, c'est la présentation des prix! Nous avons ici six jeunes habitants de La Rochelle. Alors, ces jeunes personnes, qui sont très intelligentes, ont gagné le premier prix de notre jeu national. Fantastique, non? Et ce soir, ils vont choisir leurs prix. Les filles d'abord. Vous êtes …?
– Coralie.
– Mireille.
– Stéphanie.
– Alors, Mesdemoiselles, qu'est-ce que vous allez prendre?
– Euh, moi je prends … le repas au restaurant pour quatre personnes.
– Vous êtes quatre personnes dans la famille?
– Oui monsieur, mes parents, mon frère et moi.
– Fantastique! Coralie prend le repas … et toi, Mireille, qu'est-ce que tu prends?
– Alors, moi, je prends le lecteur de CDs, j'adore la musique.
– Excellent! Mireille prend le lecteur de CDs. Et puis Stéphanie … tu prends …?
– Ben, moi, je n'ai pas de baladeur, alors je prends ça. Merci beaucoup, Monsieur, c'est génial!
– Voilà le baladeur pour toi, Stéphanie! Et maintenant les trois garçons. Vous êtes?
– Sébastien, bonsoir!
– Luc.
– Et Christophe.
– Bonsoir à tous les trois. Toi, d'abord, Sébastien, qu'est-ce que tu prends comme prix?
– Moi, le cédérom, s'il vous plaît … j'adore les jeux électroniques.
– Voilà … Sébastien prend le cédérom … et puis Luc?
– Moi, j'aime beaucoup le sport, alors je prends les billets pour le match, ça va?
– Mais, bien sûr, ça va être un grand match de football, la France contre l'Angleterre. Alors Christophe, tu prends quoi?
– Ben, moi, je prends des billets pour le Parc Astérix, c'est bien, ça. J'aime beaucoup les parcs d'attraction et j'adore Astérix. Merci beaucoup.
– Je vous en prie! Et voilà, c'est la fin de notre jeu de cette année. Félicitations à l'équipe de La Rochelle et bonne chance à tous pour l'année prochaine.

Grammar in Action 1, page 22 **GRAMMAR**

Using the verb *prendre*

Further practice of *prendre*, if required.

Area 5
Describing more food and drink
SB 102, 1–5
CD 3/18
FC 61–75
CM 9/3, 9/4
Fruit and vegetables

SB 102 **REVISION/PRACTICE GRAMMAR**

1 Le plat favori

A simple maze puzzle giving revision of animals and practice of the partitive article.

Solution:

1 *La souris mange du fromage.*

2 *L'oiseau mange du pain.*
3 *Le cheval mange du sucre.*
4 *Le chien mange de la viande.*
5 *Le perroquet mange une tomate.*
6 *Le cochon d'Inde mange une pomme.*
7 *Le chat mange du poisson.*
8 *Le lapin mange des carottes.*

Drinks

REVISION

Ask the class to give suggestions for drinks and make a list of hot drinks and cold drinks on the board. For support, write some initial letters on the board.

SB 102 **REVISION**

2 Des boissons froides

A simple puzzle practising cold drinks.

Solution: *limonade, lait, jus de fruit, coca, vin*

FC 61–75 **PRESENTATION/PRACTICE**

Des fruits et des légumes

Using flashcards, magazine pictures or the real thing, revise the words for fruit, learnt earlier in the unit (*une pomme, une banane, une poire, une orange, du/un melon*) and teach *une pêche, des raisins, des fraises*.

In a similar way, revise the words for vegetables (*des petits pois, des carottes, des pommes de terre*) and teach *des haricots verts, du chou, du chou-fleur, des oignons*.

Two games

PRACTICE

1 Qu'est-ce que c'est?

One student picks up a card, not showing it to the rest of the class. They can ask up to five 'yes/no' type questions to guess what it is, e.g.
C'est un fruit/un légume? C'est grand/petit?
C'est rouge/vert/orange/jaune/blanc?

2 J'adore les fruits et les légumes.

A chain game in which one person says a fruit or vegetable that they eat and the next person adds another one, e.g.
Je mange une pêche.
Je mange une pêche et deux bananes.
Je mange une pêche, deux bananes et trois oignons etc.

This can be played in various ways, e.g. alternating fruit and vegetables, with different subjects, e.g. *Mon chat mange* ... etc.

SB 102 **PRESENTATION** **WRITING**

3 Les fruits et les légumes

Students write the words for the fruit and vegetables with the missing vowels.

Solution: **1** *fraises,* **2** *petits pois,* **3** *melon,* **4** *haricots verts,* **5** *chou-fleur,* **6** *poire,* **7** *oignons,* **8** *pommes de terre,* **9** *carottes,* **10** *pêches*

Follow-up

PRACTICE

The ten sentences in Task 3 present various ways of expressing likes, dislikes and preferences. A simple substitution game could be played with competing teams or groups, or, if students make their own sets of cards, as a pair activity.

Write the sentences on strips of paper or card with a gap where the incomplete word was. Students pick a sentence at random and read it out, putting any suitable word in the gap. In sentences 3 and 10, the adjective will need to be changed if a noun of a different gender is used.

GRAMMAR/EXTENSION

Definite article for preferences

There is no *Dossier-langue* on using the definite article when expressing preferences. This is to avoid confusion with the partitive, but teachers may wish to point out the usage to more able students. Often, however, it is simply assimilated through usage and drawing attention to it could create rather than solve a problem.

SB 102, 3/18 **WRITING** **LISTENING**

4 Mon repas préféré

Students complete the sentences, then listen to the recording to check their answers.

Mon repas favori

1 – Mon repas favori est le goûter. Je mange des tartines avec du beurre et du Nutella et une pomme. Je bois un chocolat chaud.

2 – Mon repas favori est le petit déjeuner. J'adore les céréales et les fruits. Alors je mange souvent des céréales avec une banane. Comme boisson, je prends d'abord un jus d'orange, puis du café au lait. Et je mange des toasts aussi.

3 – Mon repas favori est le déjeuner du dimanche. Comme hors-d'œuvre, on prend souvent du potage. Ça, c'est toujours bon. Puis, comme plat principal, j'adore le poulet rôti avec des pommes de terre, des petits pois et des haricots verts. Et mon dessert favori, c'est la tarte aux pommes.

SB 102, **SPEAKING**

5 À toi!

Students practise talking about their favourite meal of the day.

CM 9/3 **SUPPORT/CONSOLIDATION**

Des jeux de vocabulaire

This copymaster provides a range of activities practising food and drink vocabulary.

Solutions:

1 Mots mêlés
pêche, raisin, poire, banane
lait, vin, eau
oignon, carotte
déjeuner

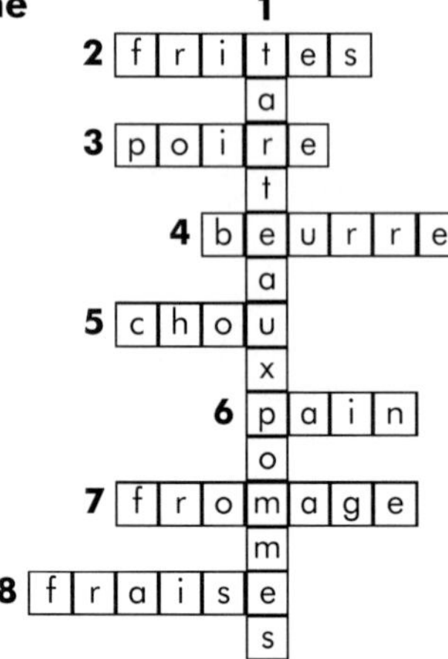

2 Un serpent
a potage, viande, pommes de terre, salade, yaourt
b limonade

3 Un acrostiche

					1			
	2	f	r	i	t	e	s	
					a			
	3	p	o	i	r	e		
					t			
				4	b	e	u	r r e
					a			
	5	c	h	o	u			
					x			
				6	p	a	i	n
					o			
	7	f	r	o	m	a	g	e
					m			
8	f	r	a	i	s	e		
					s			

CM 9/4 EXTENSION

La page des jeux

Solutions:

1 Mots croisés

2 C'est quel mot?
Possible solution: 1 *le déjeuner, le dîner,* **2** *l'eau,* **3** *une carotte, un chou, un chou-fleur,* **4** *une banane,* **5** *du melon,* **6** *du poulet, du poisson,* **7** *une tarte*

3 Invente un acrostiche
Able students may be able to make up an acrostic which could be exchanged with other students to solve. This task can be adapted for practice of any vocabulary items.

Possible version:

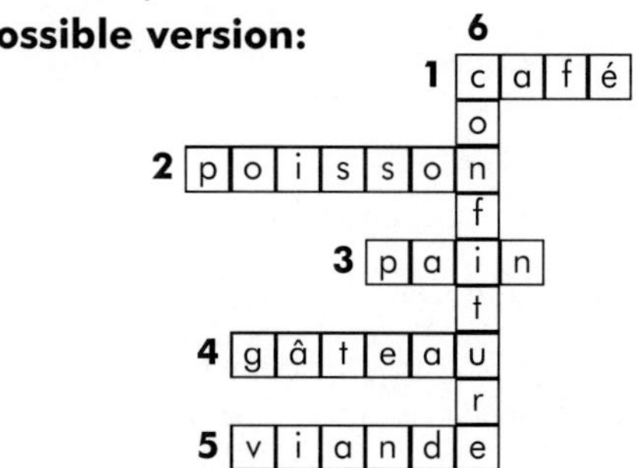

Area 6
Eating with a French family
Accepting or declining food

SB 103, 6, SB 104, 1–2
CD 3/19–21
FC 42–55; CM 9/5

FC 42–55 (ANY SELECTION) **SPEAKING PRACTICE**

Je n'aime pas beaucoup ça

Explain that if students are staying with a French family, it is useful to be able to say that they don't like something in a polite way – *(Je regrette, mais) je n'aime pas beaucoup ça.*

This phrase can then be practised by showing various flashcards of food and asking students *Tu aimes ça?*

SB 103, 3/19 **PRESENTATION LISTENING**

6 À table

This item contains some key phrases and vocabulary, which are practised in part **b** and should be learnt by heart by the majority of students.

a Students listen to the recording without looking at the text. Ask a few general questions, e.g. *C'est quel repas? Est-ce qu'on prend un dessert?*
Then play the recording, with students following in their books. To check understanding, ask what they would say in French in the following situations:
- say you'll have some water
- accept something you are offered
- say something is good
- say something is delicious
- say you don't like something very much
- say you've eaten enough of something
- say 'No thank you'
- say you'd like a banana

b Students vary the core conversation, which should help them to learn the key phrases and vocabulary.

À table

– Assieds-toi là, Alex, à côté de Laurent.
– Oui, Madame.
– Qu'est-ce que tu prends comme boisson? Il y a de la limonade et de l'eau.
– De l'eau, s'il vous plaît.
– Pour commencer, il y a du potage aux légumes.
– Bon appétit, tout le monde.
– Mmm! C'est bon, ça.
– Tu veux encore du potage?
– Oui, je veux bien.
– Voilà. Maintenant, il y a du poisson. Et comme légumes, il y a des frites et du chou-fleur.
– C'est délicieux, Madame.
– Tu veux encore du poisson?
– Non, merci, j'ai assez mangé.
– Tu prends de la salade?
– Non, merci, je regrette, mais je n'aime pas beaucoup ça.
– Comme dessert, il y a des fruits. Qu'est-ce que tu prends?
– Je voudrais une banane, s'il vous plaît. Merci.

The conversations are ideal for use with a text manipulation package such as *Fun with Texts*. A reconstruction exercise such as *Copywrite (easy)* would work well, and will help students to remember the new vocabulary accurately. Before the lesson, either type the conversations into the prepared file yourself, or encourage a student to do so (but check it carefully before letting the class loose on the activity!).

SB 104 **SPEAKING/READING**

1 Deux réponses possibles

This task provides practice of the basic phrases for having a meal. It could be done orally first in class or in groups of three, with one person asking the question and the other two giving each reply.

Solution: 1 d/f, 2 e/h, 3 a/j, 4 c/g, 5 b/i

SB 104 **GRAMMAR**

Dossier-langue
Please and thank you

Check that students remember when to use *tu/vous*.

SB 104 **EXTENSION**

2 C'est utile, le dictionnaire

Some familiar or recognisable words are listed in new combinations. Students will find that they know part of each expression. Encourage them to guess the full meaning before looking the words up in a dictionary.

Solution:

1 *une omelette aux champignons* – mushroom omelette
2 *du conconbre* – cucumber
3 *de la crème anglaise* – custard
4 *du riz au lait* – rice pudding
5 *une tarte au citron* – lemon tart/pie
6 *du jus de viande* – gravy
7 *un yaourt aux noisettes* – hazelnut yoghurt
8 *des carottes râpées* – grated carrot
9 *une glace à la vanille* – vanilla ice cream
10 *de la barbe à papa* – candy floss

SB 104 **EXTENSION**

Explain that RSVP stands for *Répondez, s'il vous plaît*.

SB 104, 3/20–21, TB 33, 38 **LISTENING SPEAKING**

Chantez! Pique-nique à la plage

The song introduces some new vocabulary, e.g. *le panier, la plage, une galette, les chips, les petits pains, il ne faut pas, oublier*. This could be written on the board and students could be asked to check the words in the glossary.

The song can be used at any convenient point in the unit. See TB 33 for notes on using the songs, and TB 38 for the musical score.

Pique-nique à la plage

1 Bonne journée! Bonne journée!
Tout le monde va pique-niquer.
Va chercher le panier!
Pique-nique, pique-nique à la plage.

2 Bonne journée! Bonne journée!
Qu'est-ce que nous allons manger?
Des sandwichs, une grande quiche.
Pique-nique, pique-nique à la plage.

3 Bonne journée! Bonne journée!
Regarde dans le panier.
Oh, chouette, une galette!
Pique-nique, pique-nique à la plage.

4 Bonne journée! Bonne journée!
Il ne faut pas oublier
Les chips, le vin, les petits pains.
Pique-nique, pique-nique à la plage.

5 Quelle journée! Quelle journée!
Tout le monde va pique-niquer.
Allons trouver le soleil!
Pique-nique, pique-nique à la plage.

CM 9/5 **READING/SPEAKING**

À table

This provides further practice of having a meal with a family, if required. In Task 2, students practise a dialogue with different variations.

Solution: 1 Questions et réponses
1g, 2e, 3c, 4d, 5f, 6a, 7b

Area 7
The negative
Expressing likes and dislikes
Talking about vegetarianism
SB 105 3–4, SB 106, 1–3
Au choix SB 142, 6–7
CD 3/22
FC 34–55; CM 9/6, 9/7
Grammar in Action 1, page 23
ne … pas; j'aime/je n'aime pas ça

Vous aimez ça? **PRESENTATION/SPEAKING**

This game introduces the idea of the negative by revising *Je n'aime pas*, and gives further practice of food and drink vocabulary.

Half the class is told that it likes vegetables but not fruit, and the other half the reverse. The teacher asks each half a question in turn, e.g. *Vous aimez les pommes?* If the 'vegetable eaters' are asked, they reply *Non, je n'aime pas ça* etc. If they make a mistake the other side wins a point. The game could begin with each half replying in chorus and then individuals could be questioned. As a variation one half could like drinks and the others food.

The first team to lose three points has lost. *J'aime ça* and *Je n'aime pas ça* could be written on the board early in the game and the teacher could point out that the *n'* and the *pas* make one sentence mean the opposite of the other.

3/22 **LISTENING**

C'est bon, ça?

Students listen to these short conversations then write down the numbers 1–8, putting a tick if the person likes the food mentioned and a cross if they don't.

Solution: 1✓, 2✓, 3 ✗, 4 ✗, 5✓, 6 ✗, 7✓, 8✓

C'est bon, ça?

1 – Tu veux encore de la salade de tomates, Jean-Claude?
– Oui, s'il te plaît. C'est délicieux. J'aime beaucoup la salade de tomates.

2 – Je voudrais encore du potage, s'il te plaît, Maman. J'adore le potage.

3 – Vous prenez un thé, Suzanne?
– Non, merci, M. Dublanc. Je n'aime pas le thé.

4 – Tu prends des pommes de terre, Guy?
– Ah non, merci. Je n'aime pas beaucoup les pommes de terre.

5 – Passe-moi du café, s'il te plaît. Mmm, c'est très bon. J'aime beaucoup le café.

6 – Tu prends du vin rouge, Christophe?
– Non, merci. Je n'aime pas le vin.

7 – Encore un peu de gâteau, Anne-Marie?
– Oui, s'il te plaît, Maman. Il est délicieux. J'aime beaucoup les gâteaux.

8 – Est-ce que tu aimes le fromage?
– Oui, j'aime le fromage, surtout le Camembert.

SB 105 **READING/PRESENTATION**

3 Être végétarien

Read the letter aloud, with the class following in their books. Give them a short time to scan through and to work out the gist. Encourage them to ask, in French, about anything they don't understand.

Write 'Nathalie' on one side of the board and 'Simon' on the other. Say a short phrase, e.g. *Cette personne adore les fruits, ne mange pas de viande, mange bien, prend beaucoup d'omelettes*, and then say, or point to, one of the names. The class says *Oui* or *Non*, as appropriate.

Students can then do the *vrai ou faux* task.

Solution: 1F, 2V, 3F, 4F, 5F, 6V, 7F, 8F

Before reading the reply, you could discuss with the class the sort of answer the editor might give (this will probably involve some English). Then read the reply aloud. Finally ask a few general questions about both letters, e.g. *Est-ce que Mme Drouot est contente de Nathalie/Simon? Qui est végétarien/ne?*

SB 105 **READING**

4 Des réponses

Students have to work out which negative phrase completes each sentence, either writing the correct letter or writing out the sentence in full. These sentences are all linked with the theme of vegetarianism.

Solution: 1a/g, 2b, 3f, 4a/g, 5e, 6d, 7h, 8c

This text would work well as a text manipulation exercise, e.g. *Fun with Texts: Clozewrite*. However, the *Clozewrite* program distributes the gaps evenly, e.g. every seventh word, so the task would not be the same as the one on the page. Other packages, e.g. *ML DevTray* do enable you to decide where to put the gaps, but the preparation beforehand is even longer as you have to enter the gaps manually (this is where a student helper is very useful!).

SB 105 **GRAMMAR**

Dossier-langue
The negative

Go through the explanation of the negative, encouraging the class to work out the pattern for themselves, and writing *ne … pas / n' … pas / ne* (verb) *pas* on the board as they are 'discovered', together with some example sentences.

FC 34–42 **SPEAKING**

Qu'est-ce que je fais?

Using the action flashcards, choose one activity and ask *Qu'est-ce que je fais?*

Hold up the flashcards, leaving the activity you have selected until last. Shake your head when showing the activities not chosen, saying *Je ne regarde pas la télé, je n'écoute pas de musique* etc. until you reach the right flashcard, e.g. *Je travaille*.

For further practice, students could be given two flashcards and asked to choose one activity, say which one they are not doing then ask the class what they are doing.

Alternatively, students could choose one activity and the class could ask questions in the negative until they eliminate all but the right answer, as above.

FC 43–55 **SPEAKING**

Où est Mangetout / le chat / etc.?

Similar activities could be based on places in a town, with the teacher or students holding three flashcards and stating, e.g. *Mangetout n'est pas au marché, il n'est pas à la piscine, alors où est-il?*

SB 106 **READING**

1 Le jeu de la carotte

First check that students recognise and remember the words for all the items illustrated.

The clues to the correct answers are in the negative. If some students need help, write the two alternatives on the board and work out one or two answers with them, letting them finish alone.

Solution: **1** *sucre,* **2** *fromage,* **3** *beurre,* **4** *poisson,* **5** *chocolats,* **6** *carotte,* **7** *viande*

SB 106 GRAMMAR

2 Les chiens et les chats

If help is needed, suggest that students pick out the verb and then 'surround' it by *ne ... pas*. The rest of the sentence should then be easily guessable.

Solution:

a **1** *Les chats ne jouent pas avec les enfants.*
2 *Les chats ne sont pas intelligents.*
3 *Les chats ne mangent pas bien.*
4 *Les chats ne restent pas à la maison.*
5 *Les chats n'aiment pas les enfants.*

b **1** *Les chiens ne sont pas indépendants.*
2 *Les chiens ne sont pas intelligents.*
3 *Les chiens ne mangent pas bien.*
4 *Les chiens ne respectent pas les jardins.*
5 *Les chiens n'aiment pas les autres animaux.*

Re-sequencing activities are particularly suited to helping students get to grips with writing negative sentences as they encourage them to think about the order of words in a sentence. The idea of putting *ne* before the verb and *pas* after it is alien to the English speaker, so tasks that reinforce this concept are invaluable.

SB 106 WRITING

3 Je n'aime pas ça!

Students use the simple substitution table to help them with the writing of negative sentences. For extension, this can be expanded to include more things that students actively dislike etc. and also, if wished, to include things which friends or members of the family dislike.

Au choix SB 142 GRAMMAR

6 Mes deux chats

This gives practice in writing negative sentences.

Solution:

1 *Noiraud n'est pas petit.*
2 *Noiraud ne chasse pas les oiseaux.*
3 *Noiraud ne va pas souvent dans la rue.*
4 *Noiraud n'est pas tigré.*
5 *Noiraud ne mange pas beaucoup.*
6 *Noiraud ne joue pas dans le jardin.*
7 *Noiraud n'est pas jeune.*
8 *Noiraud n'aime pas explorer.*

Au choix SB 142 READING/WRITING EXTENSION

7 Les jeunes

This is a more demanding task using a wider range of vocabulary and using *fumer* – to smoke, but using only the third person plural. For support, the missing phrases could be written on the board in jumbled order.

Solution: **1** *ne sont pas,* **2** *ne mangent pas,* **3** *ne fument pas,* **4** *n'ont pas,* **5** *ne portent pas,* **6** *ne regardent pas,* **7** *ne jouent pas,* **8** *ne vont pas,* **9** *ne surfent pas,* **10** *ne sont pas*

CM 9/6 GRAMMAR SUPPORT/CONSOLIDATION

Ça ne va pas!

Further practice of the negative, if required.

Solutions:

1 À la cantine
1e, 2d, 3c, 4a, 5f, 6g, 7b

2 Des problèmes au collège
1g, 2d, 3a, 4c, 5h, 6f, 7e, 8b

3 Complète les phrases
1 *Charlotte n'est pas dans la salle de classe.*
2 *Sophie n'aime pas le dessin.*
3 *Ce n'est pas intéressant.*
4 *L'ordinateur ne marche pas.*
5 *Je n'aime pas l'anglais.*
6 *Aujourd'hui, nous n'avons pas musique.*
7 *Marc ne trouve pas son livre.*
8 *Je n'ai pas de stylo.*

CM 9/7 GRAMMAR EXTENSION

La forme négative

This copymaster provides further practice of the negative.

Solutions:

1 Des expressions utiles
1e, 2a, 3d, 4c, 5b

2 Complète les phrases
a **1** *je ne suis pas,* **2** *Je n'aime pas,* **3** *ne sont pas,* **4** *je n'ai pas,* **5** *ce n'est pas*
b **1** *je ne suis pas,* **2** *ce n'est pas,* **3** *Ce n'est pas,* **4** *ne sont pas,* **5** *je ne suis pas,* **6** *je n'ai pas,* **7** *je n'aime pas, je n'aime pas, je n'aime pas*

3 Des phrases
In this open-ended task, students make up their own sentences using some negative expressions.

4 Luc et Lucie
1d, 2f, 3h, 4a, 5b, 6e, 7c, 8g

Grammar in Action 1, page 23 GRAMMAR

The negative

Further practice of the negative, if required.

This area is an ideal time to introduce expressions for describing problems with computers. There are several negative phrases in the useful expressions (SB149), e.g. *ne marche pas, ne trouve pas, il n'y a pas.* Once students have understood the basic structure, they can manipulate the language to produce many more sentences about computer problems. We hope that this will not become a regular feature of ICT lessons!

Area 8
Further activities and consolidation

SB 106, 4, SB 107
Au choix SB 143, 8
CD 3/23–25
Écoute et parle SB 158, 7, 1–8
Student CD 2/8–15, 39–41
CM 9/8–9/12

This area brings together a selection of items using the themes and language of the unit. They can be used in any order and many are optional.

SB 106, READING WRITING

4 Un message de Dominique

a Students read the message and do the vrai/faux task. More able students could give the reasons why some sentences are false.

Solution: **1F** *(c'est son repas favori)*, **2F** *(d'habitide on mange de la salade de tomates)*, **3F** *(on mange du poulet)*, **4V**, **5F** *(il n'aime pas beaucoup les légumes)*, **6F** *(il adore ça)*, **7F** *(c'est la limonade)*

b They then write a reply to Dominique, preferably on a computer. If done as an e-mail, it could be sent to a class in France or to a different class in the same school.

SB 107, SB 158, TB 179, SCD 2/14

Vocabulaire de classe

The instructions are also recorded in random order in the *Écoute et parle* section (see TB 179).

Solution: **1c, 2f, 3a, 4h, 5e, 6b, 7g, 8d**

Au choix SB 143 READING/WRITING

8 La fête autour du monde

For extension work, students could read the descriptions of four different festivals and do the related tasks.

a A dictionary task based on new vocabulary used in the text.

Solution:

agneau (m)	lamb	*dinde (f)*	turkey
bâton (m)	stick	*lumière (f)*	light
bûche de Noël (f)	Christmas log	*marron (m)*	chestnut
citrouille (f)	pumpkin	*récolte (f)*	harvest

b Students find two sentences to describe each festival.

Solution: **1 b, h; 2 d, f; 3 c, e; 4 a, g**

c Students write a description of a special meal, e.g. for a festival or a birthday celebration. A detailed example is given, but students could write a shorter description.

Students who are familiar with Eid, Thanksgiving and Diwali could give more information. The Islamic and Hindu calendars are different from the Gregorian calendar used in Europe (see TB 32), so the months do not entirely correspond. Ramadan can occur at various times of the year. Diwali is in October or November.

CM 9/8, SCD 2/39–41 INDEPENDENT LISTENING

Tu comprends?

1 Le déjeuner

Solution: **1c, 2b, 3c, 4b, 5c, 6b**

Le déjeuner

– Qu'est-ce qu'on mange aujourd'hui pour le déjeuner?
– Pour commencer, il y a du jambon.
– Alors comme hors-d'œuvre, il y a du jambon.
– Oui, et comme plat principal, il y a du poisson.
– Mmm, j'aime bien le poisson. Et comme légumes?
– Comme légumes, il y a des petits pois.
– Des petits pois, oui.
– Et ensuite, il y a du fromage.
– Ah, j'aime bien le fromage. Et comme dessert?
– Comme dessert, il y a un gâteau au chocolat.
– Un gâteau au chocolat, chouette!
– Et comme boisson, il y a de l'eau minérale.
– De l'eau minérale, bien.

2 Qu'est-ce qu'on prend?

Solutions: **A 1b, 2a, 3g, 4h, 5d, 6e**
B 1f, 2d, 3g, 4b, 5a, 6c

Qu'est-ce qu'on prend?

A Des boissons

1 – Qu'est-ce que vous prenez, comme boisson?
– Je prends un café, s'il te plaît.

2 – Pour moi, un thé.
– Un thé, oui.

3 – Et Thomas, qu'est-ce qu'il prend?
– Alors pour Thomas, du lait, s'il te plaît.
– Un verre de lait, oui.

4 – Et toi, Nicole?
– Pour moi, un coca, s'il te plaît.
– Un coca, d'accord.

5 – Et toi, Luc?
– Un jus d'orange, s'il te plaît.

6 – Très bien, et pour moi, un chocolat chaud.

B Des fruits

– Comme dessert, il y a des fruits, alors qu'est-ce que vous prenez?
1 – Pour moi, des raisins, s'il vous plaît.
2 – Moi, je prends une pêche.
3 – Mmm, moi j'adore les fraises, alors je prends des fraises.
4 – Moi, je voudrais une poire.
5 – Pour moi, une pomme, s'il vous plaît.
6 – Et moi, je prends une banane.

3 Positive ou négative?

Solution: 1 ✓, 2 ✗, 3 ✗, 4 ✗, 5 ✓, 6 ✗, 7 ✗, 8 ✗

Positive ou négative?

1 – Est-ce qu'il y a du pain?
– Voilà le pain.

2 – Et avez-vous du beurre?
– Je regrette, il n'y a pas de beurre.

3 – Est-ce qu'il y a de la confiture?
– Nous n'avons pas de confiture.

4 – Tu prends du chou-fleur?
– Je regrette, mais je n'aime pas le chou-fleur.

5 – Est-ce qu'il y a du lait?
– Bien sûr, il y a du lait.

6 – Est-ce que Claire mange de la viande?
– Elle est végétarienne, alors elle ne mange pas de viande.

7 – Tu prends du sucre?
– Merci, je ne prends pas de sucre.

8 – Tu veux du fromage?
– Merci, je n'aime pas beaucoup le fromage.

SB 107, CM 9/9

Sommaire

A summary of the main vocabulary and structures of the unit.

SB 158, SCD 2/8–15 SOUNDS AND WRITING INDEPENDENT LISTENING

Écoute et parle – Unité 9

1 Les sons français

Solution: oi: (a) 1b, 2d, 3f, 4a, 5c, 6e
ai: (a) 1c, 2b, 3a, 4d

Les sons français

Les lettres oi

a 1 boisson **2** revoir **3** quoi
4 soir **5** toi **6** boîte

b histoire, soixante, moi, emploi, droite

Les lettres ai

a 1 raison **2** raison **3** vrai **4** vaisselle

b lait, mai, maison, j'ai

2 Des phrases ridicules

Des phrases ridicules

Toi, tu as histoire ce soir, alors, moi, je dis «au revoir».
C'est vrai, tu as raison. En mai, j'ai du lait dans la maison.

3 Les mots qui riment

Solution: (a) 1d, 2h, 3g, 4b, 5f, 6a, 7c, 8e

Les mots qui riment

a

Liste A	Liste B
1 faux	**a** qui
2 vrai	**b** gare
3 sont	**c** là
4 quart	**d** beau
5 êtes	**e** je
6 si	**f** fête
7 pas	**g** mon
8 ne	**h** vais

b
1d faux, beau **5f** êtes, fête
2h vrai, vais **6a** si, qui
3g sont, mon **7c** pas, là
4b quart, gare **8e** ne, je

4 Les sons français

Solution: 1a –, b z, 2 a –, b z, 3 a z, b –, 4 a z, b –, 5 a –, b z, 6a z, b –

Les sons français

La lettre s à la fin d'un mot

1 a nous travaillons **b** nous avons
2 a vous jouez **b** vous êtes
3 a nous aimons **b** nous regardons
4 a vous habitez **b** vous pensez
5 a nous cherchons **b** nous écoutons
6 a vous ouvrez **b** vous fermez

5 Et après?

Solution: 1d, 2g, 3h, 4j, 5l, 6p, 7s, 8w, 9z, 10b, 11e, 12i, 13n, 14q, 15t, 16x

Et après?

1	c	**5**	k	**9**	y	**13**	m
2	f	**6**	o	**10**	a	**14**	p
3	g	**7**	r	**11**	d	**15**	s
4	i	**8**	v	**12**	h	**16**	w

6 Plus dix

Solution: 1 *quatre-vingt-dix,* **2** *vingt,* **3** *cinquante,* **4** *soixante-dix,* **5** *trente,* **6** *cent,* **7** *quarante,* **8** *quatre-vingts*

Plus dix

1 quatre-vingts **5** vingt
2 dix **6** quatre-vingt-dix
3 quarante **7** trente
4 soixante **8** soixante-dix

7 Vocabulaire de classe

Solution: 5, 8, 3, 1, 7, 2, 6, 4

Vocabulaire de classe

Regarde la page 107. Écoute le CD et écris le nombre de chaque instruction dans l'ordre du CD.

Ce n'est pas difficile.

Je n'ai pas fini.
Je n'ai pas mon livre.
Ne parlez pas anglais.
Ce n'est pas facile.
Je ne comprends pas ce mot.
Je ne trouve pas mon cahier.
Je n'ai pas de stylo.

8 Une conversation

Une conversation

a Écoute les questions et réponds comme indiqué.

– Qu'est-ce que tu prends normalement au petit déjeuner?
(pause)
– Des céréales, des toasts et du jus d'orange.
– Quelle est ta boisson préférée?
(pause)
– La limonade.
– Qu'est-ce que tu aimes manger?
(pause)
– J'adore les frites et la pizza.
– Est-ce qu'il y a quelque chose que tu n'aimes pas?
(pause)
– Je n'aime pas les petits pois.

b Écoute les questions et réponds pour toi.

– Qu'est-ce que tu prends normalement au petit déjeuner?
– (pause)
– Quelle est ta boisson préférée?
– (pause)
– Qu'est-ce que tu aimes manger?
– (pause)
– Est-ce qu'il y a quelque chose que tu n'aimes pas?
– (pause)

Épreuve – Unité 9

CM 9/10, 3/23–25 **INFORMAL ASSESSMENT LISTENING**

Épreuve: Écouter

A Le pique-nique (NC 1)

Solution: 1f, 2j, 3b, 4a, 5h, 6g, 7c, 8e (mark /7)

Le pique-nique

Qu'est-ce qu'il y a pour le pique-nique?

1 Il y a du pain, du pain,
2 du jambon, du jambon,
3 du fromage, du fromage,
4 des tomates, des tomates,
5 des œufs, des œufs,
6 des pommes, des pommes,
7 des raisins, des raisins.
8 Et comme boisson? Comme boisson, il y a de la limonade. Ah bon, j'aime bien la limonade.

B Le petit déjeuner (NC 2)

Solution: (mark /6: $^1/_2$ mark per correct tick)

	bread etc.	cereal	juice	coffee	milk	choc	tea
1	✔			✔			
2	✔						✔
3	✔	✔	✔				
4		✔				✔	
5	✔				✔		
6	✔	✔		✔			

Le petit déjeuner

1 – Au petit déjeuner, je prends du café au lait et des tartines avec du beurre.
– Alors, tu prends du café comme boisson et du pain avec du beurre, c'est tout?
– Oui, c'est tout.

2 – Le matin, je prends des tartines avec du beurre et de la confiture et un bol de thé.
– Tu prends du thé comme boisson et du pain avec du beurre et de la confiture, c'est ça?
– Oui, c'est ça.

3 – Pour mon petit déjeuner, je prends du jus de fruit et des céréales. Et je prends aussi des tartines au beurre.
– Comme boisson, tu prends un jus de fruit, et avec ça tu prends des céréales et des tartines avec du beurre.

4 – Et moi, je prends un chocolat chaud comme boisson et je mange des céréales.
– Alors, tu prends un chocolat chaud et des céréales, c'est tout?
– Oui, c'est tout.

5 – Le matin, je prends des tartines avec du beurre et de la confiture et je bois du lait.
– Bon, tu prends du lait comme boisson et tu manges du pain avec du beurre et de la confiture, c'est ça?
– Oui, c'est ça.

6 – Pour mon petit déjeuner, je prends des céréales et des tartines avec du beurre et je bois du café.
– Alors, comme boisson, tu prends un café, et avec ça tu prends des céréales et des tartines avec du beurre.
– Oui, c'est ça.

C À table (NC 3)

Solution: 1a, 2c, 3b, 4a, 5b, 6a, 7b, 8a (mark /7)

À table

– Assieds-toi là, Claire, à côté de Sophie.
– Oui, Madame.
– Qu'est-ce que tu prends, comme boisson? Il y a de la limonade et de l'eau.
– De la limonade, s'il vous plaît.
– Pour commencer, il y a de la salade aux tomates.
– Bon appétit, tout le monde.
– Mmm! C'est bon, ça.
...

– Voilà, maintenant, il y a de l'omelette au fromage. Et comme légumes, il y a des pommes de terre et du chou.
– C'est délicieux, Madame.
– Tu veux encore de l'omelette?
– Non, merci, j'ai assez mangé.
...
– Tu prends de la salade?
– Oui, s'il vous plaît.
– Et comme fromage, il y a du Camembert. Tu prends du fromage, Claire?
– Non, merci, je regrette mais je n'aime pas beaucoup ça.
– Comme dessert, il y a des fruits. Qu'est-ce que tu prends?
– Je voudrais une pêche, s'il vous plaît. Merci.

CM 9/11 **READING**

Épreuve: Lire

A Le déjeuner (NC 1)

Solution: **1a, 2f, 3b, 4d, 5c, 6h, 7g, 8e** (mark /7)

B Mon repas idéal (NC 2)

Solution: **1F, 2V, 3F, 4F, 5F, 6F, 7F** (mark /6)

C Une conversation (NC 2)

Solution: **1d, 2h, 3a** (accept **e**), **4f, 5b** (accept **e**), **6e** (accept **b**), **7c, 8g** (mark /7)

CM 9/12 **WRITING/GRAMMAR**

Épreuve: Écrire et grammaire

A Une liste (NC 1)

Solution: **1** *du pain,* **2** *du beurre,* **3** *de la confiture,* **4** *des carottes,* **5** *de l'eau (minérale),* **6** *des pommes* (mark /5: $^1/_2$ mark for correct partitive, $^1/_2$ mark for correct noun)

B Qu'est-ce qu'on prend? (NC 1)

Solution: **1** *prenez,* **2** *prenons,* **3** *prennent,* **4** *prend,* **5** *prends,* **6** *prends* (mark /5: 1 mark per correct answer)

C Ça ne va pas! (NC 1)

Solution: **1** *Il ne fait pas beau.* **2** *Je ne joue pas au football.* **3** *Mes amis ne téléphonent pas.* **4** *Je ne suis pas content.* (mark /6: 1 for correct verb, 1 for correct *ne ... pas*)

D Mon repas idéal (NC 3)

Solution: This is an open-ended task. (mark /4: give 1 mark for each item listed)

SB 108–109 **REVISION/CONSOLIDATION**

Rappel 4

This section can be used at any point after *Unité* 9 for revision and consolidation. It provides reading and writing activities which are self-instructional and can be used by students working individually for homework or during cover lessons.

SB 108

1 Où sont les voyelles?

Solution:

1 *juillet,* **2** *novembre,* **3** *septembre,* **4** *avril,* **5** *mai,* **6** *l'anglais,* **7** *l'histoire,* **8** *la géographie,* **9** *la musique,* **10** *la technologie*
11 *vert,* **12** *rouge,* **13** *jaune,* **14** *noir,* **15** *blanc,* **16** *le jogging,* **17** *la chemise,* **18** *le pantalon,* **19** *les chaussettes,* **20** *la cravate*

SB 108

2 Des listes

Solution: **1** *mercredi,* **2** *le soir,* **3** *il est une heure et quart,* **4** *troisième,* **5** *l'hiver,* **6** *le déjeuner*

SB 108

3 Masculin, féminin

Solution:

masculin		***féminin***	
le matin	*le fromage*	*une carotte*	*une cassette*
le dessin	*un lapin*	*la confiture*	*une disquette*
le potage	*un village*	*la limonade*	*une omelette*
		une pomme	*la salade*

SB 108

4 C'est quel verbe?

Solution: **1** *J'ai,* **2** *j'aime,* **3** *Je vais,* **4** *je prends,* **5** *je suis,* **6** *j'aime, je vais,* **7** *j'aime, je suis,* **8** *j'ai*

SB 108

5 Une lettre

Solution: **1** *mon,* **2** *mes,* **3** *ma,* **4** *mes,* **5** *leur,* **6** *leurs,* **7** *nos,* **8** *ton,* **9** *ta,* **10** *mon*

SB 109

6 La journée de Mangetout

Solution:

a **a** *entre,* **b** *reste,* **c** *commence,* **d** *mange,* **e** *retourne,* **f** *cherche,* **g** *pense,* **h** *chasse*
b **1b, 2a, 3f, 4c, 5h, 6g, 7d, 8e**

SB 109

7 Questions et réponses

Solution: **1c, 2g, 3e, 4b, 5a, 6j, 7d, 8f, 9h, 10i**

SB 109

8 À toi!

This is an open-ended task.

unité 10 Amuse-toi bien!

Areas	Topics	Grammar
1	Talking about sport	Present tense of *faire* (D-L 111)
2	Talking about music and other activities	*jouer à, jouer de* (D-L 113)
3	Discussing leisure activities and expressing opinions	
4	Helping at home Giving reasons and opinions	Using a verb + an infinitive (D-L 116)
5	Using the 24-hour clock	
6		Possessive adjectives (D-L 118)
7	Describing an ideal day Expressing opinions	
8	Further activities and consolidation	

National Curriculum information

Some students	Level 3–4
Most students	Levels 2–3+
All students	Level 2

Refer also to the information about coverage of 'Knowledge, skills and understanding' (TB 9).

Revision

The vocabulary and structures needed for the *Contrôle* at the end of this unit are mainly revised in the *Rappel* section following *Unité 9* (SB 108–109, TB 181).

Presse-Jeunesse 4 offers opportunities for reading for pleasure (SB 122–125, TB 199).

Sounds and writing

- letters *tion*, *ui*, the sound 'ye'
- final e on a word
- see *Écoute et parle* (SB 159, TB 196)

ICT opportunities

- making an electronic phrase book (TB 184, 192)
- whole class e-mail exchanges (TB 188)
- matching up suitable penfriends (TB 188)
- text reconstruction activities (TB 188)

Reading strategies

Reading to obtain specific information – scanning the text rather than reading every word.
Using grammatical clues – identifying verbs, adjectives and nouns by their context to aid understanding (CM 107–108).

Assessment

- Informal assessment is in the *Épreuves* at the end of this unit (TB 197).
- Formal assessment is in the *Troisième contrôle* following this unit (TB 203). There are also alternative tasks following *Unité 9* (TB 206).

Students' Book

Unité 10 SB 110–121

Au choix SB 144 1, 2 (TB 185), 3 (TB 187), 4 (TB 188)
SB 145 5 (TB 190), 6 (TB 192)
SB 146 7, 8 (TB 193), 9 (TB 194)

Écoute et parle SB 159 (TB 196)

Presse-Jeunesse SB 122–125 (TB 199)

Flashcards

1, 2	opinions
5, 23	gardening, riding
34–42	activities
46	swimming
90–95	leisure
96–100	household tasks

Copymasters

10/1	*Les loisirs* [extension] (TB 186)
10/2	*faire* [grammar] (TB 186)
10/3	*À la maison* [support] (TB 190)
10/4	*Sébastien et Vivienne* [speaking: information gap] (TB 190)
10/5	*24 heures* [grammar] (TB 192)
10/6	*C'est à qui?* [grammar] (TB 193)
10/7	*La page des lettres* [extension] (TB 194)
10/8	*Tu comprends?* [independent listening] (TB 195)
10/9	*Sommaire* (TB 196)
10/10	*Épreuve: Écouter* (TB 197)
10/11	*Épreuve: Lire* (TB 198)
10/12	*Épreuve: Écrire et grammaire* (TB 198)
107–108	*Presse-Jeunesse 4* (TB 199)
121–126	*Troisième contrôle* (TB 203)

Additional

Grammar in Action 1, pp 34–37

CDs

3/26–40
Student CD 2/16–21, 42–45

Language content

Sporting activities (Area 1)

Est-ce que tu aimes le sport?

Je joue *au badminton.*
au cricket.
au football.
au golf.
au rugby.
au tennis.

Je fais *de la gymnastique.*
du cyclisme.
du VTT.
de l'équitation.
de la natation
de la planche à voile.
du ski.
de la voile.
du roller.
du skate.

Music and other activities (Area 2)

Est-ce que tu aimes la musique?

Je joue *du piano.*
du violon.
de la guitare.
de la flûte.
de la batterie.

J'aime la musique, mais je ne joue pas d'un instrument.

Est-ce que tu fais autre chose?

Je fais *du dessin.*
de la peinture.
du théâtre.
des photos.

Je joue *à l'ordinateur.*
aux cartes.
aux échecs.
aux jeux vidéo.

Helping at home (Area 4)

faire la cuisine
faire la vaisselle
faire les courses
laver la voiture
passer l'aspirateur
ranger la chambre
travailler dans le jardin

24-hour clock (Area 5)

treize
quatorze
quinze
seize
dix-sept
dix-huit
dix-neuf
vingt
vingt et un
vingt-deux
vingt-trois
vingt-quatre

Holiday items (Area 6)

On part en vacances.
Qu'est-ce qu'on prend?
anorak (m)
appareil(-photo) (m)
chemise (f)
chemisier (m)
jean (m)
lunettes de soleil (f pl)
maillot de bain (m)
parapluie (m)
pyjama (m)
sandales (f pl)
valise (f)
veste (f)

Classroom language and rubrics

Qui a fini?
J'ai fini.
J'ai oublié ma trousse.
J'ai oublié mon cahier.
J'ai gagné.
Je n'ai pas fait mes devoirs.
Tu as oublié ton livre?
Vous avez fini?

On-going activities

This unit would be a suitable time for students to put the finishing touches to their self-description files, electronic phrase books and verb tables. This work could form part of consolidation or revision activities at the end of the year's work, possibly with students working in pairs or groups to compare notes and fill in any gaps.

Area 1
Talking about sport
Present tense of *faire*
SB 110–111, 1–4
Au choix SB 144, 1–2
FC 23, 38–40, 46, 91–93
CD 3/26
Grammar in Action 1, page 34

FC 23, 38–40, 46, 91–93 **PRESENTATION**

Les sports

- Begin by revising the sports taught earlier (*badminton, basket, football, golf, tennis, tennis de table, rugby, volley*) – see *Unité 6*. Use flashcards 38–40 and any others that you have. Supplementary flashcards could be made.
- Using flashcards, give plenty of question and answer work, e.g. *Qu'est-ce qu'il/elle fait? Il/Elle joue au football/tennis/tennis de table* etc. Then give flashcards out to students for practice of the first and second persons.
- Gradually introduce the following sports, e.g. using flashcards 23 (riding), 46 (swimming), 91 (skate-boarding), 92 (roller skating/blading), 93 (cycling). Ask questions, e.g.
Est-ce que tu fais de l'équitation/de la natation/du skate/du roller/du patin à roulettes/du cyclisme?

SB 110 **READING**

1 Les loisirs en France

Go through the article in the Students' Book with the class, reading the captions, teaching the other new words (*faire de la voile/de la planche à voile/du VTT/des promenades*) and asking questions, e.g. *Qu'est-ce qu'on fait comme sport dans la photo d?*

Ask volunteers to read out different captions and ask each other questions.

For reinforcement, you could play a game such as *Jeu de mémoire* (this could be a group activity, each group being asked in turn to name one of the activities described until all have been mentioned), *Effacez!* or *Le jeu des mimes* (see TB 26–28).

SB 110, 3/26 **LISTENING**

2 Faites-vous du sport?

Students listen and write down the letter of the photo illustrating the sport mentioned. The answers could be checked orally and discussion could follow, e.g. *Cette personne fait du cyclisme. Tu aimes le cyclisme, Jane? Qui fait du cyclisme le week-end?* etc.

Solution: 1g, 2f, 3c, 4a, 5h, 6e, 7d, 8b

Faites-vous du sport?

1 – Qu'est-ce que vous faites comme sport, Monsieur?
– Moi, je fais des promenades, euh, des promenades avec mon chien.

2 – Qu'est-ce que vous faites comme sport, Mademoiselle?
– Je fais de l'équitation. J'adore les chevaux, mais je ne suis pas très sportive!

3 – Et toi, Christine, toi et ton frère? Vous faites du sport?
– Oui, oui. En été, nous faisons de la planche à voile.
– Il y a un grand lac près d'ici où on fait de la planche à voile.

4 – Est-ce que vous faites du sport, Mademoiselle?
– Oui, je fais de la natation. Je vais à la piscine tous les samedis.

5 – Est-ce que vous faites du sport, les garçons?
– Oui, nous faisons du skate.
– Du skate. Où faites-vous ça?
– Au centre sportif – c'est très populaire.

6 – Qu'est-ce que tu fais comme sports, Lucie?
– Je fais du roller, avec mes copines.
– Ah, le patin à roulettes, tu aimes ça?
– J'adore ça. On va très vite, c'est fantastique!

7 – Est-ce que vous faites du sport en famille, Madame?
– Nous faisons du cyclisme – ça, c'est un sport qu'on fait ensemble. C'est bien.

8 – Quel est ton sport préféré, Richard?
Pour moi, c'est la voile. J'aime beaucoup faire de la voile avec mes cousins. C'est amusant!

SB 111 **READING**

3 Qu'est-ce qu'ils font?

Students match up captions and pictures. Check the answers orally to give practice of the different parts of *faire* as well as names of sports.

Solution: 1d, 2b, 3h, 4g, 5f, 6c, 7a, 8e

SB 111, **GRAMMAR**

Dossier-langue
Faire – a very useful verb

Students should look for the different parts of *faire* in the cartoons above to complete the paradigm. As they have been meeting parts of the present tense of *faire* since *Unité 6* and more intensively in this unit, most of them should not have much difficulty with completing the paradigm itself.

As extension, point out other uses of *faire*, for instance ask students to think of all the different examples they can remember in which *faire* is used for the weather.

Ask them to guess what the following expressions mean and eventually add them to their vocabulary lists or electronic phrase book (see TB 40): *faire les courses, faire des photos, faire un gâteau, faire les devoirs, faire de la lecture, faire un film, faire de la peinture.*

With more able students, there are a lot of possibilities for exploiting more fully the information about the use and meanings of *faire*, e.g.

- they could study the *Dossier-langue* for a few minutes, then compete in teams to answer, from memory, the question *Comment dit-on … en français?*

- students work in pairs, each setting a short test for another pair. These should be a standard length, as stated by the teacher, and could be written on paper or on computer. They could include expressions in French or English, from the *Dossier-langue*, to be translated, e.g.
  Quel temps fait-il? ....
  .... It's cold. etc.

  or French or English expressions with missing words to be supplied, e.g.
  Vous .... *de l'équitation?*
  Nous faisons les courses. We are doing ....

SB 111 **READING/SPEAKING**

4 Qu'est-ce qu'on fait?

More able students could omit this task and do instead the slightly harder version in *Au choix*, Task 1.

Some students might need guidance in how to look for the right pronoun in the answer to match it with the question. They can just jot down the matching numbers and letters, but, for more practice, they could then read out the questions and answers in pairs like short conversations.

Solution: 1b, 2g, 3c, 4f, 5a, 6e, 7h, 8d

Follow-up **CONSOLIDATION**

For further practice of *faire* some students could play a miming game, but this time asking *Qu'est-ce que je fais?* and guesses being made in sentences: *Tu fais de l'équitation?* etc.

Au choix SB 144 **EXTENSION**

1 Questions et réponses

In parts a and b, students complete the questions and answers with the correct part of *faire*. In part c they have to match up questions and answers.

Solution:

a **1** *tu fais,* **2** *elle fait,* **3** *elles font,* **4** *ils font,* **5** *je fais,* **6** *il fait,* **7** *vous faites*
b **a** *Tu fais,* **b** *il fait, je fais,* **c** *Elles font,* **d** *Nous faisons,* **e** *Il fait,* **f** *Ils font,* **g** *Elle fait*
c **1b, 2g, 3c, 4f, 5a, 6e, 7d**

Au choix SB 144 **EXTENSION GRAMMAR/WRITING**

2 On fait de la voile

This task provides practice in using all parts of *faire*. This could eventually be read aloud by groups of three students and acted like a short sketch.

Solution: **1** *fais,* **2** *fais,* **3** *fait,* **4** *font,* **5** *fait,* **6** *fait,* **7** *faisons,* **8** *faites,* **9** *faisons,* **10** *fais,* **11** *faites*

Grammar in Action 1, page 34 **GRAMMAR**

Using the verb *faire*

This would give useful consolidation of *faire* and could be used now or later, for revision.

Area 2
Talking about music and other activities
jouer à, jouer de

SB 112–113, 1–3
Au choix SB 144, 3
CM 10/1, 10/2 (or in Area 3)
FC 34–37, 41–42, 90, 94, 95
CD 3/27
Grammar in Action 1, page 36

FC 35, 94 **PRESENTATION**

Music

Teach the words for musical instruments, using flashcards, actual instruments or the photos (SB 112).

Revise *jouer* (*Unité 6*) and introduce *jouer de* + instrument with questions, e.g.

Regardez la photo. On joue de quel instrument? Qui joue d'un instrument de musique? Thomas, tu joues de quel instrument? etc.

Make sure you also teach the names of any instruments that students actually play, e.g. recorder – *une flûte (à bec)*, cello – *un violoncelle*, double bass – *une contrebasse*, trumpet – *une trompette*, clarinet – *une clarinette*.

SB 112, 3/27 **READING LISTENING**

1 On aime la musique

a Talk briefly about the pictures, e.g. *Voici de jeunes Français. Ils aiment écouter de la musique – comme vous, non? Tous ces enfants jouent d'un instrument. Regardez, on joue du piano, du violon* etc.

Then students choose the right instrument from the box to complete the captions, jotting down the numbers and letters.

Solution: 1c, 2e, 3d, 4f, 5a, 6b

b Play the recording so the answers can be checked against it. Then ask volunteers to read out the captions and follow this with questions, asking some yourself and then asking students to question each other, e.g. *Alain joue de quel instrument? Qui joue du violon? Il joue dans un groupe – c'est qui?* etc.

On aime la musique

En France, presque tous les jeunes aiment écouter de la musique, la radio, des cassettes, mais surtout des CDs.
Souvent, ils jouent d'un instrument, par exemple, Alain joue de la flûte à bec et sa sœur, Marie, joue du piano.
Voici Natalie qui joue du violon.
Voici Christophe et Luc. Ils jouent de la batterie au Club de Jeunes.
Et voici leur ami, David, qui joue de la guitare.
Il fait de la musique pop et il joue dans un groupe.

FC 41, 42, 90, 95 **PRESENTATION**

Other activities

Teach the words for any of these other activities which have not been met already: *jouer aux jeux vidéo/aux cartes/aux échecs/à l'ordinateur, faire de la peinture/du dessin/des photos/du théâtre/de la lecture.*

Continue with oral question and answer work as above, but enlarge the range to include the new vocabulary and use lots of examples of *jouer de* + instruments and *jouer à* + games and other activities.

SB 112 **READING SPEAKING**

2 D'autres activités

Read aloud the introductory paragraph and then students do the short task matching captions to the pictures.

Check this orally asking for complete sentences, then ask questions about who does/likes/dislikes the five activities pictured here.

Solution: 1b, 2e, 3a, 4c, 5d

SB 112 **EXTENSION**

This short item encourages dictionary work to find the two meanings of *un trombone*.

SB 113 **GRAMMAR**

Dossier-langue
Jouer (to play) + *à* or *de*

Most students will by now have understood the pattern *jouer de* + instruments and *jouer à* + games.

Ask one or two to explain the point and to make up some examples to illustrate it.

SB 113 **READING WRITING**

3 C'est quelle activité?

Students complete the captions with the various forms of *à* or *de* and match up the captions and pictures. They could just write the prepositions, but it would be good practice to write out the sentences in full.

Solution: **1b** *du*, **2g** *de la*, **3f** *de la*, **4c** *de la*, **5h** *au*, **6e** *aux*, **7d** *aux*, **8a** *de la*

Follow-up **SUPPORT**

Most students could do at least part of CM 10/1 and 10/2. In addition, more able students could do the dictionary activity, *Au choix*, Task 3 (see below).

As an alternative to the *Au choix* task, other students could play one of these games to practise leisure activities.

1 Chain game

There are several possible versions of this, e.g.

- the first person says *Je joue de la flûte*. The next repeats this and adds on another instrument etc.
- as above, but alternating sports and musical activities
- as above, but adding days of the week, e.g. *Le lundi, je joue de la flûte; le mardi, je fais du dessin* etc.

2 Qu'est-ce que tu fais?

Students write symbols for an activity or activities that they do (possibly in the form of a diary) and then take it in turns to guess what their partner does. The winner is the first to guess the activity or activities of their partner.

GRAMMAR IN ACTION 1, PAGE 36 **GRAMMAR**

Using *jouer à* and *jouer de*

This page of graded activities could be used now or later, for revision.

CM 10/1 **EXTENSION**

Les loisirs

This copymaster has an incline of difficulty. The first two items offer support for spelling and writing sport and other leisure vocabulary.

The other two tasks also practise this vocabulary but require more reading. Either use the complete sheet with all students, letting them see how much they can do, or differentiate by setting the first two tasks to some and the others to the more able.

Solutions:

1 Des sports et des loisirs
1e, 2c, 3b, 4a, 5j, 6h, 7i, 8g, 9d, 10f

2 Où sont les voyelles?
1. *la peinture* = painting
2. *des promenades* = walks
3. *la voile* = sailing
4. *faire de la natation* = to go swimming
5. *la lecture* = reading
6. *jouer aux échecs* = to play chess
7. *jouer du violon* = to play the violin
8. *faire des photos* = to take photos
9. *faire du ski* = to go skiing
10. *jouer de la batterie* = to play the drums

3 Le jeu des définitions
1b, 2d, 3f, 4c, 5h, 6e, 7g, 8a

4 Une semaine active
1. *Lundi, je joue au badminton.*
2. *Mardi, je joue sur l'ordinateur.*
3. *Mercredi, je joue au football.*
4. *Jeudi, je fais de l'équitation.*
5. *Vendredi, je fais du skate.*
6. *Samedi, je fais de la natation.*
7. *Dimanche, je fais du cyclisme/vélo/VTT.*

CM 10/2 **GRAMMAR**

faire

This gives practice of *faire*. There is some incline of difficulty, but most students should be able to cope with all the tasks.

Solutions:

2 Questions
1 *fait,* 2 *faites,* 3 *font,* 4 *fais,* 5 *fait,* 6 *fait,* 7 *fait,* 8 *font*

3 Réponses
a *fait,* **b** *fait,* **c** *fait, fait,* **d** *faisons,* **e** *fait,* **f** *font,* **g** *fais,* **h** *fait, fait*

4 Trouve les paires
1c, 2d, 3f, 4g, 5a, 6b, 7e, 8h

5 Mots croisés

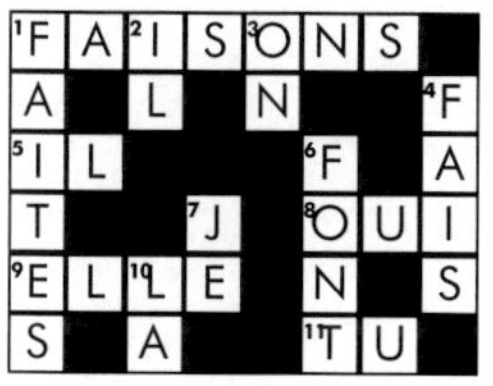

Au choix SB 144 **EXTENSION**

3 C'est utile, le dictionnaire

This gives dictionary practice with some different sports and activities.

Solution:

athlétisme (m) = athletics
babyfoot (m) = table football
boules (f pl) = bowls
boxe (f) = boxing
jeu (m) de société = board game
mots croisés (m pl) = crossword puzzle
pêche (f) = fishing
plongée (f) = diving
puzzle (m) = jigsaw puzzle
sports (m pl) d'hiver = winter sports

Area 3
Discussing leisure activities and expressing opinions

SB 113, 4, SB 114, 1–2
Au choix SB 144, 4
CD 3/28–29

This area adds little new vocabulary, but the tasks are a bit harder than in the previous two areas, so it could be omitted by the least able students.

Leisure **PRESENTATION**

Begin with more discussion about leisure, bringing in questions about preferences and giving plenty of practice of other activities, asking *Est-ce que tu fais autre chose/d'autres activités?*

SB 113, 3/28,  **SPEAKING WRITING EXTENSION**

4 Le jeu des interviews

In parts a and b, students listen to a sample conversation, then interview each other in pairs about what leisure activities they like and do. They write down the responses they receive on a piece of paper, giving a mini-portrait of the person interviewed. Ask students to read through part b and see what they are supposed to do, before listening to the example.

Le jeu des interviews

– Est-ce que tu aimes le sport?
– Oui, j'aime le sport.
– Qu'est-ce que tu fais comme sport?
– Je fais de la natation et je joue au tennis.
– Est-ce que tu aimes la musique?
– Oui, j'aime beaucoup la musique.
– Est-ce que tu joues d'un instrument de musique?
– Non, je ne joue pas d'un instrument, mais j'aime écouter des CDs.
– Est-ce que tu as d'autres activités comme loisirs?
– Oui, j'aime la lecture et je joue aux cartes avec mes amis.

For support, the teacher could pause the recording and write the reported (3rd person) replies on the board after each exchange, e.g.

1 *Elle aime le sport*
2 *Elle fait de la natation et elle joue au tennis.*
3 *Elle aime la musique*
4 *Elle ne joue pas d'un instrument.*
5 *Elle aime la lecture et elle joue aux cartes.*

c The sheets with the mini-portraits on are then collected and re-distributed. Students have to identify the person who gave the responses on their paper by interviewing each other again till they find a match. (For practical reasons, it would be best to divide the class into groups and collect and re-distribute the sheets within each group to make identification more feasible.)

d As an alternative to just noting down the answers, students could prepare questionnaires on the computer and print them out for use in this activity, so they only have to tick boxes or write in a word or two. It would be best to keep these simple and the teacher could choose one or two to use as the standard class version (see the sample, SB 113).

SB 114 **READING WRITING**

1 On cherche un(e) correspondant(e)

Before they work on the two tasks below, students read this correspondence, perhaps with volunteers reading some letters aloud. The letters give further practice with leisure vocabulary and include quite a lot of opinions.

a Students identify the person referred to by looking for relevant information in the letters.

Solution: **1** *Jean,* **2** *Sandrine,* **3** *Paul,* **4** *Caroline,* **5** *Caroline,* **6** *Paul,* **7** *Sandrine,* **8** *Paul,* **9** *Sandrine,* **10** *Sandrine*

b Students write answers in complete sentences.

Solution: (other answers might also be correct)

1 *Non, il n'est pas sportif.*
2 *C'est le tennis.*
3 *Il s'appelle Pistache.*
4 *Il joue de la guitare.*
5 *Non, il n'habite pas en ville / il habite à la montagne.*
6 *Elle joue aux échecs avec son frère.*
7 *Sandrine habite en Normandie.*
8 *Sandrine fait des promenades à cheval.*

Penfriends

Some students may be interested in finding a penfriend, or at least looking at the details of penfriends on various websites (see TB 207–208).

A whole class e-mail exchange is very effective. For advice on organising this, see the list of publications (TB 208, TB 154).

SB 114,  **WRITING**

2 À toi!

This is the culmination of work in Areas 1–3. Using the *Pour t'aider* box to help them, students write their own self-portrait, slotting their preferred activities into the model letter. Encourage them to add further information and illustrations. If preferred, this letter could be done on the computer and include clip art.

If students have started a self-description file, they could now include this information (see TB 40, TB 86).

AU CHOIX SB 144, 3/29, **LISTENING CONSOLIDATION**

4 Spécial-loisirs

Students should listen to the complete item first, read through the text, then listen to each person individually and complete the descriptions.

This would be ideal as an individual listening activity, if equipment is available, or could also be used as a text re-sequencing exercise, e.g. *Fun with Texts, Textsalad* (see TB 41).

Solution: *Benoît* – **b**, **f**, **a**, **g**;
Céline – **i**, **c**, **e**;
Dominique – **k**, **d**, **h**;
Agnès – **l**, **n**;
Malik – **m**, **j**

Spécial-Loisirs

– Les jeunes en France, comment passent-ils leurs loisirs? Notre reporter, Chantal Sabrine, parle à des jeunes à Paris.

– Bonjour. Comment t'appelles-tu?
– Je m'appelle Benoît Laroche.
– Alors, Benoît, qu'est-ce que tu fais, comme loisirs?
– Je fais du sport – j'aime beaucoup ça ... et je regarde la télévision.
– Qu'est-ce que tu fais, comme sport?
– Alors ... au collège, je joue au football ... et je fais de l'athlétisme. Puis, le week-end, quand il fait beau, je fais du cyclisme avec mon père. C'est bien, ça.
– Merci, Benoît. Maintenant je vais parler à une jeune fille. Bonjour, comment t'appelles-tu?
– Céline Marceau.
– Alors, Céline, est-ce que tu aimes le sport aussi?
– Ah non. Je n'aime pas du tout ça!
– Alors qu'est-ce que tu fais, comme loisirs?
– Bon, alors moi, j'aime les jeux de société, comme le Monopoly et je fais des puzzles ... et je joue aux échecs et aux cartes aussi. Puis, le samedi soir, je vais en discothèque avec mes amis.
– Merci, Céline. Maintenant, je parle à ...
– Dominique Puisseux.
– Alors, Dominique, qu'est-ce que tu fais, le mercredi et le week-end?
– Ça dépend. J'aime la lecture et j'aime la musique.
– Est-ce que tu joues d'un instrument de musique?
– Oui, je joue du piano et de la flûte. Et je joue avec l'orchestre des jeunes.
– Et les sports, est-ce que tu fais du sport?
– Non, pas beaucoup, mais en été, je fais de la voile.
– Merci, Dominique. Et toi, comment t'appelles-tu?
– Agnès Laroche.
– Alors, Agnès, qu'est-ce que tu fais comme loisirs?
– Moi, j'aime faire de l'ordinateur. Nous avons un ordinateur à la maison et je travaille sur l'ordinateur ou je fais des jeux.
– Merci, Agnès. Et maintenant je parle à ...
– Malik Kessel.
– Alors, toi, Malik, qu'est-ce que tu fais, comme loisirs?
– Je fais un peu de tout. J'aime le sport. Je joue au tennis dans un club de jeunes, et j'aime la musique aussi ... mais je ne joue pas d'instrument. Et je fais du dessin et de la peinture.
– Et qu'est-ce que tu aimes dessiner?
– Les voitures. J'aime beaucoup dessiner les voitures, surtout les voitures de sport.
– Merci, Malik, et merci à tout le monde qui a participé à notre enquête sur les jeunes et les loisirs.

Area 4
Helping at home
Giving reasons and opinions
Using a verb + an infinitive

SB 115, 3–5, SB 116–117, 1–3
Au choix SB 145, 5
CD 3/30–31
Écoute et parle SB 159, 6
Student CD 2/21
CM 10/3, 10/4
FC 5, 96–100

FC 5, 10, 96–100 **PRESENTATION**

Household tasks

Teach the following, using flashcards and other pictures: *faire la vaisselle/la cuisine, laver la voiture, ranger la chambre, passer l'aspirateur, travailler dans le jardin, aider à la maison*. Revise *faire une promenade, faire les courses*.

Ask some questions, e.g. *Est-ce que tu aides à la maison / fais la vaisselle?* etc.

3/30 **LISTENING**

Quiz sonore

Write on the board the following lettered statements (which can be used afterwards for a game of *Effacez!* – see TB 26).

a *On fait la cuisine.*
b *On range la chambre.*
c *On fait une promenade.*
d *On fait les courses.*
e *On travaille dans le jardin.*
f *On fait la vaisselle.*
g *On lave la voiture.*
h *On passe l'aspirateur.*

Students listen to the recording and jot down the number and letter to identify the sounds. Check the answers by replaying the quiz and pausing after each sound to ask the answer, which could be given as a complete sentence.

Solution: Ex. b, 1h, 2f, 3e, 4a, 5d, 6g, 7c

Quiz sonore

– Quiz sonore!
– Salut et bienvenue à notre quiz sonore. Écoutez bien pour identifier les sons. Écoutez l'exemple d'abord.
– **Exemple** *(sound of tidying room* + Zut, alors!*)*
– Qu'est-ce qu'on fait? … Oui, c'est ça. On range la chambre – c'est la phrase b. Maintenant, écoutez les sept autres sons.
– **Numéro 1** *(sound of hoovering)*
– **Numéro 2** *(sound of washing up)*
– **Numéro 3** *(sound of gardening)*
– **Numéro 4** *(sound of cooking* + Mmm, c'est délicieux!*)*
– **Numéro 5** *(sound of shopping* + C'est combien?*)*
– **Numéro 6** *(sound of washing car* + Oh, pardon!*)*
– **Numéro 7** *(sound of going for a walk)*
– Et voilà, c'est tout! C'est la fin du quiz sonore. Au revoir tout le monde!

SB 115 **READING**

3 Au travail

The captions in this matching task include different persons of the verb, so it will be useful for the students to say the whole sentence when giving the answers.

Solution: 1b, 2a, 3h, 4f, 5e, 6g, 7d, 8c

SB 115, 3/31 **LISTENING SUPPORT/EXTENSION**

4 Tu aides à la maison?

a For support, students listen to the recording and match the task mentioned with the pictures from Task 3.

Solution: 1 5, 2 1, 3 4, 4 2, 5 3, 6 7, 7 8, 8 6

b For extension, students listen to the recording again and match the opinion or reason mentioned by each speaker with the opinions listed below.

Solution: 1b, 2a, 3e, 4c, 5d, 6g, 7f, 8h

Tu aides à la maison?

1 – Pendant les vacances, est-ce que tu aides à la maison?
– Un peu. J'aide ma mère à faire les courses.
– Et tu aimes faire les courses?
– Oui, j'aime ça.

2 – Est-ce que tu aides tes parents à la maison?
– Ça dépend. Quelquefois, je lave la voiture pour ma mère.
– Bon, alors, toi, tu laves la voiture. Tu aimes faire ça?
– Pas beaucoup, mais je le fais, quand même.

3 – Et toi, est-ce que tu fais quelque chose pour aider pendant les vacances?
– Oui, moi, je passe l'aspirateur.
– Alors, tu passes l'aspirateur, c'est bien. Tu aimes faire ça?
– Euh, oui, ça va – j'écoute de la musique en même temps!

4 – Et toi, qu'est-ce que tu fais pour aider?
– Pas grand-chose.
– Tu ranges ta chambre, peut-être, et tu fais ton lit?
– Ah oui, je range ma chambre, mais je n'aime pas ça!

5 – Est-ce que tu fais quelque chose pour aider à la maison?
– Euh quelquefois, mais je trouve ça très ennuyeux!

– Tu fais la vaisselle, peut-être?
– Oui, c'est ça. Je fais la vaisselle – mais pas le dimanche!

6 – Vous aidez à la maison ou dans le jardin?
– Dans la maison, pas beaucoup. Mais dans le jardin, oui, quelquefois.
– Oui, oui. Travailler dans le jardin, c'est bien. Nous aimons faire ça.

7 – C'est votre chien, ça?
– Oui, c'est notre chien. Il s'appelle Drac.
– Vous faites souvent des promenades avec Drac?
– Oui, pendant les vacances. On a plus de temps pendant les vacances et puis c'est amusant!

8 – Est-ce que vous aidez vos parents dans la maison?
– Non, pas très souvent, moi.
– Oui, tu es paresseux, toi! Mais tu aides quand on fait la cuisine.
– Ah oui, faire la cuisine, ça, c'est différent! J'adore faire ça!

SB 115, **SPEAKING**

5 Inventez des conversations

Students practise this conversation in pairs, slotting in different phrases from the options given.

CM 10/3 **SUPPORT**

À la maison

This sheet on household tasks is suitable for use now or for homework. If preferred, it could be used as an alternative to the more difficult reading task on SB 116, Task 1, or later, as an alternative to *Au choix*, SB 145, Task 5.

Solution:

1 (Presque) tout le monde travaille
1b, 2f, 3a, 4i, 5c, 6h, 7d, 8g, 9e

2 Des phrases mélangées
1 *J'aime faire la cuisine.*
2 *Mon frère déteste faire la vaisselle.*
3 *Les enfants aiment laver la voiture.*
4 *Est-ce que tu aides à la maison?*
5 *Je n'aime pas beaucoup passer l'aspirateur.*
6 *Quelquefois, je travaille dans le jardin.*
7 *J'adore faire les courses en ville.*
8 *Mon père aime beaucoup faire des promenades avec le chien.*

3 Et toi, qu'est-ce que tu aimes faire?
This is an open-ended task.

SB 116 **READING**

1 D'accord ou pas d'accord?

If everyone is to do this task, some help will be needed with understanding the four letters. More able students could read through them alone and then go straight on to the true/false exercise which follows.

Solution: 1V, 2F, 3V, 4V, 5V, 6F, 7V, 8F, 9V, 10F

SB 116 **GRAMMAR**

Dossier-langue
Verb + infinitive

Go through this short explanation of the use of verb+ infinitive, asking a few questions, e.g.
Est-ce que tu aimes travailler dans le jardin?
Qu'est-ce que tu préfères faire?

SB 116 **GRAMMAR** **WRITING**

2 On aime ... on déteste

Students write out complete sentences prompted by symbols. Some might need help with vocabulary and a reminder that numbers 5–8 require a plural verb.

Solution:
1 *Luc adore jouer au football*
2 *Sophie déteste faire de la voile.*
3 *Marc n'aime pas jouer au tennis.*
4 *Claire aime faire de la peinture.*
5 *Presque tous les jeunes aiment (écouter de) la musique.*
6 *Normalement, les jeunes détestent faire la vaisselle.*
7 *Beaucoup d'enfants adorent faire la cuisine.*
8 *Mes amis aiment jouer aux cartes.*

SB 117, **SPEAKING**

3 À toi!

Students use this substitution table as a starting point for making up conversations involving verb + infinitive and expressing opinions. This might prove difficult for some students, so, as an alternative, they could do CM 10/3 (see above, TB 190), if not done already, or play a chain game, beginning first with *J'aime ...*, then going on to *Je n'aime pas ...* after, say, five additions. If they do this, try to introduce some phrases containing verb + infinitive, if possible.

CM 10/4,  **SPEAKING** **CONSOLIDATION**

Sébastien et Vivienne

This information gap activity will probably need some demonstration by the teacher and a student. The worksheet should be cut in half and the answers written on the sheet.

SB 159, TB 197, SCD 2/21 **LISTENING**

6 Une conversation

For extra practice of answering questions about leisure activities, students could use this *Écoute et parle* task (see TB 197).

Au choix SB 145 **EXTENSION**

5 Des opinions sur les loisirs

This open-ended activity gives further practice in using verb + infinitive, expressing opinions and giving reasons.

Area 5
Using the 24-hour clock

SB 117, 4–5
Au choix SB 145, 6
CM 10/5
SB 93, TB 161
CD 3/9–10, 32–33
Teaching clock with 24 hours (optional)

Date and time — REVISION

Revise orally the date and the time, using the 12-hour clock. There are several suitable games to help with this, e.g. *Et après?* (write on the board or say a day, month or number and the class have to say the one that follows), *Loto* (students write down, say, three months and three days), *Le jeu du pendu* (see also TB 25–27).

The 24-hour clock — PRESENTATION

Explain that the 24-hour clock is used much more widely on the continent, for television and radio programmes, on posters and timetables.

- Draw two columns on the board and, using figures, write a time after noon in the left-hand column, using the 24-hour clock. Then ask a student to write the equivalent time using the 12-hour clock in the right-hand column. Begin with hours only and then add in 30, 15, 45, and eventually other times, until you have a list of about twelve times. Say all the times in French as they are written up.
- Next, rub out the original times and do the whole thing again in reverse, this time seeing if the students can supply the times in French.
- Leave the times on the board and play a game of *Effacez!* (TB 26).
- For further practice, divide students into teams. Someone from each team in turn says a time in French, using the 24-hour clock, and someone from the other team has to write it on the board in figures.

3/32 — LISTENING

Vingt-quatre heures

Revise *ouvert* and *fermé* and explain *à partir de*. Play the recording and ask students to jot down the time in figures (or to write the 12-hour clock equivalents as well, if you prefer). This task uses times on the hour only.

Solution:

1 *15h* – 3pm
2 *13h* – 1pm
3 *20h* – 8pm
4 *21h* – 9pm
5 *17h* – 5pm
6 *16h* – 4pm
7 *14h* – 2pm
8 *18h* – 6pm
9 *20h* – 8pm
10 *22h* – 10pm

Vingt-quatre heures

1 Le match de rugby commence à 15 heures.
2 Le déjeuner est à 13 heures.
3 Le film commence à 20 heures.
4 Le concert commence à 21 heures.
5 Le match de football commence à 17 heures.
6 La banque est ouverte jusqu'à 16 heures.
7 L'épicerie est ouverte à partir de 14 heures.
8 Le restaurant est ouvert à partir de 18 heures.
9 L'épicerie ferme à 20 heures.
10 Le match finit à 22 heures.

SB 117 — READING

4 Attention, c'est l'heure!

Students match up the times in words and numbers. This time the full range of times is used.

Solution: 1b, 2g, 3d, 4f, 5c, 6a, 7e, 8h

SB 117 — EXTENSION

!

Draw students' attention to the use of the 24-hour clock for times of events.

SB 117, 3/33 — LISTENING

5 C'est quand?

Students listen to the short conversations, look at the advertisements and choose the correct time from the three options. For extra practice, the answers could be checked orally with students reading out all three possible times listed for each advertisement, then stating the correct one.

Solution: 1b, 2c, 3a, 4a, 5b, 6a

C'est quand?

1 – Allô! Ici le cinéma Dragon.
– Bonjour Madame. Ça commence à quelle heure, le film, s'il vous plaît?
– À 20 heures 15, Monsieur.

2 – Salut, Jacques. C'est à quelle heure, le match de football?
– À 14 heures 30.
– Ah bon.

3 – C'est à quelle heure, le bal?
– À 21 heures.
– Alors, à ce soir!

4 – Pardon, Madame. Le concert commence à quelle heure?
– À 20 heures 45, Monsieur.

5 – La discothèque est ouverte à partir de quelle heure, s'il vous plaît, Monsieur?
– À partir de 20 heures 30, Mademoiselle.

6 – La piscine ouvre à quelle heure aujourd'hui, s'il vous plaît?
– À 14 heures, Madame.

CM 10/5 — CONSOLIDATION/SUPPORT GRAMMAR

24 heures

Some students could do this copymaster as support, whilst others could do the *Au choix* task below as extension.

The first two tasks are quite easy, involving matching times in figures and words (24-hour clock and ordinary time). The third task is harder, involving finding out opening and closing times from posters. It could be developed further by asking for the English for the times.

Solutions:

1 Quelle heure est-il?
1b, 2e, 3f, 4h, 5g, 6a, 7d, 8c

2 Autrement dit
1e, 2c, 3b, 4a, 5d, 6f

3 Ça ouvre … ça ferme
1 *dix heures, dix-huit heures*
2 *quatorze heures trente, vingt heures*
3 *dix heures, vingt-deux heures*
4 *midi, dix-neuf heures trente*
5 *dix-sept heures, vingt et une heures*
6 *huit heures, treize heures*

Au choix SB 145 — EXTENSION READING SPEAKING/WRITING

6 C'est quand?

Students look for information in the advertisements and answer the questions. They should answer in words, but do not need to give complete sentences. This could be done as a writing task or students could work in pairs asking and answering questions alternately.

Solution:

1 *À partir de onze heures.*
2 *À dix-huit heures quinze.*
3 *À vingt et une heures trente.*
4 *À dix-huit heures trente.*
5 *À dix-sept heures cinquante-cinq.*
6 *À dix-neuf heures.*
7 *À vingt heures trente-cinq.*
8 *Non.*
9 *À seize heures.*
10 *À vingt heures quarante-cinq.*

SB 93, TB 161, 3/9–10 — LISTENING SPEAKING

Chantez! Attention, c'est l'heure!

For revision and for fun, sing again the rap from *Unité 8* (see TB 161).

Area 6
Possessive adjectives
SB 118–119, 1–6
Au choix SB 146, 7–9
CM 10/6
Grammar in Action 1, page 35
CD 3/34

REVISION/PRESENTATION

Clothing

Begin by revising the words for clothes, met so far (see SB 47).

Using pictures from magazines, home-made flashcards or actual garments, teach the following new items of clothing: *anorak (m), chemise (f), chemisier (m), jean (m), maillot de bain (m), pyjama (m), sandales (f pl), veste (f)* and also the words *valise (f), parapluie (m)* and *lunettes de soleil (f pl).*

When the class knows most of these words orally, write them on the board in random order and ask the class to list them, in alphabetical order, with their meanings (adding them to their vocabulary books or electronic word lists).

Students could make up wordsearches, acrostics or word-snakes on the computer, incorporating a selection of the clothing vocabulary, and print them out to set to other students.

SB 118, 3/34 — READING SUPPORT

1 Lucie part en vacances

a Students match text and illustrations to practise the new vocabulary.

Solution: 1h, 2e, 3l, 4b, 5c, 6g, 7f, 8d, 9a, 10i, 11k, 12j

b Students listen to the recording, jotting down which things Lucie takes and, by default, find out which two things she forgets.

Solution: h, b, d, i, e, f, k, c, l, a
*Elle oublie son pyjama (**g**) et son appareil-photo (**j**).*

Lucie part en vacances

– Tu fais ta valise, Lucie?
– Oui, maman.
– Qu'est-ce que tu prends?
– Je prends mon jean et mon anorak, mon parapluie et ma veste.
– Mais il fait beau en été, Lucie!
– Oui, oui, je sais! Je prends aussi mon maillot de bain et mes lunettes de soleil, avec mes sandales et mon petit chemisier en coton.
– Très bien. Est-ce que tu as la chemise qui est un cadeau pour ton cousin Daniel?
– Oui, oui, Maman. J'ai la chemise pour Daniel aussi.

SB 118 **GRAMMAR**

Dossier-langue
Possessive adjectives

This sets out all the possessive adjectives (previously taught in *Unités 3* and *8*). Practise these orally, for example in questions about clothes, before going on to the tasks which follow, e.g.
De quelle couleur est ton anorak / ton maillot de bain?
De quelle couleur sont tes baskets?
Mon anorak est ... etc.
Regardez la chemise de Richard. De quelle couleur est-elle? Sa chemise est ...

SB 118 **GRAMMAR** **READING**

2 Où sont les chaussettes?

Students complete each person's speech bubble with the correct possessive adjectives, and also read the story.

Solution: **Christophe: 1** *ma*, **2** *mes*, **3** *mon*, **4** *mon*, **5** *ma*, **6** *mon*
Anne-Marie: 7 *ta*, **8** *tes*, **9** *ton*, **10** *ton*, **11** *ton*, **12** *ton*
M. Lambert: 13 *sa*, **14** *ses*, **15** *son*, **16** *son*, **17** *sa*, **18** *son*

SB 119, **WRITING/SPEAKING** **CONSOLIDATION**

3 Tu pars en vacances

This task gives further practice of *mon, ma, mes* and *ton, ta, tes*. Ask questions to check that the class knows the words for all the objects illustrated. Each person writes down three objects from those shown. Students then work in pairs asking questions to find out the things on the other person's list. As this involves changing the person of the verb from questions to answers, less able students will need some help, or they could omit the item and, instead, start work on CM 10/6 for support.

SB 119 **GRAMMAR**

4 À toute la bande!

This task provides practice of *notre, nos* and *votre, vos*. Students complete the postcard with the correct possessive adjectives.

Solution: **1** *nos*, **2** *notre*, **3** *nos*, **4** *notre*, **5** *notre*, **6** *nos*, **7** *votre*, **8** *vos*, **9** *vos*, **10** *vos*

AU CHOIX SB 146 **CONSOLIDATION**

7 Au pique-nique

Either this or the next task could be done for further practice. As an alternative, less able students could work on CM 10/6 (see below).

Students use the substitution table to help them to make up simple sentences.This could be done as an oral or written task, depending on the ability of the students.

Solution:

1. *Où est notre pain?*
2. *Où est notre fromage?*
3. *Où est notre jambon?*
4. *Où est notre saucisson?*
5. *Où sont nos pommes?*
6. *Où sont nos chips?*
7. *Où sont nos biscuits?*

AU CHOIX SB 146 **CONSOLIDATION**

8 L'Île d'Or

a Students choose the correct word (*votre* or *vos*) to complete the gaps in the advert.

Solution: **1** *votre*, **2** *vos*, **3** *votre*, **4** *vos*, **5** *votre, votre*, **6** *votre*

b As extension, students match the sentences with the items on the poster.

Solution: **1f, 2c, 3b, 4e, 5a, 6d**

SB 119 **READING**

5 On fait des photos

This item and the next give practice of *leur* and *leurs*. Students match the pictures with the sentences, which each include the word *leur(s)*.

Solution: **1b, 2e, 3a, 4c, 5d**

SB 119 **WRITING**

6 Les photos de Dani

Using the table to help them, students say or write a sentence to describe each 'photo'.

Solution: This is an open-ended task.

GRAMMAR IN ACTION 1, PAGE 35 **GRAMMAR**

Using *notre/nos, votre/vos, leur/leurs*

This gives useful consolidation of possessive adjectives and could be used now or later, for revision.

CM 10/6 **GRAMMAR** **SUPPORT**

C'est à qui?

This copymaster brings together all the possessive adjectives. It could be done now or later, for consolidation.

Solutions:

2a Corinne va à la plage
1 *tes*, **2** *ta*, **3** *ton*, **4** *ton*, **5** *tes*

2b Patrick adore l'informatique
1 *ses*, **2** *sa*, **2** *son*, **4** *ses*, **5** *ses*

3 Notre collège
This is an open-ended task.

4 Une famille musicale
1 *Notre*, **2** *Mon, sa*, **3** *Ma, son*, **4** *Mes, leurs, leur*, **5** *Mon, son*, **6** *votre*, **7** *notre*

Au choix SB 146 **EXTENSION**

9 Au bureau des objets trouvés

This text includes examples of possessive adjectives, mainly *leur(s)*. Students read the text then write answers to the open-ended questions which follow.

Solution: (some possibilities)

1 *Non, il travaille dans un bureau des objets trouvés.*
2 *Il le trouve intéressant et quelquefois amusant.*
3 *Ils perdent souvent leurs sacs et leurs parapluies.*
4 *On laisse quelquefois ses chaussettes dans le train.*
5 *Ils laissent quelquefois leur chien dans le train.*

Saynète: J'ai perdu ... **PRACTICE**

Using similar language to the above, students could work in groups (possibly with a view to eventual presentation of the sketch to others) and make up a sequence taking place in the lost property office at a leisure park or after a pop festival.

They could bring along a selection of garments and objects as props. (The obvious need for censorship is covered if it is stated in advance that they must be things for which everyone has learnt the French!)

A variety of people could ask *Avez-vous notre/mon ...?* with the person in charge replying *C'est votre ..., ça?* This could perhaps include some funny or incongruous things.

Area 7
Describing an ideal day
Expressing opinions
SB 120, 1–2

SB 120 **READING WRITING EXTENSION**

1 Une journée idéale

This and the next task are particularly suitable for more able students and could be omitted by others.

Students read the article on Lucie's ideal day, then read the ten sentences and correct the deliberate mistakes.

Solution: **1** ~~cyclisme~~ *ski,* **2** ~~octobre~~ *avril,* **3** ~~à une heure~~ *à midi,* **4** ~~déteste~~ *adore,* **5** ~~de l'orangeade~~ *de la limonade,* **6** ~~à la fraise~~ *à la vanille,* **7** ~~un livre~~ *des magazines,* **8** ~~blanc~~ *noir,* **9** ~~dans une discothèque~~ *au restaurant,* **10** ~~à onze heures~~ *à minuit*

SB 120 **WRITING**

2 À toi!

Students write two paragraphs themselves, based on the outlines provided and with reference to the previous item. Part a is about their own ideal day and part b about a day which is definitely not ideal.

Area 8
Further activities and consolidation
SB 120
CD 3/35–40
Écoute et parle SB 159, 5, 1–6
Student CD 2/16–21, 42–45
CM 10/7–10/12

CM 10/7 **EXTENSION**

La page des lettres

Students read the selection of letters from young people seeking penfriends, then complete the summary which follows. The second item is a *vrai ou faux* activity based on two Internet letters.

Solutions:

1 Je cherche un(e) correspondant(e)
a 4, b 3, c 6, d 4, e 2, f 5,
g 2 (**6** if 'nature' includes animals)**, h 5**

2 Les loisirs
1F – *Mathilde aime/adore cuisiner,* **2F** – *Mathieu aime les voitures américaines et anglaises,* **3V,** **4F** – *Mathilde collectionne les recettes,* **5V**

SB 120, TB 39, 3/35–36 **LISTENING SPEAKING**

Chantez! Samedi, on part en vacances

A pleasant and popular way to conclude the theme of holidays and leisure would be to sing this song. See TB 33 for notes on on using the songs and TB 39 for the musical score.

Samedi, on part en vacances

Samedi, on part en vacances.
Samedi, on part en vacances.

1 Nice et Cannes, Toulouse et Sète,
Ma valise est presque faite.

Samedi, on part en vacances.
Samedi, on part en vacances.

2 Oui, c'est vrai on part demain.
Où est mon maillot de bain?
Nice et Cannes, Toulouse et Sète,
Ma valise est presque faite.

Samedi, on part en vacances.
Samedi, on part en vacances.

3 Pour le soleil, mes lunettes,
Pour le volley, mes baskets.
Oui, c'est vrai on part demain.
Où est mon maillot de bain?
Nice et Cannes, Toulouse et Sète,
Ma valise est presque faite.

Samedi, on part en vacances.
Samedi, on part en vacances.

4 Faire du vélo, faire du ski,
Faire du camping, allons-y!
Pour le soleil, mes lunettes,
Pour le volley, mes baskets.
Oui, c'est vrai on part demain.

Où est mon maillot de bain?
Nice et Cannes, Toulouse et Sète,
Ma valise est presque faite.

Samedi, on part en vacances.
Samedi, on part en vacances.

5 Sète, Toulouse et Nice et Cannes,
Nous allons en caravane.
Faire du vélo, faire du ski,
Faire du camping, allons-y!
Pour le soleil, mes lunettes,
Pour le volley, mes baskets.
Oui, c'est vrai on part demain.
Où est mon maillot de bain?
Nice et Cannes, Toulouse et Sète,
Ma valise est presque faite.

Samedi, on part en vacances.
Samedi, on part en vacances.

6 Que nous avons de la chance,
C'est bientôt les vacances.
Sète, Toulouse et Nice et Cannes,
Nous allons en caravane.
Faire du vélo, faire du ski,
Faire du camping, allons-y!
Pour le soleil, mes lunettes,
Pour le volley, mes baskets.
Oui, c'est vrai on part demain.
Où est mon maillot de bain?
Nice et Cannes, Toulouse et Sète,
Ma valise est presque faite.

Samedi, on part en vacances.
Samedi, on part en vacances.

SB 121, SB 159, TB 197, SCD 2/20 LISTENING

Vocabulaire de classe

This is a matching exercise as usual and all the expressions might have cropped up in everyday classroom routine. Each contains a perfect tense, but it is left to the teacher to decide whether to comment on this or not.

Solution: 1h, 2b, 3e, 4d, 5c, 6a, 7g, 8f

There is an *Écoute et parle* task linked with this item (see TB 197).

CM 10/8, SCD 2/42–45 INDEPENDENT LISTENING SOUNDS AND WRITING

Tu comprends?

1 On fait du sport

Solution: 1c, 2h, 3b, 4f, 5g, 6a, 7e, 8d

On fait du sport

1 – Tu fais du sport, Sophie?
– Oui, bien sûr. Je fais de l'équitation tous les dimanches.

2 – Et vous, Marc et Luc, est-ce que vous faites du sport?
– Oui, nous faisons du VTT. Ça, c'est super.

3 – Et Sika, est-ce qu'elle fait du sport?
– Oui, elle fait de la gymnastique, le mercredi.

4 – Et Claire et Nicole, qu'est-ce qu'elles font, comme sport?
– En été, elles font de la planche à voile. C'est bien, ça.

5 – Est-ce que tu fais du ski en hiver, Charles?
– Oui, j'adore faire du ski.

6 – Et toi, Karim, qu'est-ce que tu fais, comme sport?
– Pas grand-chose – mais je fais de la natation de temps en temps. J'aime bien la natation.

7 – Et toi, Lucie, qu'est-ce que tu aimes faire, comme sport?
– Moi, j'adore faire du roller avec mes amis. C'est très amusant.

8 – Et Paul et Sanjay, est-ce qu'ils font du sport?
– Oui, ils font de la voile avec le club de voile, ici à La Rochelle.

2 Enquête loisirs

Solution:

	painting	drama	chess	drums	flute	violin	computer
1			✔				
2				✔			
3					✔		
4		✔					
5	✔						
6						✔	
7							✔

Enquête loisirs

1 – Qu'est-ce que tu aimes faire, à part le sport?
– Moi, j'aime jouer aux échecs. C'est très intéressant.

2 – Et toi, Charles, tu as d'autres loisirs?
– Oui, j'aime bien la musique et je joue de la batterie.

3 – Nicole, tu joues d'un instrument de musique aussi?
– Oui, moi, je joue de la flûte. J'aime bien cet instrument.

4 – Et vous, Paul et Sanjay, est-ce que vous avez d'autres loisirs?
– Oui, nous aimons faire du théâtre. Ça, c'est toujours amusant.

5 – Magali, qu'est-ce que tu fais comme loisirs?
– Moi, je fais de la peinture. J'adore ça.

6 – Marc, est-ce que tu aimes la musique?
– Oui, j'aime la musique et je joue du violon.

7 – Et vous, Lucie et Paul, est-ce que vous faites autre chose à part le sport?
– Oui, nous jouons aux jeux vidéo à l'ordinateur. Ça, c'est vraiment bien.

3 Je n'aime pas ça!

Solution:

	Activité	Raison
1	**e**	*pas amusant*
2	**c**	*ennuyeux*
3	**a**	*difficile*
4	**f**	*pas amusant*
5	**b**	*pas intéressant*
6	**d**	*fatigant*

Je n'aime pas ça!

1 – Est-ce que tu aides à la maison?
– Oui, bien sûr.
– Qu'est-ce que tu n'aimes pas faire?
– Je déteste faire la vaisselle. Ce n'est pas amusant.

2 – Et toi, Paul, est-ce qu'il y a une activité que tu détestes?
– Oui, je déteste laver la voiture.
– Pourquoi?
– Parce que c'est ennuyeux.

3 – Et vous, les filles, qu'est-ce que vous n'aimez pas faire?
– Nous n'aimons pas faire la cuisine. C'est difficile. Nous préférons manger les choses que nos parents ont préparées.

4 – Est-ce que vous aimez faire les courses?
– Non, nous détestons faire les courses. Aller au supermarché, ce n'est pas amusant.

5 – Lucie, est-ce qu'il y a un travail à la maison que tu n'aimes pas faire?
– Oui, beaucoup, mais surtout, je n'aime pas passer l'aspirateur. Je déteste ça. Ce n'est pas intéressant.

6 – Et toi, Marc, qu'est-ce que tu n'aimes pas faire?
– Je n'aime pas travailler dans le jardin. C'est très fatigant.

4 C'est quand?

Solution: **1** *21h30,* **2** *15h,* **3** *14h30,* **4** *18h,* **5** *19h,* **6** *16h20,* **7** *20h45,* **8** *13h40*

C'est quand?

1 – Le film commence à quelle heure?
– Il commence à 21 heures 30.
– À 21 heures 30.

2 – Salut Suzanne, le match commence à quelle heure cet après-midi?
– À 15 heures.
– Bon, à 15 heures.

3 – Le musée ouvre à quelle heure aujourd'hui?
– À 14 heures 30.
– À 14 heures 30, oui.

4 – Et il ferme à quelle heure?
– À 18 heures.
– À 18 heures, bon, merci.

5 – On mange à quelle heure, le soir?
– Normalement, nous mangeons à 19 heures.
– À 19 heures, d'accord.

6 – Le train pour Paris part à quelle heure?
– Il part à 16 heures 20.
– À 16 heures 20, merci.

7 – Le concert commence à quelle heure?
– Il commence à 20 heures 45.
– À 20 heures 45, bon merci.

8 – Tes cours commencent à quelle heure, l'après-midi?
– À 13 heures 40.
– À 13 heures 40, c'est ça.

SB 121, CM 10/9

Sommaire

A summary of the main structures and vocabulary of this unit.

SB 159, SCD 2/16–21 INDEPENDENT LISTENING

Écoute et parle – Unité 10

1 Les sons français

Solution: **ui: (a) 1b, 2d, 3a, 4e, 5c**
i: (a) 1d, 2b, 3a, 4c

Les sons français

Les lettres ui

a **1** paraluie
2 minuit
3 produit
4 bruit
5 circuit

b nuit, huit, biscuit, pluie

La lettre i

a **1** conversation
2 cahier
3 nation
4 solution

b natation, viande, maillot, équitation

2 Des phrases ridicules

Des phrases ridicules

La nuit, la souris fait du bruit, quand elle mange huit fruits, à minuit.

Toute la nation écoute la conversation ou fait de la natation, mais pas de l'équitation.

3 Chasse à l'intrus

Solution:

a **1c, 2d, 3c, 4b, 5a, 6b, 7c, 8b, 9c, 10d**

b In addition to **2**, groups **3**, **4**, **5**, **6**, **7** (and to some extent **10** *-aux* and *-eau*) have a different spelling for the same sound.

Chasse à l'intrus

1 **a** délicieux, **b** paresseux, **c** cadeaux, **d** généreux

2 **a** lit, **b** riz, **c** dis, **d** lait
3 **a** mai, **b** c'est, **c** le, **d** j'ai
4 **a** trois, **b** nos, **c** droit, **d** toi
5 **a** gros, **b** nous, **c** joue, **d** où
6 **a** les, **b** je, **c** thé, **d** et
7 **a** aux, **b** beau, **c** ou, **d** vos
8 **a** saison, **b** boisson, **c** maison, **d** raison
9 **a** jeu, **b** feu, **c** beau, **d** peu
10 **a** animaux, **b** chevaux, **c** château, **d** choux

4 Comment ça s'écrit?

Solution: **1**, **3**, **4**, **7** and **9** end in -e. An important exception to this general rule is *le basket* where the final *-t* is sounded because the word is of English/American origin.

Comment ça s'écrit?

1	artiste	**6**	grand
2	art	**7**	grande
3	salade	**8**	haut
4	porte	**9**	haute
5	port	**10**	point

5 Vocabulaire de classe

Solution: **6, 8, 5, 4, 1, 3, 7, 2**

Vocabulaire de classe

Regarde la page 121. Écoute le CD et écris le nombre de chaque instruction dans l'ordre du CD.

Je n'ai pas fait mes devoirs.

Vous avez fini?

J'ai gagné.

J'ai oublié mon cahier.

Qui a fini?

J'ai oublié ma trousse.

Tu as oublié ton livre?

J'ai fini.

6 Une conversation

Une conversation

a Écoute les questions et réponds comme indiqué.

- Qu'est-ce que tu aimes faire pendant les vacances?
  (pause)
- J'aime faire de l'équitation.
- Est-ce que tu aimes jouer au golf?
  (pause)
- Non, pas beaucoup. Je préfère jouer au basket.
- Est-ce que tu aides à la maison?
  (pause)
- Je fais les courses.
- Qu'est-ce que tu n'aimes pas faire?
  (pause)
- Je déteste travailler dans le jardin.

b Écoute les questions et réponds pour toi.

- Qu'est-ce que tu aimes faire pendant les vacances?
- (pause)
- Est-ce que tu aimes jouer au golf?
- (pause)
- Est-ce que tu aides à la maison?
- (pause)
- Qu'est-ce que tu n'aimes pas faire?
- (pause)

Épreuve – Unité 10

CM 10/10, 3/37–40 **INFORMAL ASSESSMENT LISTENING**

Épreuve: Écouter

A Tu aimes ça? (NC 1)

Solution: **1b, 2c, 3g, 4e, 5a, 6f** (mark /5)

Tu aimes ça? (NC 1)

1 – Est-ce que tu joues du piano?
– Oui, je joue du piano.

2 – Tu aimes le patin à roulettes?
– Le patin à roulettes? Oui, j'aime ça.

3 – Tu aides à faire la vaisselle?
– Oui, mais je déteste faire la vaisselle!

4 – Qu'est-ce que tu fais, tu dessines?
– Oui, je dessine et je fais de la peinture. J'aime la peinture.

5 – Tu aides à la maison?
– Oui, je passe l'aspirateur.
– Tu passes l'aspirateur? C'est bien, ça!

6 – Tu aimes jouer aux échecs?
– Oui, j'aime bien jouer aux échecs, mais je ne joue pas très bien.

B Quelle heure est-il? (NC 1)

Solution: **1b, 2a, 3d, 4f, 5e, 6c** (mark /5)

Quelle heure est-il?

1 – Le film commence à 13 heures 10.
– C'est vrai? À 13 heures 10!

2 – Le musée ferme à 16 heures.
– À 16 heures! C'est extraordinaire!

3 – Le film finit à quelle heure?
– À 22 heures 45.
– À 22 heures 45?
– C'est ça.

4 – Venez ici, tout le monde! Il est 24 heures! Il est minuit!
– Hourra, il est minuit!

5 – Le train arrive à 17 heures 15.
– À 17 heures 15, merci beaucoup.

6 – Il est 18 heures 30. Est-ce que le magasin est ouvert?
– À 18 heures 30? Mais oui, bien sûr!

C On part en vacances (NC 2)

Solution: 1b, 2b, 3d, 4c, 5b, 6a (mark /5)

On part en vacances

1 – Jean-Pierre, tu as ton jean?
– Oui, j'ai mon jean et mon anorak.
– Tu as tes chaussettes?
– Bien sûr, j'ai trois paires de chaussettes.

2 – Tu as ton pyjama, Mathilde?
– Oui, oui, Maman, mon pyjama est avec mon chemisier.
– Très bien. Et n'oublie pas ton appareil-photo.
– Voici mon appareil – il est dans mon sac.

3 – Tu as tout, Christophe?
– Alors, voici mon short, mon T-shirt et ... où sont mes chaussettes?
– Voilà tes chaussettes.
– Ah, merci beaucoup!

4 – Claire, qu'est-ce que tu as dans ton sac?
– J'ai mes lunettes de soleil dans mon sac, et puis mon livre – mon livre pour lire dans le train.

5 – Mme Martin regarde sa valise. Elle a sa veste blanche, ses sandales et aussi son parapluie. Elle a toujours son parapluie. Elle est pessimiste!

6 – Et M. Dunois, qu'est-ce qu'il prend?
– Il prend sa veste, son pull et sa chemise.
– Sa veste, son pull et sa chemise? Mais il part en vacances!
– Oui, mais il est très formel.

D Au club des jeunes (NC 3)

Solution: 1V, 2V, 3F, 4V, 5F, 6V (mark /5)

Au club des jeunes

1 Ce soir, au club des Jeunes, on fait du sport, on fait de la musique et on fait de l'informatique.

2 Deux filles jouent au ping-pong et d'autres jeunes personnes font de la musique.

3 Trois filles et un garçon jouent aux cartes et les autres jouent au Monopoly.

4 Une jeune fille joue de la batterie – je pense qu'elle adore ça!

5 Un garçon joue de la trompette. Il porte un pantalon noir, très chic et une chemise blanche.

6 Il y a aussi un ordinateur et deux garçons surfent sur le Net.

CM 10/11 **READING**

Épreuve: Lire

A J'aide à la maison (NC 2)

Solution: 1f, 2e, 3c, 4d, 5a, 6b (mark /5)

B Questions et réponses (NC 2)

Solution: 1b, 2d, 3h, 4c, 5f, 6a, 7e, 8g (mark /7)

C Sébastien est en vacances (NC 3)

Solution: 1V, 2F, 3F, 4V, 5F, 6F, 7V, 8V, 9F (mark /8)

CM 10/12 **WRITING GRAMMAR**

Épreuve: Écrire et grammaire

A Un serpent (NC 1)

Solution:

la voile, la natation, le cyclisme
le violon, la guitare
le dessin, la peinture
un maillot de bain
(mark /4: $^1/_2$ mark for each item, including the example)

B Un questionnaire sur les loisirs (NC 1)

Solution: **1** *au*, **2** *au*, **3** *fais*, **4** *joue*, **5** *de la*, **6** *aux* (mark /5)

C Une lettre (NC 1)

Solution: **1** *suis*, **2** *fais*, **3** *ma*, **4** *mes baskets*, **5** *mon maillot de bain*, **6** *prendre* (mark /5)

D À toi! (NC 3)

Solution: This is an open-ended task. (mark /6)

SB 122–125, CM 107–108 **READING EXTENSION**

Presse-Jeunesse 4

These pages provide reading for pleasure. They can be used alone or with the accompanying copymaster. See the notes on TB 17.

SB 122, CM 107

Le match de football

On the copymaster, part A helps train reading for gist and getting the main story, helped by the pictures, and B helps in highlighting key vocabulary.

Solutions:

A 3, 1, 6, 2, 5, 4

B

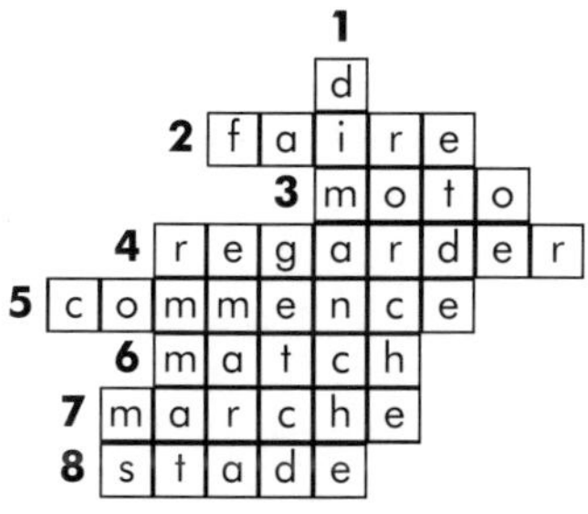

SB 123, CM 107

Connais-tu ces sports?

Solution: 1 NS, 2 E, 3 E, 4 NS, 5 E, 6 NS, 7 NS

SB 123

Les loisirs – ça montre qui tu es

A personality quiz based on leisure activities.

CM 107 **READING STRATEGIES**

4 Lire – c'est facile

This item in the series on reading strategies deals with scanning for specific information. Students look for key information from the next two factual items.

SB 124, CM 107

Une recette: mousse au chocolat

Solution: **1** *125g,* **2** *2,* **3** *oui,* **4** *les jaunes d'œufs,* **5** *oui,* **6** *le chocolat*

CM 108 **READING STRATEGIES**

5 Lire – c'est facile

In this final item on reading strategies, students are encouraged to use grammatical clues to find the answers.

Solution: **1** *prestidigitateur,* **2** *tours/efforts/adolescents,* **3** *essaie,* **4** *n'apprécient pas,* **5** *célèbre,* **6** *stupéfiants/sophistiqués*

SB 124, CM 108

Le sais-tu?

A factual item about judo and volley ball

Solutions:

A *blanc, jaune, orange, vert, bleu, marron, noir*

B *populaire, sociable, simple*

C **1** *5,* **2** *un judoka,* **3** *au Japon,* **4** *en Amérique,* **5** *représentent,* **6** *6,* **7** *la plage,* **8** *n'est pas* (negative), **9** *ne coûte pas* (negative), **10** *est* (positive)

SB 125, CM 108

Tout est bien qui finit bien

Students read the story and do the true/false task on the copymaster.

Solutions:

A 1V, 2F, 3V, 4F, 5F, 6V, 7F, 8F, 9V, 10V

B This is an open-ended task.

Encore Tricolore 1
nouvelle édition

Contrôles

The three *Contrôles* provide blocks of formal assessment of the vocabulary and structures introduced during the course. They assess all four National Curriculum Attainment Targets. See TB 20 for the Assessment Introduction.

The National Curriculum Level is indicated in brackets after the title. The tasks test elements of performance at that level.

The Listening and Reading copymasters are designed to be written on, but the Speaking and Writing (and alternative tasks) are re-usable.

Mark scheme:
Do not include a mark for the example. Each *Contrôle* has a total of 100 marks (25 for each Attainment Target).

Record sheets:
A record sheet for students is provided on CM 128. They will need one for each block of *Contrôles*.

Listening:
All items are repeated on the CD. For Level 1 assessment only, the recording can be played twice (so that students hear it four times altogether). At all levels, the pause button can be used at any time to give students time for reflection and for writing.

Speaking:
Decide how you wish to conduct this assessment:

- invite students out individually and ask the questions yourself;
- invite them in pairs, listen to the conversation and mark the answers;
- offer your students the option of recording the assessment with a partner, for you to listen to and mark afterwards. It is important, if students record their conversations at home, to obtain some assurance that they are not reading the questions and answers. In practice, this is usually patently obvious when listening to the cassette!

Premier contrôle – Unités 1–4

CM 109–110, 4/1–4 **LISTENING**

Premier contrôle: Écouter

A Loto mathématique (NC 1)

Make sure that students understand that they should only put three crosses (not including the example) on each card.

Solution: *Carte numéro un – 24, 30, 45, 3;*
Carte numéro deux – 12, 11, 17

(mark /6: 4+ shows understanding of short statements, with no interference and with plenty of repetition)

Loto mathématique

Carte numéro un:
vingt-quatre, trente, quarante-cinq, trois

Carte numéro deux:
douze, onze, dix-sept

B Dans ma chambre (NC 1)

Solution: 1a, 2b, 3b, 4a, 5a, 6b, 7a

(mark /6: 4+ shows understanding of short statements, with no interference and with plenty of repetition)

Dans ma chambre

1 Voici mon baladeur.
2 J'ai une table et deux chaises.
3 Il y a des stylos et une règle.
4 Ça, c'est mon ordinateur.
5 Mon chat s'appelle Tom.
6 Voilà trois cahiers.
7 Et voilà mon poisson.

C À la maison (NC 2)

Each item is repeated once, slowly and clearly. It is not necessary to replay the recording for the purposes of assessing at Level 2. It is acceptable, however, to pause the CD at any time to give your students more time for reflection.

Solution: 1V, 2F, 3F, 4F, 5F, 6V, 7F, 8V

(mark /7: 5+ shows understanding of a range of familiar statements)

À la maison

1 Maman est dans la cuisine.
2 Le chien est dans le jardin.
3 Le chat est sous la télé.
4 Ma sœur est dans sa chambre.
5 Mon père est dans la salle de bains.
6 Je suis dans le jardin.
7 Le téléphone est sur la chaise.
8 Mon grand-père est dans le salon.

D Deux familles (NC 2)

Solution:

	brother	sister	cat	dog	rabbit
Sylvie	1	0	2	–	–
Richard	1	2	–	1	1

(mark /6: 5+ shows understanding of a range of familiar statements)

Deux familles

– Bonjour. Je m'appelle Sylvie. Voilà des photos de ma famille. Voici Paul, mon frère. Je n'ai pas de soeurs. Voilà mes deux chats.

– Salut. Je suis Richard. J'ai des photos aussi. Voici Marie et Isabelle, mes soeurs. Voici mon petit frère, Patrick. Marie a un lapin. Moi, j'ai un chien. Voilà, il s'appelle Bruno.

CM 111 **SPEAKING**

Premier contrôle: Parler

Students should be given the sheet up to a week before the assessment, to give them time to choose whether they prefer to do 1 and 2 or 2 and 3 or 1 and 3, and to prepare and practise all three conversations (two structured ones and the open-ended one) with their partners.

Mark scheme:

Section A: mark /16: 2 marks per response

- 1 mark for conveying the requested information, but with a minimal response, e.g. one or two words. Repetition of the question and prompting by pointing to the visuals may be necessary.
- 2 marks for a response that is clear and conveys all of the information requested, in the form of a complete phrase or sentence, though not necessarily an accurate one. The question and answers may seem disjointed, like separate items rather than part of a coherent conversation.

Section B: mark /9: 2 marks per response, as above, + 1 bonus mark for one or more extra details, e.g. names of animals, their size or their colour. The extra information must be in the form of a complete phrase or sentence, though not necessarily an accurate one.

Summary:	**Marks**	7–15	16–25
	Level	1	2

CM 112–113 **READING**

Premier contrôle: Lire

A Dans la salle de classe (NC 1)

Solution: 1g, 2e, 3b, 4a, 5f, 6d, 7c

(mark /6: 4+ shows understanding of single words presented in a clear script – illustrations provide context and visual support)

B Les animaux (NC 1)

Solution: 1f, 2e, 3d, 4b, 5a, 6h, 7g, 8c

(mark /7: 5+ shows understanding of single words presented in a clear script – illustrations provide context and visual support)

C La famille (NC 2)

Solution: 1F, 2V, 3V, 4F, 5F, 6V, 7V

(mark /6: 4+ shows understanding of short phrases presented in a familiar context)

D Des questions et des réponses (NC 2)

Solution: 1c, 2b, 3g, 4f, 5d, 6a, 7e

(mark /6: 4+ shows understanding of short phrases presented in a familiar context)

CM 114 **WRITING**

Premier contrôle: Écrire

A La maison (NC 1)

Solution: **1** *la grande salle de bains,* **2** *la chambre de Lucie,* **3** *la chambre de Thomas et de Marc,* **4** *la chambre de Monsieur et Madame Duval,* **5** *la petite salle de bains,* **6** *le salon,* **7** *la salle à manger,* **8** *la cuisine,* **9** *le jardin*

(mark /8: do not allow spelling mistakes as the vocabulary is given; 6+ shows ability to copy single familiar words or short phrases correctly)

B Quelle image? (NC 2)

Solution:

1 *J'ai quatre ans.*
2 *J'habite en Écosse.*
3 *J'habite dans une ferme.*
4 *Voilà un cinéma.*
5 *J'ai huit ans.*
6 *Voilà une rue.*
7 *J'habite dans un appartement.*
8 *Voilà un café.*
9 *J'ai six ans.*
10 *J'habite en France.*

(mark /9: do not allow spelling mistakes as the vocabulary is given; 7+ shows ability to copy short familiar sentences correctly)

C Des questions (NC 2)

Solution: **1** *âge,* **2** *habites (accept es),* **3** *frères,* **4** *animal,* **5** *appelles,* **6** *ordinateur,* **7** *stylo,* **8** *couleur,* **9** *chat*

(mark /8: 6+ shows ability to write familiar words from memory – note that, at this level, it does not matter if spelling is approximate, as long as the meaning is clear and unambiguous without reference to the contextual picture)

Deuxième contrôle – Unités 5–7

CM 115–116, 4/5–8 **LISTENING**

Deuxième contrôle: Écouter

A À Granville (NC 1)

If you sense that your students would find it helpful, play the recording again so they hear the information four times altogether.

Solution: 1d, 2e, 3b, 4a, 5g, 6f, 7c

(mark /6: 4+ shows understanding of short statements, with no interference and with plenty of repetition)

À Granville

Qu'est-ce qu'il y a pour les touristes à Granville?
1 Il y a le marché, le samedi.
2 Il y a une grande piscine.

3 La tour Saint-Jacques.
4 Le camping n'est pas loin.
5 Il y a un cinéma avec trois salles.
6 La cathédrale est magnifique.
7 L'Escargot, c'est un bon restaurant.

B Les activités de la famille Giroux (NC 2)

Before the assessment, check that students understand that 20.30 means 8.30pm (item 4).

Solution: 1F, 2F, 3V, 4V, 5F, 6F, 7V, 8V

(mark /7: 5+ shows understanding of a range of familiar statements)

Les activités de la famille Giroux

1 – Je cherche un bon cadeau – c'est l'anniversaire de Pierre le 23 mai.
2 – Pierre? Il regarde un match de football avec son copain Alexandre.
3 – C'est la Fête des Mères aujourd'hui. Alette a offert des chocolats à Maman.
4 – Il y a un concert à l'église ce soir, à huit heures et demie. Je joue dans l'orchestre.
5 – Alette travaille dans sa chambre, avec sa copine Jeanne.
6 – Il y a un match de tennis de table au Collège Émile Zola. C'est le 9 octobre.
7 – Le 15 juin, je vais au Musée Maritime avec le collège.
8 – Papa … papa … PAPA!
– Je suis là. J'écoute de la musique.

C C'est où exactement? (NC 2)

Solution:

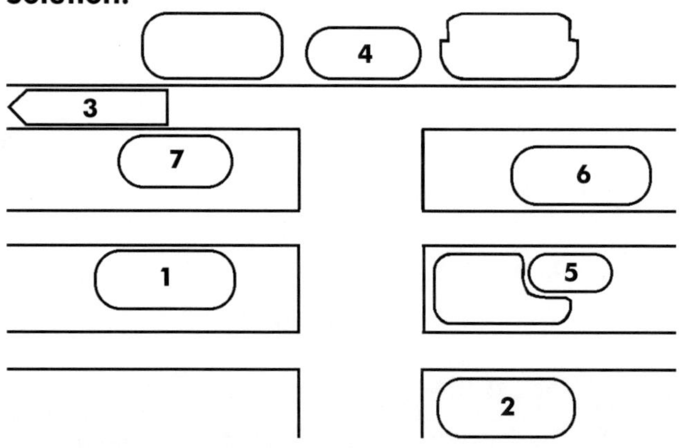

(mark /6: 4+ shows understanding of a range of familiar questions and answers)

C'est où exactement?

1 – Pour aller à la poste, s'il vous plaît?
– Prenez la deuxième rue à gauche, et c'est à gauche.
– Merci, monsieur.
2 – Pardon, il y a un supermarché ici?
– Oui, voilà, à droite!
– Oh, pardon.
3 – L'auberge de jeunesse, c'est loin?
– C'est assez loin – c'est à quinze kilomètres.
– Quinze kilomètres, ça va.
4 – Le restaurant Renaud, c'est loin?
– Non, continuez tout droit. C'est entre l'Hôtel Pasteur et l'église.
– Ah, oui, merci.
5 – Maman, il y a des toilettes ici?
– Oui, derrière l'office du tourisme.
6 – Où est l'hôpital?
– Ce n'est pas loin. Prenez la deuxième rue à droite, et c'est à gauche.
– Oh, merci.
7 – Pour aller au marché, s'il vous plaît?
– Vous prenez la troisième rue à gauche, et le marché est à gauche.
– Merci beaucoup.

D Quel temps fait-il? (NC 3)

Solution:

	temps	*opinion*	*activité*
Charles	**e**	**c**	**a**
Magalie	**a**	**d**	**d**
Robert	**d**	**b**	**c**

(mark /6: 4+ shows understanding of short dialogues, spoken at near normal speed without any interference, identifying personal responses, including opinions)

Quel temps fait-il?

– Et voici notre premier joueur. C'est Charles, qui habite à la Rochelle.
– Allô.
– Charles, c'est Annie ici!
– Ah oui, bonjour Annie.
– Il fait beau à La Rochelle?
– Euh, non – il y a du vent. Mais ça va, j'aime le vent.
– C'est vrai?
– Ah oui, je fais de la planche à voile!
– Ah.

– Et maintenant Magalie, à Lyon.
– Allô.
– Salut Magalie.
– Salut Annie.
– Quel temps fait-il à Lyon, Magalie?
– Il y a du soleil – j'adore le soleil.
– Moi aussi.
– Je vais à la piscine avec mes amis.
– Super!

– Et le numéro trois habite à Lille. Il s'appelle Robert.
– Allô.
– Salut Robert.
– Ah, bonjour Annie.
– Qu'est-ce que tu fais aujourd'hui?
– Oh, il pleut. Je n'aime pas ça. Je reste dans ma chambre et je surfe sur le Net.
– Ah, bon.

– Alors, trois personnes, Robert, Magalie et Charles. On joue!!

CM 117 **SPEAKING**

Deuxième contrôle: Parler

Students should be given the sheet up to a week before the assessment, to give them time to choose whether they prefer to do 1, 2 or 3, and to prepare and practise both conversations – the structured one (A) and the open-ended one (B) – with their partners.

Mark scheme:

Section A: mark /12: 3 marks per response

- 1 mark for conveying the requested information, but with a minimal response e.g. one or two words. Repetition of the question and prompting by pointing to the visuals may be necessary.
- 2 marks for a response that is clear and conveys all of the information requested, in the form of a complete phrase or sentence, though not necessarily an accurate one. The question and answers may seem disjointed, like separate items rather than part of a coherent conversation.
- 3 marks for a clear and complete response that conveys all of the information requested, in the form of a complete phrase or sentence, though not necessarily an accurate one. The language flows reasonably smoothly, and is recognisable as part of a coherent conversation.

Section B: mark /13: 3 marks per response, as above, + 1 bonus mark for adding one or two items of extra information about personal preferences (i.e. using knowledge of language to adapt and substitute single words and phrases).

Summary:	**Marks**	7–13	14–18	19–25
	Level	1	2	3

CM 118–119 **READING**

Deuxième contrôle: Lire

A Cico le clown (NC 1)

Solution: 1c, 2g, 3e, 4b, 5a, 6f, 7d

(mark /6: 4+ shows understanding of single words presented in a clear script)

B Sophie à Cherbourg (NC 2)

Solution: 1d, 2b, 3e, 4g, 5f, 6a, 7h, 8i, 9c

(mark /7: 5+ shows understanding of short phrases presented in a familiar context)

C En ville (NC 2)

Solution: (other answers are possible)

1 *La poste est à gauche.*
2 *Le musée est entre le parking et l'office de tourisme.*
3 *L'hôtel est derrière le café.*
4 *Le restaurant est devant la banque.*
5 *L'hôtel est dans la rue principale.*
6 *L'office de tourisme est dans la rue Saint-Joseph.*
7 *Le café est à droite.*

(mark /6: 4+ shows understanding of single words presented in a clear script – do not penalise for copying spellings incorrectly as only reading skills are being tested)

D Les cadeaux de Coralie (NC 3)

Solution: 1F, 2F, 3V, 4F, 5V, 6F, 7F

(mark /6: 4+ shows understanding of a short text, identifying and noting main points, including likes, dislikes and feelings)

CM 120 **WRITING**

Deuxième contrôle: Écrire

A Les activités (NC 1)

Solution: **1** *téléphone,* **2** *dansent,* **3** *surfes,* **4** *jouons,* **5** *dessine,* **6** *écoute,* **7** *allez,* **8** *chantent,* **9** *regarde*

(mark /8: 1/2 mark for correct word; 1/2 mark for correct spelling – round up the odd 1/2 mark; 5+ shows ability to select appropriate words to complete sentences and copy them correctly)

B Quel temps fait-il? (NC 2)

Solution: *À Marseille, il fait beau. À Paris, il y a du vent. À Cherbourg, il y a du brouillard. À Bordeaux, il fait chaud. À Grenoble, il fait froid. À Toulouse, il y a du soleil.*

(mark /9: 1 mark for key weather word, even if the spelling is inaccurate (this includes completing the *Paris* sentence); 1 mark for each correctly-constructed sentence, apart from *Marseille* and *Paris*, accepting only the smallest spelling errors; 5+ shows ability to adapt given patterns correctly and add further vocabulary from memory)

C Le week-end (NC 3)

This is an open-ended task.

(mark /8: 1/2 mark for comprehensible phrase, even if the spelling is inaccurate; further 1/2 mark for each of the four phrases that is accurate or virtually accurate; 5+ shows ability to write two or three short sentences on familiar topics, adapting a model and adding own vocabulary)

Troisième contrôle – Unités 8–10

CM 121–122, 4/9–12 **LISTENING**

Troisième contrôle: Écouter

A La soirée d'Anne-Marie (NC 2)

Solution: 1a, 2b, 3a, 4b, 5a, 6a, 7b

(mark /6: 4+ shows understanding of a range of familiar statements)

La soirée d'Anne-Marie

1 Je quitte le collège à cinq heures.
2 À cinq heures et quart, j'arrive à la maison.
3 Je prends le goûter dans la cuisine.
4 Après le goûter, je regarde la télé.
5 Nous mangeons à sept heures et demie.
6 Je commence mes devoirs après le dîner.
7 Je me couche à dix heures.

B Rendez-vous à quelle heure? (NC 3)

Solution: **1** *1h30,* **b**, **2** *6h30/18h30,* **d**, **3** *8h00/20h00,* **e**, **4** *10h15,* **c**

(mark /6: 4+ shows understanding of short dialogues, spoken at near normal speed without any interference)

Rendez-vous à quelle heure?

1 – Tu veux aller en ville cet après-midi?
– Oui, je veux bien.
– Alors, rendez-vous à la gare à une heure et demie, ça va?
– Très bien, une heure et demie à la gare.

2 – Tu veux aller voir un film ce soir?
– Ce soir, ce n'est pas possible, mais vendredi soir, oui.
– Alors, rendez-vous à six heures et demie devant le cinéma?
– Six heures et demie. À vendredi.

3 – Tu veux fêter l'anniversaire de Pierre avec nous samedi soir?
– Oui, super!
– Alors rendez-vous à la maison de Pierre à huit heures?
– Huit heures. OK. À samedi.

4 – Tu veux jouer au tennis dimanche matin?
– Oui, nous deux?
– Et Lucie et Claire. Rendez-vous au parc à dix heures et quart, ça va?
– Ça va. Dix heures et quart. À dimanche.

C Deux interviews (NC 3)

Solution:

Sabine		*Paul*	
lettres	*symboles*	*lettres*	*symboles*
d	♡♡	**c**	💔💔
h	💔	**e**	♡

(mark /7: 5+ shows understanding of short dialogues, spoken at near normal speed without any interference, identifying and noting personal responses, including likes and dislikes)

Deux interviews

Sabine
– Sabine, qu'est-ce que tu aimes manger ou boire?
– Moi, j'adore le chocolat chaud, surtout quand il fait froid.
– Et ... est-ce qu'il y a quelque chose que tu n'aimes pas?
– Je ne sais pas ... Ah oui, le chou-fleur. Je n'aime pas le chou-fleur.

Paul
– Et Paul, il y a quelque chose que tu n'aimes pas manger ou boire?
– Il y a beaucoup de choses que je n'aime pas, mais je déteste surtout le lait.
– Et qu'est-ce que tu aimes? Beaucoup de choses aussi, je suppose.
– Bien sûr, mais surtout, j'aime les fraises. Mmm.

D Luc parle à Patrick (NC 4)

Only use this task if the class has completed *Unité 10*, as it is based on vocabulary and structures taught in this unit. If you wish to carry out an assessment when the class has only reached the end of *Unité 9*, use the alternative Level 4 listening task on CM 127.

Solution: 1c, 2a, 3c, 4b, 5a, 6c, 7c

(mark /6: 4+ shows understanding of longer passages, spoken at near normal speed with little interference, identifying main points and some details)

Luc parle à Patrick

– Ça va, Luc?
– Oui, j'adore le ski. Il y a beaucoup de neige pour le ski, mais il fait du soleil!
– Tu fais du ski le matin et l'après-midi?
– Oui, il y a une classe de dix heures à douze heures, et une classe de quatorze heures à seize heures.

****

– Et qu'est-ce que tu fais à midi?
– Nous allons au restaurant et nous mangeons un grand repas chaud.
– Il y a des activités le soir aussi?
– Oui, ce soir, on fait de la natation. Mercredi, il y a un match de basket. J'aime jouer au basket!

****

– Et les autres soirs, qu'est-ce que tu fais?
– On fait du shopping, on va au cinéma. Mais aussi, on range les chambres et on fait la vaisselle – ça, c'est ennuyeux.
– Mais le ski, c'est bien, non? Tu as ton appareil-photo avec toi?
– Oui, j'ai un appareil-photo numérique. Il y a un café avec Internet en ville. Je t'écris un e-mail avec des photos.
– Ça, c'est une bonne idée!

CM 123 **SPEAKING**

Troisième contrôle: Parler

Students should be given the sheet up to a week before the assessment, to give them time to choose whether they prefer to do 1, 2 or 3 (or, if they have not yet completed *Unité 10*, 1 or 2), and to prepare and practise both conversations – the structured one (A) and the open-ended one (B) – with their partners.

Mark scheme:

Section A: mark /12: 3 marks per response

- 1 mark for a response that is clear and conveys all of the information requested, in the form of a complete phrase or sentence, though not necessarily an accurate one. The questions and answers may seem a little disjointed, like separate items rather than parts of a coherent conversation.
- 2 marks for a response that is clear and conveys all of the information requested, in the form of a complete phrase or sentence, though not necessarily an accurate one. The language must flow reasonably smoothly and be recognisable as part of a coherent conversation.

- 3 for a clear and complete response that flows smoothly as part of a coherent conversation. The language must be in complete sentences or phrases that are reasonably accurate and consistent as far as grammar, pronunciation and intonation are concerned.

Section B: mark /13: 3 marks per response, as above, + 1 bonus mark for adding one or two items of extra information about personal preferences (i.e. using knowledge of language to adapt and substitute single words and phrases).

Summary:	**Marks**	7–13	14–18	19–25
	Level	2	3	4

CM 124–125 **READING**

Troisième contrôle: Lire

A L'emploi du temps (NC 2)

Solution: **1** *mardi,* **2** *jeudi,* **3** *jeudi,* **4** *lundi,* **5** *samedi,* **6** *vendredi,* **7** *mardi*

(mark /6: 4+ shows understanding of short phrases presented in a familiar context)

B Le déjeuner au restaurant (NC 3)

Solution:

	hors-d'œuvre	*plat principal*	*dessert*	*autres informations*
M. Martin	**b**	**c**	**–**	**b**
Mme. Dubois	**–**	**b**	**a**	**e**
M. Colin	**a**	**d**	**c**	**c**

(mark /7: 5+ shows understanding of short texts, identifying and noting main points, including likes, dislikes and feelings)

C Au Centre Picolle (NC 3)

Only use this task if the class has completed *Unité 10*, as it is based on vocabulary and structures taught in this unit. If you wish to carry out an assessment when the class has only reached the end of *Unité 9*, use the alternative Level 3 reading task on CM 127.

Solution:

	Activité 1	*Activité 2*	*Activité 3*	
Brigitte	**B**	**D**	**I**	
	Activité 1	*Activité 2*	*Activité 3*	*Activité 4*
Simon	**F**	**G**	**J**	**K**

(mark /6: 4+ shows understanding of short printed texts, identifying main points, including likes and dislikes)

D Le message de Richard (NC 4)

Solution: **1F, 2V, 3V, 4F, 5F, 6F, 7V**

(mark /6: 4+ shows understanding of a longer text, identifying and noting main points and details, including likes, dislikes and feelings)

CM 126 **WRITING**

Troisième contrôle: Écrire

A Une boisson ou un fruit? (NC 2)

Solution:

1 *Monsieur Mally prend un café.*
2 *Adèle prend une banane.*
3 *Madame Bijou prend une pomme.*
4 *Robert prend une limonade.*
5 *Julien prend une poire.*

(mark /8: 1 mark for each key word, even if the spelling is inaccurate; 1 mark for each correctly-constructed sentence, accepting only the smallest spelling errors; 5+ shows ability to adapt given patterns correctly)

B Au terrain de camping (NC 3)

Only use this task if the class has completed *Unité 10*, as it is based on vocabulary and structures taught in this unit. If you wish to carry out an assessment when the class has only reached the end of *Unité 9*, use the alternative Level 3 writing task on CM 128.

Solution:

1 *Alors, Papa n'est pas là, il fait les courses.*
2 *Annette, tu fais la vaisselle.*
(*fais* = 1 mark, *fait* = 1/2 mark, *faire* = 0 marks)
3 *Christophe et Gilles, vous rangez la tente.*
(*rangez* = 1 mark, *rangerz* = 1/2 mark, *ranger* = 0 marks)
4 *Et moi, je prépare le déjeuner.*
(*prépare* = 1 mark, *prépares* = 1/2 mark, *préparer* = 0 marks)
5 *Après, nous allons à la piscine.*
(*allons* = 1 mark, *allerons* = 1/2 mark, *aller* = 0 marks)

(mark /8: 1 mark for each correctly conjugated verb, or 1/2 mark for an attempt that shows understanding of the conjugation, rounding up an odd 1/2; 1 mark for each reasonably accurate sentence; 5+ shows ability to write short sentences on familiar topics, adapting a model and vocabulary from a word bank)

CM 126

C Un week-end typique (NC 4)

Although there is potential to use the vocabulary and structures learned in *Unité 10*, if you have not yet completed this final unit with the class, there are still plenty of pieces of information from the other units available to students.

This is an open-ended task.
(mark /9: 6+ shows ability to write simple sentences, relying largely on memorised language)

Mark scheme:

- for each weekend activity comprehensibly mentioned: 1 mark (up to max. of 2)
- for each comprehensible reference to time of activities: 1 mark (up to max. of 2)
- for each comprehensible expression of an opinion of an activity: 1 mark (max. of 2)
- for fairly accurate spelling throughout (comprehensible with a little effort): 1 mark

or for generally accurate spelling throughout (easily comprehensible): 2 marks

Troisième contrôle – Unités 8–9 (alternative tasks)

CM 127, 4/13 **LISTENING**

Troisième contrôle: Écouter (alternative task)

D Nathalie change de collège (NC 4)

Only use this task if you wish to carry out an assessment when the class has reached the end of *Unité* 9. It is designed to be used instead of the main Task D and is based on vocabulary and structures taught before the end of *Unité* 9. It is of a similar nature and Level to the main Task D and also has a total of 6 marks.

Solution: 1c, 2a, 3c, 4b, 5a, 6c, 7b

(mark /6: 4+ shows understanding of longer passages, spoken at near normal speed with little interference, identifying main points and some details)

Nathalie change de collège

– Alors Nathalie, tu vas au collège en Angleterre maintenant! C'est différent?

– Oui, mais ce n'est pas très différent. Je préfère notre collège en France.

– Tu portes un uniforme scolaire?

– Oui, bien sûr. J'ai une jupe bleu marine, une chemise blanche et une cravate jaune et bleue.

– C'est vrai?

– Oh, ça va. Et on mange au collège aussi. Notre maison est trop loin pour rentrer pour le déjeuner. C'est à quinze kilomètres du collège.

****

– Et les repas sont bons?

– Oui, il y a une grande cantine. Chaque jour il y a un repas chaud avec de la viande et des légumes, mais il y a aussi une sélection de frites, pizzas et salades. Je prends ça, normalement.

– Et tu commences à quelle heure le matin?

– À neuf heures moins le quart.

– Ça, c'est super! Ici, on commence à huit heures.

– Je sais.

****

– Tu rentres à la maison plus tard aussi?

– Non, le bus arrive à trois heures et demie, et à quatre heures et quart, je suis chez moi, devant la télé avec mon goûter!

– Pas de devoirs!

– Si, beaucoup. Mais je commence mes devoirs à cinq heures moins le quart.

CM 127–128 **READING**

Troisième contrôle: Lire (alternative task)

C Une semaine d'activités (NC 3)

Only use this task if you wish to carry out an assessment when the class has reached the end of *Unité* 9. It is designed to be used instead of the main Task C, and is based on vocabulary and structures taught up to the end of *Unité* 9. It is of a similar nature and Level to the main Task C, and also has a total of 6 marks.

Solution: **1** *dimanche,* **2** *vendredi,* **3** *mardi,* **4** *samedi,* **5** *mercredi,* **6** *lundi,* **7** *jeudi*

(mark /6: 4+ shows understanding of short printed texts, identifying main points, including likes and dislikes)

Troisième contrôle: Écrire (alternative task)

B La famille Boulot va au cinéma (NC 3)

Only use this task if you wish to carry out an assessment when the class has reached the end of *Unité* 9. It is designed to be used instead of the main Task B, and is based on vocabulary and structures taught up to the end of *Unité* 9. It is of a similar nature and Level to the main Task B, and also has a total of 8 marks.

Decide whether you want your students to write the times out in full and make sure they are aware of this.

Solution:

1 *Maman travaille, elle rentre à la maison à cinq heures et quart.*

2 *Julien, tu manges/prends le dîner à cinq heures et demie/5h30.* (*manges/prends* = 1 mark, *mange/prend* = $^1/_2$ mark, *manger, prendre* = 0 marks)

3 *Nous prenons le bus à six heures moins dix/5h50.* (*prenons* = 1 mark, *prendrons/prennons* = $^1/_2$ mark, *prendre* = 0 marks)

4 *Le film commence à six heures vingt/6h20.* (*commence* = 1 mark, *commences* = $^1/_2$ mark, *commencer* = 0 marks)

5 *Après, maman et moi, nous allons/mangeons/prenons le dîner au restaurant à neuf heures/9h.* (*allons/mangeons/prenons* = 1 mark, *alons/mangons/prendons* = $^1/_2$ mark, *aller/manger/prendre* = 0 marks)

(mark /8: 1 mark for each correctly conjugated verb, or $^1/_2$ mark for an attempt that shows understanding of the conjugation, rounding up an odd $^1/_2$; 1 mark for each reasonably accurate sentence; 5+ shows ability to write short sentences on familiar topics, adapting a model and vocabulary from a word bank)

Useful websites, addresses and other information

1 Websites

Finding sites on the Internet

Yahoo France (**www.yahoo.fr**) is a good search engine to use since it has sites listed under different categories but also has a search facility. Thus, if you want to find a website to do with Camembert, you could just type in Camembert in the search box or you could click on the *nourriture* category and click on sub-categories until you get to cheeses.

There are other French search engines which work in similar ways. There are also multi-lingual search engines, for example *Altavista* (**www.altavista.com**), which can be set to search in any language or in a particular language.

Students might like to carry out searches to find information about towns in France or about places they have heard of such as *Parc Astérix* or *Disneyland Paris*.

Saints' days and festivals

Saints' days and festivals are mentioned in *Unité 5*, Area 1. For information about festivals consult:

http://perso.wanadoo.fr/rene.oster

And for information on the saint of the day consult:

www.micronet.fr/~fize/

This site also allows you to look up any name and find the appropriate Saint's day, if there is one. You can even download the database and install it on any PC. You can then use it on machines that are not connected to the Internet. The information on the Saint of the day is a little difficult for beginners but is short and to the point and those students interested could probably make sense of it with the help of a dictionary.

The following *Yahoo* category has lists of special festivals planned for the year:

www.yahoo.fr/Societe/Evenements/An 2000
(or type in current year)

Virtual greetings cards

A virtual birthday card is featured in *Unité 5* (SB 39). Students may well wish to follow up this activity by producing their own virtual greetings card in French.

It is difficult to recommend a specific site as these sites may not always be active. However, there is a category of virtual greeting card sites on *Yahoo*:

www.yahoo.fr/Commerce_et_economie/Societes/Cadeaux/Cartes_de_voeux/

Virtual postcards can also be sent to penfriends or even to someone else in the school. Websites for virtual postcards can be found with a simple search on *Yahoo France*. Just type *cartes virtuelles* in the search box and click on *Recherche*.

Weather information

The weather is covered in *Unité 6*.

Students may like to visit the following website to discover the weather today in various French towns.

www.meteo.fr

2 CALL software (Computer Aided Language Learning)

Many ICT materials are available for helping language learners, some as CD-ROMs, some as disks, others in both formats. Sometimes site licences are included in the price and sometimes they are extra. It is important to check that the desired item is available in a form that is compatible with the system in your school.

Fun with Texts

This is the most well known of the text manipulation packages (see Section 2 TB 40–41 for suggestions for use). It can be obtained from:

Camsoft Ltd., 10 Wheatfield Close, Maidenhead, Berkshire, SL6 3PS (Tel: 01608 825206)

You can also find out more about *Fun with Texts* and other Camsoft materials at their website:

http://www.camsoftpartners.co.uk

There are many more packages available offering cloze and text manipulation exercises, e.g. *Gapkit* (also from Camsoft, this package allows cloze with multi-media).

Over 200 cloze packages on the Web are listed on the following site along with software reviews and a list of sites with downloadable demos:

http://www.linguasy.com/linguasy

CD-ROMs

Each CD-ROM program will have its own strengths and they often cater to a very specific purpose, e.g. the *French Grammar Studio*. There are a number of programs that are specifically designed for beginners and which offer a good range of listening and reading practice activities in the topics of ***Encore Tricolore 1 nouvelle édition***. Some of the more common ones are:

All in one Language Fun

Triple Play Plus French

The BBC's *French Experience* double CD

CD-ROM reviews can be found at the BECTA Website. The most recent review at the time of writing was completed in 1998.

http://www.becta.org.uk/information/cd-roms/index.html

On-line materials

Some websites offer on-line learning materials developed by languages teachers. Many of these have been developed using the *Hot Potatoes* software which is available free of charge from the University of Victoria, Canada:

http://web.uvic.ca/hrd/halfbaked

You can download the program from their website and then develop your own activities or you can direct your pupils to sites made by other languages teachers – the Hot Potatoes site has a list of these.

3 La Rochelle

The following information links up with the background information in Section 2 (TB 32). La Rochelle features in the Students' Book in *Unité* 2 and *Unité 7*.

Websites

Students may wish to make a *Visite Virtuelle à La Rochelle*. Below are two sites that were operative at the time of writing:

www.ville-larochelle.fr/

www.ville-la-rochelle.com/

Websites for tourist information from other French towns can be found through the *Yahoo France* Geography category – click on France and then towns. This gives an A–Z of French towns with several websites each for medium size towns. Larger cities have their own *Yahoo* listing, e.g. Paris, Marseille, Lyon, Bordeaux, Toulouse, Nice, Strasbourg, Nantes, Lille, Rennes, Grenoble, Montpellier, Nancy, Aix-en-Provence, Montréal, Québec, Bruxelles, Liège, Genève, Lausanne, Neuchâtel.

Useful addresses

Office de tourisme – Syndicat d'Initiative, Place de la Petite Sirène, Le Gabut, 17025, La Rochelle

Comité départemental du Tourisme, 11 bis, rue des Augustins, 17025 La Rochelle

Auberge de Jeunesse, Centre International de Séjour, Les Minimes, 17025 La Rochelle.

4 Books relating to ICT

Atkinson, T (1992): *Hands off – it's my go!* London, CILT/NCET

Atkinson, T (1998): *WWW: The Internet*, London, CILT (InfoTech 3)

Buckland, D (2000): *Putting achievement first. Managing and leading ICT in the MFL department*, London, CILT (InfoTech 5)

Hewer, S (1997): *Text manipulation*, London, CILT (InfoTech 2)

NCET (1997): *Accent on IT – practical training and support for KS3*, Coventry, NCET (Video pack).

Slater, P & Varney-Burch, S: *Multimedia in language learning*, London, CILT (InfoTech 6)

Townsend, K (1997): *E-mail*, London, CILT (InfoTech 1)

5 Useful websites for teachers and students

French search engines *(Des moteurs de recherche)*

www.yahoo.fr

www.voila.fr

www.lycos.fr

Many of the French search engines have useful junior sections, e.g.

http://fr.dir.yahoo.com/Societe/Groupes_et_communautes/Enfants/

www.voila.fr/Chaine/Loisirs_sorties/Sites_pour_les_enfants/

www.lycos.fr/webguides/juniors

General interest sites for children

Premiers pas sur Internet – general interest site, with discussions and contributions from children from French-speaking countries.
www.momes.net

Okapi (French teenage magazine)
www.okapi.bayardpresse.fr

General information about France
http://ambafrance.org.uk/zipzap/boussole.html

Language teaching

Association for Language Learning (ALL)
www.languagelearn.co.uk

CILT, the National Centre for Languages
www.cilt.org.uk

Lingu@net (This site provides useful links to other websites for languages.)
www.linguanet.org.uk

Exchanges

Central Bureau for International Education and Training
www.centralbureau.org.uk
www.wotw.org.uk

ICT organisations

British Education Communications and Technology Agency (BECTA)
www.becta.org.uk

Modern Foreign Languages and Information Technology Project (MFLIT)
www.vtc.ngfl.gov.uk/resoucre/cits/mfl

The Microelectronics in Education Unit in Wales (MEU)
www.meucymru.co.uk

Scottish Council for Educational Technology (SCET)
www.scet.org.uk

Education in England

Department for Education and Skills
www.dfes.gov.uk

National Curriculum
www.nc.uk.net

Standards
www.standards.dfes.gov.uk

Qualifications and Curriculum Authority (QCA)
www.qca.org.uk

Education in Wales

Currciulum and Assessment Authority for Wales
www.accac.org.uk

Education in Scotland

Scottish Qualifications Authority
www.sqa.org.uk

Scottish Virtual Teachers' Centre
www.svtc.org.uk

Scottish Consultative Council on the Curriculum
www.scca.ac.uk

Education in Northern Ireland

Northern Ireland Council for the Curriculum, Examinations and Assessment
www.ccea.org.uk